NEWCOMER'S HANDBOOK®

FOR MOVING TO

Washington D.C.

Including Northern Virginia
and Suburban Maryland

3rd Edition

FIRST BOOKS

6750 SW Franklin
Portland, OR 97223
503-968-6777
www.firstbooks.com

3rd edition

Author: Mike Livingston
Publisher: Jeremy Solomon
Editor: Bernadette Duperron
Contributor: Ricia Anne Chansky
Design: Erin Johnson
Maps provided by DesignMaps.com

ISBN 0-912301-49-X
ISSN 1535-4407

Printed in the USA on recycled paper.

Published by First Books, 6750 SW Franklin Street, Portland, OR 97223.

What readers are saying about Newcomer's Handbooks:

I recently got a copy of your Newcomer's Handbook for Chicago, and wanted to let you know how invaluable it was for my move. I must have consulted it a dozen times a day preparing for my move. It helped me find my way around town, find a place to live, and so many other things. My only suggestion is a more detailed map of the area. It's just a small gripe however, as your book helped me so much. Thanks.

—Mike L.
Chicago, Illinois

Excellent reading (Newcomer's Handbook for San Francisco and the Bay Area) ... it seems balanced and trustworthy. One of the very best guides if you are considering moving/relocation. Way above the usual tourist crap.

—Gunnar E.
Stockholm, Sweden

I was very impressed with the latest edition of the Newcomer's Handbook for Los Angeles. It is well organized, concise and up-to-date. I would recommend this book to anyone considering a move to Los Angeles.

—Jannette L.
Attorney Recruiting Administrator for a large Los Angeles law firm

I recently moved to Atlanta from San Francisco, and LOVE the Newcomer's Handbook for Atlanta. It has been an invaluable resource – it's helped me find everything from a neighborhood in which to live to the local hardware store. I look something up in it everyday, and know I will continue to use it to find things long after I'm no longer a newcomer. And if I ever decide to move again, your book will be the first thing I buy for my next destination.

—Courtney R.
Atlanta, Georgia

In looking to move to the Boston area, a potential employer in that area gave me a copy of the Newcomer's Handbook for Boston. It's a great book that's very comprehensive, outlining good and bad points about each neighborhood in the Boston area. Very helpful in helping me decide where to move.

—no name given (online submit form)

TABLE OF CONTENTS

CONTENTS

CONTENTS

WELCOME TO WASHINGTON! "AMERICA'S HOMETOWN" IS NOW *your* hometown. Perhaps you've moved "inside the Beltway" where, according to legend, everyone is a policy analyst or a bureaucrat. Not true—while many folks come here to work on "The Hill" or in the real-life West Wing, Washington isn't just a government town. You'll find America's best and brightest coming here to work in academia, the high-tech or bio-tech industries, national and international nonprofits, corporate law, and in the services and trades it takes to feed, shelter, transport, and entertain a city of three million people.

So, what's it like here? Northerners consider Washington a southern city and Southerners consider it northeastern. Both have a point. Hot and steamy summer days, tree-lined avenues, and old mansions converted into offices give Washington the physical feel of a southern city, but the frenetic "type A" culture makes it seem more northern. Newcomers from Maine or Georgia are equally likely to find people here to be self-absorbed, hurried, and seemingly rude. It is President Kennedy who is credited with the observation, now a cliché, that Washington combines northern charm with southern efficiency.

Washington isn't just one city. In addition to the District of Columbia, the Washington metropolitan area includes parts of two states, Virginia and Maryland. (In this book, "Washington" refers to the metropolitan area and "D.C." refers to the city itself.) Northern Virginia, suburban Maryland, and "the District" have some things in common—most notably, high levels of income and education, congested roads and commuting issues, and a high cost of living. Recent analysis from Runzheimer International, a management consulting firm specializing in travel and living costs, put the cost of a 2,200 sq. ft. home in Washington—four bedrooms and 2.5 baths—at an average cost of $332,300; much higher than Atlanta's average of $207,900, but close to Chicago's price tag of $333,800. For more about relocation expenses and city comparisons go to www.runzheimer.com.

The Virginia suburbs are conservative and southern compared to the rest of Washington. Subdivisions with names like Fox Mill Estates and Hunter's Valley reflect Northern Virginia's not-too-distant past as horse country. Through here the Potomac River is a striking cultural boundary—many Virginians seldom venture into Maryland, and many Marylanders only go to Virginia to work in Tysons Corner or to scour antique stores in the countryside. Suburban Maryland is more liberal and more closely tied to the city. In fact, many Marylanders are former city dwellers who have moved out of D.C. and into Maryland to get their kids into some of the best public schools in the country. These are "soccer mom" suburbs, where many parents are active in the PTA and quite a few residents actually show up for zoning hearings about new roads or strip malls. The District of Columbia generally attracts a younger crowd than the suburbs—many new residents are singles or young couples, some fresh out of college and eager to change the world. Many opt to put up with the city's high taxes and slow services in exchange for the ability to walk home from a neighborhood nightclub or a late night at the office. In terms of local government, the District, a federal colony governed by Congress, was granted limited "home rule" in 1973, allowing residents to choose their city council and school board. A whopping 90% of the District's registered voters are either Democrats or independents. In 1980 District residents voted to become the 51st state, a move blocked by Congress. More recently, the District added the words "Taxation Without Representation" to its license plates, hoping to remind out-of-towners that they're visiting the only place in America without the right to self-government.

> MORE RECENTLY, THE DISTRICT ADDED THE WORDS "TAXATION WITHOUT REPRESENTATION" TO ITS LICENSE PLATES, HOPING TO REMIND OUT-OF-TOWNERS THAT THEY'RE VISITING THE ONLY PLACE IN AMERICA WITHOUT THE RIGHT TO SELF-GOVERNMENT.

Most people arrive here with a lot of preconceptions. Let's try to sort out the myths from the reality:

- **Washington is not a revolving door**. Since administrations come and go every four to eight years, there's a perception that Washington's population is transient. Actually, more than half of the area's adult residents have been here for 20 years or more, and there are proud lifelong residents here as well. So yes, new people are always arriving, but this is not a government camp—it's a living city where people raise families, walk the dog, go to the movies, and get picked for jury duty.
- **Washington is not just government**. Tourism and hospitality are big business here, of course, but the late 1990s also saw a boom in

startup high-tech and bio-tech businesses. Neighboring Montgomery County in Maryland is a hotbed of genetics research. In 2000, Black Entertainment Television and XM Satellite Radio opened their new headquarters in a once desolate industrial area just off Capitol Hill, near the offices of CNN and Amtrak. These industries provide a growing share of this region's jobs and a growing market for support services.

- **Washington is home to a diverse population**. Many people settle here from all over the world—some coming directly from their home countries, but many move to Washington from other US communities. There was never a mass immigration here, like the Irish immigration to Boston or the Russian immigration to Baltimore. There are some neighborhoods in D.C. with a large Latino population, such as Mt. Pleasant and Columbia Heights, and there's an official Chinatown, but mostly Washington is a city where hyphenated Americans come to lose their hyphens. That's not to say Washington is a paradise of racial harmony, but social and political tension here has less to do with race than with economic class. It is often said that Washington is "a tale of two cities"—indeed, D.C. has a bigger income gap than any state, with the richest fifth of the population 27 times as wealthy as the poorest fifth. (Nationwide, the richest fifth is 10 times as wealthy as the poorest.) The District has some 20,000 residents earning more than $100,000 a year, and about twice as many residents living in homeless shelters or on the street. And the nation's capital leads the nation in rates of infant mortality, diabetes, and HIV/AIDS. That said, you'll find incomes and property values tend to be higher to the west of Rock Creek Park than to the east—the most affluent neighborhoods are concentrated in Northwest D.C. and the western suburbs, and almost all of the struggling neighborhoods are east of the Park. There are plenty of exceptions, though—while some neighborhoods are exclusively rich and some poor, many are in fact economically diverse.

- **Washington is expensive**. Real estate, like the rest of the economy, boomed here in the late 1990s; by the end of 2000, property taxes were catching up, and as this book goes to press, many real estate agents believe housing prices will decline in the first decade of the new century. Be assured, though, Washington will still have a higher cost of living than most US cities—and, on a brighter note, high wages and salaries to match. Among the 20 largest metropolitan areas in the United States, your housing dollar will go farther in any city except New York, San Francisco, Boston, or Chicago than in Washington. If you earned $50,000 a year in L.A. and you want to maintain the same standard of living in D.C., you'll need to earn $59,000 here; if you moved from Denver or Atlanta, the amount is roughly $65,000; from St. Louis or Houston, it's $86,000 or more.

- **Washington is inside and outside the Beltway**. The Capital Beltway is a highway that circles the District and the inner suburbs. The Beltway is also the symbol for a stereotype of Washingtonian thinking: politicians and pundits talk about the culture "inside the Beltway" as a delusional never-never land where policy is made by people who are out of touch with the rest of us. There are certainly plenty of bureaucrats who could stand to "get a life," but their cubicles are not necessarily located inside the Beltway. With so many federal agencies located in the suburbs, including the Census Bureau, the National Institute of Standards & Technology (formerly the National Bureau of Standards), the National Institutes of Health, the CIA, and major facilities for NASA and the Department of Agriculture, thousands of federal employees live and work outside the Beltway. And not all policy wonks are sheltered in an ivory tower. According to studies by the market research firm Claritas, Washingtonians tend to read books, jog, play tennis, drink Scotch, travel, and take adult-education courses more than residents of other US cities. This is also the place with the nation's highest percentage of women in the workforce and two-career couples.
- **Washingtonians talk like lawyers and bureaucrats**. While not everyone in Washington is a "fed," practically everyone speaks the language. In a city where people actually watch "Meet the Press" and "Face the Nation," the latest policy jargon makes its way quickly into everyday conversation, as do acronyms and initials—NASA, EPA, NIH, GSA, SEC, OSHA, FOIA, and OMB, just for example. And everyone here knows that "GS-9" indicates a rank on the federal pay scale, and that form SF-171 is the all-purpose federal job application.
- **Washington is wired—and wireless**. In 1999 the *Washington Business Journal* proclaimed Washington to be "the nation's most-wired metropolitan area"—that is, the area with the nation's highest percentage of households connected to the internet. By 2000, according to some estimates, half the homes in the area were online—and nearly 70% in Northern Virginia. Washington is also a leading market for wireless phones, and many Washingtonians chatter away on the Metro, in restaurants, in elevators, and, watch out, behind the wheel.
- **Washington is safer than you think**. While personal safety is not guaranteed anywhere, it seems Washington has a much worse reputation than it deserves. In any metropolitan area in the US, there are some neighborhoods to avoid, and Washington is no exception. Most violent crime in D.C. is related to gang feuds, which are usually confined to a single block or intersection. While it makes for grisly stories on the evening news, most Washingtonians never encounter violent crime firsthand. (See the chapter on **Getting Settled** for safety tips.)

- **Washington is a *nice* place to live**. To many visitors, this place is white marble monuments, historic buildings, and museums. It doesn't stop there. The area is full of elegant homes and downtown buildings built before the Civil War, and the city's historic preservation laws keep them close to their original appearance. Rock Creek Park is one of the largest urban parks in the world, and on its woodland trails you can easily forget you're in a city. Several bald eagles, including a nesting pair, live along the Anacostia River. There are smaller parks and open spaces in every neighborhood. Even little wedges formed by traffic patterns are landscaped and tended by the National Park Service. Many small parks feature statues of early American heroes—obscure as well as famous ones. And no building may be built to a height higher than the top of the Capitol dome—so no matter where you are in Washington, you can always see the sky.

THE L'ENFANT PLAN FOR THE FEDERAL CITY

The District of Columbia is renowned as an eye-catching city with lots of trees and open space—and the lowest skyline of any East Coast city its size. None of that happened by accident. Long before any schools offered degrees in "urban planning," John Adams and Thomas Jefferson commissioned architects to design the capital city—at a site personally selected by former land surveyor George Washington—in unprecedented detail.

One of the nation's first government contractors was Pierre L'Enfant, hired to turn a 68-square-mile expanse of swamps and hills into a capital city of broad, tree-lined avenues and panoramic views. The principal government buildings would boast classical columns, domes, and friezes worthy of Greek and Roman temples, and nothing would block the view of the Capitol from anywhere in the city. To the west of the Capitol, there would be a "vast esplanade" lined with "the sort of places as may be attractive to the learned and afford diversion to the idle." And, in the spirit of federalism, the national capital would honor the states it served by naming an avenue after each one.

Track down a map drawn by L'Enfant—or his assistant, Benjamin Banneker, the son of two former slaves—and you would find it to be mostly applicable to D.C.'s current layout. Most of the principal streets would be recognizable, although the antique map would show a canal along the path of present-day Constitution Avenue; Tiber Creek had not yet been buried in a tunnel; and there was a J Street in those days. But the L'Enfant Plan is largely intact today—thanks to Banneker, who copied the maps from memory after President Jefferson fired L'Enfant and the hot-tempered architect took the originals with him.

In the planning stages the District of Columbia was divided into four jurisdictions: Washington City, the area south of Florida Avenue NW (which was then called Boundary Avenue); Washington County, the "uptown" part of the modern city, which was still mostly farmland; and the independent cities of Georgetown and Arlington, which had their own mayors. Georgetown remained independent until 1871, and Arlington was returned to Virginia in 1847 (a long story made short in the **Neighborhood Profile** for Arlington). L'Enfant was mainly concerned with Washington City, but the rules L'Enfant devised for the names of streets apply to the whole city, all the way to the four moss-covered stones marking the corners of the diamond-shaped District.

South of Florida Avenue, the land between the Potomac and Anacostia rivers was mostly swamp, now filled in and paved over. The Capitol and the White House are situated on dry ground, but the Washington Monument is slowly sinking at the rate of an inch per century.

THREE VISIONARIES: SHEPHERD, MCMILLAN, AND OLMSTED

Despite the grand layout by L'Enfant, as the nation celebrated its centennial, the capital city was still lined with muddy dirt roads. Pigs and chickens ran around loose in the streets, and malaria-bearing mosquitoes bred in puddles in the carriage ruts. Ambassadors from northern Europe got high-risk pay for spending the summer in Washington. It remained in such a state until Alexander "Boss" Shepherd, the director of public works, decided to pave the city and get it ready for the 20th century—never mind the niceties of bookkeeping and bureaucracy. Skipping bureaucratic red tape, he gathered a bunch of laborers and had these work crews lay sewers and asphalt faster than anyone could ask how the city was going to pay for it. For his efforts he was appointed governor of the District (a position that no longer exists), he then drained the city treasury to flatten hilly streets, bury obsolete canals, install streetlights, build parks, and plant some 60,000 trees. When the bills came due, he fled to Mexico and lived out his days making questionable investments in silver mines.

> PIGS AND CHICKENS RAN AROUND LOOSE IN THE STREETS, AND MALARIA-BEARING MOSQUITOES BRED IN PUDDLES IN THE CARRIAGE RUTS.

Sure, the Boss was corrupt and a bit of a maverick, but none deny that he made Washington a nicer and safer place to live. Today, in fitting tribute both to his important work and his unsavory methods, his statue stands at the entrance to the city's sewage treatment plant.

In 1901, Congress created the Park Improvement Commission of the District of Columbia, chaired by Sen. James McMillan. The McMillan

Commission, as it came to be called, picked up where L'Enfant left off, outlining the growth of parks and greenspace in the expanding city. The commission created the Mall, fulfilling L'Enfant's vision of the nation's front lawn, and called on Congress to establish Rock Creek Park and to preserve the "Fort Circle"—the ring of forts that defended the city during the Civil War. Many of the small parks throughout the uptown residential neighborhoods are Civil War sites preserved at the initiative of the McMillan Commission.

One of the commissioners was Frederick Law Olmsted, the renowned landscape architect who designed New York's Central Park as well as the Capitol grounds and the National Zoo. Olmsted shares with L'Enfant much of the credit for the prominence of greenspace in the nation's capital.

THE 21ST CENTURY

The National Capital Planning Commission, the successor to the McMillan Commission, is a federal agency with three commissioners appointed by the President of the United States and two appointed by the Mayor of the District of Columbia. Certain public officials are also commissioners ex officio: the Interior and Defense secretaries, the head of the General Services Administration, the chairs of the House and Senate committees on government affairs, and the mayor and council chair. Their job is to provide the District and surrounding jurisdictions with a general framework for development decisions affecting federal land and buildings.

In 1996, the commission unveiled the third master plan for the District—the "Legacy Plan," short for Extending the Legacy: Planning America's Capital for the 21st Century. The Legacy Plan seeks to preserve the spirit and effect of the L'Enfant Plan while responding to the needs of a growing and changing city. In the commission's words, "The Legacy Plan preserves the historic character and open space of the Mall and its adjacent ceremonial corridors while accommodating growth and new development. The plan expands the reach of public transit and eliminates obsolete freeways, bridges, and railroad tracks that fragment the city. It reclaims Washington's historic waterfront for public enjoyment, and adds parks, plazas, and other amenities to the urban fabric. Using federal resources to generate local investment, the Legacy Plan will spur community renewal well into the twenty-first century." (For more go to www.ncpc.gov.) It is important to understand that the details of the Legacy Plan are offered as possibilities or guidelines illustrating the sort of development that may be

"THE LEGACY PLAN PRESERVES THE HISTORIC CHARACTER AND OPEN SPACE OF THE MALL AND ITS ADJACENT CEREMONIAL CORRIDORS..."

considered in the new century; these are not actual projects that have been authorized or funded. That said, the Legacy Plan envisions these changes within the 21st century:

- Since the Mall is "full," with no room for new museums, a second Mall will be built along South Capitol Street from the Capitol to the Anacostia River. An important monument or public building will "anchor" the south end of the new Mall; perhaps the Supreme Court will be moved to this prestigious site.

- The Southeast-Southwest Freeway will be removed, since the Beltway will be able to carry more traffic between Prince George's County and Alexandria when the new, improved Woodrow Wilson Bridge is finished. The waterfront along the Anacostia and Potomac will be lined with parks and promenades, and a network of "water taxis" will provide public transportation to riverside offices and attractions.

- A sports and entertainment complex at the site of aging RFK Stadium will serve as an eastern gateway to the heart of the city.

- Downtown D.C. will be served by a paratransit network or "circulator" providing cheap, frequent trips for people traveling a short distance within the city.

- As needed, new federal buildings will be built along 16th Street NW or North Capitol Street, and more museums and monuments will be located outside the Monumental Core, especially along the improved waterfront.

Whether or not these particular visions come to pass, it's a good bet that the District in 2100 will still fit the description set forth in the L'Enfant Plan of 1790. Olmsted's vision, too, is in good hands: with a gift of $100 million from philanthropist Betty Brown Casey, the District is building a mayoral mansion on a 17-acre park in Foxhall and spending $50 million citywide to plant new trees and keep them healthy.

FINDING YOUR WAY AROUND

Today the city is divided into four quadrants whose center is the Capitol and whose boundaries are North Capitol Street, East Capitol Street, South Capitol Street and the Mall. In relation to the Capitol, the quadrants are known as Northwest, Northeast, Southeast, and Southwest, and every street name in the District includes a two–letter abbreviation indicating the quadrant. Downtown, east–west streets are named with letters of the alphabet, proceeding away from the Capitol; numbered streets run north–south and count away from the Capitol. So the corner of 7th & D streets NW is seven blocks west of North Capitol Street and four blocks north of the Mall; 7th Street NE is 14 blocks away, parallel to 7th Street NW.

After the alphabet streets (and actually there's no X, Y or Z Street, and no J Street either), crosstown streets bear two–syllable names in alphabetical order: Adams, Belmont, Clifton, and so on; this is the "second alphabet." Beyond Webster, the "third alphabet" bears three–syllable names—Allison, Buchanan, Crittenden. Finally, near the northern tip of the District, there's a "fourth alphabet" named after plants and flowers—Aspen, Butternut, Cedar.

Avenues run diagonally, and most are named after states—and yes, there is an avenue or street for every state.

Simple, right? Usually, but there are exceptions: Constitution and Independence avenues run east–west along the Mall, and East Executive Avenue and West Executive Avenue run north–south along the White House grounds. There's no J Street. And there are the notorious traffic circles ("rotaries" if you're from New England, "roundabouts" if you're from Old England, intimidating messes if you're from anywhere else), and square parks seemingly plunked in the middle of many major through streets. Some streets, such as Park Road NW and Military Road NW, simply violate the naming convention.

THE CITY'S MOST FAMOUS PHYSICAL FEATURE, CAPITOL HILL, ISN'T MUCH OF A HILL, BUT IT OFFERS GREAT VIEWS BECAUSE L'ENFANT WANTED TO PROVIDE GREAT VIEWS FROM THE CAPITOL.

Perhaps the most confusing twist is that while many of the inner suburbs follow the same nomenclature as the District; streets with the same name may be separate short neighborhood streets, not continuous thoroughfares. For example, the Rittenhouse Street crossing 16th Street NW doesn't connect to the Rittenhouse Street crossing Wisconsin Avenue NW, likewise, the Hamilton Street you encounter on Georgia Avenue NW doesn't connect to the Hamilton Street in Hyattsville, MD. (But cross-streets of the same name *are* the same distance north of the Capitol.)

If you know the general rules and the major exceptions, you'll do fine, but if you invest in a good street atlas and study it, you will quickly find it time and money well spent. (See the section on **Maps** below.)

Cyclists and pedestrians should bear in mind that the city is hilly. Just north of Florida Avenue NW, lofty Meridian Hill stretches from Rock Creek east to Howard University, and it's a steep climb of three or four blocks. Neighborhoods that border Rock Creek Park can also exercise your leg muscles or your parking brakes. The city's most famous physical feature, Capitol Hill, isn't much of a hill, but it offers great views because L'Enfant wanted to provide great views from the Capitol.

TRAFFIC CIRCLES

The District has 18 **traffic circles**, most dating from the L'Enfant Plan or the Civil War. Some are attractive parks; others are little more than a bend in the road. A few are just D–shaped remnants of old circles. The five downtown circles—Dupont, Logan, Scott, Thomas, and Washington—are major landmarks and chronic traffic jams; others, such as Sherman and Pinehurst, are little known and seldom visited except by those who live nearby. Here are the principal streets intersecting at each circle:

- **Barney**: K Street SE, Kentucky Avenue, Pennsylvania Avenue
- **Chevy Chase**: Connecticut Avenue NW, Western Avenue
- **Columbus**: Massachusetts Avenue NE between 1st and 2nd streets
- **Dupont**: 19th Street NW, P Street, Connecticut Avenue, Massachusetts Avenue, New Hampshire Avenue
- **Grant**: 5th Street NW, Illinois Avenue, New Hampshire Avenue
- **Kalorama**: Belmont Road NW, Kalorama Road
- **Logan**: 13th Street NW, P Street, Rhode Island Avenue, Vermont Avenue
- **Memorial**: encircles the Lincoln Memorial at the western end of the Mall—23rd Street NW, Henry Bacon Drive NW, Ohio Drive SW, Daniel French Drive SW
- **Observatory**: 34th Street NW, Massachusetts Avenue
- **Pinehurst**: 33rd Street NW, Western Avenue, Utah Avenue
- **Scott**: 16th Street NW, N Street, Massachusetts Avenue, Rhode Island Avenue
- **Sheridan**: Massachusetts Avenue NW between 22nd and R streets
- **Sherman**: 7th Street NW, Crittenden Street, Illinois Avenue, Kansas Avenue
- **Tenley**: Nebraska Avenue NW, Wisconsin Avenue
- **Thomas**: 14th Street NW, M Street, Massachusetts Avenue, Vermont Avenue
- **Ward**: Massachusetts Avenue NW, Nebraska Avenue, Loughboro Road
- **Washington**: 23rd Street NW, K Street, New Hampshire Avenue, Pennsylvania Avenue
- **Westmoreland**: Massachusetts Avenue NW, Western Avenue, Dalecarlia Parkway

Note that all traffic goes counterclockwise in traffic circles; in other words, you turn right to enter the circle and turn right again to leave it.

MAPS

- **ADC Street Atlases,** available at most bookstores and large drugstores, are detailed, reliable, and indexed to show post offices, libraries, police stations, recreation centers, and other useful facilities. Atlases of the District and of each neighboring county are available for around $10 each; the regional atlas, which covers the entire area profiled in this book, is a bargain at $30. A poster-sized ADC map of the District is available from the D.C. Board of Elections & Ethics at One Judiciary Square; it doesn't have an index and it doesn't show Metro stations, but it's just $3.50. ADC also publishes an excellent bicycle map of the District.
- **Flashmaps, Washington DC,** published by Fodor's, is an elegant "map guide" to the metro area.
- **Rand McNally** street atlases are almost as good as ADC's, and Rand McNally has a retail store at 7988 Tysons Corner Center, 202-223-6751.
- **Thomas Brothers** provides online maps at www.thomas.com/ poi/wdc, indexed to show government buildings,airports, shopping centers, schools, and other points of interest, as well as their fabulous, detailed "Thomas Guide."
- See the **Washington Reading List** for special topical maps and walking tours. And if you're buying real estate and you need to look at a precise surveyor's map, visit the Washingtoniana Division at Martin Luther King Jr. Library, 901 G Street NW, 202-727-1213.

Note: you can purchase all the above maps from First Books, www.firstbooks.com, 503-968-6777, in Oregon (no sales tax).

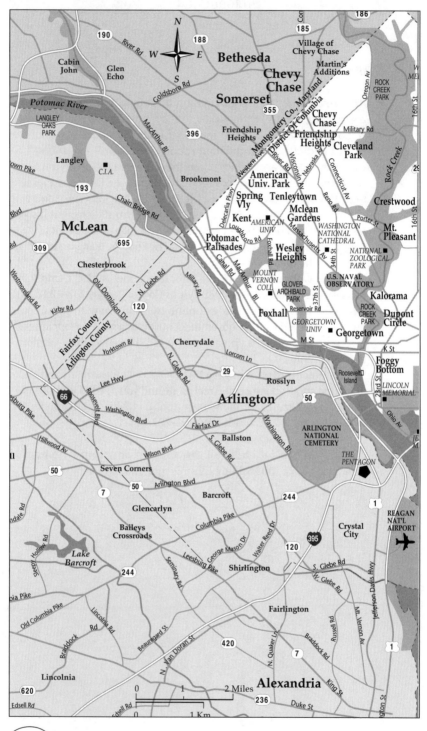

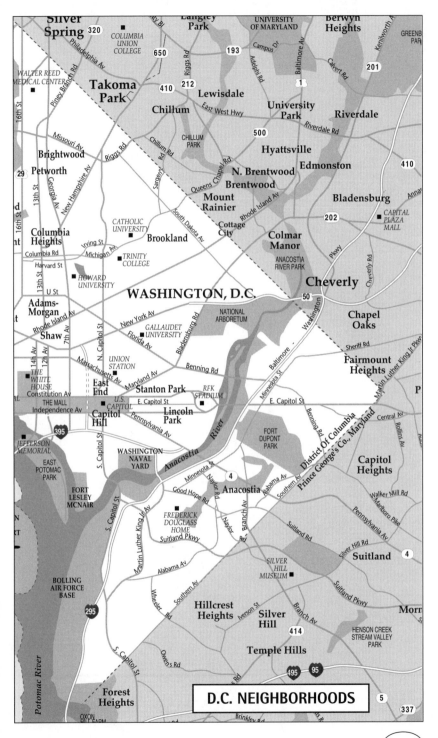

D.C. NEIGHBORHOODS

NEIGHBORHOODS IN THE WASHINGTON AREA ARE KNOWN LESS for distinctive housing styles or geography and more for the profile of their residents. Coming here you'll have about 3.5 million new neighbors—572,000 of them in the District and three million around the Beltway—and they tend to settle in clusters based on culture and lifestyle.

In workaholic Washington, a lot of accurate guesses can be made about a neighborhood by looking at the major employers nearby. Active and retired military officers gravitate toward Northern Virginia neighborhoods, near the Pentagon; congressional aides and lobbyists tend to be in Capitol Hill; diplomats cluster in Embassy Row; and non-profit staffers trying to change the world are usually within biking distance of Dupont Circle. The inner suburbs, especially to the north of D.C., attract civil service workers in search of affordable homes and good public schools. In the outer suburbs, it's more complicated—in the land of sprawling subdivisions and office parks, employees of America Online in Dulles or Digex in Beltsville might not find housing close to the office and therefore may have a lengthy commute.

If you move here with a job lined up, it's a good idea to find a home near your job. It will save you a lot of time and frustration, not to mention money, and it's easier on the environment. In this city where many work 50 or 60 hours a week, where the unwritten rule at some firms is "if you don't come in on Sunday, don't come in on Monday," the most common complaint about the quality of life in the Washington area has to do with traffic congestion and long commutes. Mass transit is such an attractive alternative to clogged commuter thoroughfares that many Washingtonians rate Metrorail access among their main considerations when looking for housing—and a house within a quarter-mile of a Metro station can cost 30% to 40% more than an identical house a mile away.

The following neighborhood profiles are intended to help you get a feel for the character of each neighborhood. Included are those neighborhoods most likely to appeal to newcomers. There is no substitute for meeting face-to-face with a local real estate agent or scouting out a neighborhood where you've seen an attractive listing in the classified ads, but these introductions will let you know what to expect.

THE DISTRICT OF COLUMBIA

D.C., the nation's capital is home to 572,000 people, 330,000 of whom are registered voters—the only voters in the United States who are not represented in Congress. District residents pay federal taxes—more, per capita, than residents of most states—but have no voting voice in the branch of government that collects and spends those taxes. And D.C. is the only city in the nation where every law passed by the city council and signed by the mayor must be approved by Congress before it goes into effect.

The home of Duke Ellington and Howard University, the District was once nicknamed "Chocolate City," and the majority of the population has always been so-called minorities. The District still has a strong African-American heritage, but the Latino and Asian communities are large and growing. There are plenty of international residents, too—including diplomats, journalists, students, translators, and their families—adding to the cultural diversity of many D.C. neighborhoods.

In 1980, District residents voted to join the Union as the 51st state—and Congress laughed the matter off the floor. Some citizens continue to push for statehood; others advocate "retrocession"—returning the District to Maryland, which donated the land to the federal government in 1790—and still others would settle for voting seats in Congress, though Congress would still have the power to overturn local laws and micromanage local affairs. D.C. voters elect the "shadow" congressional delegation of the proposed state of New Columbia—two shadow Senators and a shadow US Representative, who serve as elected lobbyists for D.C. statehood. There is also a nonvoting D.C. "delegate" to the House of Representatives—a position with some influence, perhaps, but no real power.

Meanwhile, the District government features an innovative layer of local representation: 37 elected "Advisory Neighborhood Commissions" have the power to hold hearings on zoning decisions, liquor licenses, building permits, and other local matters. Each commissioner represents about 2,000 households. The city council and regulatory agencies are required by law to give "great weight" to recommendations made by ANCs. In some neighborhoods, the local ANC is an active group of dedicated civic leaders; in others, few residents can name their commissioner and seats may go vacant for years. Some people attend ANC meetings, or run for a seat on the commission, out of genuine concern for quality of life in the neighborhood; others, it seems, get involved just to debate or to fatten a political résumé.

Almost every neighborhood also has a neighborhood association, a non-profit corporation working to improve living conditions and, in mixed residential and commercial neighborhoods, the business atmosphere. Call the Mayor's Office of Community Outreach, 202-442-8150, to find a civic association in your community.

Some civic-minded residents gather in cyberspace in a twice-weekly e-mail forum called "Themail," hosted by the editors of the online magazine www.dcwatch.com. It's the digital equivalent of the cracker barrel at the general store—a place to chat with neighbors, share reviews of neighborhood businesses, swap advice about dealing with city bureaucrats, and debate current events in the community.

As in any big city, residents have plenty of things to complain about. In Washington, potholes, traffic, and the humidity are perennial favorites, along with a few serious and contentious concerns: management of the public schools, federal/District relations, and displacement issues involving gentrification of long neglected neighborhoods—the great paradox of urban planning. Since the spring of 2000, an epidemic of underground electrical fires has caused power failures in Georgetown, Dupont Circle, and the downtown business district, and has sent manhole covers flying. (A report issued in late 2001 suggested that the network of underground power lines can't keep up with the city's growing demand for energy.) Still, Washingtonians are proud of their city, and take particular joy in showing off the non-tourist sites—the dark staircase from the film *The Exorcist*, the panoramic view from 13th and Euclid, the Japanese springhouse on the Capitol grounds, and their second-favorite restaurant (first is Ben's Chili Bowl).

If the District's lettered and numbered streets, grid quadrants, and traffic circles are making you dizzy, grab your trusty *ADC Street Atlas* and read the introductory section on the **L'Enfant Plan** to get your bearings.

Government: www.washingtondc.gov, 202-727-1000
Mayor: 202-727-2980, http://dc.gov/mayor
D.C. Council: 13-member legislature with eight members representing wards, four elected at large and one chairperson elected at large: 202-724-8000, www.dccouncil.washington.dc.us
Advisory Neighborhood Commissions: 202-727-2525, http://anc.washingtondc.gov
Public Schools: 202-724-4222, www.k12.dc.us; charter schools, 202-328-2660, www.dcpubliccharter.com
Libraries: 202-727-0321, http://dclibrary.org
Police: 202-727-1010, www.mpdc.org
Online Guides: www.washington.org, www.dclibrary.org/community, www.exploredc.org, www.dcpages.com, www.dcwatch.com, www.washdc.org

Area Code: 202
Sales Tax: 5.75%

CAPITOL HILL

STANTON PARK
LINCOLN PARK
POTOMAC AVENUE

Boundaries: North: H Street NE, H Street NW; **East**: 12th Street NE, 12th Street SE; **South**: South Carolina Avenue SE; **West**: 2nd Street NW, Washington Avenue SW

Location: North of the Washington Navy Yard; east of Judiciary Square and Penn Quarter; south of Union Station rail yards; west of the Southeast Waterfront; north of the Washington Navy Yard

Given the inherent prestige of Capitol Hill, many people claim to live there even though their addresses lie well to the south and east of the high ground. There really is a hill. Known as Jenkins Hill before the Capitol was built here, Capitol Hill also boasts the Supreme Court, the Library of Congress, and the offices of national newsmakers ranging from the Heritage Foundation to the Sierra Club. Members of Congress and their staffers live on the Hill, of course, as do lobbyists and journalists—but plenty of people live here just because they love the well-maintained townhouses from the late 19th and early 20th centuries.

These vintage homes are delightful—many feature exposed brick, hardwood floors, molded plaster, and even some working gaslights. On practically every block, there are a few homes bearing nameplates identifying them as historic landmarks. Naturally, residents pay dearly to live so close to the Capitol—often half a million dollars or more. Groups of recent graduates—or even freshmen members of Congress—share houses in order to save on rent, and prices drop a bit on the north side of the neighborhood, around **Stanton Park** east of Union Station. Capitol Hill, like many D.C. neighborhoods, is an area where housing prices and quality of life can vary dramatically in the space of a few blocks. H Street NE, a few blocks north of Stanton Park, is just now beginning to recover from the race riots of 1967. Even street corners in the shadow of the Capitol are not immune to late-night drug deals and gang activity, and if you read the police reports in Thursday's *Washington Post*, you'll see more muggings around the Hill than in most comparably wealthy neighborhoods. Some drug trafficking is evident in the nearby **Lincoln Park** and **Potomac**

Avenue neighborhoods east of 11th Street—where, as a result, many townhouses are bargains.

Almost every corner has a little market or convenience store, and there are plenty of eateries. Hill residents work long hours and eat out a lot, and Pennsylvania Avenue and 8th Street SE are lined with neighborhood restaurants. Taverns are a popular place to unwind—ask any lobbyist or congressional aide for directions to the Tiber Creek Pub, the Dubliner, Politiki, Tunnicliff's, or the Hawk & Dove. Those who do cook at home shop for groceries at Eastern Market, a cavernous red-brick hall along 7th Street SE, north of Pennsylvania Avenue. Here greengrocers, butchers, dairy farmers, and fishermen have been hawking their goods since 1873. Across the street is a weekend flea market, and the neighboring blocks are lined with funky little shops and delis. For upscale shopping and dining, go to Union Station, www.unionstationdc.com, on Massachusetts Avenue NE just a block north of the Capitol. Union Station has been a busy railway station since 1907 and a busy shopping mall since 1988. For many city dwellers it's a convenient place to see a movie—in fact, it houses the District's only commercial movie theater east of Rock Creek—and it's popular with tired tourists in need of a quick lunch or a sit-down dinner. (Soon after the shopping and dining concourses opened, Union Station dethroned the National Air & Space Museum as the top tourist attraction in the nation's capital.)

Web Sites: www.capitolhill.org, www.voiceofthehill.com, www.hillrag.com
Zip Codes: 20002, 20003
Post Offices: Postal Square, 2 Massachusetts Avenue NE, 202-523-2022; Southeast Station, 7th Street and Pennsylvania Avenue SE, 202-523-2173; Union Station Shops, 202-523-2057
Police Station: First District Substation, 5th & E streets SE, 202-727-4660
Emergency Hospital: D.C. General Hospital, 19th Street and Massachusetts Avenue SE, 202-675-5000
Libraries: Northeast, 330 7th Street NE, 202-698-3298; Southeast, 403 7th Street SE, 202-698-3377
Public High School: Eastern, 1700 East Capitol Street NE, 202-698-4500
Government: Ward 6
Parks: Capitol grounds; Folger Park (North Carolina Avenue between 2nd & 3rd streets SE); Garfield Park (off 3rd & G streets SE); Lincoln Park (East Capitol Street between 11th & 13th streets); Stanton Square (C Street NE between 4th & 6th); Seward Square (Pennsylvania & North Carolina avenues SE); Union Station Plaza (between Union Station and the Capitol)
Community Resources: Eastern Market & Market Five Gallery, 225 7th Street SE, 202-546-2698, www.easternmarket.net; Library of Congress, 101 Independence Avenue SE, 202-707-5000, www.loc.gov (see **Cultural Life**); Folger Shakespeare Library, 201 East Capitol Street SE,

202-544-4600, www.folger.edu (see **Cultural Life**); Georgetown University Law Center, 600 New Jersey Avenue NW, 202-662-9000, www.georgetown.edu; Capitol Hill Arts Workshop is a nonprofit facility featuring a theater, darkroom, and studio space for painting, pottery, music, and dance: 545 7th Street SE, 202-547-6839, www.chaw.org.

Public Transportation: Metro: Union Station (Red Line); Capitol South (Blue & Orange lines), 2nd & D streets SE; Eastern Market (Blue & Orange lines), 7th Street & Pennsylvania Avenue SE; Metrobus routes: 30-36 (Pennsylvania Avenue SE); 91-97 (1st Street); X8 (Maryland Avenue NE); D6 (C Street); MARC: Union Station (Penn, Brunswick, and Camden lines); Virginia Rail Express: Union Station (Fredericksburg and Manassas lines)

EAST END/PENN QUARTER

NOMA
CHINATOWN
JUDICIARY SQUARE

Boundaries: **North**: New York Avenue NW; **East**: Louisiana Avenue NW, railroad tracks; **South**: Pennsylvania Avenue NW; **West**: 15th Street NW

Location: north of the Mall; east of downtown; south of Shaw; west of Judiciary Square and Capitol Hill

East End and Penn Quarter are not residential areas, but locals and tourists come here for dining, entertainment, and work. **East End**, east of the MCI Center and overlapping with the eastern part of Shaw, is the focal point of big commercial development in the early 21st century. The old and new convention centers are both here, and there's perennial talk of adding a baseball stadium, if the city ever acquires a team. In the meantime, XM Satellite Radio and Black Entertainment Television have headquarters here, in the section sometimes called **NoMa** (**No**rth of **Ma**ssachusetts Avenue), and District officials hope to attract additional information technology firms to the area.

There are a few residential blocks in NoMa, west of New Jersey Avenue NW, and gentrification has not reached this area, so you may be able to find a good deal on a townhouse, some in exquisite shape, despite their innocuous-looking exteriors. East of New Jersey Avenue, toward North Capitol Street, are some of the most forlorn blocks in the District, with tracts of decaying public housing barely a 15 minute walk from the Capitol.

South of Massachusetts Avenue, along H Street NW between 5th and

7th, is **Chinatown**—or what's left of it. A festive Chinese arch still spans H Street outside the Gallery Place-Chinatown Metro station, but the only contemporary nod to the neighborhood's ethnic heritage is Chinese lettering in the windows of the Starbucks and the CVS drugstore. Most of the Chinese families have long since moved out to the suburbs. There are still plenty of good Chinese restaurants here, however, and the dean of them all is Tony Cheng's—downstairs for Mongolian barbecue cooked in front of you, upstairs for seafood, and in the foyer for photos of every President since Kennedy dining here.

Penn Quarter, a triangular area formed by Mt. Vernon Square, the Treasury Department, and the National Archives, emerged in the 1990s as a popular nightspot for the next age bracket past the club scene. Four of the city's most prominent theaters are here—the Warner, the Shakespeare, the National, and historic Ford's—and a hopping restaurant scene nourishes the theater crowds. Families with kids visit Planet Hollywood, Hard Rock Café and ESPN Zone, and there are popular local restaurants here too—notably Jaleo, which shares the historic Lansburgh department store building at 7th and E with the Shakespeare Theatre and luxury condos. Jaleo doesn't take reservations, and many people are willing to wait an hour for a table to sample the city's most renowned tapas. The meat-and-potatoes crowd goes a block south to the District Chophouse & Brewery, while nouveau cuisine fans head a few blocks west to Red Sage at 12th and Pennsylvania.

Artists and art lovers flock here, too, for the National Portrait Gallery at 7th & F streets and the National Gallery of Art at 7th and Constitution Avenue. The stretch of 7th street between the two museums is lined with little galleries and studios. The US Navy Memorial and the Martin Luther King Memorial Library (the main D.C. public library) are nearby, and some of the shops and office buildings around 9th and F streets date from the late 19th century.

You aren't likely to live in Penn Quarter unless your timing is impeccable—there's not much housing, and vacancies are scarce. If you do find an apartment at the Lansburgh, or at Market Square at 7th and Pennsylvania NW, expect to pay an astronomical price. Despite perennial talk of the need for more downtown housing, no developer wants to pass up this "trophy" real estate where exclusive office towers and hotels—much more profitable than housing—could go.

Between Penn Quarter and the Capitol is **Judiciary Square**, Pennsylvania Avenue to F Street and 4th to 5th streets NW, named for the concentration of federal and local courthouses and Justice Department offices. The Metropolitan Police Department is also headquartered here, and the National Law Enforcement Officers Memorial occupies a broad plaza just outside the Judiciary Square Metro station. At the north end of the square, the National Building Museum, housed in the historic Pension

Building, is one of the most underrated museums in Washington—both for its exhibits on architecture and infrastructure and for its intrinsic beauty. Parts of East End and Penn Quarter are within the **Downtown Business Improvement District (BID)**, www.downtowndc.org, a special tax zone in which business owners have actually *asked* the city to collect a slightly higher tax on commercial property. The added revenue pays for certain extra services, such as private street cleaning contractors, security cameras, and perky "ambassadors" who patrol the sidewalks to greet tourists and make homeless people feel unwelcome. (The **Golden Triangle BID**, www.gtbid.org, adjoins the Downtown BID to the west and covers the area between Dupont Circle and Pennsylvania Avenue NW.)

Web Site: www.downtowndc.org

Zip Codes: 20001, 20002, 20005

Post Offices: Ben Franklin Station, 12th Street & Pennsylvania Avenue NW, 202-523-2386; Techworld, 8th & K streets NW, 202-523-2400

Police Station: Metropolitan Police Department Headquarters, 4th & D streets NW, 202-727-1010, http://mpdc.dc.gov

Emergency Hospital: Howard University Hospital, 2401 Georgia Avenue NW, 202-865-6100

Library: Martin Luther King Jr. Memorial, 9th & G streets NW, 202-727-0321

Government: Ward 2, School District 1

Neighborhood Festivals: Arts On Foot (September), www.artsonfoot.org; Taste of D.C. (October), www.washington.org

Park: Freedom Plaza/Pershing Park (Pennsylvania Avenue NW between 13th & 15th streets)

Community Resources: National Portrait Gallery/National Museum of American Art, 8th & F streets NW, 202-357-1300, www.npg.si.edu; Ford's Theatre, 511 10th Street NW, 202-347-7833, www.fordstheatre.org; National Theatre, 1321 Pennsylvania Avenue NW, 202-628-6161, www.nationaltheatre.org; Shakespeare Theatre, 450 7th Street NW, 202-207-1122, www.shakespearedc.org; Warner Theatre, 13th & E streets NW, 202-783-4000, www.warnertheatre.com; National Law Enforcement Officers Memorial Visitors Center, 605 E Street NW, 202-737-3400; National Building Museum, 401 F Street NW, 202-272-2448, www.nbm.org

Public Transportation: Metro: Metro Center (Red, Blue, and Orange lines), entrances on G Street NW at 11th, 12th and 13th streets, and at 12th & F streets NW; Gallery Place-Chinatown (Red, Yellow, and Green lines), entrances on 7th Street NW at F and H streets; Judiciary Square (Red Line), entrances at the National Law Enforcement Officers Memorial and at 4th & D streets NW; Metrobus routes: D1-D6 (K Street NW), S2/S4 (I Street NW), 42 (11th Street NW), 54 (Pennsylvania Avenue NW)

DUPONT CIRCLE

Boundaries: North: S Street NW; **East:** 14th Street NW; **South:** N Street NW, Rhode Island Avenue NW; **West:** Rock Creek

Location: north of downtown; east of Shaw; south of Kalorama and Adams Morgan; east of West End

Dupont Circle is home to dozens of non-profit advocacy groups, and home to many recent college graduates hoping to get paid for their idealism and commitment to social causes. It's also the capital of Washington's large gay and lesbian community, and many stores and restaurants display a pink triangle or rainbow flag in the window. Lambda Rising and Outlook, among other retailers, cater especially to the gay community, as do several bars and cafés along 17th Street NW. Dupont Circle—along with Adams Morgan to the north—is the heart of Washington's nightlife. An array of restaurants and bars, movie theaters, bookstores with long hours, and ample boutique shopping make this a neighborhood where the sidewalks don't roll up at sundown—indeed, not even at midnight.

Kramerbooks & Afterwords was Washington's first combined bookstore/cafe, and still leads the city's short list for late night dining and spotting political celebrities. Its upstairs bulletin board is a good place to look for short-term sublets or apartment rental postings. The original Teaism teahouse, now a local chain, still draws standing-room crowds to 2009 R Street NW. The Brickskeller, at 1523 22nd Street NW, serves some 700 kinds of beer from all over the world; expect at least a half-hour wait on weekends. Kramerbooks and other local favorites, including Luna Grill & Diner and Second Story Books, have opened locations in the suburbs. If you don't want to dine out every night, there's an abundance of gourmet markets, bakeries, and eateries geared toward carryout; and there's a bustling farmers' market on Sunday mornings at the Q Street entrance to the Dupont Circle Metro station. A word to the wise: the Safeway supermarket at 17th & R streets is known as the "Soviet Safeway" because of the notoriously long lines. If you're in a hurry, it might actually be quicker to take the No. 42 bus to the Safeway at 1747 Columbia Road.

The Circle itself is a gathering place for bicycle couriers, executives from nearby office buildings, and street people. At lunchtime and early evening, many come to play chess at tables with built-in chessboards, and there's often a small crowd of spectators. Between two concentric rings of benches, which are always crowded, grassy lawns serve as the neighborhood "beach." The fountain in the center of the circle is unique—most circles and squares downtown are dominated by the standard bronze statue of a 19th-century general or admiral. At the other extreme, a tiny patch of grass at 20th Street & New Hampshire Avenue NW was "adopted" by one local citizen and unofficially dedicated as the Sonny Bono Memorial Park. It features one bench, lovingly maintained flowerbeds, and a simple plaque in memory of the entertainer and congressman.

There are some art galleries on Connecticut Avenue and along the side streets north of the Circle, but rising rents have forced some struggling artists to 7th Street NW and Shaw, where zoning "overlays" encourage the development of studios and galleries. South of N Street NW, Connecticut Avenue is lined with office buildings whose storefront restaurants and clothing stores cater to the downtown office crowd. The Improv comedy club is here, at 1140 Connecticut Avenue, and several plain-looking buildings nearby camouflage swanky SoHo-type nightclubs—the kind with fashion police at the door.

Many row houses off the Circle have been converted into apartments of all sizes, and elegant old mansions have been turned into embassies or offices housing non-profit groups, including Public Citizen and the Church of Scientology. One of the finest houses in Washington, the Christian Heurich mansion at 20th Street and New Hampshire Avenue, serves as the headquarters of the Historical Society of Washington, D.C. "English basements"—apartments below row houses, with their own separate entrances—make popular rentals for singles and young couples just getting started, but even these fetch $1,000 or more for a one-bedroom. An efficiency or studio apartment can approach $1,000 in the postwar high-rises along New Hampshire Avenue south of the Circle; in prestigious old apartment buildings to the east, between 14th & 17th streets NW, condo units command even higher rent.

For most young newcomers, the Dupont Circle area is one of the first stops on a house-hunting tour. If you're willing and able to pay a four-figure rent (or to buy a six-figure condo), you'll have a dazzling assortment of restaurants, shops, and nightlife within walking distance.

Web Sites: www.dupont-circle.com, www.intowner.com

Zip Codes: 20009, 20036

Post Offices: Temple Heights Station, 1921 Florida Avenue NW, 202-232-7613; 20th Street, 1111 20th Street NW, 202-523-2410

Police Station: Third District Headquarters, 1620 V Street NW, 202-673-6930

Emergency Hospital: George Washington University Hospital, 901 23rd Street NW, 202-715-4000

Library: West End, 24th & L streets NW, 202-724-8707

Public High Schools: Cardozo, 13th & Clifton streets NW, 202-673-7385; School Without Walls, 2130 G Street NW, 202-724-4889

Government: Ward 2

Neighborhood Festivals: Capital Pride Parade (June), www.capital-pride.org; Kramerbooks & Afterwords Block Party (August), 202-387-1400; Halloween High Heels Race

Parks: Dupont Circle, Rock Creek (points of access west of 23rd Street NW), Rose (26th & P streets NW), Scott Circle

Community Resources: Phillips Collection, rivaled only by the Corcoran as the city's leading private art museum; 21st & Q streets NW, 202-387-2151, www.phillipscollection.org (see **Cultural Life**); Visions Cinema Bistro Lounge, 1927 Florida Avenue NW, 202-667-0090; Church Street Theatre, 1401 Church Street NW, 202-265-3748. D.C. Jewish Community Center offers a health club, theater, after-school programs, and social activities: 1529 16th Street NW, 202-518-9400, www.dcjcc.org. The neighborhood probably has more bookstores and special-interest libraries per square mile than anywhere else in the country—see **Cultural Life** for details. Also visit www.dkmuseums.com for a directory of more than a dozen small museums in the Dupont-Kalorama area.

Public Transportation: Metro: Dupont Circle station (Red Line), entrances at Connecticut Avenue & Q Street NW and south side of Dupont Circle at 19th Street NW; Metrobus routes: 42 (Connecticut Avenue NW), G2 (P Street NW), L2 (New Hampshire Avenue NW), N2-N6 (Connecticut Avenue NW downtown, Massachusetts Avenue NW uptown)

KALORAMA

KALORAMA TRIANGLE

Boundaries: **North**: Rock Creek; **East**: Connecticut Avenue NW, Columbia Road NW, 19th Street NW; **South**: S Street NW; **West**: Rock Creek

Location: north of Dupont Circle; east of Embassy Row (across Rock Creek); south of Woodley Park (across Rock Creek); west of Adams Morgan

Just up the hill from Dupont Circle, straddling Connecticut Avenue NW, is Kalorama, where every home that isn't an embassy or museum is a mansion or luxury apartment. Kalorama, Greek for "beautiful view," is perched on hills above Rock Creek, and many homes offer postcard-perfect views. Indeed, it was a view of the White House—now obstructed by downtown office buildings—that lured affluent Washingtonians to build homes here in the late 19th and early 20th centuries.

Presidents Hoover and Franklin Roosevelt lived in Kalorama before they moved to 1600 Pennsylvania Avenue, and President Wilson retired here.

Today, residents include senators, retired Cabinet secretaries, and members of the city council. Nearly a quarter of the houses here are embassies or chanceries, and in 1989, the whole neighborhood was added to the National Register of Historic Places.

Many homes have ballrooms and formal gardens, and some have servants' quarters. Some houses are actually made up of parts of European castles or chalets that were moved here. Generally, houses start at half a million dollars, though a few have sold for nearly $3 million. Even if money is no object, you will have to watch patiently and move quickly to buy a home here—homes often sell before they're even listed.

Many area apartment buildings were built before World War I and are still among the most elegant residences in town—and the most expensive. Condos often start at a million dollars. If you're lucky, however, you might find an efficiency renting for $900 in the area bounded by Columbia, Calvert and Rock Creek—the area known as **Kalorama Triangle** in the lingo of real estate classifieds.

If your Kalorama address leaves you a little short on bus fare, you can walk down Connecticut Avenue to shop and dine in Dupont Circle; walk across the Duke Ellington Bridge into Adams Morgan; or walk across the majestic Taft Bridge into Woodley Park. Get used to those walks—pleasant, but hilly—for groceries, videos, and other basics. Kalorama is all residential.

Web Site: www.intowner.com

Zip Codes: 20008, 20009

Post Offices: Kalorama Station, 2300 18th Street NW, 202-523-2904; Temple Heights Station, 1921 Florida Avenue NW, 202-232-7613

Police Station: Third District Headquarters, 1620 V Street NW, 202-673-6930

Emergency Hospital: George Washington University Hospital, 901 23rd Street NW, 202-715-4000

Library: West End, 24th & L streets NW, 202-724-8707

Public High Schools: Cardozo, 13th & Clifton streets NW, 202-673-7385; School Without Walls, 2130 G Street NW, 202-724-4889

Government: Ward 1

Neighborhood Festival: Dupont-Kalorama Museum Walk (June), 202-667-0441, www.dkmuseums.com

Parks: Mitchell (off Massachusetts Avenue NW west of Sheridan Circle); Rock Creek (points of access off Waterside Drive NW)

Community Resources: Textile Museum, 2320 S Street NW, 202-667-0441, www.textilemuseum.org; other small museums in the Dupont-Kalorama area are listed at www.dkmuseums.com. The Woodrow Wilson House, where the Nobel laureate and ex-President lived, is the only presidential museum in the District: 2340 S Street NW, 202-387-4062, www.woodrowwilsonhouse.org.

Public Transportation: Metrobus routes: L1 (Connecticut Avenue NW); 42 (Columbia Road NW); walk to Metro, Dupont Circle or Woodley Park-Zoo stations (Red Line)

FOGGY BOTTOM/WEST END

Boundaries: **North**: N Street NW; **East**: 17th Street NW, Connecticut Avenue NW; **South**: Constitution Avenue NW; **West**: Potomac River, Rock Creek

Location: north of the Mall; east of Georgetown (across Rock Creek); south of Kalorama; west of Dupont Circle and downtown

Nestled between the White House and Georgetown, at the "foggy bottom" of a hill overlooking the Potomac, **Foggy Bottom** is home to the State Department, the International Monetary Fund, and the World Bank. To the north, between Dupont Circle and Georgetown, are the upscale hotels and restaurants of **West End**. Together, these two areas essentially create one neighborhood—a diverse zone of overlap between elite Georgetown, powerful Pennsylvania Avenue, and hip Dupont Circle. George Washington University is here, and so are the headquarters of the American Red Cross, the Federal Reserve, the Pan-American Health Organization, the Bureau of National Affairs, and the General Services Administration—the "landlord" of government office buildings.

Most of the homes here are luxury apartments in modern high-rises, but there are a few blocks of old row houses west of New Hampshire Avenue. Many were built more than a century ago for workers at the Christian Heurich Brewery, which once stood where the Kennedy Center is today. The neighborhood attracts a lot of diplomats and prominent journalists; Mayor Anthony Williams also lives here. At the end of New Hampshire Avenue NW, between the Kennedy Center and the mouth of Rock Creek, is perhaps the most famous address in Washington besides 1600 Pennsylvania Avenue: The Watergate. Scene of the 1972 burglary of the Democratic National Committee headquarters, The Watergate is a towering mixed-use complex with luxury apartments and condominiums, offices, the posh Swissotel Watergate, designer boutiques, and four-star restaurants. Justice Ruth Bader Ginsburg, Senator Bob and Secretary Elizabeth Dole, and the most famous White House intern in history have all called The Watergate home. In its shadow, to the north, is the old water gate at the south end of the C&O Canal.

Between the Potomac and George Washington University (GW), you'll find apartments for more varied budgets, but even student-friendly housing isn't exactly cheap. High-rise luxury condos in the vicinity of 22nd and M are not known for their dazzling views, but they do offer a convenient location, lots of space, and modern trimmings. With rooftop pools, concierge services, and carpeted hallways, these buildings look and feel like hotels. Like many urban universities, GW is more like a neighborhood than a distinct campus, and longtime residents of the West End and Foggy Bottom are constantly at odds with the school about student housing, parking, and proposals to expand school facilities. Parking can be a problem here.

Foggy Bottom and West End are just a few minutes walk from the fine restaurants and clubs of Georgetown, Dupont Circle, and the downtown business district, but there are neighborhood attractions here too: the jazz club One Step Down; Lulu's nightclub and Blackie's House of Beef, together filling a whole block of 22nd Street; restaurants and taverns that cater to GW students; and Asia Nora. For the city's favorite mashed potatoes, peach cobbler, and cornbread, visit Sholl's Colonial Cafeteria in the basement of the office building at 20th and K streets NW. Sholl's, a venerable Washington institution, attracts patrons from all walks of life, and the people-watching is at least as good as the food.

Some residents continue to fume about the closure of Pennsylvania Avenue NW near the White House, a precaution taken by the Secret Service after several security incidents in the mid-1990s. While a six-lane crosstown thoroughfare was severed, requiring tedious detours around Lafayette Square, the resulting pedestrian zone in front of the White House is popular with sightseers, photographers, street hockey players, and (of course) placard-waving protesters.

Zip Code: 20037
Post Office: Watergate, 2512 Virginia Avenue NW, 202-965-2730
Police Station: Second District Headquarters, 3320 Idaho Avenue NW, 202-282-0070
Emergency Hospital: George Washington University Hospital, 901 23rd Street NW, 202-715-4000
Library: West End, 24th & L streets NW, 202-724-8707
Public High School: School Without Walls, 2130 G Street NW, 202-724-4889
Government: Ward 2
Parks: Edward R. Murrow (18th Street and Pennsylvania Avenue NW); Rock Creek (access off 26th & M streets NW); Rose (26th & P streets NW); Washington Circle
Community Resources: George Washington University, 2121 I Street NW, 202-994-1000, www.gwu.edu; John F. Kennedy Center for the

Performing Arts, New Hampshire Avenue and Rock Creek Parkway NW, 202-467-4600, www.kennedy-center.org
Public Transportation: Metro: Foggy Bottom-GWU (Blue & Orange lines), 23rd & I streets NW; Metrobus routes: 30-36 (Pennsylvania Avenue NW), D5 (K Street NW), L2 (20th Street NW northbound, 21st Street NW southbound)

GEORGETOWN

BURLEITH
FOXHALL

Boundaries: **North**: Whitehaven Parkway, Whitehaven Park; **East**: Rock Creek; **South**: Potomac River; **West**: Potomac River

Location: north of the Potomac River; east of Palisades; south of Glover Park; west of West End and Dupont Circle (across Rock Creek)

Before upstart colonials dreamed of a nation, let alone a nation's capital, Georgetown was a bustling port on the Potomac River at the point where the water becomes too shallow for further navigation. One of the oldest urban neighborhoods in North America, Georgetown remained an industrial center throughout the 19th century and did not become a fashionable address until the 1950s. Today residential Georgetown, with its 200-year-old buildings and cobblestone side streets, boasts a world-renowned university and a disproportionate share of Washington's powerful newsmakers. The commercial strips of Wisconsin Avenue and M Street NW are favorite evening and weekend destinations for tourists, suburbanites and students from area universities.

Most Georgetown homes are beautiful rowhouses on tree-lined streets; apartments are rare, other than "English basement" apartments below townhouses. Historic preservation rules limit the alteration of exteriors, but inside most homeowners have added air conditioning and modern kitchens. The appeal here is genuine; the houses, storefronts and converted industrial buildings are all of a "they don't make 'em like that anymore" quality. Georgetown University adds to the charm, with Gothic stone buildings and the towering steeple of Healy Hall marking the west end of the neighborhood. Not coincidentally, housing is expensive—many homes fetch at least twice the citywide median price. Georgetown University students cram into group houses, rent apartments across the Key Bridge in Virginia, or head uptown.

There is one cluster of 1980s high-rises: Washington Harbour, by the river and the mouth of Rock Creek. The view is worth a million bucks, so the condos here—at half a million—are sort of a bargain. The complex is designed to be accessible by yacht, and boaters come ashore to the waterfront bars and restaurants.

Wisconsin Avenue and M Street feature upscale specialty shops, boutiques, and neighborhood cafes and restaurants; increasingly, however, you'll also find the same Starbucks, Ben & Jerry's and Barnes & Noble stores you'll find in any other city.

No other city has the Chesapeake & Ohio Canal, though. This 19th-century barge canal ran from Georgetown to Cumberland, MD, past rocky stretches of the Potomac. Today, C&O Canal National Historical Park offers some of the best places for cycling and jogging in the Washington area. (See the chapter on **Greenspace** for details.)

Just one cautionary note about Georgetown: watch out for exploding manhole covers! Beginning in the spring of 2000, several mysterious explosions under M Street sent these heavy iron discs flying 10 feet into the air—and caused power failures throughout the neighborhood. The culprit is the aging electrical system serving the neighborhood east of Wisconsin Avenue. Pepco has begun a $30 million project to replace the old wires and cable throughout the affected area—but Pepco officials say the task might not be finished until 2005.

Georgetown has its own little suburbs—the posh neighborhoods of **Foxhall** to the west and **Burleith** to the north. These areas feature big homes with big yards behind privacy hedges. In Burleith, one Whitehaven Parkway mansion is the home of Senator and Bill Clinton. In 2001, philanthropist Betty Brown Casey gave $50 million to the city, partly to build a mayoral mansion on a 17-acre parcel in Foxhall. And the Foxhall Village enclave, just west of the university, is an award-winning complex of stucco Tudor houses built in the 1920s.

Know how to make a Georgetown resident laugh? Ask about parking. If you must park here, plan to spend *half an hour* looking for a space. Better yet, get on the bus.

Web Sites: www.georgetowndclife.com, www.georgetowner.com, www.burleith.org, www.foxhall.org

Zip Code: 20007

Post Office: Georgetown, 3050 K Street NW, 202-523-2405

Police Station: Second District Headquarters, 3320 Idaho Avenue NW, 202-282-0070

Emergency Hospitals: Georgetown University Hospital, 3800 Reservoir Road NW, 202-687-2000; George Washington University Hospital, 901 23rd Street NW, 202-715-4000

Library: West End, 24th & L streets NW, 202-724-8707

Public High Schools: School Without Walls, 2130 G Street NW, 202-724-4889; Duke Ellington School of the Arts, 1698 35th Street NW, 202-292-0123

Government: Ward 2

Parks: C&O Canal (between M Street NW and the Potomac River); Dumbarton Oaks-Montrose (north of R Street NW between Wisconsin Avenue and Rock Creek); Glover Archbold (points of access off 44th Street NW and Reservoir Road); Rock Creek (points of access off Pennsylvania Avenue and M Street NW, east of 28th Street); Whitehaven (connecting Dumbarton Oaks and Glover Archbold parks north of T Street NW)

Community Resources: Georgetown University, 37th & O streets NW, 202-687-4328, www.georgetown.edu; Junior League of Washington, 3039 M Street NW, 202-337-2001, www.jlw.org; Cineplex Odeon Foundry shows movies at a discount several months after their initial release, 1055 Thomas Jefferson Street NW, 202-333-FILM ext. 827.

Public Transportation: Metro: Foggy Bottom-GWU (Blue & Orange lines), 23rd & I streets NW; Metrobus routes: 30-36 (Pennsylvania and Wisconsin avenues NW), D1/D2 and D6 (Q Street NW); G2 (P Street NW westbound, O Street NW eastbound)

UPPER NORTHWEST

EMBASSY ROW
MCLEAN GARDENS
AMERICAN UNIVERSITY PARK
FRIENDSHIP HEIGHTS
TENLEYTOWN
SPRING VALLEY
PALISADES
KENT
WESLEY HEIGHTS
GLOVER PARK

Boundaries: **North**: Maryland; **East**: Reno Road NW, 34th Street NW; **South**: Whitehaven Parkway, Whitehaven Park; **West**: Maryland, Potomac River

Location: north of Georgetown and Burleith; east of the Potomac River; south of Bethesda, MD; west of the Connecticut Avenue corridor

A classified ad listing a home in "Upper Northwest" might mean a spacious colonial in the leafy hills of Foxhall Road, a luxury apartment on the stretch of Massachusetts Avenue known as **Embassy Row**, a brick townhouse in the self-contained residential village of **McLean Gardens**, a detached house with a white picket fence in **American University Park** north of Ward Circle, or an older brick or stone house off the bustling retail corridor of Wisconsin Avenue in **Friendship Heights**. In any case, it is likely to mean an expensive home, but probably more spacious and cheaper per square foot than homes in Dupont Circle or Capitol Hill. It will mean an older home in a stable, upscale neighborhood, and proximity to elite private schools such as Sidwell Friends, St. Alban's, National Cathedral, and the public Duke Ellington School of the Arts, as well as excellent public elementary schools. And unless you live just off Wisconsin or Massachusetts avenues, it will mean a lot of driving—west of American University, even buses are scarce.

East of the university is **Tenleytown**, a commercial strip along Wisconsin Avenue. This is some of the highest ground in Washington, prime real estate for radio and TV towers. NBC, CBS, and Fox have studios nearby, and residents routinely face off against wireless phone companies seeking to add even more towers to the Tenleytown skyline.

In American University Park, south of River Road NW, a nice colonial house with a fenced yard and two or three bedrooms might rent for the price of a one-bedroom apartment on Connecticut Avenue. Across Massachusetts Avenue are posh enclaves in the western corner of the District: **Spring Valley**, on the north side of Loughboro Road, and **Palisades**, on the south, with **Kent** and **Wesley Heights** lying west and east of Foxhall Road. Houses here are spacious, elegant, and shaded by big trees in big yards. Spring Valley lost some of its luster in the 1990s when construction crews unearthed live ammunition and chemical weapons that the Army was testing nearby during World War I. Many residents are concerned about possible effects of long-term exposure to the buried chemicals, though the Army made a major cleanup effort from 1993 to 1995 and maintains that there is no danger to the public. Currently the Army Corps of Engineers is in the process of certifying that each property is free of munitions and harmful chemicals. Despite this sour note, this area is much sought after. Houses demand premium prices and often sell within a matter of days.

Heading east along Massachusetts Avenue is Embassy Row, an accurate nickname for the area between Dupont and Westmoreland circles. Japan, the United Kingdom, India, Ireland, New Zealand, Greece, and Finland are just a few of the dozens of countries whose official representatives in the US are based here. Almost all embassies have visitors' centers and exhibits, and are listed in the business White Pages under "Embassy of..." There are a few apartment buildings here, too—big, elegant prewar buildings. Expect to pay $1,000 or more for a one-bedroom rental. West of

Embassy Row, the cottages and townhouses of **Glover Park** make afford-able rentals for young families and groups of recent graduates.

Ambassadors aren't the only VIPs with official residences in Upper Northwest—there's also the Episcopal Archbishop of Washington, whose house is on the grounds of the National Cathedral, and the Vice President of the United States, whose mansion is on the grounds of the US Naval Observatory. The observatory, on a hill above Massachusetts Avenue NW at 34th Street, is also the home of the Navy's atomic clock, the official time-piece of the US government.

Web Sites: www.palisadesdc.org, www.s6000.com/md-dc/friendshipheights
Zip Codes: 20007, 20016
Post Offices: Calvert, Wisconsin Avenue & Calvert Street NW, 202-523-5907; Friendship, 4005 Wisconsin Avenue NW, 202-635-5304; Palisades, 5136 MacArthur Boulevard NW, 202-523-2562
Police Station: Second District Headquarters, 3320 Idaho Avenue NW (39th Street), 202-282-0070
Emergency Hospitals: Georgetown University Hospital, 3800 Reservoir Road NW, 202-687-2000; Sibley Memorial Hospital, 5255 Loughboro Road NW, 202-537-4000
Libraries: Tenley-Friendship, 4450 Wisconsin Avenue, 202-282-3090; Palisades, 49th & V streets NW, 202-282-3139
Public High School: Woodrow Wilson, 3950 Chesapeake Street NW, 202-282-0120
Government: Ward 3
Neighborhood Festivals: Glover Park Day (June); Palisades Fourth of July Parade; Spring Valley 5K to benefit Children's Hospital (September), 202-895-2705
Parks: Battery Kemble (off Chain Bridge Road NW between Loughboro Road and the Potomac River); C&O Canal (points of access along Clara Barton Parkway and Canal Road NW); Glover Archbold (east of 44th Street NW between Massachusetts Avenue and the Potomac River); Palisades (Canal Road and Arizona Avenue NW); Wesley Heights (con-necting Battery Kemble and Glover Archbold parks south of Garfield Street NW); Whitehaven (south of W Street NW between Wisconsin Avenue and Glover Archbold Park)
Community Resources: Washington Islamic Center, 2551 Massachusetts Avenue NW, 202-332-8343 (see **Places of Worship**); Washington National Cathedral, Wisconsin & Massachusetts avenues NW, 202-966-2171; www.cathedral.org/cathedral (see **Places of Worship**). Iona House Senior Services, 4125 Albemarle Street, 202-895-9448, www.iona.org/privatecare; Capital Crescent Trail is a Rails-to-Trails bike path along the route of a rail line that once carried coal to the federal

power plant serving the Capitol. The commuter-oriented trail connects Georgetown with downtown Silver Spring via Palisades, Bethesda, and Chevy Chase; 202-234-4874, www.cctrail.org.

Public Transportation: Metro: Tenleytown-AU (Red Line), Wisconsin Avenue and Albemarle; Friendship Heights, Wisconsin and Western avenues NW; Metrobus routes: N2-N8 (Massachusetts Avenue NW), 30-36 (Wisconsin Avenue NW), M4 (Nebraska Avenue NW), D5/D6 (MacArthur Boulevard NW)

CONNECTICUT AVENUE CORRIDOR

WOODLEY PARK
CLEVELAND PARK
VAN NESS
CHEVY CHASE

Boundaries: **North**: Maryland; **East**: Rock Creek; **South**: Taft Bridge; **West**: 34th Street NW, Reno Road NW

Location: north of Kalorama; east of Embassy Row, Tenleytown, and Friendship Heights; south of Chevy Chase, MD

Connecticut Avenue NW from the Taft Bridge over Rock Creek to Chevy Chase Circle at the Maryland line, is a charming series of "urban village" neighborhoods that combine the best elements of urban and suburban living. Most of the homes are in grand old apartment buildings, but there are plenty of single-family houses on tree-lined side streets. The houses here don't all look alike, they have fenced yards, and some are even made of stone. Just off Connecticut Avenue, you'll find many 1930s townhouses with basements converted into separate apartments. Commercial strips punctuate Connecticut Avenue, drawing locals to Woodley Park, Cleveland Park, Van Ness and Chevy Chase for shopping and dining.

This area attracts a political crowd—a favorite local hangout is Politics & Prose, a bookstore and cafe that hosts readings by big-name political authors. And more personal checks written to political campaigns bear zip code 20008 than any other zip code outside Hollywood or Manhattan.

From Taft Bridge north to Klingle Valley is **Woodley Park**, whose east-side residents are privy to the early morning sound of trumpeting elephants from the nearby National Zoo. Affordable ethnic restaurants with outdoor seating face the Woodley Park-Zoo Metro station. Around the corner, the city's largest hotel, the Marriott Wardman Park, is perched high above Rock Creek.

North of Woodley Park, Connecticut Avenue crosses a bridge over Klingle Valley Park, the newest addition to the District's extensive park system. Klingle Road, once used as a commuting back door into Mt. Pleasant, was closed in 1990 due to storm damage. While tree removal crews were busy clearing storm debris from residential streets throughout Northwest D.C., residents of Mt. Pleasant and Cleveland Park took the opportunity to use the closed road for walking and jogging. Many residents decided this area served their neighborhood much better as a park rather than as a commuter shortcut, and asked the city *not* to repair the road.

North of Klingle Valley is **Cleveland Park**, summer retreat of President Grover Cleveland. Cleveland, like many Washingtonians, came to this high ground to enjoy the cooling breezes that bring some relief from the swampy August heat. Many of the 19th-century cottages here were built with wraparound porches to catch the breeze. Some of those vintage homes are palatial, but there are more modest three-bedroom houses on the side streets, with back-alley garages instead of driveways.

Some of the District's best public schools are here, including John Eaton and Oyster Bilingual elementary schools, as well as prestigious private schools such as the Washington International School, Maret, and the National Cathedral School. Consequently, Cleveland Park attracts many families with school-aged children. Students in other neighborhoods compete for limited "out-of-boundary" admission to the top public schools here. (See **Childcare and Education** for more on the process.)

The biggest commercial movie screen in the Washington area is in Cleveland Park, at the vintage Uptown Theater, complete with balcony seats. A commercial strip on Connecticut Avenue between Macomb and Porter streets features two gourmet markets and a health food store, a Petco pet superstore, several coffee bars, two Irish pubs and an assortment of neighborhood restaurants.

North of Cleveland Park, across another little valley leading to Rock Creek, is the main campus of the University of the District of Columbia. The stores lining Connecticut Avenue here in **Van Ness** are more utilitarian than the destination shops of Cleveland Park—here it's office supplies, photocopying, fast food and groceries. There's a Pier One Imports home furnishing store, too, and Calvert Woodley Liquors has a nice selection of fine cheeses. Off Connecticut Avenue on Van Ness Street is Howard University Law School.

From Yuma Street north to Chevy Chase Circle is the D.C. neighborhood known as **Chevy Chase**, not to be confused with the neighboring town of Chevy Chase, MD. Just off Connecticut Avenue, you'll find assorted cottages, split-levels, and brick and stone colonials, all beautiful and expensive. Mansions border Rock Creek Park. Some of the District's most desirable schools are in Chevy Chase: Lafayette and Murch elementary schools, Deal Junior High, and the private St. John's and Georgetown Day high schools.

Connecticut Avenue, the commercial main street of Chevy Chase, caters to locals in a high income bracket: gourmet markets, good restaurants, and bookstores, but also video stores, a library, a post office, and Chevy Chase Community Center.

Web Site: www.clevelandpark.com

Zip Codes: 20008, 20015

Post Offices: Cleveland Park, 3430 Connecticut Avenue NW, 202-523-2395; Northwest Station, 5632 Connecticut Avenue NW, 202-523-2569

Police Stations: Second District Headquarters, 3320 Idaho Avenue NW (39th Street), 202-282-0070; Sixth District Headquarters, 100 42nd Street NW (Albemarle Street), 202-727-4520

Emergency Hospitals: Georgetown University Hospital, 3800 Reservoir Road NW, 202-687-2000; George Washington University Hospital, 901 23rd Street NW, 202-715-4000

Libraries: Chevy Chase, 5625 Connecticut Avenue NW (Oliver Street), 202-282-0021; Cleveland Park, 3310 Connecticut Avenue NW (Macomb Street), 202-282-3080

Public High School: Woodrow Wilson, 3950 Chesapeake Street NW, 202-282-0120

Government: Ward 3 (except the eastern part of Chevy Chase, which is Ward 4)

Neighborhood Festival: Cleveland Park Day (September)

Parks: Chevy Chase Circle; Klingle Valley (south of Macomb Street NW from Rock Creek west to Woodley Road); Melvin C. Hazen (south of Tilden Street NW from Rock Creek west to 34th); Muhlenberg-Fort Reno (off Nebraska Avenue NW just west of Connecticut Avenue); Normanstone (along Massachusetts Avenue NW across from the Naval Observatory); Rock Creek (points of access east of Connecticut Avenue NW and off Military Road); Soapstone Valley (south of Albemarle Street NW from Rock Creek west to Connecticut Avenue)

Community Resources: National Zoo, 3001 Connecticut Avenue NW, 202-673-4800, www.si.edu/natzoo (see **Greenspace**); Hillwood Museum, 4155 Linnean Avenue NW, 202-686-5807 (see **Greenspace**); Cineplex Odeon Uptown Theater, 3426 Connecticut Avenue NW, 202-333-FILM ext. 799; University of the District of Columbia, 4200 Connecticut Avenue NW, 202-274-5000, www.udc.edu; Howard University Law School, 28th & Upton streets NW, 202-806-8000, www.law.howard.edu

Public Transportation: Metro: Woodley Park-Zoo/Adams Morgan (Red Line), Connecticut Avenue & Garfield Street NW; Cleveland Park (Red Line), Connecticut Avenue & Ordway Street NW; Van Ness-UDC (Red Line), Connecticut Avenue & Veazey Terrace NW; Metrobus routes: L1/L2 (Connecticut Avenue NW), H2-H4 (Porter Street NW)

BRIGHTWOOD

PETWORTH
TAKOMA
CRESTWOOD

Boundaries: **North**: Aspen Street NW; **East**: New Hampshire Avenue NW, railroad tracks; **South**: Spring Road; **West**: Rock Creek

Location: north of Mt. Pleasant; east of the Connecticut Avenue corridor (across Rock Creek); south of Walter Reed Army Medical Center and Takoma Park, MD; west of the Soldiers' & Airmen's Home

Brightwood is one of the last nice neighborhoods where you can buy a house for $150,000 or so—if anyone's selling. Some of the sturdy town-houses built before World War II are still occupied by the original owners or their children. Families also cling to the elegant detached houses off 16th Street NW, many also built before the war. The leafy residential belt between 16th Street and Georgia Avenue NW resembles a cross-section of greater Washington: 16th Street is lined with grand Federal and Tudor homes, and just three blocks east, Georgia Avenue is a struggling swath of laundromats, pager stores and storefront tax preparers. In between the two sections is a quiet, economically diverse residential enclave. There are a few run-down apartment complexes along 14th Street, between Military Road and Walter Reed Army Medical Center, but mostly the side streets resemble the inner suburbs: children at play, people walking dogs and washing cars, and front porches shaded by mature trees.

In addition to stately homes and embassies, 16th Street hosts a variety of houses of worship, including a selection of Protestant churches, Buddhist and Baha'i temples, a synagogue, Greek and Russian Orthodox churches, and the secular humanist congregation of the Washington Ethical Society. Also here, at 16th Street and Colorado Avenue, is the William H.G. Fitzgerald Tennis Stadium. Beware: each August brings the Legg Mason Tennis Classic and, along with, world-famous athletes and ludicrous traffic jams. Surrounding the tennis stadium is a carpet of soccer fields, used frequently by local youth teams. In the woods of Rock Creek Park, behind the fields, the Carter Barron Amphitheatre attracts crowds in the summer and fall to free performances by the Shakespeare Theater Company, D.C. Blues Society artists, and the National Symphony Orchestra.

The crescent-shaped hill near 13th Street and Georgia Avenue is a remnant of Fort Stevens, which repelled a Confederate attack on Washington during the Civil War. Near the fort, housing is relatively inexpensive—in the shadow of a huge radio antenna reminiscent of the Eiffel Tower, and just beyond walking distance to the Takoma and Georgia Avenue-Petworth Metro stations. Good houses under $200,000 are rare in the District, but you may find them here. Most of the townhouses here are more spacious than they look from outside, and their porches and tiny front yards are nicely landscaped and well maintained.

The triangle of Missouri, Georgia, and New Hampshire avenues is **Petworth**, a vast, mostly residential area. There's a pocket of liquor stores and gang activity along Kennedy Street NW between 5th and 9th streets; 508 Kennedy Street is the Northwest D.C. field office for Medicaid and food stamps. Just a few blocks north, though, you'd hardly notice the depressed strip. The green campus of the US Soldiers' & Airmen's Home, a few blocks east of New Hampshire Avenue, is a retirement community for distinguished enlisted veterans.

North of Brightwood, along Piney Branch Road NW, **Takoma** is a less-expensive version of neighboring Takoma Park, MD, and offers affordable detached houses in every size and shape. There's a waiting list to get into Takoma Village Cohousing, 202-546-4654, www.takomavillage.org, a planned community of some 70 households, located just inside the D.C. line. Cohousing is a model of resource-sharing that aims to strike a balance between independent home ownership and a communal lifestyle: residents live in their own condos, but the community shares certain amenities—one laundry room, one set of home and garden tools, and even some shared cars, computers, and TVs. The community strives for diversity—not just ethnic and economic, but also a balance of young families, singles, and retirees.

Crestwood is an enclave of big, elegant houses nestled between 16th Street and Rock Creek Park south of Colorado Avenue. Old split-levels and colonials line the hillside leading to the park, and there's a cluster of mansions in Tudor and Spanish styles just off 16th and Colorado. Like most of the Brightwood area, this is a secluded and stable community with little turnover.

Web Site: www.crestwood-dc.org

Zip Codes: 20011, 20012

Post Offices: Brightwood, Georgia Avenue and Piney Branch Road NW, 202-523-2392; Petworth Station, 4211 9th Street NW, 202-523-2682

Police Station: Fourth District Headquarters, 6001 Georgia Avenue NW, 202-576-6745

Emergency Hospital: Washington Hospital Center, 110 Irving Street NW, 202-877-7000

Libraries: Takoma, 416 Cedar Street NW, 202-576-7252; Petworth, 4200 Kansas Avenue NW, 202-541-6300

Public High School: Coolidge Senior High School, 6315 5th Street NW, 202-576-6143

Government: Ward 4

Parks: Fort Slocum (east of 3rd Street NW between Madison and Oglethorpe streets); Grant Circle; Rock Creek (points of access along 16th Street & Colorado Avenue NW); Sherman Circle

Community Resources: Carter Barron Amphitheatre, 16th Street & Colorado Avenue NW, 202-426-0486, www.nps.gov/rocr/cbarron; National Museum of Health and Medicine, Walter Reed Army Medical Center, Georgia Avenue and Butternut Street NW, 202-782-2200; Rock Creek Park Tennis Center and William H.G. Fitzgerald Tennis Stadium, 16th & Kennedy streets NW, 202-722-5949; Fort Stevens and Battleground National Cemetery, site of the only Civil War battle in the District of Columbia; the fort is at 13th & Rittenhouse streets NW and the cemetery is a few blocks north at 6625 Georgia Avenue NW. President Lincoln dedicated this memorial park for Union soldiers killed in the successful defense of Fort Stevens. Free and open during daylight hours; for more information, visit www.nps.gov/batt.

Public Transportation: Metro: Takoma (Red Line), 4th & Cedar streets NW; Georgia Avenue-Petworth (Green Line), Georgia & New Hampshire avenues NW; Metrobus routes: S2-S4 (16th Street NW); 52-54 (14th Street NW); 70-73 (Georgia Avenue NW); 62 (5th Street NW); 64 (New Hampshire Avenue NW); E2-E4 (Kennedy Street NW); K2 (Blair Road NW)

MT. PLEASANT

COLUMBIA HEIGHTS

Boundaries: **North**: Piney Branch Park; **East**: 16th Street NW; **South**: Euclid Street NW, Calvert Street NW; **West**: Rock Creek Park

Location: north of Adams Morgan; east of the National Zoo; south of Crestwood; west of Howard University

Mt. Pleasant, west of 16th Street atop Meridian Hill, is the heart of the District's growing Latino community, and it also attracts many recent graduates. Red brick townhouses, many for rent, line the side streets from Hobart to Newton. Quite a few of these homes date from World War I, and some are just as nice inside as those in pricier neighborhoods closer to Dupont Circle. Hardwood floors, exposed brick, and detailed plasterwork are common features here.

This is a favorite neighborhood for groups of young adults sharing a house—it's an easy walk or bike ride to Dupont Circle, where many non-profit employers are located, and landlords here are accustomed to group rentals. Four people can share a four-bedroom townhouse for half the price of a one-bedroom apartment. If you prefer your very own digs, 16th Street and the side streets north of Park Road are lined with charming old apartment buildings. Like a vintage convertible with tail fins and some duct tape on the seats, these buildings might not be in mint condition, but they have character.

Mt. Pleasant Street attracts locals and visitors alike to its dollar stores and *tiendas*, to beloved eateries like Haydee's and Heller's Bakery, and to newer hangouts including The People Garden juice bar and Dos Gringos café, all in a two-block stretch between Kenyon Street and Park Road NW. And the nightlife of Adams Morgan is just around the corner. In addition, no Mt. Pleasant address is more than a few blocks from Rock Creek Park, perfect for walkers and cyclists (see **Greenspace**).

Across 16th Street, **Columbia Heights** stretches east toward Georgia Avenue NW. This is a changing neighborhood—after decades of decline, young homebuyers are buying inexpensive townhouses near the new Columbia Heights Metro station. Commercial developers have big plans for the land around the decaying old Tivoli Theater at 14th Street and Park Road, but it's not clear whether neighbors of modest income will be able to stay and enjoy the area's recovery. Like neighboring Mt. Pleasant, the neighborhood is mostly Latino, and Spanish is the primary language in many of the carry-outs lining 14th Street on the hill down toward Shaw.

Web Sites: www.lcsystems.com/mtp, www.innercity.org/columbiaheights, www.intowner.com
Zip Code: 20010
Post Office: Kalorama Station, 2300 18th Street NW, 202-523-2904
Police Station: Third District Headquarters, 1620 V Street NW, 202-673-6930
Emergency Hospital: Howard University Hospital, 2401 Georgia Avenue NW, 202-865-6100
Library: Mt. Pleasant, 3160 16th Street NW, 202-671-0200
Public High School: Bell Multicultural High School, 3145 Hiatt Place NW, 202-673-7314
Government: Ward 1
Neighborhood Festival: Mt. Pleasant Day (June)
Parks: Lamont (Mt. Pleasant & Lamont streets NW); Piney Branch (points of access off 17th and Mt. Pleasant streets NW); Rock Creek (points of access off Park Road and Porter Street NW)
Community Resources: Gala Hispanic Theatre, 1625 Park Road NW, 202-234-7174, www.galatheatre.org (see **Cultural Life**).
Public Transportation: Metrobus routes: 42 (Mt. Pleasant Street NW), S2-S4 (16th Street NW); walk to Metro, Columbia Heights (Green Line)

ADAMS MORGAN

Boundaries: **North**: Euclid Street NW, Calvert Street NW; **East**: 16th Street NW; **South**: T Street NW; **West**: 19th Street NW

Location: north of Dupont Circle; east of Kalorama; south of Mt. Pleasant; west of Columbia Heights (across Malcolm X Park)

Adams Morgan is a hopping, culturally diverse neighborhood, where locals and visitors can dine out on Ethiopian, West African, Italian, Mexican, Thai, Salvadoran, French, South American, Indian, Chinese, Middle Eastern and Jamaican cuisine, and adjourn for coffee and dessert at any of three neighborhood coffeehouses: Franklyn's, at 18th & U streets NW, for milkshake-like iced mochas; Tryst, at 2459 18th Street NW, a couch-and-coffee-table nightspot; and Jolt 'n' Bolt, at 18th & T, featuring a cozy courtyard and a good selection of pastries and fruit smoothies. Little grocery stores, gift shops, and magazine stores catering to the Latino, Ethiopian, and West African communities dot the neighborhood. In addition, the bustling commercial strips along 18th Street and Columbia Road offer the practical basics—a hardware store, a post office, and a Safeway supermarket. City Bikes, at Columbia Road and Champlain Street, is the outfitter of choice for bicycle commuters and couriers.

Adams Morgan got its name when the principals of the predominantly white Adams School and the predominantly black Morgan School called residents together to improve the neighborhood. That 1956 meeting was called "the Adams Morgan Better Neighborhood Conference," and the same cooperative spirit still characterizes the neighborhood today. Many young professionals, especially non-profit workers from Dupont Circle offices a few blocks south, reside here. Most of the housing here is prewar apartment houses or row houses converted to apartments, and just about every building has a roof deck.

Living in a popular neighborhood has its price: $1,200 for a modest one-bedroom apartment is common, up from about $800 in 1996. There are a few blocks south of Columbia Road near 16th Street where rentals are less expensive, but for most young professionals, living in Adams Morgan means sharing an apartment or house.

The enticing shopping and dining strip along 18th Street is always crowded with pedestrians and choked with traffic; however, poorly lit side streets can be unsafe late at night. Muggings are a persistent problem—not an epidemic, statistically, but always a concern for pedestrians. The biggest problem in Adams Morgan, though, is parking—particularly on weekends, which here seem to begin on Thursdays. The chronic parking shortage is being addressed with a new parking garage at 18th and Belmont, out of sight behind the shops. Also, in an attempt to ease the parking problem, "Adams Morgan" was added to the name of the Woodley Park-Zoo Metro station in 1999. The addition was intended to inspire more people to take public transportation to Adams Morgan, but the station is actually a 15-minute walk away, across Rock Creek Park. Evenings and weekends, there are shuttle buses every 15 minutes from the station and from the U Street-Cardozo station; also, the Dupont Circle station is a short ride away on the crowded No. 42 bus.

Web Sites: http://adamsmorgan.net, www.anc1c.org, www.intowner.com
Zip Code: 20009
Post Offices: Kalorama Station, 2300 18th Street NW, 202-523-2904; Temple Heights Station, 1921 Florida Avenue NW, 202-232-7613
Police Station: Third District Headquarters, 1620 V Street NW, 202-673-6930
Emergency Hospital: Howard University Hospital, 2401 Georgia Avenue NW, 202-865-6100
Library: Mt. Pleasant, 3160 16th Street NW, 202-671-0200
Public High Schools: Bell Multicultural High School, 3145 Hiatt Place NW, 202-673-7314; Cardozo Senior High School, 1300 Clifton Street NW, 202-673-7385
Government: Ward 1
Neighborhood Festivals: Latino Summer Fiesta (Marie Reed Elementary School, August); Adams Morgan Day (September), www.adamsmorganday.org
Parks: Malcolm X (16th Street NW between W and Euclid streets), Rock Creek (points of access off Harvard Street NW and the Duke Ellington Bridge)
Community Resources: D.C. Arts Center, gallery and performance space, 2438 18th Street NW, 202-462-7833; Meridian International Center, a non-profit agency promoting international exchange through the arts, 1630 Crescent Place NW, 202-667-6800, www.meridian.org; One World Media Center, a non-profit video production studio providing equipment and training to amateur filmmakers, 2390 Champlain Street NW, 202-667-9038, www.owmc.org; Scottish Rite Center for Language Disorders, Children's National Medical Center, 1630 Columbia Road NW, 202-939-4703, www.cnmc.org.
Public Transportation: Metrobus routes: 42 (Columbia Road NW), 90-98 (U Street NW)

SHAW

Boundaries: **North**: Florida Avenue NW; **East**: North Capitol Street; **South**: Massachusetts Avenue NW; **West**: 16th Street NW

Location: north of Penn Quarter; east of Adams Morgan and Dupont Circle; south of Columbia Heights and Howard University; west of Eckington and NoMa

If you saw Matthew Broderick in *Glory*, you're familiar with Col. Robert Gould Shaw, who commanded the Army's first African-American regiment during the Civil War. The neighborhood that bears his name is vast and diverse, spanning the heart of midtown D.C. This is where jazz legend Duke Ellington made his debut, in an auditorium in the city's first office building designed, built and owned by African-Americans—the True Reformer Building, which still stands at 13th & U streets NW.

After two decades of decline and middle-class flight, Shaw began a slow, steady recovery in the 1990s. Young professionals moved into under priced townhouses off U Street NW between 7th and 16th, driving property values back up—and driving some longtime residents out. For now, the neighborhood is racially and economically diverse, but lower-income residents and lower-rent businesses are struggling to stay. In the long run, it's a good bet that Shaw will manage to retain its diversity and heritage—old and new residents alike take pride in the community, attend civic association meetings, and do volunteer work. It's not unusual to see someone fixing a bike for a kid next door, or getting up early on Saturday to remove graffiti from a public playground.

Shaw is home to dozens of charitable organizations, most notably the Whitman-Walker Clinic (one of the world's first and largest AIDS clinics, headquartered at 14th and S); Bread for the City, a multi-service center at 7th and P; and Manna, the city's largest non-profit housing developer. One of the city's biggest playgrounds is here, too: John F. Kennedy Memorial Playground at 7th and O.

The Reeves Center, at 14th & U streets NW, is a municipal office building—the Department of Public Works, the Office of Campaign Finance, the Lottery Commission, and other D.C. agencies are headquartered here. Outside, there are a few sit-down restaurants and many fast-food outlets. A block north, at 2114 14th Street, is one of the city's oldest soup kitchens, Martha's Table. Head east along U Street for some of the city's most prominent nightspots, including Republic Gardens, State of the Union, and the Velvet Lounge. Ben's Chili Bowl, the city's sentimental favorite restaurant, is at 12th and U streets NW, next to the historic Lincoln Theatre. To the south are three community theaters: the Source, the Studio, and Living Stage, all on 14th Street NW between P and U streets. Head west on U Street for antique furniture and vintage clothing.

The **Logan Circle** area, around 13th and P, is known as a red light district, though it is also known for grand, expensive brick townhouses and historic mansions. A new Fresh Fields supermarket at 14th & P caters to the upscale Logan Circle crowd.

At the south end of Shaw, the new Washington Convention Center, opening in 2003, is the largest construction project in D.C. history. Two industrial sump pumps will hum around the clock for decades to come, trying to keep the underground river displaced by the gargantuan building from gushing into people's basements.

Web Sites: www.shawdc.com, www.logancircle.org, www.intowner.com

Zip Codes: 20001, 20009

Post Office: T Street Station, 1915 14th Street NW, 202-483-9580

Police Stations: Third District Headquarters, 1620 V Street NW, 202-673-6930; Traffic Branch, 5th Street and New York Avenue NW, 202-727-4435

Emergency Hospital: Howard University Hospital, 2401 Georgia Avenue NW, 202-865-6100

Libraries: Watha T. Daniel, 8th Street & Rhode Island Avenue NW, 202-671-0212; Sursum Corda, 1st Street & New York Avenue NW, 202-724-4772

Public High Schools: Cardozo, 1300 Clifton Street NW, 202-673-7385; Dunbar, 1301 New Jersey Avenue NW, 202-673-7233

Government: West of 14th Street, Ward 2 south of U Street and Ward 1 to the north; east of 14th Street, Ward 2 south of S Street and Ward 1 to the north

Neighborhood Festivals: One Common Unity Festival, http://themovement.org

Parks: Logan Circle; Malcolm X (16th Street NW between W and Euclid streets)

Community Resources: African-American Civil War Memorial, "Spirit of Freedom" statue and museum, Vermont Avenue & U Street NW, 202-667-2667, www.afroamcivilwar.org; Howard University, 2400 6th Street NW, 202-806-2250, www.howard.edu; Bread for the City, 1525 7th Street NW, 202-265-2400, www.breadforthecity.org; Martha's Table, 202-328-6608; Whitman-Walker Clinic, 202-797-3500, www.wwc.org. The Shaw EcoVillage Project, www.shawecovillage.com, trains young people to take leadership roles in improving the quality of life in their neighborhood. Theaters (see **Cultural Life**): Lincoln Theater, 1215 U Street NW, 202-328-6000; Source Theatre, 1835 14th Street NW, 202-462-1073; Studio Theatre, 1333 P Street NW, 202-332-3300; Living Stage, 1901 14th Street NW, 202-234-5782; Greater U Street Heritage trail is a self-guided tour of historical and cultural sites from the age of Duke Ellington. Free trail guides available from the DC Heritage Coalition, 202-828-8255 or www.dcheritage.org.

Public Transportation: Metro: Shaw-Howard University (Green Line), entrances at 7th & S streets NW and 8th & R streets NW; U Street-Cardozo (Green Line), entrances at 13th & U streets NW and 10th Street & Vermont Avenue NW; Mt. Vernon Square, (Green and Yellow lines), 7th & M streets NW). Note that the "Shaw-Howard University" station is actually more than half a mile downhill from Howard University. Metrobus routes: 52/54 (14th Street NW), 70-73 (7th Street NW), 90-98 (U Street NW)

BROOKLAND

Boundaries: **North**: Providence Hospital; **East**: South Dakota Avenue NE; **South**: Rhode Island Avenue NE, Franklin Street NE; **West**: Catholic University

Location: north of Brentwood and Eckington; east of Catholic University; south of Providence Hospital and Michigan Park; west of Mt. Rainier, MD

Nuns, monks, and priests are a common sight on the streets of Brookland, home of the Catholic University of America and the flagship Roman Catholic Church in the US, the blue-domed Basilica of the National Shrine of the Immaculate Conception. Across the railroad tracks from campus and the Shrine, Brookland has the look and feel of a suburban town—there is a garden club, lots of settled families, and well-attended community meetings. There are also plenty of opportunities to give back to the community; at Byte Back, for instance, volunteers help homeless adults learn computer skills in order to get jobs. Others help stock the shelves at nearby Capital Area Food Bank, where the city's soup kitchens and shelters do their wholesale shopping.

You'll also find comfortable nightspots close by, including the venerable Col. Brooks' Tavern and Kelly's Ellis Island Pub. On 12th Street NE, a funky coffee bar, Brookland's Cup of Dreams, anchors a strip of practical shops, including a pharmacy, hardware store, gas station, and eateries. A few blocks away, at 3225 8th Street NE, Dance Place offers classes and recitals.

East of 12th Street, Brookland is a quiet residential neighborhood, with tree-lined streets and an eclectic assortment of houses—Victorians, Georgians, Queen Annes, bungalows, even the occasional ranch house. Many are a century old, and most have bigger yards than the typical D.C. home. Some of the larger houses are actually monasteries or convents.

Walk to the Brookland Metro station for a 10-minute ride downtown, or use the station as an underpass to cross the railroad tracks and take in a concert at the Shrine or the university. As you ride the Metro on elevated tracks toward Capitol Hill, you can see the route of the planned Metropolitan Branch Trail, a commuter-oriented bike path that will eventually link Silver Spring to Capitol Hill.

Zip Codes: 20017, 20018
Post Office: Brookland Station, 12th and Monroe streets NE, 202-635-5315
Police Station: Fifth District Headquarters, 1805 Bladensburg Road NE, 202-727-4510
Emergency Hospital: Providence Hospital, 1150 Varnum Street NE, 202-269-7000
Library: Woodridge Regional Library, 18th Street & Rhode Island Avenue NE, 202-541-6226
Public High School: Moore Academy, 1001 Monroe Street NE, 202-576-7005
Government: Ward 5
Neighborhood Festival: Brookland Community Day (September)
Parks: Fort Bunker Hill (east of 13th Street NE between Otis and Perry streets); Turkey Thicket (west of Michigan Avenue NE north of Perry Street)
Community Resources: Byte Back, 3430 9th Street NE, 202-529-3395, www.byteback.org; Capital Area Food Bank, 645 Taylor Street NE, 202-526-5344; Catholic University of America, 620 Michigan Avenue NE, 202-319-5000, www.cua.edu; Dance Place, 202-269-1600, www.danceplace.org; Franciscan Monastery, 1400 Quincy Street NE, 202-526-6800 (see **Greenspace**); National Shrine, 4th Street & Michigan Avenue NE, 202-526-8300, www.nationalshrine.com (see **Places of Worship**); Trinity College, 125 Michigan Avenue NE, 202-884-9050, www.trinitydc.edu
Public Transportation: Metro: Brookland (Red Line), off Michigan Avenue at the railroad tracks; Metrobus routes: H2-H6 (Michigan Avenue), R4 (Michigan Avenue), G8 (Monroe Street)

ANACOSTIA

Boundaries: **North**: Anacostia River, Pennsylvania Avenue SE; **South**: St. Elizabeths Hospital; **East**: Alabama Avenue SE; **West**: South Capitol Street

Location: north of St. Elizabeths Hospital and Congress Heights; east of the Washington Navy Yard (across the Anacostia River) and Bolling Air Force Base; south of Marshall Heights; west of Hillcrest

Here's a secret: You can visit Anacostia, even live here, and not get shot. Despite its reputation as a tough neighborhood, police statistics show that the number of violent crimes per year in the Anacostia police district is consistently below the citywide average. There are signs of drug trafficking—tiny plastic bags on the sidewalk, the kind of bags used for crack cocaine—but the drug trade and related gang strife seldom involves people who are minding their own business. It's not a good place to raise kids, but young adults shouldn't automatically skip real estate listings just because they're "east of the river"—the Anacostia River.

The neighborhoods east of the river are almost exclusively African-American. Though the struggling parts of Southeast D.C. are dotted with pockets of middle-class housing, Anacostia did not benefit from the economic boom of the late 1990s, and even now this area struggles to attract grocery stores and sit-down restaurants to its neglected streets. However, living here is cheap and convenient. It's a 60-cent bus ride to the Anacostia Metro station, and from there, Capitol Hill and the Smithsonian are less than 10 minutes away. For young federal workers at the Transportation, HUD, or Energy departments, it certainly would make commuting easy. And the Navy offices and contractors in the renovated Southest Federal Center complex are just one Metro stop away, near the Navy Yard station.

The name "Anacostia" is applied loosely to most of Southeast D.C. east of the river. The Anacostia historic district is the area straddling Good Hope Road, overlooking the river. To the south along Martin Luther King Jr. Avenue is St. Elizabeth's Hospital, the federal mental institution whose sprawling campus dates back to the Civil War. South of the hospital, at 2737 Martin Luther King Jr. Avenue SE, is Players Lounge, one of the few popular nightspots east of the river.

There's a lot of parkland east of the river, as well as one of the Smithsonian's more obscure museums. The Anacostia Museum in Fort Stanton Park is the Smithsonian's museum of African-American history. And, throughout all the ups and downs of his political career spanning five decades, Marion Barry has lived in Anacostia, not far from the historic home of abolitionist Frederick Douglass. The Douglass estate, Cedar Hill, is a museum of the abolitionist movement. The human rights activist lived here, at 14th & W streets SE, from 1877-1895. For a tour, call 202-426-5961 or visit www.nps.gov/frdo.

Again, it's not right for everybody, but worth investigating.

Zip Code: 20020
Post Offices: Anacostia Station, 2650 Naylor Road SE, 202-635-5307; Randle Station, 2306 Prout Street SE, 202-584-3241
Police Station: Seventh District Headquarters, 2455 Alabama Avenue SE, 202-698-1500
Emergency Hospital: Greater Southeast Community Hospital, 1310 Southern Avenue SE, 202-574-6000

Libraries: Anacostia, 1800 Good Hope Road SE, 202-698-1190; Francis Gregory, 3660 Alabama Avenue SE, 202-645-4297
Public High Schools: Anacostia, 1601 16th Street SE, 202-645-3000; Ballou, 3401 4th Street SE, 202-645-3400
Government: Ward 8
Neighborhood Festival: Unifest (May), 202-678-8822
Parks: Anacostia (along the Anacostia River between the Whitney Young Bridge and Bolling Air Force Base); Fort Stanton (off Naylor Road SE near 27th Street)
Community Resources: Anacostia Museum, 1901 Fort Place SE, 202-357-1300, www.si.edu/anacostia; Frederick Douglass National Historic Site (details above)
Public Transportation: Metro: Anacostia (Green Line), Howard Road & Firth Sterling Avenue SE; Congress Heights (Green Line), 13th Street & Alabama Avenue SE; Metrobus routes: A2-A48 (Martin Luther King Jr. Avenue SE); W1-W8 (Alabama Avenue SE); 90-93 (8th Street SE)

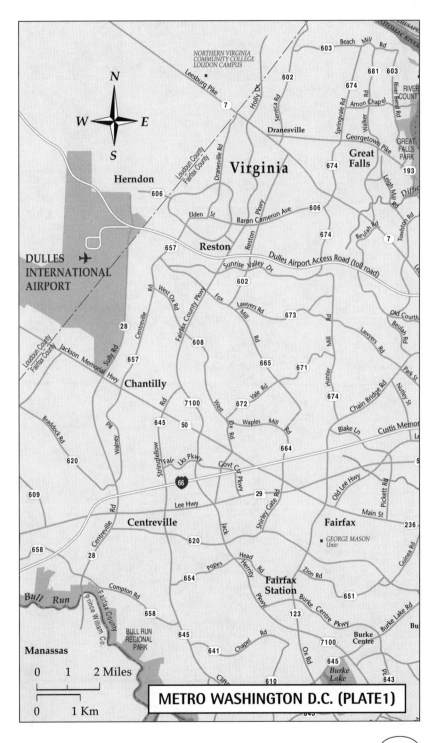

METRO WASHINGTON D.C. (PLATE1)

49

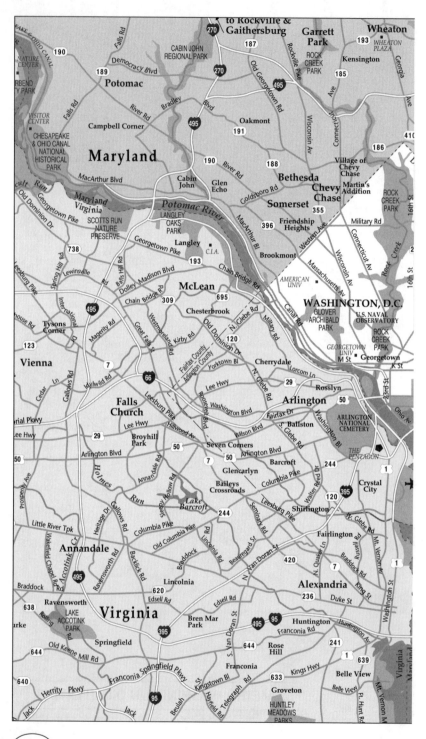

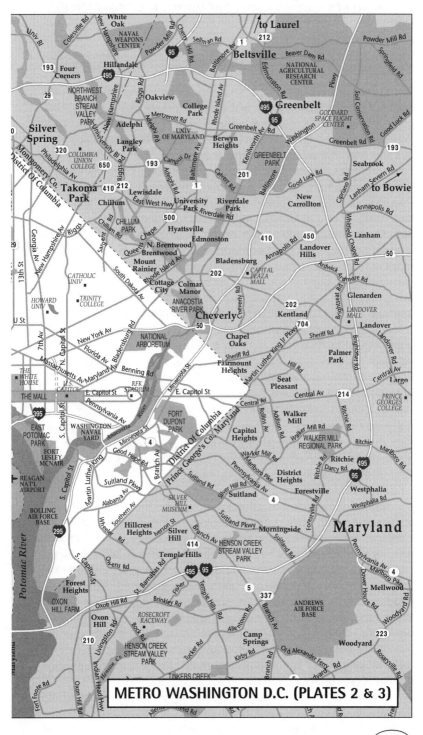

METRO WASHINGTON D.C. (PLATES 2 & 3)

MARYLAND

Long before the First Amendment guaranteed religious freedom in the United States, the colonial settlement at St. Mary's City adopted the first religious tolerance law in North America. Today, the Maryland suburbs of Washington are a cultural melting pot, the cosmopolitan population center of a little state that calls itself "America in Miniature." Barely 300 miles from corner to corner, Maryland encompasses coal mines and paper mill towns in the Allegheny Mountains; crab and oyster fishing on the Chesapeake Bay; shipping in the busy port of Baltimore, with most imported cars sold in the eastern US arriving at Dundalk Marine Terminal; and vast poultry farms, including the Perdue conglomerate on the eastern shore. There are tobacco farms in Southern Maryland— which, culturally, is more southern than much of Virginia; software and information technology firms are clustered in Greenbelt and Columbia; and one of the world's leading centers of biotechnology research, with companies like MedImmune and Human Genome Sciences, lines the I-270 corridor from Bethesda to Frederick.

Nearer D.C. proper, Maryland is home to hundreds of square miles of major federal facilities: the US Naval Academy, Andrews Air Force Base, Patuxent River Naval Air Station, Camp David, the National Agricultural Research Center, the Goddard Space Flight Center, the National Institutes of Health, Aberdeen Proving Ground, and Fort Meade. The Naval Surface Warfare Center has several facilities here, including an eye-catching 1,800-foot-long tank just outside Bethesda where the Navy tests scale models of new ships. On the Gaithersburg campus of the National Institute for Standards & Technology (formerly the National Bureau of Standards), you can visit a small exhibit and see a gray metal block and stick: the nation's official, definitive kilogram and meter.

Naturally, the suburbs attract a lot of government workers and techies—educated, white-collar, middle-income folks employed at federal campuses in the suburbs. As in the District, Rock Creek provides a rough dividing line between upscale neighborhoods, mostly to the west of the creek, while more moderate neighborhoods are generally found to the east. There is little abject poverty in the suburbs, although some neighborhoods near the eastern corner of the District are struggling—even though the demographics in Prince George's County show plenty of buying power, the county has not had an easy time attracting high-end shops and restaurants. The eastern suburbs are often perceived as a stepping stone for those moving out of decaying neighborhoods in the District—an image uncharitable to both jurisdictions.

Beyond the Baltimore-Washington corridor, Maryland is a farming and fishing state, and there is some industry in Western Maryland and on the upper reaches of the Bay. The culture clash between urban and rural

Maryland often leads to tense politics in Annapolis, and a divided delega-tion in Congress. In a traditionally Democratic state, rural conservatives grew increasingly vocal in the 1980s and '90s; the 1994 election of Governor Parris Glendening (D) was so close that, after a week of recounts, the Republican candidate never did concede. Even within the suburbs, though, the Democratic majorities of the Montgomery and Prince George's county councils wage heated perennial debates about sprawl, highways, mass transit, and the growing pains of a region that is expected to gain another million residents by 2025.

In the cultural sense, you're still "inside the Beltway" here—people actually attend zoning hearings, speak in federal jargon and acronyms, carry cellular phones everywhere, work long hours, and consider them-selves devoted public servants. And many are.

Capital: Annapolis
Governor: 410-974-3901 or 800-811-8336, www.gov.state.md.us
Maryland General Assembly: 301-970-5400 or 800-492-7122, mlis.state.md.us
Internet Guide: Sailor, www.sailor.lib.md.us
Citizen Handbook: www.mdarchives.state.md.us; available on CD-ROM for $35 + $2 shipping from Maryland State Archives, 350 Rowe Boulevard, Annapolis 21401, 410-260-6400. Or, to find your elected officials, visit http://mdelect.net and enter your zip code.
Newspaper of Record: *Baltimore Sun*, 410-332-6000 or 800-829-8000; circulation, 410-539-1280; www.sunspot.net

MONTGOMERY COUNTY

Montgomery County is one of the most educated places in the world—roughly 90% of residents over age 25 have college degrees. Home to the National Institutes of Health and the National Institute of Standards & Technology, the county is emerging as a center of the biotech industry.

Rapid population growth is changing the county. There are roughly 857,000 people here; about 100,000 arrived in the 1990s, many settling into newly built subdivisions in the northern part of the county. In fact, in the '90s, the population of the outer suburbs here surpassed that of the inner suburbs, and urban sprawl became the dominant issue in local pol-itics. Schools and transportation systems are struggling to keep up with the growth.

Housing, however, is readily available here. There are plenty of gov-ernment workers, military and diplomatic families, scientists, and other mobile types coming and going, putting houses on the market for rent and for sale. If suburban life is for you renting here can be a huge bargain compared to the District. A three-bedroom house in Silver Spring might cost no more than a one-bedroom apartment in D.C.

Montgomery County stretches from the Potomac to the Patuxent, and north from D.C. to Sugarloaf Mountain, a 1,300-foot mound that looms over I-270. At White's Ferry, at the western tip of the county, the last auto ferry making regular trips across the Potomac bears the name of General Jubal Early, whose Confederate troops crossed the river here in 1864 to attack Washington. Across the county, the tiny village of Brookeville proudly reminds visitors that it served as the nation's capital for a day, in 1814, when President Madison retreated there during the British invasion of Washington.

The county takes its name from General Richard Montgomery, who was killed in 1775 leading the Continental Army against the British in Quebec.

Government: Executive Office Building, 101 Monroe Street, Rockville, 240-777-1000, www.co.mo.md.us

County Executive: 240-777-2500; www.co.mo.md.us/executive

County Council: nine members—five representing districts, four elected at large: Council Office Building, 100 Maryland Avenue, Rockville, 240-777-7900, www.co.mo.md.us/council

Public Schools: 301-279-3000, www.mcps.k12.md.us

Libraries: 240-777-0002, www.montgomerylibrary.org

Police: 301-279-8000, www.co.mo.md.us/services/police

Online Guide: www.co.mo.md.us

BETHESDA

FRIENDSHIP HEIGHTS
NORTH BETHESDA
SOMERSET
POTOMAC

Boundaries: North: Montrose Road; **East**: Maryland Route 355; **South**: District of Columbia; **West**: Seven Locks Road

Located between the old-money citadels of Chevy Chase and the semi-rural estates of Potomac, Bethesda attracts professionals and their families. Some work nearby as doctors or scientists at the National Institutes of Health or the National Naval Medical Center, both of which occupy huge campuses off Wisconsin Avenue.

The **Friendship Heights** area, which straddles the D.C./Maryland line, is a shopping and dining destination. This upscale stretch of Wisconsin Avenue offers a melting pot of cuisine, from Mongolian barbecue to local microbrews. Chevy Chase Pavilion at Wisconsin Avenue and Military Road NW is home to the original Cheesecake Factory, where some 40 kinds of cheesecake always make up for the long lines. To the north, along Rockville Pike in **North Bethesda**, is a meat-and-potatoes shopping mecca; people come here in droves to shop for everything from home furnishings and toys to major appliances and cars.

Between Friendship Heights and the naval hospital, Bethesda has its own "downtown," with offices and retail space surrounding the Metro station. Bethesda even has its own suburb, the little incorporated town of **Somerset**, located between the Chevy Chase County Club and Little Falls Branch Park. Lining the streets in this little town (population 1,000) are old cottages and colonials. Somerset was one of Maryland's first designated "Tree Cities."

Most of the homes in North Bethesda are standard postwar suburban styles—ramblers, split-levels, bungalows—with garages and ample yards; closer to the District line are older colonials with smaller yards and bigger trees. There are several huge apartment high-rises just off Rockville Pike, and smaller high-rises closer to downtown Bethesda, built after World War II. Bethesda is a safe community with first-rate schools and convenient access to the District, yet housing is more affordable and abundant than you might expect. Thanks to families whose work takes them overseas for a few years at a time, there is a steady rental market here.

To the west of Bethesda, **Potomac** is mansion country. This, the Maryland side of Great Falls, is just as fashionable and pricey as the Virginia side—but Potomac tends to have residents with "newer" money: celebrities, senators, doctors, and lawyers, not the 18th-century families of Northern Virginia. The homes are newer here than across the river, but the yards are just as vast, the winding lanes just as long, and the public transportation just as nonexistent.

Web Sites: www.bethesda.org, www.erols.com/friendshiphtsvillage, www.townofsomerset.com

Area Codes: 301, 240

Zip Codes: 20814, 20815, 20817, 20852, 20854

Post Offices: Bethesda, 7400 Wisconsin Avenue, 301-941-2664; Bethesda Annex, 7001 Arlington Road, 301-941-2680; Friendship Heights, 5530 Wisconsin Avenue, 301-941-2694; West Bethesda, 9601 Seven Locks Road, 301-365-8673

Police Station: Bethesda District, 7359 Wisconsin Avenue, 301-657-0119 (commander), 301-279-8000 (Community Concerns Line)

Emergency Hospital: Suburban Healthcare System, 8600 Old Georgetown Road, 301-896-3100

Libraries: Bethesda Regional, 7400 Arlington Road, 301-986-4300; Davis,

6400 Democracy Boulevard, 301-897-2200; Little Falls, 5501 Massachusetts Avenue, 301-320-4880; Potomac, 10101 Glenolden Drive, 301-983-4475

Public High Schools: Bethesda-Chevy Chase, 4301 East-West Highway, 301-649-8280; Walter Johnson, 6400 Rock Spring Drive, 301-571-6900; Walt Whitman, 7100 Whittier Boulevard, Bethesda, 301-320-6600; Winston Churchill, 11300 Gainsborough Road, Potomac, 301-469-1220

Public Transportation: Metro: Bethesda, Medical Center, Grosvenor and White Flint stations (Red Line); Metrobus routes: J1-J3 (Silver Spring, Montgomery Mall), J8-J9 (Gaithersburg), and 14 series (Tysons Corner); Ride-On routes: 27-42 & 46 (local) and 70 (I-270 corridor)

Government: 8th Congressional District; Montgomery County Council District 1: Somerset Town Hall, 301-657-3211

Neighborhood Festivals: Literary Festival (various locations, April); Imagination Bethesda Children's Arts Festival (Woodmont Avenue & Elm Street, June); Bethesda Grand Prix of Cycling (Woodmont Avenue, June); Taste of Bethesda (along Norfolk Avenue, October); Bethesda Row Arts Festival (Bethesda & Woodmont avenues, October); for more information, call the Bethesda Urban Partnership, 301-215-6660, or visit www.bethesda.org/events.

Major Parks: Cabin John (off Westlake Drive south of Tuckerman Lane); C&O Canal (points of access along MacArthur Boulevard); Little Falls Branch (along Little Falls Branch between Bradley Boulevard and the Potomac River); Rock Creek (points of access off Cedar Lane, Grosvenor Lane, and Kensington Parkway); Watts Branch Stream Valley (along Watts Branch between Wootton Parkway and River Road)

Community Resources: Discovery Trail is a self-guided tour of two dozen works of public art—sculptures, fountains, and murals—in downtown Bethesda. Start at Bethesda Metro Center (outside the Metro station) and follow the signs, or contact the Bethesda Urban Partnership for a map: www.bethesda.org or 301-215-6660. The web site also lists private art galleries and studios in Bethesda. Capital Crescent Trail commuter bike path from Georgetown to Silver Spring—for information, call 202-234-4874 or visit www.cctrail.org. Glen Echo, Goldsboro Road & MacArthur Boulevard; see **Greenspace** for details. National Library of Medicine, 10301 Baltimore Avenue; see **Cultural Life** for details. Strathmore Hall Arts Center, Strathmore Avenue & Rockville Pike; see **Cultural Life** for details. The Writer's Center is a facility and a membership organization offering workshops, classes, and special events for local writers. The center also publishes the nation's oldest poetry journal (*PoetLore*, established 1889) and a newsletter for writers: 4508 Walsh Street, Bethesda, 301-654-8664, www.writer.org.

CHEVY CHASE

MARTIN'S ADDITIONS
FARMINGTON
VILLAGE OF CHEVY CHASE

Boundaries: North: Jones Bridge Road; **East**: Rock Creek; **South**: District of Columbia; **West**: Wisconsin Avenue

Named for a medieval English estate, Chevy Chase, nestled between the District and the East-West Highway, is a patrician bastion of stately homes, big trees, and two of the area's oldest country clubs, Chevy Chase and Columbia. This is where the "old" families of Washington, known to society-page readers as "cave dwellers," play tennis and entertain in drawing rooms. Among the nation's wealthiest neighborhoods, Chevy Chase does not feel as ostentatious as one might expect; the streets are lined with more Volvos and SUVs than luxury cars.

While Chevy Chase proper is decidedly upscale, there are some more affordable sections closer to Rock Creek. Postwar ramblers and split-levels line the winding streets of the neighborhoods officially called **Martin's Additions** and **Farmington**—but politely just called Chevy Chase.

In addition to picture-perfect houses, there is picture-perfect green space here, at the Woodend estate, 8940 Jones Mill Road, which belongs to the Audubon Naturalist Society (a local organization not to be confused with the National Audubon Society). The 40-acre grounds bordering Rock Creek Park, are a flourishing nature preserve, attracting deer, foxes, owls, and other woodland species to this rich habitat. Annual events at the mansion include a wildlife art show and a holiday fair.

Local government can be confusing here—the separate jurisdictions of the town of Chevy Chase and the incorporated **Village of Chevy Chase** look and feel the same. The Village is the area between Chevy Chase Country Club and the District, and parts of the area east of Connecticut Avenue.

Web Sites: www.townofchevychase.org, www.ccvillage.org
Area Codes: 301, 240
Zip Code: 20815
Post Office: Chevy Chase Branch, 5910 Connecticut Avenue, 301-652-8508
Police Station: Bethesda District, 7359 Wisconsin Avenue, 301-657-0119 (commander), 301-279-8000 (Community Concerns Line)
Emergency Hospital: Suburban Healthcare System, 8600 Old Georgetown Road, Bethesda, 301-896-3100

Library: Chevy Chase, 8005 Connecticut Avenue, 301-986-4313
Public High School: Bethesda-Chevy Chase, 4301 East-West Highway, Bethesda, 301-649-8280
Government: 8th Congressional District; Montgomery County Council District 1; mayor chosen from five-member town council: Town Hall, 4301 Willow Lane, 301-654-7144; Chevy Chase Village Town Hall, 301-654-7300
Major Park: Rock Creek (points of access off East-West Highway and Jones Mill Road)
Community Resources: The National 4-H Center is a conference facility with the look and feel of a small college campus, and is one of the few visitor destinations in this predominantly residential area: 7100 Connecticut Avenue, 301-961-2840 or 800-368-7432, www.fourhcouncil.edu/4hcenter. Woodend Mansion is available for private functions, and the grounds are open to the public. Call 301-652-9188 or visit www.audubonnaturalist.org for seasonal hours and events.
Public Transportation: Metrobus routes: J1-J3 (Montgomery Mall, Silver Spring), L7/L8 (Friendship Heights); Ride-On routes: 1 & 11 (Friendship Heights, Silver Spring)

GAITHERSBURG/MONTGOMERY VILLAGE

WASHINGTON GROVE
KENTLANDS
GERMANTOWN
CLARKSBURG

Boundaries: **North**: Warfield Road; **East**: Rock Creek Park, Airpark Road; **South**: Darnestown Road, Shady Grove Road; **West**: Seneca Creek State Park

For more than a century, the **City of Gaithersburg**, right in the center of Montgomery County, marked the end of the suburbs and the beginning of the farm belt. But, by 1990, new subdivisions began springing up in the northern part of the county, and now a majority of the county's population is in Rockville and points north. Gaithersburg is a railroad town, founded in 1878, six years after the arrival of the Baltimore & Ohio Railroad; today, there's a stop on the commuter train line from D.C. to Brunswick, and there are still a few industrial parks along the tracks. The county fairgrounds are here, along the tracks, just west of the authentic Old Town district.

If you live in Gaithersburg and work in D.C., plan for a long commute—you'll need to take a bus, or drive, to the outermost Metro station, where you can settle in for a 35-minute ride downtown. If you work on the

Hill, the MARC commuter train can get you there in 45 minutes from the heart of Old Town Gaithersburg, but there are only half a dozen trips a day. There are plenty of jobs in the Gaithersburg area, though—not just with the biotech research firms in the I-270 corridor, but with some major non-profit employers and federal agencies. The National Geographic Society occupies a big campus north of Darnestown Road, stretching to the park-like headquarters of the Izaak Walton League off Muddy Branch Road. Between these green spaces and West Diamond Avenue is the vast campus of the National Institute of Standards & Technology (NIST—still "the Bureau" to those who lived here when it was called the National Bureau of Standards). These sites buffer Muddy Branch Park with plenty of green space; if you live nearby, don't be surprised to see an occasional deer in your front yard.

Many homes in Gaithersburg are modern townhouse condos or plain, rectangular garden apartments. There are some detached homes, especially between Old Town and Lakeforest Mall, and in the alluring, leafy old village of **Washington Grove** where no two cottages or bungalows are alike. Residents of the village buy fresh meat at an old-fashioned butcher shop, dine at the old Hershey family restaurant, and assist with an all-volunteer children's library.

North of incorporated Gaithersburg, the planned community of **Montgomery Village** offers housing at varied levels of luxury and convenience, but it's still mostly townhouses and garden apartments, and all postwar. (Hootie and some of the Blowfish grew up here). Newcomers are lured here by the open space, from Lake Whetstone and the smaller ponds that line Montgomery Village Avenue, to the little parks that link the community golf course with the busy airstrip at Montgomery County Airpark.

A smaller planned community, **Kentlands**, was built in the late 1980s and early '90s in the southwest corner of Gaithersburg, with a promise of varied housing stock and an economically diverse suburban village. The jury is still out on this emerging neighborhood; while there are some housing bargains, the "village" features more Starbucks and Subway franchises than corner drugstores.

Great Seneca Creek State Park protects a vast forest west of Kentlands. North and west of the park, in **Germantown** and **Clarksburg**, old farms are giving way to new subdivisions.

The future of these communities—especially Kentlands and the still-mostly-rural **Olney** to the east—hinges on the decades-old debate about the proposed Intercounty Connector (ICC) highway, the northern arc of a proposed outer Beltway. The ICC would link northern Prince George's County with the Shady Grove Metro station south of Gaithersburg and, if Virginia lawmakers have their way, a new Potomac River bridge. Governor Parris Glendening cancelled the ICC project in 1999, but quietly cleared the way for a series of road upgrades—widening a highway here, adding an interchange there—that amount to building the ICC one little piece at a time. County and state elections since the early 1990s have revolved around this issue alone, and the controversy isn't going away anytime soon. If you're looking for a home anywhere between Gaithersburg and Rockville, ask detailed questions about the latest highway plans—or you could end up living next to a superhighway in a few years.

Web Sites: www.ci.gaithersburg.md.us, www.kentlandsusa.com, www.washgrov.sailorsite.net

Area Codes: 301, 240

Zip Codes: 20877, 20878, 20879

Post Offices: Gaithersburg, 21 South Summit Avenue, 301-208-3700; Diamond Farms Branch, 23 Firstfield Road, 301-208-3708; Montgomery Village Branch, 10079 Stedwick Road, 301-208-3715

Police Station: Gaithersburg City Police, 7 East Cedar Avenue, 301-258-6400

Emergency Hospitals: Shady Grove Adventist, 9901 Medical Center Drive, Rockville, 301-279-6000; Montgomery General, 18101 Prince Philip Drive, Olney, 301-774-8882

Libraries: Gaithersburg Regional, 18330 Montgomery Village Avenue, 301-840-2515; Quince Orchard, 15831 Quince Orchard Road, 240-777-0200

Public High Schools: Gaithersburg, 314 South Frederick Avenue, 301-840-4700; Quince Orchard, 15800 Quince Orchard Road, 301-840-4686; Watkins Mill, 10301 Apple Ridge Road, 301-840-3959

Government: 8th Congressional District; Montgomery County Council district 3; mayor and five-member city council: City Hall, 31 South Summit Avenue, 301-258-6300; Washington Grove Town Hall, 301-926-2256

Neighborhood Festivals: Olde Towne Gaithersburg Day (along East Diamond Avenue, September); Labor Day parade (East Diamond Avenue); Oktoberfest at Kentlands; for information about these and other community events, call the Gaithersburg Arts & Special Events Team, 301-258-6310.

Major Parks: Green Farm (off Snouffer School Road north of Centerway Road); Muddy Branch (along Muddy Branch from I-270 to the Potomac River); Rock Creek (points of access along Needwood Road and Muncaster Mill Road); Seneca Creek (points of access along Clopper Road, Great Seneca Highway, and Riffle Ford Road)

Community Resources: Activity Center at Bohrer Park offers sports and fitness facilities, classes, leagues, and arts activities for all ages, and after-school and summer activities for teens. User fees vary: 506 South

Frederick Avenue, 301-258-6350. Free summer concerts at City Hall Concert Pavilion and at Montgomery Village Lawn Theater, 18850 Montgomery Village Avenue; check newspapers for schedules. Montgomery County Fairgrounds, off North Frederick Avenue with entrances on Chestnut Street and Perry Parkway, are a busy venue for commercial and civic events throughout the year—craft fairs, computer shows, concerts, a Fourth of July celebration, and more—in addition to the county fair in August. Check newspapers.

Public Transportation: Metro: Shady Grove (Red Line); MARC: Washington Grove, Gaithersburg, and Germantown stations (Brunswick Line); Ride-On: 50 series (Lakeforest Mall), 60 series (Montgomery Village), and 70 series (Germantown)

GARRETT PARK

Boundaries: **North**: cul-de-sac off Rokeby Avenue; **East**: railroad tracks; **South**: Rock Creek; **West**: west of Kenilworth Avenue

Garrett Park, a leafy little incorporated town nestled between Rock Creek and Rockville Pike, is eccentric and always has been. The town was founded in 1898 for the express purpose of electing a local government to outlaw one high-tech resident's newfangled indoor privy. In 1982, a year ahead of Takoma Park, the town passed an ordinance boycotting companies that make nuclear weapons—in fact, Garrett Park claims to be the world's first official nuclear-free zone. The whole town is a designated arboretum and is listed on the National Register of Historic Places.

Probably the quirkiest of quirks, though, is that Garrett Park doesn't have any mail carrier routes—every residence has a post office box at the old post office down by the railroad tracks. This time-honored tradition of heading in town for your mail, and chatting with neighbors along the way seems to fit comfortably with most everyone.

Practically every house and garden here is picturesque, and the town is a sampler of architectural styles from old Victorians to post-war bungalows. Long before Bill Gates rediscovered the concept of "bundling," each of the distinctive "Chevy houses" in Garrett Park originally came with a new Chevy in the driveway! If anyone ever decided to move away, just about every home in Garrett Park would fetch more than a quarter million dollars. Good luck!

Web Site: www.garrettpark.org
Area Codes: 301, 240
Zip Code: 20896
Post Office: Garrett Park, 4600 Waverly Avenue, 301-933-2580

Police Station: Bethesda District, 7359 Wisconsin Avenue, 301-657-0119 (commander), 301-279-8000 (Community Concerns Line)

Emergency Hospital: Suburban Healthcare System, 8600 Old Georgetown Road, Bethesda, 301-896-3100

Library: Kensington Park, 4201 Knowles Avenue, Kensington, 301-897-2211

Public High School: Walter Johnson, 6400 Rock Spring Drive, 301-571-6900

Government: 8th Congressional District; Montgomery County Council District 1; mayor and five-member town council: Town Hall, 10814 Kenilworth Avenue, 301-933-7488

Neighborhood Festivals: Pool Opening Picnic (Memorial Day weekend) and Closing Picnic (Labor Day weekend) at Cambria and Knowles avenues; Attic-in-the-Street Sale (various locations, September)

Major Park: Rock Creek (points of access off Knowles Avenue)

Community Resources: Penn Place, Waverly and Rokeby avenues, houses the post office, Garrett Park Cafe, and a few shops and offices—it's the one-stop "downtown" Garrett Park.

Public Transportation: MARC: Garrett Park (Brunswick Line); Ride-On routes 5 (Silver Spring, Twinbrook), 6 (Wheaton, North Bethesda), 38 (Wheaton, Montgomery Mall)

ROCKVILLE

FALLSMEAD
TWINBROOK

Boundaries: North: Gude Drive; **East**: Rock Creek Park; **South**: Montrose Road; **West**: Lakewood Country Club, Watts Branch Stream Valley Park

The City of Rockville is dominated by a little cluster of office towers housing county government offices, and north of downtown Rockville, light industrial sites line the railroad tracks. "Downtown" begins at the north end of the Rockville Pike commercial strip stretching south to Bethesda. "The Pike" here becomes Hungerford Drive, the city's Main Street—not the pedestrian-friendly kind, but a busy six-lane thoroughfare. In residential **Fallsmead** to the west, and in **Twinbrook**, south along Veirs Mill Road, plain postwar colonials, ramblers, and split-levels made of brick and siding line the winding streets and cul-de-sacs of stable neighborhoods. The prices are good as long as you're not too close to the tracks or the constant hum of traffic on I-270, the Pike, or Veirs Mill Road.

Rockville is the population center and county seat of the most affluent county in Maryland, and the city's clout in state politics is almost equal to

Baltimore's. Not surprisingly, Rockville attracts a government related crowd—contractors, lobbyists, and ambitious lawyers. Rockville, like most of the Maryland suburbs, is overwhelmingly Democratic, but there's always a referendum or ballot initiative to keep things divisive. From May to November in even-numbered years, campaign signs bloom like weeds in front of many homes.

Web Sites: www.ci.rockville.md.us, www.rocknet.org

Area Codes: 301, 240

Zip Codes: 20850, 20851, 20852

Post Offices: Rockville, 500 North Washington Street, 301-838-2900; Courthouse Station, West Montgomery Avenue & South Washington Street, 301-838-2922; Pike Station, 143 Rollins Avenue, 301-231-5973; Twinbrook Shopping Center, 2001 Veirs Mill Road, 301-838-2933

Police Stations: Rockville City Police, City Hall, 111 Maryland Avenue, 301-309-3100; Montgomery County Police Department, Rockville District, 1451 Seven Locks Road, 301-279-1591 (commander), 301-279-1992 (Community Concerns Line)

Emergency Hospitals: Shady Grove Adventist, 9901 Medical Center Drive, 301-279-6000

Libraries: Rockville Regional, 99 Maryland Avenue, 240-777-0140; Twinbrook, 202 Meadow Hall Drive, 240-777-0240

Public High Schools: Richard Montgomery (International Baccalaureate magnet providing European-style curriculum), 50 Richard Montgomery Drive, 301-279-8400; Thomas S. Wootton, 2100 Wootton Parkway, 301-279-8550

Government: 8th Congressional District; Montgomery County Council District 3; mayor and 4-member city council: City Hall, 301-309-3000

Neighborhood Festivals: Rockville's Hometown Holidays (Washington Street & Middle Lane, May) and Spirit of Rockville (Civic Center Park, September), 301-309-3330

Major Parks: Civic Center Park/Norbeck Gardens (Edmonston Drive off Baltimore Road); Rock Creek (points of access off Norbeck Road and Avery Road); Upper Watts Branch (off Nelson Street)

Community Resources: Civic Center Park, off Edmonston Drive in the northeast corner of the city, includes the F. Scott Fitzgerald Theatre; historic Glenview Mansion, which houses an art gallery and ballrooms available for weddings and other private functions; and acres of woodland park along tributaries of Rock Creek. For more information, call 301-309-3001 or visit the Recreation & Parks page of the city's web site (see above). The Rockville Little Theater Company, 301-545-5660 or www.srbnet.com/rlt, is based at the F. Scott Fitzgerald Theatre. The Civic Center also houses the Rockville Civic Ballet, Community Chorus,

Brass Band, Concert Band, and a Dixieland jazz band. The F. Scott Fitzgerald Literary Conference is held every September at the Rockville campus of Montgomery College; for information, call 301-309-9461 or visit www.ci.rockville.md.us. The Musical Theater Center at Wintergreen Plaza, 837-D Rockville Pike, 301-251-5766, www.musicaltheatercenter.org, offers classes in acting, dance, music, and stagecraft for children and adults; two companies in residence perform here and on stages around Washington. Rockville Arts Place, 100 East Middle Lane, 301-309-6900, offers classes, camps, exhibits, studio space, and a shop selling works by local artists and craftspeople. Suto Dance Studio, 4511 Bestor Drive, 301-871-1000, offers classes in a variety of dance disciplines and skill levels.

Public Transportation: Metro: Rockville and Twinbrook (Red Line); MARC: Rockville station (Brunswick Line); Metrobus routes: Q1/Q2 (Veirs Mill Road), Y7 (Norbeck Road), and T2 (Falls Road); Ride-On routes: 48-52 (Olney), 44-47 & 54-59 (local)

SILVER SPRING

Boundaries: **North**: Dennis Avenue, Columbia Pike; **East**: Prince George's County; **South**: District of Columbia, Takoma Park; **West**: railroad tracks, 16th Street

Silver Spring is the name applied loosely to most of southern Montgomery County east of Connecticut Avenue. A real estate listing for Silver Spring might turn out to be half an hour's drive north on US Route 29, in the middle of nowhere, but usually the name refers to downtown Silver Spring—a distinct commercial area capping the northern tip of D.C.—or the postwar suburbs along Sligo Creek.

Downtown Silver Spring is dominated by a skyline of office towers—mostly housing AT&T and the National Oceanic & Atmospheric Administration. There are apartment towers, too, taller than those allowed in the District. After years of abortive attempts to attract big-name retailers to the declining old downtown area, a new Fresh Fields and a Borders Books & Music bring evening crowds to the busy corner of Georgia Avenue and Colesville Road. City Place, on Colesville a block north of Georgia, is the only outlet mall inside the Beltway, and a variety of tempting restaurants line Georgia Avenue nearby. Seafood connoisseurs keep Crisfield's, at Georgia and Colesville, at the top of their lists; south of Colesville is a strip of neighborhood ethnic restaurants, including Japanese, Irish, and Salvadoran; and the vintage Tastee Diner at Georgia Avenue and Cameron Street is the perfect stop for a "short stack," key lime pie, or fries smothered in brown gravy.

In 2000, by popular demand, this 1950s institution was saved from a wrecking ball—the whole diner was physically moved from its original location a few blocks away. Up Georgia Avenue, near the north end of 16th Street, venerable Woodside Deli is also the real thing—crusty rye bread, pastrami, and matzo ball soup, as if transplanted straight from Baltimore. While downtown Silver Spring is expected to become more of a nightspot after 2002, when the American Film Institute moves from its current digs at the Kennedy Center to the vintage Silver Theater at Georgia and Colesville, right now it's mostly an office district and transit hub. Dozens of Ride-On and Metrobus lines converge at the Silver Spring Metro station, just a few blocks from a MARC/Amtrak stop and a Greyhound station.

The residential neighborhoods flanking Sligo Creek Park are quintessential suburbs: detached houses built just after World War II, with front and back yards, on tree-lined streets, with lots of kids running around. Most of the houses are colonials, split-levels, and ramblers, but east of Northwest Branch and Columbia Pike there are several pockets of big, stately houses with loop driveways.

Web Site: www.silverspringcenter.com

Area Codes: 301, 240

Zip Codes: 20901, 20902, 20910

Post Offices: Silver Spring, 8616 Second Avenue, 301-608-1300; Aspen Hill, 14030 Connecticut Avenue, 301-871-4441; Colesville, 13217 New Hampshire Avenue, 301-879-2333; Forest Glen, 2460 Linden Lane, 301-295-7594; Silver Spring Centre, 8455 Colesville Road, 301-608-1305; Woodmoor, 110 University Boulevard West, 301-593-6819

Police Station: Silver Spring District, 801 Sligo Avenue, 301-565-7744

Emergency Hospital: Holy Cross, 1500 Forest Glen Road, Silver Spring, 301-754-7000

Libraries: Silver Spring, 8901 Colesville Road, 301-565-7689; Long Branch, 8800 Garland Avenue, 301-565-7585

Public High Schools: James Hubert Blake (fine arts magnet), 300 Norwood Road, 301-879-1300; Montgomery Blair (science and communications magnets), 51 University Boulevard East, 301-649-2800; Springbrook, 201 Valley Brook Drive, 301-989-5700

Government: 5th Congressional District; Montgomery County Council District 5

Major Parks: Nolte (points of access off Dale Drive south of Wayne Avenue); Sligo Creek (points of access off Colesville Road, Wayne Avenue, and Piney Branch Road); Woodside (Georgia Avenue and Spring Street)

Community Resources: National Capital Trolley Museum preserves the memory of street railways in Washington and offers rides in vintage streetcars: 1313 Bonifant Road, 301-384-6088, www.dctrolley.org. Silver Spring Shared Community ArtSpace is used by a variety of performing arts organizations and individual performers; at City Place, 8661 Colesville Road, on the fourth floor; 301-589-1091.

Public Transportation: Metro: Silver Spring (Red Line); MARC, Silver Spring station (Brunswick Line); major bus system hub served by 26 Metrobus routes and 19 Ride-On routes

TAKOMA PARK

LANGLEY PARK

Boundaries: **North**: Sligo Avenue, Piney Branch Road, University Boulevard; **East**: 14th Avenue, New Hampshire Avenue; **South**: District of Columbia; **West**: Chicago Avenue

In the Birkenstocks-and-incense community of Takoma Park, the 2000 presidential race was between Al Gore and Ralph Nader. City government here boycotts the nuclear industry (so you won't find GE light bulbs in schools or libraries) and companies that do business in Burma (so no Pepsi machines in municipal buildings). Legal aliens who own or rent homes here are allowed to vote in municipal elections and serve on the city council or school board. In addition, it has won awards for its recycling efforts and tree conservation, and has been given the nickname "Azalea City" for the colorful bushes that bloom in many front yards in late spring. A thriving food co-op and two farmers' markets meet the huge demand for natural and organic food, and the neighborhood eateries along Carroll Avenue—an authentic neighborhood main street—are careful to provide vegetarian and vegan selections as well. There is a serious campaign to ban gas-burning lawnmowers in the city, and many residential streets have "speed humps" (much bigger than speed bumps, residents explain) to keep traffic from endangering cyclists, pedestrians, and children at play.

The town didn't develop its hippie reputation by accident. Takoma Park was built in 1883 as a planned community, and the Seventh-Day Adventist Church—whose adherents are strictly vegetarian—became one of the first and biggest landowners here. With an Adventist hospital, college, bookstore, and churches here, Takoma Park naturally featured some of the Washington area's earliest health food stores, and the Woodstock generation settled here in search of silken tofu and veggie burgers. The town has always been on the leading edge of gay liberation, and many same-sex couples raise families here. Occasionally, a letter to the editor in the Takoma Voice reminds residents that there are a few conservatives in town, but most residents don't mind the affectionate references to their community as the "People's Republic of Takoma Park."

Except for a few boxy apartment high-rises west of Maple Avenue, Takoma Park's hilly, winding streets are lined with nice houses in varied styles: brick Cape Cods, clapboard Victorians, postwar split-levels, and duplexes or big cottages that have been broken up into apartments. Annual building inspections ensure that landlords (and tenants) keep their rental units in good shape. Shaded with mature trees, the typical block is charming; in the spring and summer many yards burst with colorful blooms, particularly forsythia and azaleas. Some homes have tidy little watch-pocket yards, while a house across the street might have Sligo Creek Park for a backyard.

Takoma Park straddles the line between Montgomery and Prince George's counties, and in fact, until 1996 the town government had to deal with courts, police departments, fire marshals, and other agencies in two counties. With hard-won permission from the state legislature, the town held a referendum on "unification" and voted to join Montgomery County.

The 1990s saw a rise in muggings—mostly pedestrians being followed from the Metro station onto dark side streets. In response, the city police department bought a fleet of bicycles, noting that a quiet bike is much better than a noisy squad car for sneaking up on a suspect. There are still occasional outbreaks of muggings, but the community keeps a vigilant eye on the streets; pedestrians alone after dark should use caution, but the crime rate here is not especially high.

Crime is a bigger concern across University Boulevard in **Langley Park**, in apartment complexes politely described as "affordable housing" and strip malls dominated by liquor stores. It's an inhospitable place to walk, but if you're driving, there are some good ethnic restaurants in Langley Park—most notably, vegetarian Udupi Palace, 1329 University Boulevard East, 301-434-1531. Expect a long wait, with crowds of U of M students and Indian immigrants clamoring for the cheap, authentic Indian fare and the carryout dessert counter.

Web Site: www.cityoftakomapark.org

Area Codes: 301, 240

Zip Code: 20912

Post Office: Takoma Park, 6909 Laurel Avenue, 301-270-4392

Police Station: Municipal Building, 7500 Maple Avenue, 301-270-8724 (routine) or 301-270-1100 (emergency)

Emergency Hospital: Washington Adventist, 7600 Carroll Avenue, Takoma Park, 301-891-7600

Libraries: Takoma Park, 101 Philadelphia Avenue, 301-270-1717 (municipal library; nearest county library is Long Branch, 8800 Garland Avenue, 301-565-7585)

Public High School: Montgomery Blair (science and communications magnets), 51 University Boulevard East, Silver Spring, 301-649-2800

Government: 5th Congressional District; Montgomery County Council District 5; mayor and six-member city council: Municipal Building, Philadelphia & Maple avenues, 301-270-1700

Neighborhood Festivals: Jazz Festival (Takoma Avenue & Fenton Street, May); Folk Festival (Municipal Building and grounds, September); Takoma Park Street Festival (along Carroll Avenue, October); see **A Washington Year** for details. Also Fourth of July parade (Maple Avenue).

Major Parks: Long Branch (along Long Branch between Wayne Avenue and New Hampshire Avenue); Sligo Creek (points of access off Maple Avenue, Piney Branch Road, and Park Valley Road)

Community Resources: Institute of Musical Traditions sponsors a concert series and special events, call 301-587-4434 or visit www.imtfolk.org. The Institute is a spin-off of the House of Musical Traditions, 7040 Carroll Avenue, 301-270-9090, www.hmtrad.com. "HMT" sells hard-to-find instruments, recorded music and related books and videos from around the world, and provides referrals to local music teachers. A Tool Library run by the Department of Housing & Community Development provides city residents with free access to hand and power tools stored in a trailer in the parking lot of the Municipal Building. Open 4 to 8 p.m. Tuesdays and Fridays and 9 a.m. to 1 p.m. Saturdays; for more information, call 301-589-8274.

Public Transportation: Metro: Takoma (Red Line); Metrobus routes: 52-54 (L'Enfant Plaza), 62 (Georgia Avenue), F1/F2 (Cheverly), K2 (local); Ride-On routes: 12-16 & 24/25 (local)

WHEATON

GLENMONT

Boundaries: **North**: Randolph Road; **East**: Northwest Branch; **South**: Dennis Avenue, Plyers Mill Road; **West**: Georgia Avenue, Veirs Mill Road

Wheaton is the archetypal suburb: grids of similar single-family houses built quickly after World War II. Wheaton Plaza was one of the Washington area's first shopping malls, and it anchors the commercial "downtown" Wheaton. Built around the triangle of Georgia Avenue, University Boulevard, and Veirs Mill Road, Wheaton is home to a good selection of restaurants and specialty stores, including *four* used bookstores. (The basement of Wheaton Regional Library is a vast catacomb of used books for sale, cheap. Proceeds benefit the county library system.) A trip to Chuck Levin's Washington Music

Center, 11151 Veirs Mill Road, is a rite of passage for practically every kid in southern Montgomery County taking music lessons.

If you've heard that Wheaton has a great roots rock and blues scene, sorry, you're a few years too late. Most of the clubs that were old haunts of D.C. native Danny Gatton ("the world's greatest unknown guitar player," according to *Guitar World* magazine) closed around the turn of the new century, as Wheaton's nightlife drifted from music to dining.

Most of the homes in Wheaton are single-family detached houses that resemble a child's drawing of "a house"—a simple brick box with a tree in the front yard, picket fence optional. Many streets are looping courts or cul-de-sacs, making neighborhoods cozy and safe—but the nearest bus stop may be a 10-minute walk, and some blocks don't have sidewalks. East of Georgia Avenue there are a few low-rise apartment complexes—simple, affordable 1960s rectangles in beige and brown. North of Randolph Road, in **Glenmont**, there's more of the same.

Wheaton Regional Park is a 500-acre oasis at the headwaters of Sligo Creek, just south of Randolph Road. There's an ice rink, nature center, stables, a huge playground, a miniature train ride for kids, a lake, even a little campground. Brookside Gardens, a section of the park devoted to formal gardens, conservatories, and picture-perfect gazebos dotting a series of fish ponds, is one of the most romantic spots in the Washington area, and indeed it's booked for outdoor weddings almost every weekend from April to September.

If you know any subway buffs, invite them to visit you here: the Wheaton Metro station on the Red Line has the world's longest escalator, 230 feet, and the next station to the south, Forest Glen, is even deeper underground—21 stories beneath Georgia Avenue, and accessible only by high-speed elevators.

Web Site: www.wheatonnet.com

Area Codes: 301, 240

Zip Code: 20902

Post Office: Wheaton Branch, 11431 Amherst Avenue, 301-929-7830

Police Station: Wheaton District, 2300 Randolph Road, 240-773-5500 (emergency), 240-773-5525 (routine calls)

Emergency Hospital: Holy Cross, 1500 Forest Glen Road, Silver Spring, 301-754-7000

Library: Wheaton Regional, 11701 Georgia Avenue, 301-929-5520

Public High Schools: Albert Einstein, 11135 Newport Mill Road, Kensington, 301-929-2200; John F. Kennedy, 1901 Randolph Road, Silver Spring, 301-929-2100; Wheaton, 12601 Dalewood Drive, 301-929-2050

Government: 8th Congressional District; Montgomery County Council District 5

Neighborhood Festival: Taste of Wheaton (Grandview and Ennalls Avenues, May), 240-777-8122

Major Parks: Sligo Creek (points of access off Dennis Avenue, University Boulevard, and Arcola Avenue); Wheaton Regional (points of access off Arcola Avenue, Kemp Mill Road, and Glenallan Avenue)

Community Resources: Brookside Gardens & Nature Center (see description above), 301-949-8230, www.mc-mncppc.org/parks. Round House Theatre, 12210 Bushey Drive, 301-933-1644 (see **Cultural Life** for details).

Public Transportation: Metro: Wheaton and Glenmont (Red Line); Metrobus routes: C2 (Greenbelt), L7 (Friendship Heights), Q1/Q2 (Rockville), Y7/Y9 (Olney); Ride-On routes: 6 (North Bethesda), 7 (Kensington), 8/9 (Silver Spring), 34-38 (Bethesda), 48 (Rockville)

PRINCE GEORGE'S COUNTY

Prince George's County has a bad reputation, and residents are justifiably defensive. A few pockets of crime along Southern Avenue, just outside D.C., taint the county's image in the minds of many Washingtonians. As a result, even the nicer neighborhoods—and there are plenty, mostly in the north end of this largely rural county—are much more affordable than comparable places in Montgomery County; the tradeoff is a shortage of restaurants and practically no upscale shopping.

Most of the older communities here grew up with the railroads: the little towns along US Route 1 just outside Northeast D.C.—such as Mt. Rainier, Hyattsville, Riverdale Park, and Bladensburg. The old mill towns of Laurel and Bowie to the east have long histories, and the houses don't all look alike. In many places, these neighborhoods aren't pedestrian-friendly; if you want to find a house where you can walk to the grocery store, the bank, or a neighborhood pizza joint, you may have a long search ahead. If you don't mind relying on a car or public transportation, though—and if you think of your home as a place to live, not mainly as an investment— northern Prince George's County is one of the best bargains in the Washington area.

The county stretches from the Potomac to the Patuxent, and from Laurel south to the heart of Maryland's tobacco country. Giant C-5 cargo planes churn the sky above the Beltway on their way to Andrews Air Force Base, home of Air Force One. Government scientists study crops and soil in Beltsville, wetlands in Laurel, and satellite telemetry in Greenbelt. Local high schools offer special science and technology concentrations to take advantage of those resources.

Ironically, one of the county's biggest problems is the opposite of street crime: for decades the police department has faced tough and persistent questions about overzealous conduct, especially involving African-American suspects, and several high-profile stories have drawn unfavorable national attention to the county. Whether it's a real pattern or a perception, it stigmatizes the county's 780,000 residents on the basis of the actions of a few.

Civic boosters get especially annoyed by the nickname "P.G." County. Since the county doesn't seem to get enough respect from retail businesses, homebuyers, or its neighboring jurisdictions, residents appreciate at least hearing the three-syllable name unabbreviated. (The name refers to Prince George of Denmark, whose wife, Queen Anne of Great Britain, chartered the first European colonies here in the early 18th century.)

Government: County Administration Building, 14741 Governor Oden Bowie Drive, Upper Marlboro, www.co.pg.md.us
County Executive: 301-952-4131, www.co.pg.md.us
County Council: nine members, each representing a council district; 301-952-3600, www.co.pg.md.us/council
Public Schools: 301-952-6300, www.pgcps.pg.k12.md.us
Libraries: 301-699-3500, www.prge.lib.md.us
Police: 301-772-4740, www.co.pg.md.us
Online Guide: www.co.pg.md.us/about

BOWIE

OLD BOWIE
SOUTH BOWIE/MITCHELLVILLE

Boundaries: **North**: Duckettown Road, Bowie State University, Patuxent River; **East**: US Route 301; **South**: Central Avenue; **West**: Church Road, Collington Branch, Hillmeade Road

The nation's capital has been missing major-league baseball since 1971, but the sprawling old railroad town of Bowie has its own professional baseball team—the Baysox, a minor-league affiliate of the Baltimore Orioles. By far the largest city in the Maryland suburbs, Bowie offers old and new housing in old and new neighborhoods.

On a map, Bowie looks like a cane, and the handle is **Old Bowie**, the 19th-century stomping ground of railroad barons. The modern city of Bowie grew to the south along the tracks, and it was still horse country when Oden Bowie's trains rolled through the rail junction off Chestnut Avenue.

Today, strip malls and modern subdivisions line Annapolis Road, and office parks cluster along US Route 50, known locally as the John Hanson Highway; to the south, you can find attractive bargains. The **Mitchellville** area, from Allen Pond Park south to Central Avenue, is an upscale enclave where spacious houses on big lots sell for considerably less than comparable homes in Montgomery County. Good luck finding one for rent. There are still a few semi-rural pockets here, but developers are moving in quickly; some low-rise luxury apartments off Mitchellville Road have rental rates approaching those in the District.

Southern Bowie, known locally as "South Bowie" and technically a part of Mitchellville, has the highest average household income in the county. When affluent African-American families left the District in droves in the early 1990s, this is where many settled. Despite this evidence of ample purchasing power, Prince George's County officials complain that upscale retail chains continue to flock to Montgomery County.

Web Site: www.cityofbowie.org
Area Code: 301
Zip Codes: 20715, 20716, 20720
Post Office: Bowie, 6710 Laurel-Bowie Road, 301-464-0707
Police Station: District II Station, 601 Crain Highway, 301-390-2100
Emergency Hospital: Bowie Health Center, 15001 Health Center Drive, 301-262-5511
Library: Bowie, 15210 Annapolis Road, 301-262-7000
Public High Schools: Bowie, 15200 Annapolis Road, 301-805-2600; Tall Oaks Vocational, 2112 Church Road, 301-390-0230
Government: 5th Congressional District; Maryland General Assembly District 23; Prince George's County Council Districts 4 and 6; mayor and six-member city council: City Hall, 2614 Kenhill Drive, 301-262-6200
Major Parks: Allen Pond (Mithcellville Road & Northview Drive); Black Sox (off Mitchellville Road south of Mt. Oak Road); Collington Branch Stream Valley (along Collington Branch between US Route 50 and Central Avenue); Foxhill (Collington Road & Faith Lane); White Marsh (off Route 3 south of Annapolis Road)
Community Resources: Artist of the Month exhibit at City Hall (see above under **Government**); Belair Mansion is the historic home of colonial Governor Samuel Ogle, circa 1745; open from 1 to 4 p.m., Thursday-Saturday, free: 12207 Tulip Grove Drive, 301-809-3089. Belair Stable Museum was part of the Belair Stud Farm; when it closed in 1957, it was the oldest continuously working horse farm in the country; located at 2385 Belair Drive, 301- 809-3089. Bowie Playhouse/Theatre in the Woods, White Marsh Park, offers performances by the Bowie Community

Theater Company. For information, call 301-805-0219. Bowie Railroad Station & Huntington Museum honors Oden Bowie, railroad executive and governor of Maryland in the early 20th century; open noon to 4 p.m., weekends, free. Located at 11th Street & Chestnut Avenue, 301-809-3089. Bowie City Gymnasium, 4100 Northview Drive, 301-809-3009; other public athletic facilities include the Bowie Ice Arena, 301-809-3090, and Bowie Senior Center, 301-809-2300. Prince George's Genealogical Library is at 12219 Tulip Grove Drive, 301- 262-2063. The Radio-Television Museum opened in 1999 under the auspices of the Radio History Society; 2608 Mitchellville Road, 301-390-1020, www.radiohistory.org.

Public Transportation: MARC: Seabrook and Bowie State stations (Penn Line); Metrobus routes: B21-B29 & C28 (New Carrollton), C29 (Addison Road)

CHEVERLY

Boundaries: **North**: Landover Road; **East**: US Route 50; **South**: US Route 50; **West**: Baltimore-Washington Parkway

Cheverly is a leafy oasis surrounded by industrial parks along the railroad. For a small municipality, Cheverly has a lot of neighborhood parks, which are hardly distinguishable from the town's broad, grassy medians and big residential front lawns. This is lawnmower-and-lemonade territory, and it's a bargain.

A planned community built in 1918, Cheverly carefully avoided the prefabricated look and feel of most planned communities. Distinctive cottages and bungalows line winding streets and lush hillsides. Many locals consider this to be one of the most attractive suburban towns in the area, and you can still find a nice prewar house for well under $200,000.

Bumper stickers indicate a gay-friendly community, but it's not Dupont Circle hip. This is a settled suburb for families and couples; young renters—especially a group sharing a house—may be greeted with a bit of suspicion.

The southern part of Cheverly and neighboring Tuxedo Park, along US Route 50, is industrial—wholesale warehouses cluster around the railroad tracks just outside the District.

US Route 50 between Washington and Annapolis is called the John Hanson Highway—Maryland native John Hanson was, in a manner of speaking, the first president of the United States. (The Constitution was adopted nine years after the American Revolution, and in those early years, the Articles of Confederation gave executive power to the president pro tempore of the Senate—Hanson.) And yet, from the bridge where Cheverly

Avenue crosses the tracks, it's not the Hanson Monument you can see in the distance.

Web Site: www.cheverly.com
Zip Code: 20785
Area Code: 301
Post Office: Landover Branch, 3312 Dodge Park Road, 301-322-5055
Police Stations: Cheverly Police Department, Town Hall, 301-773-8362; Prince George's County Police Department, District I Station, 5000 Rhode Island Avenue, Hyattsville, 301-699-2626
Emergency Hospital: Prince George's Hospital Center, 3001 Hospital Drive, 301-618-2000
Library: Bladensburg, 4820 Annapolis Road, 301-927-4916
Public High School: Fairmont Heights High School (biotechnology magnet), 1401 Nye Street, Capitol Heights, 301-925-1360
Government: 4th Congressional District; Prince George's County Council District 5; mayor and six-member town council: Town Hall, 6401 Forest Road, 301-773-8360
Major Park: Anacostia River (points of access west of Kenilworth Avenue)
Community Resources: Publick Playhouse, a restored Art Deco performance hall featuring local and touring theater companies and live jazz, gospel, and world music; 5445 Landover Road, 301-277-1710.
Public Transportation: Metro: Cheverly (Orange Line); MARC: New Carrollton, (Penn Line); Metrobus routes: F1/F2 (Takoma), F8 (Langley Park), F12/F13 (New Carrollton); The BUS route 23 (Addison Road)

GREENBELT/BELTSVILLE

Boundaries: North: Muirkirk Road, Laurel-Bowie Road; **East**: Patuxent Wildlife Research Center, Good Luck Road; **South**: Capital Beltway; **West**: Interstate 95

Much larger than any local city except the District of Columbia, the National Agricultural Research Center in **Beltsville** is a major complex of US Department of Agriculture laboratory farms. If you get lost on the facility's service roads—like Sheep Road or Soil Conservation Road—you might come across a herd of government cows, some of which have plastic portholes installed in their sides, allowing scientists access to samples of the cows' stomach contents. Sounds like an urban legend, but it's true, and it's here.

Beltsville is a newer suburb—siding, not red brick, and fewer mature trees than some older communities in Prince George's County, with no downtown area.

As Beltsville is synonymous with the USDA facility, neighboring **Greenbelt** is synonymous with the Goddard Space Flight Center, one of NASA's main satellite tracking stations. Goddard hosts a model rocket competition every year in honor of the center's namesake, the first actual rocket scientist. Not coincidentally, Greenbelt is home to a public magnet school emphasizing science and technology: Eleanor Roosevelt High School, with 3,100 students, is the largest public school in Maryland. Students at nearby DuVal High School, meanwhile, have designed experiments carried by NASA on space shuttle missions.

Old Greenbelt, along Crescent Road, was one of three federal planned communities built by FDR's Resettlement Administration under the New Deal. An experiment in social engineering, the original homes were awarded to applicants screened not only to ensure diverse levels of income but a high level of civic participation. Even today, the town has many cooperative institutions, including a nursery school, supermarket, and a 250-acre, 1,600-unit housing co-op (see below under **Community Resources**).

The modern sections of Greenbelt, east of the Baltimore-Washington Parkway and west of Kenilworth Avenue, are a little "downtown" with high-rise office buildings, though it's not the most pedestrian-friendly place—even the Metro station is hard to reach on foot.

Web Sites: www.ci.greenbelt.md.us, www.greenbelt.com, www.beltsville.com
Zip Codes: 20770, 20705
Area Code: 301
Post Offices: Beltsville, 11301 Rhode Island Avenue, 800-275-8777; Greenbelt, 119 Centerway Road, 800-275-8777
Police Stations: Greenbelt Police Department, 550 Crescent Road, 301-474-7200 (routine), 301-474-5454 (emergency); Prince George's County Police, District VI Station, 4321 Sellman Road, Beltsville, 301-937-0910
Emergency Hospitals: Laurel Regional Hospital, 7300 Van Dusen Road, Laurel, 301-725-4300; Doctors Community Hospital, 8118 Good Luck Road, Lanham, 301-552-8118
Libraries: Beltsville, 4319 Sellman Road, 301-937-0294; Greenbelt, 11 Crescent Road 301-345-5800
Public High Schools: Eleanor Roosevelt (science magnet), 7601 Hanover Parkway, Greenbelt, 301-513-5400; High Point, 601 Powder Mill Road, Beltsville, 301-572-6400; DuVal, 9880 Good Luck Road, Lanham, 301-918-8600
Government: 5th Congressional District; Prince George's County Council Districts 1 and 4; Greenbelt Mayor serves on five-member town council: Town Office, 25 Crescent Road, 301-474-8000
Neighborhood Festival: Greenbelt Day (various locations, June); Labor Day parade (Crescent Road) and festival (various locations)

Major Parks: Greenbelt (points of access off Greenbelt Road and Good Luck Road)

Community Resources: National Agricultural Library, 10301 Baltimore Avenue, 301-504-5755; see **Cultural Life** for details. The USDA National Visitor Center offers tours of the 7,000-acre Beltsville agricultural lab. Call 301-504-9403 for reservations or visit www.ars.usda.gov/is/nvc. Goddard Space Flight Center offers tours and exhibits at its Visitor Center off Greenbelt Road. Annual public events include Space Day, with model rocket contests and interactive exhibits, and Community Day, with opportunities to meet astronauts and mission scientists. For information, call 301-286-8981 or visit http://pao.gsfc.nasa.gov. Greenbelt Homes Inc. is the city's housing co-op. By joining the co-op, you purchase the right to live in one of the co-op's homes and to earn and sell equity in that home; the title remains with the member-owned non-profit corporation. For details, call 301-474-4161. Greenbelt Community Center includes a gym, stage, co-op nursery school, dance studio, ceramics studio, city museum, and meeting rooms: 15 Crescent Road, 301-397-2208; for information about art classes, call the Greenbelt Association for the Visual Arts, 301-474-2192, and for the Greenbelt Concert Band, 301-552-1444.

Public Transportation: Metro: Greenbelt (Green Line); MARC: Seabrook (Penn Line), Greenbelt and Muirkirk stations (Camden Line); Metrobus routes: C2 (Wheaton), R3 (Fort Totten), T15-T17 (New Carrollton), Z series (Silver Spring), 81-86 (Rhode Island Avenue), 87-89 (Laurel); The BUS routes: 11 (local), H (Laurel)

LAUREL

SAVAGE
MONTPELIER
KONTERRA

Boundaries: **North**: Patuxent River; **East**: Patuxent River; **South**: Muirkirk Road; **West**: Interstate 95

Historic Laurel has its share of stereotypical postwar suburban tracts: one cookie-cutter subdivision after another, with plain townhouses built quickly in the 1950s to house the young families of World War II veterans—and Army intelligence "spooks" at nearby Fort Meade. In the northern part of town, though, some houses along Main Street were built for 19th-century mill workers.

This is one of the oldest industrial sites in the Washington area—Welsh Quakers arrived here in 1658 and set up ironworks and cotton mills, trading on the Patuxent River when ships were smaller and the river, now filled with sediment, was bigger. When the town was incorporated in the 1870s, it was known as Laurel Factory.

Some of the homes from that era have been carefully restored, with pine floors and leaded-glass windows. They don't change hands often, but when they do, you might be able to steal one for half the price of a comparably historic home in the District. You would not only have a house that could pass for Georgetown or Old Town Alexandria, but a location ideal for couples employed both in Washington and Baltimore.

Laurel's factory days are over, and the big local industries are cryptology and horse racing. Fort George G. Meade, five miles east, is the home of the NSA—the National Secur- uh, "No Such Agency." It's one of those secrets that everyone knows: this is where the Army makes and breaks encryption codes, and there is a military and civilian complement of 34,000 here to do it. Between the town and the base, Laurel Racetrack has its own train station on the MARC line from Capitol Hill to Baltimore's Camden Yards.

Just across the Baltimore/Washington Parkway, the 13,000-acre Patuxent Research Refuge is the federal government's main scientific facilities involved in wildlife conservation. Here the US Fish & Wildlife Service studies forest, meadow, and wetland ecosystems, including migratory birds and a pair of bald eagles nesting here since 1989.

A few miles up US Route 1 is the town of **Savage**, where historic Savage Mill produced bolts of canvas from 1822-1947: sails for Baltimore clipper ships, tents for the Union army, backdrops for early movie sets, and Army cloth during both World Wars. Now the complex is an arts center and antiques mall, drawing weekend crowds in search of distinctive furniture, collectibles, and works by local artists.

South of Laurel, **Montpelier** and the planned city of **Konterra** are modern subdivisions. Konterra—mostly an office park—was envisioned in the 1990s to take advantage of the planned Intercounty Connector (ICC) superhighway. The ICC was the most divisive topic in Maryland politics in the 1990s and isn't likely to be built, conclusively cancelled, or otherwise resolved anytime soon—so Konterra might be little more than an office park for years to come.

Web Sites: www.laurel.md.us, www.ftmeade.army.mil
Zip Code: 20707
Area Code: 301
Post Office: 324 Main Street, 301-498-1400; Montpelier Branch, 12625 Laurel-Bowie Road, 301-490-1818
Police Stations: Laurel Police Department, 350 Municipal Square, 301-498-0092; Prince George's County Police, District VI Station, 4321 Sellman Road, Beltsville, 301-937-0910

Emergency Hospital: Laurel Regional Hospital, 7300 Van Dusen Road, Laurel, 301-725-4300

Library: Laurel, 507 7th Street, 301-776-6790

Public High School: Laurel, 8000 Cherry Lane, 301-497-2050

Government: 5th Congressional District; Prince George's County Council District 1; mayor and five-member city council: Municipal Center, 8103 Sandy Spring Road, 301-725-5300

Neighborhood Festivals: Main Street Festival (May); Monpelier Spring Festival (May—see Montpelier under "Community Resources" below); Riverfest (Riverfront Park, October)

Major Park: Patuxent (points of access off Laurel-Bowie Road north of the B-W Parkway and along Brooklyn Bridge Road west of I-95)

Community Resources: Patuxent Research Refuge—North Tract and the National Wildlife Visitor Center are open daily, 10 a.m. to 5:30 p.m. The Visitor Center, offering tours and exhibits, is located off Powder Mill Road between Maryland Route 197 and the Baltimore-Washington Parkway. For more information, call 301-497-5760. Montpelier Mansion & Cultural Arts Center is the 18th-century Georgian home of Maj. Thomas Snowden, crowning a 70-acre estate, where the barns now house the Montpelier Cultural Arts Center. You can tour the preserved mansion and rent banquet rooms where George Washington and Abigail Adams once were guests. The Arts Center, open daily 10 a.m. to 5 p.m., shows juried exhibits of local, national, and international works, and the work of artists in residence. Classes and performances are also held here. Entrance to the grounds is off Muirkirk Road just west of Laurel-Bowie Road (Maryland Route 197). For more information, call 301-953-1376 (mansion) or 301-953-1993 (Arts Center), or visit www.pgparks.com. Savage Mill is open daily; 8600 Foundry Street, Savage, 800-788-6455, www.savagemill.com.

Public Transportation: MARC: Muirkirk, Laurel, and Laurel Racetrack stations (Camden Line); Metrobus routes: 87 & 89 (Greenbelt), 88 (New Carrollton); The BUS routes: A-C (local), D (Burtonsville), E (Columbia), F (Fort Meade), H (Greenbelt)

ROUTE 1 CORRIDOR

MT. RAINIER
COTTAGE CITY
COLMAR MANOR
BRENTWOOD
EDMONDSTON
BLADENSBURG
NORTH BRENTWOOD
HYATTSVILLE
UNIVERSITY PARK
RIVERDALE PARK
COLLEGE PARK
BERWYN HEIGHTS

Boundaries: **North**: Capital Beltway; **East**: Baltimore-Washington Parkway; **South**: Eastern Avenue; **West**: Northwest Branch, Riggs Road

The D.C./Maryland line across Rhode Island Avenue is unceremonious, noticeable mainly because traffic lights are painted gray in the District and yellow in the suburbs. But the cluster of old suburban communities along US Route 1, from D.C. to Beltsville, is a diverse area where young University of Maryland graduates and junior federal workers from the USDA facilities in Beltsville, or the NASA facilities in Greenbelt, can actually afford to own a home—with trees in the yard and the obligatory white picket fence.

Don't try to follow this without a map: Clustered just outside the District are the towns of **Mt. Rainier**, from Queens Chapel Road east to Rhode Island Avenue; **Cottage City**, from Rhode Island Avenue east to Bladensburg Road; and **Colmar Manor** east to the Anacostia River. **Brentwood** is just north of Mt. Rainier, extending to the Northwest Branch of the Anacostia and east to the railroad tracks. Hyattsville stretches from the Northwest Branch north to Route 410 and east to the tracks; **Edmondston** straddles the Northeast Branch; and **Bladensburg** stretches from the Anacostia east to the Baltimore/Washington Parkway.

These are all similar communities, but each is an incorporated town with its own little police and fire departments and town council. The homes may look the same from one town to the next—some plain modern homes mixed in with plenty of bungalows and cottages built before World War I—but most of these towns have distinct histories. Cottage City is, to the chagrin of longtime residents, known mainly as the home of the child about whom *The Exorcist* was based. Tiny **North Brentwood**, population 500, was the first predominantly African-American town in Prince George's

County, founded on land purchased by black Civil War veterans from their commanding officer. And "Historic Bladensburg" may sound like a silly pretense—the town doesn't look especially old—but in fact Bladensburg, MD is the only place where the United States was ever successfully invaded. During the War of 1812, the British navy made it all the way to the head of the Anacostia River (now the Prince George's Marina) and put troops ashore to march on Washington. They burned the Capitol and the White House while First Lady Dolley Madison smuggled the Constitution out of the city in a trunk of clothes. A stone cross at the junction of US Route 1 and Landover Road marks the landing site; few of the commuters who pass the memorial every day are aware of its significance.

Nearby Mt. Rainier attracts the area's biggest granola contingent outside Takoma Park. Neighborhood amenities include the Glut Food Co-op, under the sign of the giant carrot at 4005 34th Street, and a strip of alternative medicine shops, New Age bookstores and storefront churches just off Rhode Island Avenue.

Hyattsville is a larger town with its own commercial districts—along Hamilton Street and Ager Road and the south end of Queens Chapel Road—and a mall, Prince George's Plaza, across Route 410. The USDA fills two large office buildings near the mall. This is the childhood home of Jim Henson; in fact, Kermit the Frog was born just up the street, when Henson was a student at U of M.

University Park, nestled between the University of Maryland and Route 410 and between Adelphi Road and US Route 1, is a strictly residential enclave—all detached homes, mostly red brick, and no commercial buildings. In the 1990s, the town closed the north end of Queens Chapel Road to through traffic, ending commuter shortcuts through the neighborhood. It's an oasis of high SAT scores, active civic culture, and housing prices lower than in comparable neighborhoods in other suburbs; it's in image-challenged Prince George's County, not fashionable Montgomery County, and buyers benefit from the stereotype.

Across US 1 is **Riverdale Park**, an older suburb straddling the railroad tracks—many residential streets have grade crossings. Catering to student group rentals, there are some large houses here with many small rooms—note though, a nine-bedroom house might include some lofts and some very tiny or irregularly shaped rooms. Older maps of this area just show "Riverdale"; in a 1998 referendum, voters added "Park" to the town's name.

To the north and west, the main campus of the University of Maryland, with its own zip code and 33,000 students, defines the city of **College Park**: a college-town commercial strip along Route 1 with a lot of bookstores, delis, liquor stores, laundromats and travel agencies. There are some apartment buildings, but most of the housing stock is detached houses on quiet residential streets. Student group rentals are quite common. So are bicycles, as the "College Park" Metro station (Green Line) is nowhere near campus. It's a 10-minute shuttle ride away, serving the residential east side of town. If you drive, note that the city and the university both rely on parking tickets for a certain percentage of their annual revenue, and here you do have to feed the parking meters on weekends.

College Park Airport, a tiny airstrip off Calvert Road near the Metro and MARC stations, is the oldest working airport in the world: it was built by Wilbur Wright in 1909 as the first flight school for the Army.

Right across the railroad tracks from College Park is the town of **Berwyn Heights**, a leafy suburb where junior faculty members might buy a home. It's also a granola enclave—a strip of cottage businesses along Berwyn Road includes an herb shop, an independent health food store, and several consignment shops. There's an REI outdoor sporting goods co-op off Route 193 on a fragment of Rhode Island Avenue that doesn't connect to the road of the same name leading into D.C.

Street names can be confusing here. Many major suburban roads change names as they pass through different communities; to be on the safe side, ask for directions using route numbers. Maryland Route 410 is known as East-West Highway from Bethesda to Langley Park; in Takoma Park, it becomes Ethan Allan Avenue and then Philadelphia Avenue; after another stretch as East-West Highway, it crosses the B-W Parkway and becomes Riverdale Road. Likewise, US Route 1 between D.C. and the Beltway is known variously as Rhode Island Avenue, Bladensburg Road and Baltimore Avenue; and Route 193 is called University Boulevard west of US Route 1, and Greenbelt Road to the east. Seriously, you'll need a good map.

Web Sites: www.inform.umd.edu/Route1, http://berwyn-heights.com, www.bladensburg.com, www.inform.umd.edu/collegepark, www.hyattsville.org, http://users.erols.com/mrainier, www.ci.riverdale-park.md.us, www.upmd.org

Zip Codes: 20710, 20712, 20722, 20781, 20782, 20740

Area Code: 301

Post Offices: Brentwood, 4314 41st Street, 301-699-8841; College Park, 9591 Baltimore Boulevard, 301-345-1714; Hyattsville, 4325 Gallatin Street, 301-209-8900; Kenilworth Station, 6270 Kenilworth Avenue, 301-699-3215; Mt. Rainier, 3709 Rhode Island Avenue, 301-699-8856; Prince George's Plaza, 301-209-8903; Riverdale, 6411 Baltimore Avenue, 301-699-8859; West Hyattsville, 301-209-8932

Police Stations: District I Station, 5000 Rhode Island Avenue, Hyattsville, 301-699-2626; each municipality has its own small police force—call the town hall at the number listed below under "Government."

Emergency Hospitals: Doctors Community Hospital, 8118 Good Luck Road, Lanham, 301-552-8118; Prince George's Hospital Center, 3001 Hospital Drive, Cheverly, 301-618-2000

Libraries: Bladensburg, 4820 Annapolis Road, 301-927-4916; Hyattsville, 6532 Adelphi Road, 301-985-4690; Mt. Rainier, 3409 Rhode Island Avenue, 301-864-8937

Public High School: Bladensburg, 5160 Tilden Road, 301-985-1470

Government: 4th Congressional District (except College Park and Berwyn Heights, 5th district); Prince George's County Council District 2 (Brentwood, Colmar Manor, Cottage City, Hyattsville, Mt. Rainier) and 3 (Berwyn Heights, College Park, Riverdale Park, University Park). Each municipality has a mayor and town council—contact the **town hall** for more information: Berwyn Heights, 5700 Berwyn Road, 301-474-5000; Bladensburg, 4229 Edmonston Road, 301-927-7048; Brentwood, 4300 39th Place, 301-927-7395; College Park, 4500 Knox Road, 301-864-8666; Colmar Manor, 3701 Lawrence Street, 301-277-4920; Cottage City, 3820 40th Avenue, 301-779-2161; Edmondston, 5005 52nd Avenue, 301-699-8806; Hyattsville, 4310 Gallatin Street, 301-985-5000; Mt. Rainier, One Municipal Place, 301-985-6585; North Brentwood, 4507 Church Street, 301-699-9699; Riverdale Park, 5008 Queensbury Road, 301-927-6381; University Park, 6724 Baltimore Avenue, 301-927-2997

Neighborhood Festivals: Maryland Day (various locations at the University of Maryland, April), www.marylandday.umd.edu

Major Parks: Anacostia River (access off Bladensburg Road on the west side and Kenilworth Avenue on the east side); Greenbelt (points of access off Greenbelt Road and Good Luck Road); Northeast Branch (points of access along Kenilworth Avenue); Northwest Branch (along Northwest Branch between US Route 1 and the Metro bridge on the Green Line); Paint Branch/Berwyn Stream Valley (east of the railroad tracks between Berwyn Road and Calvert Road)

Community Resources: College Park Aviation Museum features vintage aircraft including one of the Wright Brothers' first military planes. Interactive exhibits include flight simulators, a wind tunnel, and live audio monitors from the control towers at regional airports. Open daily. Admission $4/adult; discounts for children, seniors, and groups; 1985 Cpl. Frank Scott Drive, College Park, 301-864-6029, www.pgparks.com. Riversdale mansion and estate was built in the early 19th century for George and Rosalie Calvert, whose family founded Maryland. The historic site is open for tours and rentals; 4811 Riverdale Road, Riverdale Park, 301-864-0420, www.pgparks.com. The University of Maryland-College Park offers many cultural events open to the public, including recent movies at a low cost in the Hoff Theater. Check the film, stage and exhibit listings in the Weekend section of Friday's *Washington Post*, pick up the U of M *Diamondback* on campus, or visit the Campus Activities or Student Union pages at www.inform.umd.edu/Student. Mt. Rainier Nature Center offers interpretive programs and guided nature walks: 4701 31st Place, 301-927-2163.

Public Transportation: Metro: West Hyattsville, Prince George's Plaza, and College Park stations (Green Line); MARC: Riverdale and College Park stations (Camden Line); Metrobus routes: C8 (Glenmont), F1/F2 (Takoma Park), F4/F6 (New Carrollton), R3 (Greenbelt, Fort Totten), R4 (Brookland), 80 series (Rhode Island Avenue); The BUS routes: 12/13 (local)

VIRGINIA

The Commonwealth of Virginia is the oldest settlement of European people in the Western hemisphere, and the names on the state road map sound like the index of an American history book: Lee Highway, Dolley Madison Boulevard, Jefferson High School, Lake Braddock, Wilson Boulevard, George Mason University, and even Jefferson Davis Highway. Virginia schoolchildren learn to think of their state as the "Birthplace of Presidents," and indeed, in its first two centuries, nearly one in five of our nation's chief executives were born here, including Washington, Jefferson, Madison, Monroe, and Wilson.

Virginia, the "Old Dominion," is a conservative state by any standard. A state holiday, Lee-Jackson Day, honors two Confederate generals, and until recently, the Martin Luther King Jr. holiday was combined with it—observed as "Lee-Jackson-King Day!" Head west on I-66 a little over five miles past the Beltway, and you can visit the National Rifle Association museum and headquarters. Even in cosmopolitan Northern Virginia, the two biggest employers attract a conservative set: the Pentagon and the information technology sector.

While horse farms may still occupy large expanses, the state's leading private industry is information technology. Network Solutions, AOL, Nextel, GTS, Primus Telecommunications, BTG, and Microstrategy have headquarters in a growing high-tech corridor from Tysons Corner to Dulles Airport. The aerospace industry is well represented too, with US Airways, General Dynamics, Fairchild, Orbital Sciences, Atlantic Coast Airways, World Airways, and SpaceHab based here. These company names flank the entrances to modern office parks and corporate campuses in the outer suburbs. Closer to the Potomac, big homes with big yards in airy, modern, elegant subdivisions house descendants of families that have lived in the area for generations as well as some of the newest high-tech millionaires. Closer still, Arlington and Alexandria are little cities themselves, with downtowns and varied residential areas and commercial strips blooming with nightlife.

Populous and urban Northern Virginia is a far cry from the rural towns and hamlets dotting the rolling hills of tobacco country and apple orchards that make up the rest of the state. From Hampton Roads to Massanutten Mountain, from colonial Jamestown to the new National Air & Space Museum annex at Dulles Airport, Virginia relies heavily on tourism—especially on visits from Washingtonians on day trips or weekend getaways.

Capital: Richmond
Governor: 804-786-2211, www.thedigitaldominion.com
Virginia General Assembly: 804-698-7410 (Senate), 804-698-1500 (House), 800-889-0229 (comment line); www.legis.state.va.us
Internet Guide: Virginia Information Providers Network, www.vipnet.org
Newspaper of Record: *Richmond Times-Dispatch,* 800-468-3382, www.timesdispatch.com

---

CITY OF ALEXANDRIA

HUNTINGTON
SPRINGFIELD
ANNANDALE

Boundaries: **North**: King Street, Quaker Lane, South Glebe Road; **East**: Potomac River; **South**: Capital Beltway; **West**: cul-de-sacs west of Van Dorn Street and Holmes Run

The tall, pointy tower looming over Alexandria is the Washington Monument—the other one. Many of the founders were Freemasons, and the George Washington National Masonic Memorial here houses General Washington's own gavel, which he used in the Masonic ceremony dedicating the cornerstone of the Capitol. Across the railroad tracks from the monument, Old Town Alexandria stretches east to the Potomac, and from the Beltway north to Potomac Yard, an old rail terminal site now boasting more big-box chain stores than boxcars.

George Washington shopped in Alexandria, and the historic district is so well maintained that he wouldn't seem out of place strolling through the cobblestone streets and the historic buildings—though he might be eating Ben & Jerry's ice cream or drinking a Starbucks latte. Many homes and stores bear bronze historical plaques, and woe unto any owner who tries to alter an original facade. Owning a house in Old Town is an expensive endeavor, and even some new townhouses here start in the high six figures.

For the over-30 crowd, after graduating from the taverns of neighboring

Arlington, **Old Town** is the center of nightlife on the Virginia side of the river. Bistros and bars line the streets, and one of the riverboat restaurants on the Potomac, the Dandy, is docked here. Antique stores, boutiques, and art galleries attract weekend crowds. The Torpedo Factory Art Center, once an actual torpedo factory, dominates the waterfront. The cavernous building now houses dozens of artists' suites with galleries in front and studios in back. Many classes are offered here, but it's educational just to sit and chat with the painters, sculptors, weavers, potters, jewelers, and other artists in residence, many of whom are happy to let visitors watch them work. The complex also houses a small museum devoted to Alexandria history and archaeology.

North of Potomac Yard, brick row houses off Glebe Road and Mt. Vernon Avenue are relatively cheap for Alexandria. The Birchmere, at 3701 Mt. Vernon Avenue, is the Washington area's preeminent folk music venue, with bluegrass every week and the best Irish, country, and folk singer-songwriters.

Just off Quaker Lane and I-395 is **Park Fairfax**, a complex of townhouse condominiums built just after World War II. As newcomers, Richard Nixon and Gerald Ford lived here.

West of the monument, Alexandria does have some low-income housing and scattered pockets of crime. Redevelopment plans for the industrial strip that follows Cameron Run along Eisenhower Avenue and the Beltway include the future home of the Patent & Trademark Office. The incorporated city of Alexandria works hard on public safety and the underlying social tensions, and has never experienced the middle-class flight that hurt D.C. in the late 1980s and early '90s. In 2000, Alexandria was ninth on the *Ladies' Home Journal* list of "Best Cities for Women Today and Tomorrow," citing the low crime rate, the quality of schools, jobs, health care, and child care, and the representation of women in local government.

Alexandria's own suburbs, **Huntington** to the south and **Springfield** and **Annandale** to the west, are vast residential areas consisting mainly of single-family homes. Between the Beltway and Mt. Vernon, expect to find stately old colonials; west of Van Dorn Street, newer split-level homes with large bay windows and skylights are placed in sprawling subdivisions. One of the nation's first public magnet schools for math and science, Thomas Jefferson High School, is here, on Miner Lane off Braddock Road.

The **Hollin Hills** development in Huntington, near the bird-watchers' paradise of Dyke Marsh by the Potomac, is one of the few postwar developments near Mt. Vernon. These low houses nestled in rolling hills were cited in a 1951 issue of *Life* magazine as among the "best houses for under $15,000." Today they go for up to half a million dollars.

Two noise warnings: the north side of Alexandria is close to Reagan

National Airport, and if you live near Mt. Vernon, you might occasionally hear the 21-gun salute rendered by any US Navy ship that passes by the home of the first Commander-in-Chief.

Web Site: www.ci.alexandria.va.us
Zip Codes: 22003, 22301, 22302, 22304, 22311, 22314
Area Code: 703
Post Offices: Alexandria, 1100 Wythe Street, 703-549-4201; Belle View, 1626 Belle View Boulevard, 703-765-4100; Community Branch, 7676 Richmond Highway, 703-765-4251; Engleside, 8758 Richmond Highway, 703-780-6540; Franconia, 5221 Franconia Road, 703-971-0991; Jefferson Manor, 5834 North Kings Highway, 703-960-4440; Lincolnia, 6137 Lincolnia Road, 703-354-1622; Memorial Annex, 2226 Duke Street, 703-549-1837; Park Fairfax Station, 3682 King Street, 703-379-6017; Potomac Station, 1908 Mt. Vernon Avenue, 703-549-2854; Trade Center Station, 340 South Pickett Street, 703-379-6017
Police Station: Alexandria Police Department, 2003 Mill Road, 703-838-4444; http://ci.alexandria.va.us/police
Emergency Hospital: Inova Alexandria Hospital, 4320 Seminary Road, 703-504-3000
Libraries: Charles E. Beatley Jr. Central Library, 5005 Duke Street, 703-519-5900; for branch information, call the central library or visit www.alexandria.lib.va.us.
Public High Schools: T.C. Williams, 3330 King Street, 703-824-6800; school district, 703-824-6600, www.acps.k12.va.us
Government: 8th Congressional District; Mayor and six-member City Council; City Hall, 301 King Street, 703-838-4500; www.ci.alexandria.va.us/city/amacc
Neighborhood Festivals: Alexandria Red Cross Waterfront Festival (June), 703-549-8300; Alexandria Birthday (various locations, July), 703-838-4200
Major Parks: Cameron Run (Eisenhower Avenue west of Telegraph Road); Daingerfield Island (George Washington Parkway south of Four Mile Run); Dyke Marsh (George Washington Parkway south of Belle View Boulevard); Holmes Run (along Holmes Run between Columbia Pike and Duke Street)
Community Resources: The Birchmere, 3701 Mt. Vernon Avenue; see **Cultural Life** for details. Torpedo Factory Arts Center, 105 North Union Street, 703-838-4565 www.torpedofactory.org; see **Cultural Life** for details. George Washington National Masonic Memorial is open daily, 9 a.m. to 4 p.m.; tours available. The monument includes ceremonial rooms, a museum, library, and auditorium. For information, call 703-683-2007 or visit www.gwmemorial.org.

Public Transportation: Metro: Braddock Road & King Street (Blue & Yellow lines), Van Dorn Street (Blue Line), Eisenhower Avenue (Yellow Line); VRE: Alexandria Station (Fredericksburg & Manassas lines), Franconia/Springfield Station (Fredericksburg Line), Backlick Road Station (Manassas Line); Metrobus routes: 9A/9E (Pentagon, Fort Belvoir), 10A/10E (Rosslyn), 10B-10D (Falls Church), 11Y (Fort Belvoir, Farragut Square), 28 series (Tysons Corner), 21 series (Pentagon, Landmark Mall), 25 series (Ballston), 29 series (Little River Turnpike), P13 (Pentagon); Fairfax Connector routes: 101-109 (local); ART shuttle routes (local)

ARLINGTON COUNTY

On a map, D.C. looks like somebody took a bite out of a perfect square. The missing "bite" is Arlington County, and indeed, it once was part of the District. The Constitution gives Congress control over "such District (not exceeding ten miles square) as may, by Cession of particular States, and the Acceptance of Congress, become the Seat of the Government of the United States." So Maryland and Virginia each donated land to Congress in 1791. The District was then divided into several smaller jurisdictions: the City of Washington, the City of Georgetown, and Washington County—collectively, the area now known as the District of Columbia—and, across the Potomac was "Arlington, D.C." Half a century later, it turned out that the residents of Arlington didn't identify with the city across the river, the federal government wasn't using much land in Arlington, and tensions were heating up between the North and South, which were separated more clearly by the Potomac than by the Mason-Dixon Line. In 1846, Congress agreed to let Arlington residents hold a referendum to choose whether their county would remain in D.C. or be "retroceded" to Virginia; retrocession won.

Arlington is inside the Beltway, and it's the only county in the Washington suburbs that doesn't have a problem with sprawl—because there's no room to grow.

Government: Arlington County Board, 703-228-3130, www.co.arlington.va.us
Public Schools: 703-228-6008, www.arlington.k12.va.us
Libraries: 703-228-5990, www.co.arlington.va.us/lib
Police: 703-228-4252, www.co.arlington.va.us/police
Online Guide: www.co.arlington.va.us

ARLINGTON

NORTH ARLINGTON
SOUTH ARLINGTON
ROSSLYN
CLARENDON
BALLSTON
PENTAGON CITY
CRYSTAL CITY
FAIRLINGTON
SHIRLINGTON

Boundaries: **North**: US Route 29; **East**: Potomac River; **South**: Four Mile Run, Quaker Lane, King Street; **West**: George Mason Drive

Arlington offers some of the best views of the Washington skyline, and most of the signature photos of the Capitol, the Jefferson Memorial, the Washington Monument, and the Lincoln Memorial are taken from the Arlington banks of the Potomac.

North Arlington and **South Arlington** are separated by Arlington National Cemetery, the Pentagon, Fort Myer, and the Marine Corps Memorial—more commonly known as the Iwo Jima Memorial. North Arlington's concrete jungle stretches along Wilson and Clarendon boulevards, and from "downtown" Rosslyn to more suburban Clarendon. South Arlington, just west of Reagan National Airport, includes Pentagon City, Crystal City, and Shirlington. Street names indicate north or south relative to the cemetery and Arlington Boulevard (US Route 50).

Rosslyn, just north of the Pentagon, is dominated by the metallic skyscraper known to locals as "the USA Today building" (until 2001 publishing giant Gannett was headquartered here). The building has had a few close calls with low-flying planes landing at National Airport. Other office high-rises attract military contractors and some offices are leased by the armed forces—even the vast Pentagon can't house everybody. The Rosslyn area is almost all commercial and closes by 7 p.m.; weekends, forget it.

The Newseum, the Freedom Forum's national museum of journalism, is located in the Gannett tower and under a distinctive futuristic dome connected to the base of the skyscraper. Outside, a memorial plaza honors slain journalists. The museum is slated to move to D.C.—to a coveted Pennsylvania Avenue site across from the National Archives—in 2005.

Up the hill from Rosslyn, Courthouse Square in **Clarendon** takes its name from the presence of the Arlington County courts and municipal complex. Scattered among major employers like SRA and Verizon, there are high-rise apartments—some offering spectacular views, costing up to 30% more than those that don't—and some prewar brick houses and modern townhouses. The weekday lunch and happy-hour crowds keep a variety of good restaurants hopping—Italian, Thai, Indian, Southwestern, Middle Eastern and all-American. Clarendon is emerging as a nightspot, thanks to neighborhood clubs like Whitlow's and Iota, and its retail strips, which include several thrift stores, bookstores, and a growing number of coffee bars.

Beyond Clarendon, marking the northwest corner of commercial Arlington, the **Ballston** neighborhood is dominated by Ballston Common Mall and big-box stores including REI and Barnes & Noble, most clustered along Wilson Boulevard and Fairfax Drive. A few modern apartment complexes off Wilson Boulevard attract mostly young workers looking for a convenient location; many eventually head for South Arlington or Alexandria to raise a family.

South of the Pentagon, whose 17.5 miles of corridors and four zip codes make it a city in itself, is the vast building's own little suburb, **Pentagon City**. It's mostly retail; a small pocket of apartments attracts some of the 23,000 military personnel and civilians who work in the 3.8 million square feet of offices in the world's largest office building.

Between National Airport and US Route 1 is Crystal City, a cluster of office high-rises, hotels, and tall apartment buildings surrounding the original complex of three dozen golden brick buildings. Because of the proximity to the airport, many conventions and trade shows are held here. Just west of the airport, the Patent & Trademark Office has dominated the US Route 1 skyline for decades; it's slated to move to Eisenhower Avenue in Alexandria in a few years, but for now, many Crystal City residents are lawyers dealing with intellectual property. And of course there are defense contractors and military offices galore in Crystal City. Here's the surprising part: most of the principal buildings in Crystal City are connected by a vast network of pedestrian tunnels, which are lined with shops and restaurants. If you live and work in Crystal City, you never have to go outside. In fact, some ambitious young patent attorneys take advantage of this arrangement to set their bodies to an artificial day/night cycle, to maximize the hours they can work without sleep!

To the west, the rest of Arlington is more traditional—an old, established residential area with substantial colonials and little subdivisions with brick townhouses sold as condos. Between 1900 and 1910, there were 70 subdivisions built in Arlington County, and not the dull beige boxes so familiar in the outer suburbs. These older subdivisions are shaded by mature trees, and strips of sturdy brick homes are separated more by grassy commons and walkways than by streets and parking lots. Among others, lawmakers, journalists, and high-ranking military officers reside here.

In the small section of Arlington south of Four Mile Run, **Shirlington** is becoming the suburban annex of Dupont Circle. In the past decade, cafés, late-night dining, and a substantial gay and lesbian community have filtered in. It's more affordable for young professionals than comparable neighborhoods in D.C.—but partly because it's not the most convenient location. Although it's a short distance from the 14th Street Bridge via Interstate 395, it's a struggle at rush hour.

South of I-395, **Fairlington** attracts young families to affordable low-rise apartment complexes. Southeast Asian immigrants settled here after the Vietnam War, perhaps because many of them had ties to the military; some eventually moved to the outer suburbs, but not before opening a plethora of Asian restaurants and establishing one of the area's few genuine ethnic neighborhoods. Pho noodle houses are a particular hallmark of South Arlington.

The Gunston Arts Center, on Arlington Ridge Road off South Glebe Road, is a unique facility for the performing arts. The center comprises two theaters and rehearsal space, scene shops, and costume shops, all serving local performing companies and offering classes for children and adults. On any given day, there might be opera signers rehearsing in one room and tap dancers practicing next door.

Arlington supports its mom-and-pop stores too. Locals are devoted to the Heidelberg Pastry Shoppe on North Culpeper Street; on Wilson Boulevard, Attila himself will serve your falafel at Attila's; and at Gene's Deli on North 14th Street, Gene always remembers his regular customers.

Web Site: www.co.arlington.va.us
Zip Codes: 22201-22213, 22216
Area Code: 703
Post Offices: Arlington, 3118 Washington Boulevard, 703-525-4838; Buckingham Station, 235 North Glebe Road, 703-525-4170; Courthouse Station, 2043 Wilson Boulevard, 703-525-4441; Crystal City Station, 1735 Jefferson Davis Highway, 703-413-9267; Eads Station, 1720 South Eads Street, 703-979-2108; Rosslyn Station, 1101 Wilson Boulevard, 703-525-4336; Shirlington Annex, 2850 South Quincy Street, 703-979-2106; South Station, 1210 South Glebe Road, 703-979-2245
Police Station: Arlington County Police Department, 1425 North Courthouse Road, 703-228-4252
Emergency Hospital: Arlington Hospital, 1701 North George Mason Drive, 703-558-5000
Government: 8th Congressional District; five-member County Board; county offices at Courthouse Square, 2100 Clarendon Boulevard, 703-228-3130

Library: Arlington County Central Library, 1015 North Quincy Street, 703-228-5990, www.co.arlington.va.us/lib

Public High Schools: Wakefield, 4901 South Chesterfield Road, 703-228-6700; Washington-Lee, 1300 North Quincy Street, 703-228-6200; Yorktown, 5201 North 28th Street, 703-228-5400

Neighborhood Festival: Neighborhood Day (various locations, May), 703-228-7710

Major Parks: Four Mile Run (along Four Mile Run between I-66 and the Potomac River); Gravelly Point (George Washington Parkway just north of Reagan National Airport); Lady Bird Johnson (George Washington Parkway at Memorial Bridge); Roaches Run Waterfowl Sanctuary (south end of Boundary Channel Drive)

Community Resources: Arlington National Cemetery is open daily, 8 a.m. to 7 p.m. April-September, 8 a.m. to 5 p.m. October-March. For information, call 703-695-3250 or visit www.arlingtoncemetery.com. Commuter Store locations in Rosslyn and Crystal City (see **Transportation**). Gunston Arts Center, 2700 South Lang Street, 703-228-6960. Newseum, 1101 Wilson Boulevard, 888-639-7386, www.newseum.org; see **Cultural Life** for details. Performing arts organizations: attracted by Gunston Arts Center there are a dozen professional and amateur theater companies based in Arlington, a community symphony orchestra and opera company, barbershop chorus, half a dozen dance companies, and several private galleries and visual arts studios. For a community arts directory, visit www.arlingtonarts.org or call the Arlington Cultural Affairs Division at Gunston Arts Center.

Public Transportation: Metro: Rosslyn (Blue & Orange lines), Court House, Virginia Square, Ballston-Marymount University (Orange Line), Arlington Cemetery (Blue Line), Pentagon, Pentagon City, Crystal City, National Airport (Blue & Yellow Lines); VRE: Crystal City station (Fredericksburg & Manassas lines); the Pentagon is a major bus system hub served by 73 Metrobus routes

FAIRFAX COUNTY

Fairfax County is the old stomping ground of George Washington, George Mason, Patrick Henry, J.E.B. Stuart, and the Lees, from Lighthorse Harry to Robert E., as well as quite a few slaves—around 40% of the population at the time the Constitution was ratified. This was tobacco country until the soil was depleted; after the Civil War, dairy farming took over for a few generations, and then suburban sprawl. There are still semi-rural estates here, the remnants of colonial plantations, and Fairfax County ranks among the nation's leading jurisdictions in internet use—as of 2000, well over half the homes here were online. This is where Clara Barton set up her field hospital during the Civil War, inspiring both the American Red Cross and the MASH unit. John Mosby's Rangers waged guerilla war against the Union supply lines here, and Bull Run looks much the same today as it did to Stonewall Jackson.

The county stretches from Watkins Island in the Potomac south to Mason Neck (the wetlands surrounding historic Gunston Hall), and from Arlington west to Bull Run and the Occoquan River. On the northwest county line, where corporate campuses give way to rolling farms, Dulles International Airport occupies as much land as all the cities in Fairfax County combined.

The names of entrepreneur John McLean and Senator Stephen Elkins also show up on the map. They built a trolley line connecting the Old Dominion Railroad to Great Falls and later to Herndon, and built housing along the route; unwittingly, perhaps, they invented sprawl. Today, with Fairfax County population around a million, up from 819,000 in 1990, many schoolchildren attend class in "portable classrooms."

Residents began to draw the line on sprawl in the mid-1990s, when Disney sought to build an American history theme park just outside Manassas National Battlefield Park. Disney was run out of town by a coalition of Civil War re-enactors, environmentalists, former city slickers seeking peace and quiet, 10th-generation horse farmers, Native Americans whose ancestors lived here for millennia, and descendants of slaves and Civil War veterans. Land use and related quality-of-life issues have dominated Fairfax County politics ever since.

The school system here is good, and the county claims to be the "birthplace of the internet"—a claim it shares with the inner reaches of neighboring Loudoun and Prince William counties.

Government: www.co.fairfax.va.us
County Board of Supervisors: 10 members, nine representing districts and chair elected at large; 703-324-2000; www.co.fairfax.va.us/government/board
Public Schools: 703-246-2502, www.fcps.k12.va.us
Libraries: 703-324-3100, www.co.fairfax.va.us/library
Police: 703-691-2131, www.co.fairfax.va.us/ps/police
Online Guide: www.co.fairfax.va.us; recorded information, 703-324-INFO
Area Code: 703

FAIRFAX

FAIRFAX STATION
CENTREVILLE
CHANTILLY
BURKE

Boundaries: **North**: Interstate 66; **East**: Pickett Road, Long Branch; **South**: Braddock Road; **West**: Route 645

The City of Fairfax is just about the only place in the suburbs west of the Beltway where you can find high-rise apartments as well as condos, some under $100,000, and plenty of rentals. There's upscale housing here too—detached houses and luxury condos in a variety of styles—but Fairfax is an oasis of affordable living in one of the nation's most expensive counties.

There has been a town here since the early 1700s, but the old town was ravaged by the Civil War, so most of the historic district, along Main Street, between East and West streets, dates from the late 19th century. A monument at Chain Bridge Road and Main Street honors Captain John Quincy Marr, the first Confederate officer killed in the Civil War. The history page of the town web site says, "Note that the cannons are facing north, as do all cannons at Confederate monuments."

The Fairfax mailing address extends west of town to include the county government complex off West Ox Road and Interstate 66. The Fairfax County Government Center here houses county offices, and the courtyard of the horseshoe-shaped building is the venue for the annual Fairfax Fair in June.

If you have at least half a million dollars and good luck, you might find a home along the secluded wooded country roads of **Fairfax Station,** south of town off Route 123. These are beautiful houses in eclectic styles, many on several acres of woodland.

Centreville to the west and **Chantilly** to the northwest are modern outer suburbs—nice ones, if you like sprawling subdivisions and lots of driving. **Burke**, to the south, is similar, but it's better served by public transportation and it has several lakes; a few homes sit on lakefront property, and many are within a short walk. These are all pricey areas, though, with spacious designer homes—many with garage space for at least two cars.

Web Sites: www.ci.fairfax.va.us, www.fairfaxstationvirginia.com
Zip Codes: 22030, 22031, 22032
Area Code: 703
Post Offices: Fairfax, 3951 Chain Bridge Road, 703-273-5571; Turnpike Station, 3601 Pickett Road, 703-239-2900

Police Stations: City of Fairfax Police Department, John C. Wood Municipal Complex, 3730 Old Lee Highway, 703-385-7960; Fairfax County Police Department, Fair Oaks District Station, 12300 Lee-Jackson Highway, 703-591-0966

Emergency Hospitals: Inova Fair Oaks, 3600 Joseph Siewick Drive, Fairfax, 703-391-3600; Inova Fairfax, 3300 Gallows Road, Falls Church, 703-698-1110

Library: Fairfax City Regional, 3915 Chain Bridge Road, 703-246-2281

Public High Schools: Fairfax, 3500 Old Lee Highway, 703-219-2200; Woodson, 9525 Main Street, 703-503-4600; Robinson Secondary (grades 7-12), 5035 Sideburn Road, 703-426-2100

Government: 11th Congressional District; mayor and six-member City Council; City Hall, 10455 Armstrong Street, 703-385-7855

Neighborhood Festivals: Chocolate Lovers Festival (Old Town Hall, February); Spotlight on the Arts (various locations, April); Blenheim Civil War Encampment (Blenheim, 3610 Old Lee Highway, May); Fourth of July celebration, various locations; Fall Festival (various locations, October); for information, call 703-385-7855. Fall for the Book literary fair (various locations, September), www.fallforthebook.org; Fairfax Fair (Fairfax County Government Center, June), 703-324-FAIR

Major Parks: Difficult Run (along Difficult Run west of Miller Heights Road); Eakin (along Accotink Creek south of US Route 50)

Community Resources: Fairfax Art League organizes exhibits and special events featuring local artists, and runs a gallery at Old Town Hall, 703-273-2377. For information, call 703-352-ARTS or visit http://nuovo.com/fal. Old Town Hall at 3999 University Drive is available for rentals. Call Historic Fairfax Inc. at 703-385-7858. Patriot Center, Braddock Road and Roanoke Lane, George Mason University, 703-993-3000

Public Transportation: Metro: Vienna-Fairfax/GMU (Orange Line); VRE: Burke Centre station (Manassas Line); Metrobus routes: 1B-1Z (Ballston), 2A-2G (Ballston), 12 series (Centreville), 17 series (Pentagon), 20 series (Chantilly), 29K (Alexandria); Fairfax Connector routes 402-404 (local)

GREAT FALLS/McLEAN

Boundaries: **North**: Potomac River; **East**: Potomac River; **South**: Arlington County; **West**: Dulles Access Road, Leesburg Pike

The Fairfax County banks of the Potomac are home to genteel, traditional, conservative estates belonging to old money of colonial pedigree and to the political elite. The only time you're likely to find a lot of turnover here is just after an election, when those lawmakers and Cabinet secretaries who aren't joining K Street law firms put their spacious houses and acreage on the market. If your tastes are modest and you shop around, you might find a cottage or luxury townhouse here for as little as a quarter million, but expect to see prices mostly in the high six figures—and sevens, especially for homes with great Potomac River views. After all, it's nice country—this is the Old Dominion, and if you face away from the road you might think the area hasn't changed much in two centuries.

In contrast to Potomac, MD, across the river, the horse fences here aren't just for show. Winding roads follow the terrain, making for picturesque communities, albeit hazardous driving conditions in the rain and snow. And forget about public transportation in this patrician countryside—in fact, some addresses don't even have trash and recycling collection service, and when you drive to the Great Falls dump on Saturday morning, you might run into an entire congressional committee.

The parks along the Potomac protect land that has attracted weekend explorers since John Smith came up from Jamestown in 1608, looking for gold and the legendary Northwest Passage. As it turns out, you can't sail to the Pacific from here—you run into a wall of big rocks across the Potomac where thundering whitewater spills 80 feet down from the piedmont plateau onto the coastal plain. Every year, a few unlucky souls perish here, losing their footing on the slippery rocks, and the place should not be underestimated by climbers and kayakers.

There are plenty of elite private schools in this area, but few schools in the world rival the social prestige of the Madeira School, whose cupola peeks through the treetops on prime real estate overlooking the river.

Downstream toward Arlington, a federal reservation just off Route 123 in Langley was known for years as the "Turner-Fairbank Highway Research Center," though everyone knew it was actually CIA headquarters. At some point in the 1980s, a tiny green sign marked the exit "CIA." No visitor center, no gift shop, and you're not likely ever to visit the memorial wall of 77 stars each honoring a slain CIA "asset"—many of whose names are still classified. However, according to the agency's web site, www.cia.gov, tours aren't entirely out of the question: there is "an extremely limited number of visits annually for approved academic and civic groups."

The Langley complex isn't the only cloak-and-dagger landmark in the area. Just outside Arlington, Fort Marcy Park is a major stop on the conspiracy buff's tour. Here John Dean handed briefcases full of Nixon campaign money to E. Howard Hunt to buy the Watergate burglars' silence, and here Clinton aide Vince Foster's body was found with a suicide note. Such dramatic episodes reflect the character of the Great Falls and McLean community; this is the home of money and power. Pronounce it right: "McLane."

Web Site: www.gfcitizens.com

Zip Codes: 22101, 22102, 22066

Area Code: 703

Post Offices: Great Falls, 748 Walker Road, 703-759-2885; McLean, 6841 Elm Street, 703-790-9100

Police Station: McLean District Station, 1437 Balls Hill Road, 703-556-7750

Emergency Hospitals: Reston Hospital Center, 1850 Town Center Parkway, 703-689-9000; Inova Fairfax Hospital, 3300 Gallows Road, Falls Church, 703-698-1110

Libraries: Dolley Madison, 1244 Oak Ridge Avenue, McLean, 703-356-0770; Great Falls, 9830 Georgetown Pike, 703-757-8560

Public High Schools: Langley, 6520 Georgetown Pike, McLean, 703-287-2700; McLean, 1633 Davidson Road, 703-714-5700

Government: 11th Congressional District; Dranesville District, Fairfax County Board of Supervisors

Neighborhood Festivals: Taste of McLean (McLean Community Center, 1234 Ingleside Avenue, March); McLean Day (various locations, May), 703-790-0123

Major Parks: Great Falls (north end of Old Dominion Drive); Dranesville (north of Georgetown Pike just outside the Beltway); Langley Oaks/Turkey Run (George Washington Parkway just inside the Beltway); Riverbend (Jeffery Road off River Bend Road)

Community Resources: McLean Community Center features art studio space, a theater, a teen center, classes, and recreational programs: 1234 Ingleside Avenue, 703-790-0123, www.mcleancenter.org. For information about solid waste disposal and recycling, call 703-324-5040.

Public Transportation: Metrobus routes: 23C (Langley, Crystal City), 23A/B & 23T (Tysons Corner, Crystal City)

HERNDON

Boundaries: **North**: Herndon Centennial Golf Course, Folly Lick Branch, Herndon High School; **East**: Sugarland Run; **South**: Dulles Access Road; **West**: Loudoun County

If you work in the Dulles corridor, and if planned communities like Reston remind you of *The Truman Show,* Herndon offers the convenience of a Reston location with a less manicured feel. Herndon's main street, Elden Street, is surrounded by older neighborhoods, and offers a good selection of restaurants for a town of 20,000. There are lots of upscale townhouse condos in and around Herndon, some designed to recall the Old

Dominion with cupolas and gables. Brick houses still stand in the neighborhoods that grew along the old railroad, which has now been transformed into the Washington and Old Dominion bike trail. Sales and rentals are, as in most of the western suburbs, expensive—but nothing compared to nearby Great Falls, where more homes are inherited than rented.

The Herndon area appeared on colonial charters as early as 1688, but the town wasn't incorporated until 1858. According to local legend, the town founders were debating possible names for the new municipality, and a survivor of a shipwreck proposed that the town be named in honor of Captain William Lewis Herndon, who had gone down with the ship after ensuring the safety of the women and children. Herndon, a former naval officer who helped establish the US Naval Observatory and wrote the first scholarly report on the Amazon, was among more than 400 men who died aboard the packet ship Central America in a storm off Cape Hatteras in 1857.

Sixty years after its incorporation, the town was almost as unlucky when a fire destroyed downtown Herndon. Rebuilt in brick, some of the new homes were sturdy prefabricated houses made by Sears & Roebuck and hauled into town on freight trains. Today, these are some of the oldest homes in the Dulles Corridor, and most of their occupants work nearby.

Web Sites: www.town.herndon.va.us, http://herndonweb.com
Zip Code: 20070
Area Code: 703
Post Office: Herndon, 590 Grove Street, 703-437-3740
Police Station: Herndon Police, 1481 Sterling Road, 703-435-6846
Emergency Hospital: Reston Hospital Center, 1850 Town Center Parkway, 703-689-9000
Library: Herndon Fortnightly, 768 Center Street, 703-437-8855 (founded by the Fortnightly Club in 1889)
Public High School: Herndon, 700 Bennett Street, 703-810-2200
Government: 11th Congressional District; Hunter Mill District, Fairfax County Board of Supervisors; Mayor and six-member Town Council; Herndon Municipal Center, 777 Lynn Street, 703-435-6800
Neighborhood Festivals: Labor Day Jazz Festival (Town Green), 703-435-6868; Mayor's Cup golf tournament (Herndon Centennial Golf Course, October), 703-471-5769; Herndon Folk Festival (Town Green, October), 703-435-6868
Major Parks: Runnymede/Sugarland Run (along Sugarland Run north of Herndon Parkway)
Community Resources: entertainment on the Town Green includes a Thursday evening summer concert series, 703-435-6868, and Friday

Night Live performances, 703-437-5556. Washington & Old Dominion Trail (see **Vienna** below).

Public Transportation: Fairfax Connector routes: 551, 901-904, 951/952, 980 (Falls Church), 924 (Dranesville), 927/929 (Chantilly), 941/942, 984 (Tysons Corner)

RESTON

Boundaries: **North**: Leesburg Pike; **East**: Hunter Mill Road; **South**: Fox Mill Road, Lawyers Road; **West**: Herndon, Loudoun County

Reston is a planned community built in the 1960s and named with the initials of its designer, Robert E. Simon. Deliberately eclectic housing stock, with sizes and styles to command a variety of price brackets, surrounds a retail "town center," and residential clusters or "villages" were planned for pedestrians and bicyclists. While planned communities are never quite as charming as they sound in brochures, Reston is more walkable than other modern suburbs, and economically more diverse than most.

The vast community, designed for 70,000 and not quite "full," is sort of a giant condominium: every resident, whether a homeowner or a renter, is a member of the Reston Association and pays mandatory dues—typically $370 per household, less for the few whose property tax assessment is under $71,000 or for households qualifying for certain county tax breaks. These fees maintain 1,300 acres of open space and 125 acres of artificial lakes; 55 miles of pathways with 95 bridges; ballfields, playgrounds, tennis and basketball courts, and fitness trails; Walker Nature Education Center and environmental education programs for all ages; summer camps; special events for children, seniors, and families; 15 swimming pools; a facility for boat and RV storage; community gardens; and a chapel, meeting rooms, and pavilions available for rent.

Residents also agree (by being residents) to abide by certain covenants governing the use, maintenance, and exterior appearance of their homes. It may sound Orwellian, but in practice it's no different from the zoning ordinances and building codes in any incorporated town in the suburbs; instead of municipal taxes and a town council, Reston—like many smaller subdivisions—has association dues and an elected board of directors.

Streets named after Isaac Newton, Michael Faraday, Roger Bacon, and Samuel Morse underscore the importance of the technology sector in Reston. Many employees from the nearby campuses of America Online, Network Solutions, and Xerox live here. DynCorp and Sallie Mae have headquarters here, along with a slew of smaller computer and telecom companies, and their workforce spills over into neighboring Herndon. Office parks with names like Worldgate, Dulles Technology Center, and Parkway Trade Center loom over the tollbooths of the Dulles Access Road. Virginia Tech has a Reston campus on Isaac Newton Square.

Web Sites: http://reston.org, www.restonweb.com

Zip Codes: 20090, 20091, 20094

Area Code: 703

Post Offices: Reston 20090, 11110 Sunset Hills Road, 703-437-6677; Reston 20091, 1860 Michael Faraday Drive, 703-437-7822

Police Station: Reston District Station, 12000 Bowman Towne Drive, 703-478-0904

Emergency Hospital: Reston Hospital Center, 1850 Town Center Parkway, 703-689-9000

Library: Reston Regional, 11925 Bowman Towne Drive, 703-689-2700

Public High School: South Lakes, 11400 South Lakes Drive, Reston, 703-715-4500

Government: 11th Congressional District; Hunter Mill District, Fairfax County Board of Supervisors; nine-member Reston Association Board of Directors (four members representing districts, one representing apartment owners, and three elected at large); Reston Association office, 1930 Isaac Newton Square, 703-437-9580

Neighborhood Festival: Reston Festival (north shore of Lake Anne, July), www.restonfestival.com; community events recording, 703-435-6558

Major Parks: Difficult Run (Hunters Valley Road off Hunter Mill Road); Fox Mill (Fox Mill Road south of Lawyers Road); Frying Pan (West Ox Road east of Centreville Road); Lake Fairfax (Lake Fairfax Drive south of Baron Cameron Avenue)

Community Resources: Reston Newcomers Club offers monthly social and informational programs, a newsletter, and a directory for a one-year membership fee of $21, 703-689-3388; for information about any Reston amenities, contact the Reston Association office at 703-437-9580 or http://reston.org.

Public Transportation: Fairfax Connector routes: 551-557 & 901-905 (Falls Church), 574 (Tysons Corner); RIBS bus service (local)

VIENNA

TYSONS CORNER
WINDOVER HEIGHTS

Boundaries: **North**: Dulles Access Road; **East**: Dulles Access Road; **South**: Interstate 66; **West**: Hunter Mill Road, Vale Road, Nutley Street

Beware! An office with a Vienna mailing address is most likely located in the **Tysons Corner** complex just outside the town of Vienna. If you like big shopping malls and car dealerships, you might like Tysons Corner; otherwise, this permanent traffic jam at the junction of Routes 123 and 7, just outside the Beltway, embodies all the worst stereotypes about congested roads and grim-looking office towers. Thousands of people work here, but practically none live here in this little city that's only open during the day. One Tysons skyscraper, visible from miles away, has twin arches on the roof that resemble a pair of handles; commuters refer to it, with a hint of sarcasm, as "the shopping bag building."

Route 123 south from Tysons leads to Vienna proper, where a few luxurious modern houses sell for close to half a million dollars often to executives from the technology firms and defense contractors up the road. Most of the homes here are modern suburban designs, but affordable as the Virginia suburbs go—some under $250,000; there are also a few garden apartment and townhouse complexes, both condominiums and rentals, at prices comparable to all but the most prestigious neighborhoods in D.C.

Originally called Ayr Hill, Vienna is 22 years older than the United States. Its name was changed when a wealthy doctor from Vienna, NY moved here in the 1850s on the condition that the town change its name.

During the Civil War, Vienna changed hands so many times that many families moved away to escape the continual upheaval. According to the history page of the town web site, a battle at the Park Street railroad crossing was "the first time in history a railroad was used tactically in battle." After the war, the railroad was used for industry, and Vienna boomed with sawmills, blacksmiths, a cannery, and a funeral home, which is now the town's oldest business. Now the railroad is a rails-to-trails bike path making an off-road paved link from rural Purcellville to Mt. Vernon.

In the **Windover Heights** Historic District, off Maple Avenue and Lawyers Road, a preservation review board must approve exterior changes to the historic homes and businesses. Throughout Vienna, an architectural review board ensures that construction "is not bizarre or garish and is harmonious and compatible with existing buildings." Young Tysons techies may be adversely affected by the fact that, by law, group houses are limited to no more than four unrelated adults.

Web Site: www.ci.vienna.va.us

Zip Codes: 22043, 22180, 22182

Area Code: 703

Post Office: Vienna, 200 Lawyers Road NW, 703-938-2125

Police Station: Vienna Police Department, 215 Center Street South, 703-255-6366

Emergency Hospitals: Inova Fair Oaks, 3600 Joseph Siewick Drive, Fairfax, 703-391-3600; Inova Fairfax, 3300 Gallows Road, Falls Church, 703-698-1110

Library: Patrick Henry Community Library, 101 Maple Avenue East, 703-938-0405

Public High School: Madison, 2500 James Madison Drive, 703-319-2300; Oakton, 2900 Sutton Road, 703-319-2700

Government: 11th Congressional District; Providence District, Fairfax County Board of Supervisors; mayor and 6-member town council; Town Hall, 127 Center Street South, 703-255-6300

Neighborhood Festival: Fourth of July celebration, Cherry & Center streets

Major Parks: Wolf Trap Farm (off the Dulles Access Road west of Leesburg Pike); Wolftrap Stream Valley (along Wolftrap Run between Old Court House Road and Westwood Country Club)

Community Resources: The Women's Center provides affordable counseling to women, men, and families, and sponsors an annual women's leadership conference, 133 Park Street NE, 703-281-2657, www.thewomenscenter.org. Vienna Arts Society sponsors exhibits, workshops, classes, and trips to out-of-town galleries, 703-319-3971, www.viennaartssociety.org. Vienna Community Center, 120 Cherry Street SE, 703-255-6360. Washington & Old Dominion Trail is a 45-mile paved bike path from Arlington, where it meets the Mt. Vernon Trail along the Potomac, to rural Loudoun County. For information and maps, contact the Northern Virginia Regional Park Authority at 703-729-0596, www.nvrpa.org/wod, or Friends of the W&OD Trail at www.wodfriends.org. Wolf Trap Farm Park for the Performing Arts, 703-225-1800 (see **Cultural Life** for details).

Public Transportation: Metro: Vienna-Fairfax/GMU and Dunn Loring/Merrifield (Orange Line); Metrobus: 1B/1D (Ballston), 2 series (Ballston, Fair Oaks Mall), 3A (Annandale), 3B-3F (Rosslyn), 3W/3Z (Falls Church), 12 series (Centreville), 14 series (Bethesda), 20 series (Chantilly); 23 series (Crystal City); Fairfax Connector bus hub with 19 routes serving Tysons Corner and Metro stations

CITY OF FALLS CHURCH

SEVEN CORNERS
BAILEYS CROSSROADS

Boundaries: **North**: Route 703, Interstate 66; **East**: Arlington County; **South**: Washington Street South, Hillwood Avenue; **West**: Route 703

An independent city since 1948, Falls Church was first colonized in 1699. According to a pamphlet published for the community's tri-centennial, the site once was a busy intersection of native Tauxenent trails—now marked by Leesburg Pike and Lee Highway—for 12,000 years. The city takes its name from a colonial church whose congregation included George Washington and the author of the Bill of Rights, George Mason; the church, in turn, was named for its location along the ancient trail leading to Great Falls.

The National Arbor Day Foundation consistently gives Falls Church an annual Tree City USA award. The *Falls Church News-Press*, at www.fcnp.com, boasts that the city "has the fourth highest per capita income of any juris-diction in the US, and the second highest percentage of college graduates." And residents pay for all that: in 2000, property tax assessments jumped almost 14% from the year before, with taxes on detached homes rising 17.5% and taxes on apartments and townhouses rising between 8% to 15%—an increase of nearly $200 per person.

That's within the little city. The name Falls Church is loosely applied to the suburbs west to the Beltway and south to Holmes Run. Along commer-cial Leesburg Pike, the retail districts of **Seven Corners** and **Baileys Crossroads** are the places where your neighbors in the inner Virginia sub-urbs go for practical shopping; Pentagon City and Tysons Corner are good for luxuries and gifts, not for lawnmowers. There are some reasonably-priced apartments and condos off Leesburg Pike too, and upscale condos and detached modern houses to the south near Lake Barcroft.

Web Site: www.ci.falls-church.va.us
Zip Code: 20046
Area Code: 703
Post Office: Falls Church, 301 West Broad Street, 703-250-9188
Police Station: Falls Church Police Department, City Hall, 703-241-5053 (routine) or 703-241-5050 (emergency)
Emergency Hospitals: Arlington Hospital, 1701 North George Mason Drive, 703-558-5000; Inova Fairfax, 3300 Gallows Road, 703-698-1110
Library: Mary Riley Styles Public Library, 120 North Virginia Avenue, 703-248-5030; www.falls-church.lib.va.us

Public High Schools: George Mason, 7124 Leesburg Pike, 703-248-5500 (Falls Church City Public Schools, www.fccps.k12.va.us); Falls Church, 7521 Jaguar Trail, 703-207-4000; Marshall, 7731 Leesburg Pike, 703-714-5400; J.E.B. Stuart, 3301 Peace Valley Lane, 703-824-3900 (Fairfax County Public Schools)

Government: 8th Congressional District; mayor serves on seven-member city council; City Hall, 300 Park Avenue, 703-248-5014

Major Parks: Four Mile Run (along Four Mile Run south of I-66)

Community Resources: Falls Church Recreation & Parks Division, 703-248-5077, www.ci.falls-church.va.us/services/park; the Northern Virginia Center, 7504 Haycock Road, is a satellite campus shared by Virginia Tech and the University of Virginia, specializing in continuing education and high tech career development. Contact the Virginia Polytechnic Institute at 703-538-TECH or www.nvgc.vt.edu, or the University of Virginia at 703-536-1100 or http://uvace.virginia.edu/northern. Washington & Old Dominion Trail (see **Vienna** above).

Public Transportation: Metro: East Falls Church and West Falls Church-VT/UVA (Orange Line); Metrobus routes: 3A-3F (Rosslyn), 3W/3Z and 24T (Tysons Corner), 10C (Alexandria); Fairfax Connector routes: 421/427 (Tysons Corner), 551 & 901-980 (Herndon), 552-557 and 585 (Reston)

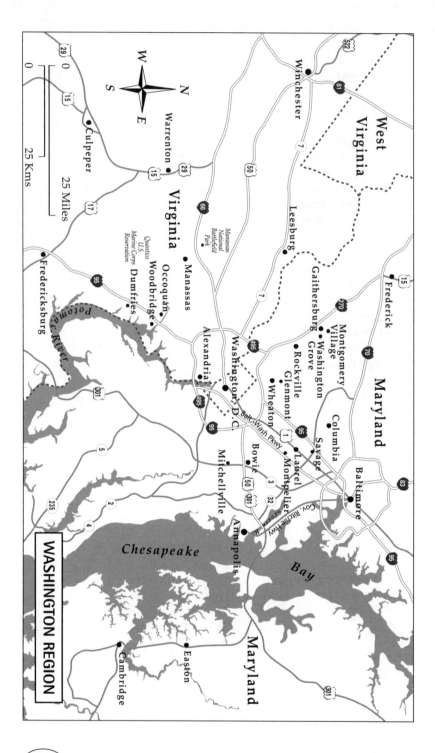

WASHINGTON REGION

OUTER SUBURBS

People have been known to commute from Washington's sprawling outer suburbs to jobs in downtown D.C., but for most Washingtonians, the outer suburbs are weekend excursions—except Columbia, which is a long-established bedroom community for long-haul commuters to Washington and Baltimore. However, if you are moving to the Washington area with a job lined up in the outer suburbs, you might find one of the following communities more convenient than those around the Beltway.

MARYLAND

ANNAPOLIS (ANNE ARUNDEL COUNTY)

The capital city of Maryland and the home of the US Naval Academy is about 45 minutes from the Beltway—by car, which is the only way to get there. (The only way by land, that is. The Chesapeake Bay and the Severn River make Annapolis a boater's paradise, and broad, sleepy creeks provide ample marina space and waterfront property.) You can find spacious cottages here at much lower prices than in Washington, and there are brokers who specialize in waterfront homes. The colonial-era old town, between the city docks and the green dome of the nation's oldest statehouse, attracts weekend window-shoppers and still feels like a colonial fishing village. There are period homes, cobblestone streets, and oysters on the half shell available on every corner, and minutes uptown, the strip malls along Route 2 and Route 70 meet modern shopping needs.

Web Sites: www.ci.annapolis.md.us, www.co.anne-arundel.md.us
Government Information: 410-263-1183
Newspaper: *The Capital*, 410-268-5000; circulation, 410-268-4800, www.hometownannapolis.com

BALTIMORE

Just 45 miles away but a world apart, Baltimore is a working port city whose tall skyline is a downtown financial district. There have been many efforts to connect Baltimore and Washington economically and culturally, but it has never worked—Baltimore is a blue-collar city and Washington is elitist. However, the two cities are planning to make a joint bid in 2005 to host the 2012 Summer Olympics. As a Washingtonian, you might spend a lot of time in Baltimore on business or in search of good crab cakes, Irish pubs,

Italian restaurants, Jewish delis, baseball, and the Fells Point seafood joint made famous by thousands of green-and-white bumper stickers that say "Eat Bertha's Mussels." The touristy Inner Harbor area and the midtown arts district around the University of Baltimore are both easily accessible from D.C. by a one-hour MARC train ride. Once you're there, Baltimore has a mixed-bag public transportation system: there's one Metro line, one light rail line, and buses; every trip is a flat $1.35, and it's simple and reliable—if your destination happens to be on one of those few routes.

Web Site: www.ci.baltimore.md.us
Government Information: 410-396-3100 (government switchboard) or 410-837-4636 (visitor information)
Newspaper: *Baltimore Sun*, 410-332-6000 or 800-829-8000; circulation, 410-539-1280, www.sunspot.net

COLUMBIA (HOWARD COUNTY)

Columbia, MD, like Reston, is a planned community whose 14,000 acres were divided into nine "villages"—mapped out in the 1960s by developer James Rouse, who went on to design most of the mid-Atlantic region's biggest shopping malls. As in most planned communities, a huge percentage of the town is parkland and recreational amenities; most kids can walk to school; and there is diverse modern housing stock, from efficiency apartments to lakefront bungalows, intended to attract an economically diverse population. Columbia is unique, though, for its location: halfway between Washington and Baltimore along Interstate 95, it was supposed to be a bridge between the two cities, but it's more of an island—rather than identifying with both cities, Columbia is remote from either. Many little high-tech firms have offices in Columbia's sprawling "flex" parks, where offices and light industrial outfits share utilitarian, hangar-like buildings, but mostly Columbia interests couples with one job in Washington and one in Baltimore.

Web Sites: www.columbia-md.com, www.co.ho.md.us
Community Information: 410-992-6099
Newspaper: *Columbia Daily Tribune*, 410-997-8000

FREDERICK (FREDERICK COUNTY)

Just north of Montgomery County, and accessible by MARC commuter trains, Frederick has been "on the map" since 1765, when colonial citizens rallied in Court House Square to burn the announcement of the Stamp Act of the British government. Today it is the northern anchor of the 270 Corridor, a biotech industry mecca stretching 35 miles south along I-270 to Bethesda. A few telecommunications companies are major employers here, too—notably Bechtel and, in upper Montgomery County, Comsat. If you want to live in a city and work in the 270 Corridor, it's certainly much cheaper to live 15 miles north of your office than 15 miles south. Many of the brick townhomes here are at least a century old, and some survived the Civil War. Visit Frederick's historic district for the antiques and a breath of clean air, upwind from most of the Washington area's exhaust and illegal levels of smog-producing ozone, and decide whether it's too remote or just right. Don't expect much cosmopolitan nightlife, though—local teens refer to their town as "Fredneck."

Web Sites: www.cityoffrederick.com, www.co.frederick.md.us
Government Information: 301-360-3842
Newspaper: *Frederick News-Post*, 301-662-1177, www.fredericknewspost.com

VIRGINIA

FREDERICKSBURG (STAFFORD COUNTY)

On the Rappahannock River 50 miles south of D.C. on I-95, modern Fredericksburg surrounds a 40-block old town where George Washington grew up. Because of its age and pedigree, Fredericksburg is the only area within potential commuter range of D.C.—almost 90 minutes by VRE train—with housing prices as high as the District's. Historic Fredericksburg is replete with stately old Victorian cottages and gabled colonials that can sell for half a million or more; even the more modern homes weren't built yesterday and are nicer, sturdier, and more expensive than most homes in outlying areas. Nearby Aquia Harbour features big modern homes near secluded marinas off the lower Potomac. Stafford County advertises itself as a "pro-business community," meaning low taxes and little patience with the "smart growth" movement seeking to limit sprawl in other parts of the outer suburbs. GEICO, Intuit, and Coca-Cola have major facilities here, and Stafford Regional Airport caters to executive charters.

Web Sites: www.efredericksburg.org, www.fredericksburgva.com, www.co.stafford.va.us
Government Information: 540-372-1010
Newspaper: *Free Lance-Star*, 540-374-5002, www.fredericksburg.com

LEESBURG (LOUDOUN COUNTY)

Historic Leesburg, where you and your car can still cross the Potomac River on a cable ferry to Poolesville, MD, is just upstream from Fairfax County along Route 7 or the Washington & Old Dominion bike trail. The 18th-century old town is surrounded by varied housing, from historic townhouses to modern detached houses in condo subdivisions, much more affordable than comparable homes closer to the Beltway. Many homes here still sell for less than $200,000 and rent for less than $700. Not coincidentally, sprawl has pushed many employers out here, including the main offices of the Federal Aviation Administration, and the population of Leesburg grew from 16,000 to 28,000 during the 1990s.

Web Sites: www.leesburgva.org, http://leesburgva.com, www.co.loudoun.va.us
Government Information: 703-777-2420
Newspaper: *Leesburg Today*, 703-771-8800, www.leesburg2day.com

MANASSAS

Best known as the scene of two Civil War battles, Manassas marks the western edge of urban sprawl. A few horse-country diehards commute to D.C.—an hour by VRE train and, depending on traffic, much longer by Interstate 66. On a clear night, the lights of Manassas can be seen from the mountains of Shenandoah National Park, 60 miles west. It's a modern suburb, with strip malls and inexpensive subdivision housing—you can rent a two-bedroom garden apartment for under $800 or buy a townhouse for under $100,000, impossible half an hour's drive east of here. For employees of Lockheed Martin and other companies in the western Dulles Corridor, it's a short commute; but the main attraction here is the genuine countryside, including the starry skies above the 5,000-acre Manassas National Battlefield Park, situated just minutes away.

Web Site: www.manassascity.org
Government Information: 703-257-8200
Newspaper: *Manassas Journal Messenger*, 703-368-3101; circulation, 703-368-3134, www.manassasjm.com

PRINCE WILLIAM COUNTY

To most Washingtonians, the area south of Bull Run and the Occoquan River conjures up images of discount shopping at Potomac Mills Outlet Mall or "antiquing" in **Occoquan**. (It's pronounced AHH-kuh-kwahn.) Prince William County is also the home of Quantico Marine Corps Base—6,600 Marines, 33,000 acres—and the bedroom suburbs of **Woodbridge** and **Dumfries**, both on the Virginia Railway Express line. Until the 1990s, the county was mostly rural, but booming population growth—including a significant Latino community—make it feel more like the older suburbs of Northern Virginia. Prince William County campaigns hard to attract businesses to its major corridors along I-95 and I-66. There are modern subdivisions here with townhouse condos and garden apartments, but to find a single-family home in Prince William County, you may need a broker.

Web Site: www.co.prince-william.va.us
Government Information: 703-792-4660
Newspaper: *Prince William Journal, 703-846-8500, www.jrnl.com*

I N MOST CITIES, THE HOUSING MARKET TENDS TO FOLLOW THE STOCK market and the general economy. In the Washington area, the housing market is more stable and somewhat recession-proof—after all, in any economic conditions, the federal government remains the world's largest employer, consumer, and client.

Housing prices fell in the District in the early 1990s as declining city services pushed middle-class families out to the suburbs. Now that the sprawling suburbs are getting crowded and the District government is getting higher marks from many residents, people are moving back into the city, driving prices back up. Young couples and singles flock to hip neighborhoods like Dupont Circle, Adams Morgan and Mt. Pleasant, where rents have doubled since 1996. In Georgetown or Capitol Hill, don't be surprised to see condos selling for six figures or three-bedroom homes selling for seven. From 1996 through 2001, according to the quarterly statistics in the *Washington Post*, the median price of home sales increased every year in almost all of the city's 22 zip codes. In the heart of the city—Shaw, Adams Morgan, Mt. Pleasant, and Columbia Heights—median prices rose by more than 20%; now, a well-kept, spacious townhouse in Adams Morgan or Dupont Circle can command as much rent as a prestigious Georgetown address. The good news is that housing is plentiful—it's much easier to find a home here than in, say, Manhattan or Seattle. A few blocks off the beaten path can make a huge difference in price, too; there are bargains to be found in many of the District's quiet residential neighborhoods. And if you're buying your first home in the District, you may be eligible for a $5,000 tax credit. (See **Assistance for First-time Homebuyers** below.)

Here are a few **things to watch out for** as you search for a place to live:
- **Airport noise**: Reagan National Airport is just across the river from downtown D.C., and air traffic roars over Georgetown and neighboring parts of Maryland as well as Arlington and Alexandria. During business

hours, air traffic is constant. There are noise-abatement rules that restrict takeoffs and landings at night, but the only sure bet is to visit a neighborhood several times, at different times of day. In Virginia, the western suburbs—Herndon and Chantilly—have noise problems from Dulles Airport to the west, and the Maryland suburbs just east of D.C. experience noise from huge cargo planes serving Andrews Air Force Base.

- **Civic involvement and public safety**: find out whether a neighborhood has high turnover or a lot of settled residents. Bonus points for the neighborhood if a lot of residents are active in the local civic association, the PTA, or local politics. Also check with the local police station and interview patrol officers about area safety. Good schools, safe neighborhoods, and sound property investments are found where neighbors care about the community and devote time and effort to its improvement.

- **Termites**: Washington's temperate climate makes it termite heaven. A termite inspection is part of any home sale, and it's advisable to go along on the inspection to make sure it's thorough and to talk with the inspector about any potential problems. See the **Pest Control** section of the **Helpful Services** chapter for more information.

- **Traffic noise**: during rush-hour commutes, when major thoroughfares are crowded, many commuters use residential streets as shortcuts. Some neighborhoods have speed bumps, frequent stop signs, and one-way streets to discourage commuters, but many streets that are tranquil on weekends turn into speedways on Monday morning. Highway noise is a problem for some suburban neighborhoods along the Beltway; concrete walls muffle the roar a bit, but they certainly don't make it go away. Again, the best way to check out noise problems in a prospective neighborhood is to visit several times, at different times of day.

RENTING VS. BUYING

In the long run, buying may be cheaper than renting, and you end up with an asset to show for it; but many newcomers buy a house or condo too soon after moving to town, only to discover that the neighborhood, the commute, or the home itself is more than they bargained for. Property taxes are high—2.15% in the District and even higher in Maryland, compared to an average of 1.83% in the nation's 75 biggest metropolitan areas. (The lowest property tax rate in the area is 0.99%, in little Arlington.) As the District continues to recover from the real estate lull during the crack epidemic of the late 1980s and early '90s, many homeowners are being caught off guard by significant hikes in their tax assessments. In the District, property values can vary dramatically from one block to the next—along with noise, traffic, graffiti, and signs of drug activity. But even inexpensive housing in the Washington area is expensive by nationwide standards. Based on statistics compiled by the *Washington Business Journal* and the Meyers Group, the average price of a house here is nearly $210,000—37% higher than the national average of $153,000.

If you're not in a hurry to get kids settled into a school, it might be wise to sign a one-year lease to allow time to get to know the city before deciding where to put down permanent roots. Throughout the Washington area, you'll find a good selection of rental houses as well as apartments. Some are owned by local families as investments; others are owned by military or diplomatic families who don't want to leave their permanent homes empty while they're posted overseas. In a typical week, the *Washington Post* Sunday classifieds list hundreds of homes for rent, and the *Washington City Paper* lists dozens of homes for rent and dozens of rooms in shared houses. And the rental market is varied enough to suit practically anyone's housing needs: from efficiency apartments in modern high-rises to pedigreed mansions in the country, from postwar suburban duplexes to 19th-century carriage houses. Townhouses, old and new, are especially abundant—tall, narrow houses adjoining similar houses on either side. A common type of rental in D.C. is the "English basement," a basement apartment with its own entrance separate from the townhouse above. In fact, for added income, many townhouse owners convert their basements into studio or one-bedroom apartments.

Most apartments in D.C. are housed in stately brick apartment buildings built before World War II, but there are plenty of newer high-rises, which tend to have more amenities and less visual charm. In the suburbs, you'll find postwar high-rises and garden apartments—low-rise buildings of two or three stories. There are suburban townhouses, too—in self-contained complexes resembling garden apartment developments. Some townhouses in suburban subdivisions are sold as condo units.

RENTING A HOUSE OR APARTMENT

Generally speaking, D.C. is a tenant-friendly jurisdiction. Most renters will find buildings maintained to the high standards required by law. It is difficult for a landlord to evict a tenant, particularly in the winter. And, unless a landlord can give a good reason not to renew a lease when it expires, the tenant has a statutory right to renew it.

The District passed a rent control statute in 1975, just a year after it first elected a mayor and city council. The law applies only to major landlords—those who own no more than four units are exempt, unless they have more than three business partners. In addition, the following properties are not subject to rent control:

- government-owned or subsidized housing
- new housing (generally, housing built after 1975)

- housing managed or overseen by certain programs of the Department of Housing & Community Development
- foreign-owned housing for embassy staff
- nursing homes and other residential health care facilities
- student housing owned by a college or university
- low-income housing owned by a charitable organization and rented below cost

For all other rental properties, the landlord may raise the rent once a year by the same percentage as the increase in the Consumer Price Index (CPI), calculated by the Bureau of Labor Statistics. (To check the CPI or learn how it is derived, call 202-691-5200 or visit http://stats.bls.gov) The rent ceiling for a vacant unit may be raised by 12% or to the rent ceiling of comparable occupied unit in the same complex. Landlords may also request an increase in the rent ceiling on the basis of economic hardship (if the current rent ceiling does not allow a at least a 12% profit margin), capital improvements, added services, or a voluntary agreement with at least 70% of the tenants affected. The tenant has a right to be notified in writing 30 days in advance of any rent increase. Landlords may not raise the rent for a unit with elderly or disabled tenants on the basis of capital improvements, but may claim an offsetting tax credit instead.

In the suburbs, the only jurisdiction with rent control is Takoma Park. For details, contact the Takoma Park department of Housing & Community Development at 301-270-5900 or www.cityoftakomapark.org/dhcd.

Don't assume that rental houses are more expensive than apartments—especially in the suburbs, where houses may be much cheaper per square foot. On the other hand, don't assume that a house will necessarily offer more living space—especially in D.C., where two-bedroom apartments in older buildings are often more spacious and luxurious than modern two-bedroom townhouses. The quoted rent for an apartment often includes utilities, and the quoted rent for a house often doesn't, but always ask. (Keep in mind: If you make an effort to save energy using high-efficiency lighting, water-saving aerators and a frugal hand on the thermostat, rent that includes utilities can be a rip-off.) In most of the neighborhoods profiled in this book, you should expect to pay $600 to $900 a month for an efficiency apartment and $1,000 or more for a one-bedroom. In hip neighborhoods like Dupont Circle and Adams Morgan, even an efficiency can fetch $1,000. For a house, expect to pay $400 to $500 per bedroom.

Sound steep? It is. Among the nation's 20 largest metropolitan areas, according to the cost-of-living calculator at www.jobrelocation.com, only six have more expensive rental markets: New York, Chicago, Minneapolis-St. Paul, San Francisco, Boston, and Detroit. But nearly two out of three

District residents are renters—some because they don't qualify for a mortgage, yes, but many Washingtonians prefer the freedom and convenience of renting to the major commitments and chores of home ownership.

FINDING RENTAL HOUSING

DIRECT ACTION

Be prepared to pound some pavement. Start by scanning the classifieds, either online or in print, but don't forget to go out and visit prospective neighborhoods and look for "For Rent" signs. Also check for vacancy notices tacked on bulletin boards at neighborhood coffeehouses or grocery stores. In the outer suburbs, follow the "open house" signs on the medians of any main road on any weekend, or call a building's rental office or condo association and simply ask about upcoming vacancies.

Old school and hometown connections can be immensely helpful in choosing a neighborhood and a home. As soon as you know you're moving to Washington, call or e-mail your old college friends or former neighbors who have moved here, or who know someone here, and ask them to keep their eyes and ears open. In this city where almost half the adult population has lived here for less than 20 years, and where old friends and acquaintances often substitute for an extended family, they won't be surprised to hear from you.

Also check with your college alumni office for help finding housing here. Many large universities around the United States have offices in D.C. that can assist alumni; even if you attended a tiny college, its alumni office may be able to put you in touch with a local contact person.

Finally, if you're being transferred to Washington by your employer, or you already have a job lined up here, be sure to ask about any relocation assistance your employer might provide. Many large companies have staff or contractors whose job is to help employees find temporary and permanent housing.

CLASSIFIED ADS

Newspaper classifieds list hundreds of houses and apartments for rent every week—even thousands, especially in May and late August, when students and interns come and go. Since most newspapers now post classifieds online the night before they appear in print, you should head first for your computer. The classifieds will give you a good sense of the rental market—the going rate for an efficiency or studio apartment in Adams Morgan, a two-bedroom apartment in Clarendon, a townhouse off Dupont Circle, or a detached house in Wheaton. There are also slick advertising circulars packed with photos and profiles of apartment complexes; you'll see these publications in newspaper boxes at Metro stations and busy street corners.

- **The Washington Post** offers an extensive real estate section on Saturdays, although there are hundreds of houses and apartments listed every day. The Saturday section adds detailed articles about the housing market—trends, styles, changing neighborhoods, and a weekly chart listing mortgage rates at local lenders. *Post* classifieds are searchable online at www.washingtonpost.com, and are posted the evening before they appear in print. The online apartment guide **www.apartments.com** is affiliated with the *Post.*
- The **Washington City Paper** lists plenty of homes for rent and a few for sale, but is most valuable for those in search of short-term rentals, sublets, house-sitting jobs, a room in a shared house, or a roommate. Check www.washingtoncitypaper.com Tuesday evenings. The paper hits the streets on Thursdays.
- **The Washington Times** has daily classifieds and a special Friday "Home Guide" section featuring expanded listings and articles about the real estate market. Listings and related articles can be searched at www.washtimes.com.
- **The Journal Newspapers** in Montgomery, Prince George's, Arlington, and Fairfax counties, and in Alexandria, include the "Journal Friday Home Report," a special section of real estate listings and related articles. Also available at www.jrnl.com.
- The **Washington Blade**, available on Fridays at restaurants, bars, bookstores and newspaper boxes around town, carries extensive listings of gay-friendly housing to share. Also available at www.washblade.com.
- **Washingtonian** magazine lists beach and mountain houses for sale or rent, and a few high-end homes in and around the city. Also available at www.washingtonian.com.
- **Neighborhood papers** listed in the **Getting Settled** chapter are short on actual listings, but carry lots of display ads from real estate agents specializing in those neighborhoods. It's a safe bet that an agent who buys a half-page ad in, for instance, the *Hill Rag* every month knows a thing or two about the real estate market on Capitol Hill.

In addition, these **free booklets** include profiles, photos, and floor plans of many major apartment complexes in the D.C. area. You won't find rental rates listed here, only display ads providing overviews of apartment complexes and the amenities they offer. Look for these publications on racks around town, or browse their contents on the web:

- **The Apartment Shoppers Guide**, www.apartmentguide.com
- **Apartments For Rent**, www.aptsforrent.com
- **Washington Post Apartment Showcase**, www.apartment-showcase.com

Other **online listings** include:

- **The Apartment Connection**, www.theapartmentconnection.com
- **ProRent Washington, D.C.**, www.apartments-in-washington-dc.net
- **UrbanApartments**, www.urbanapartments.com

REAL ESTATE BROKERS—RENTAL

Most brokers say they're happy to assist people who are looking for rentals, but be realistic: rental commissions are not a real estate broker's bread and butter, and you aren't likely to get the same level of service as clients looking to buy. (Unless you're interested in renting a mansion—and you can, in areas like Potomac and McLean, from owners who go overseas for years at a time.) For help finding a more ordinary house to rent, stick to real estate agencies that specifically advertise rental services. **Weichert** has a rental division with a database of 40,000 properties throughout the Washington area—visit www.weichert.com or call 877-301-7368. Other brokers with rental divisions include:

- **Avery-Hess**, www.averyhess.com (seven locations), 800-220-9797 or 703-266-5810 (seven locations in the suburbs)
- **Cathie Gill**, 3201 New Mexico Avenue, Suite 245; 202-364-3066; www.cathiegill.com
- **Evers & Co.**, 4400 Jenifer Street, NW, Suite 260; 202-364-1700; www.eversco.com

APARTMENT SEARCH FIRMS

These agencies are funded by property owners to find tenants to fill their buildings—so, like a real estate broker, they work for you for free:

- **The Apartment Connection**, www.theapartmentconnection.com, 800-916-APTS or 202-237-8000
- **Apartment Detectives**, 202-246-6056
- **Apartment Locators**, 800-999-RENT, 301-585-RENT, www.southernmanagement.com
- **Apartment Search**, www.apartmentsearch.com, 800-APARTMENT

SHARING AND SUBLETS

If you're on your own, renting a room in an established group house can be a great way to get acquainted with the city without spending a whole lot on rent. Sometimes a group will get together and find a home, though more often one or two people will rent a house and then seek roommates through advertising, word-of-mouth referrals, or a roommate referral service. There is a brisk market for summer sublets, particularly near colleges and universities. Or, with luck and connections, you might even find a house-sitting position.

Many people find roommates through the bulletin boards in neighborhood bookstores and cafes, and, of course, in main buildings on college and university campuses. (Try the bulletin boards at Kramerbooks & Afterwords and Lambda Rising, listed in the **Literary Life** section of the **Cultural Life** chapter; Savory Cafe, 7071 Carroll Avenue, Takoma Park; or any of the food co-ops listed in **Shopping for the Home**.) There are hundreds of listings each week in the *City Paper* under "Housing to Share" and in the *Post* under "Rooms for Rent." You can browse listings at the web sites below, or call one of the roommate matchmakers who advertise in the *City Paper* "Housing to Share" section. Always ask if there is a finder's fee.

- **www.roommateexpress.com**
- **www.dcroommatefinders.com**
- **www.rentnetroommates.com**
- **www.thesublet.com**

If you call a group house in response to an ad and you're too late, don't hesitate to ask whether they know of any other vacancies. Especially in neighborhoods like Adams Morgan and Mt. Pleasant, where group houses are common, many vacancies are filled by word-of-mouth referrals.

Several times in the 1990s, the city council considered bills to prohibit or regulate house-sharing by more than three unrelated adults. Rarely has the council heard such an outcry; group housing is a common practice throughout D.C., where the high cost of living and escalating rents compel many young adults to share a house or large apartment. It's increasingly commonplace to find older singles sharing housing too, and to find group houses in the suburbs, especially Takoma Park and near the University of Maryland.

CHECKING IT OUT

You sign a lease on a cozy efficiency, and two months later, it starts to feel a little *too* cozy. Noise from traffic outside—and from your neighbor's daily soaps—penetrates the thin walls at all hours. The dishwasher is leaking all over the kitchen floor. And there aren't enough washing machines to go around, so you've been hauling your clothes to a laundromat. To minimize the risk of such unpleasant surprises, make a checklist of your musts and must-nots; when you visit a prospective home, allow a few minutes to make a close inspection to be sure its beauty is not just skin deep. A little time and a few questions now can save you a lot of aggravation later on. For example:

- Are the kitchen appliances clean and in working order? Do the stove's burners work? How about the oven? Is there enough counter and shelf space? Will the owner provide you with manuals for any appliances that come with the home, and who is responsible for routine maintenance?

- Do the windows open, close and lock? Do the bedroom windows face a noisy or potentially dangerous area? Are there bars on the ground floor windows? Is there a window air conditioner or central air?
- Is there enough storage space? In an apartment building, is there a basement locker room for additional storage? If you have a bike, where can you park it indoors or lock it securely?
- Are there enough electrical outlets, and do they work? In a house, do the circuit breakers or fuses overload often?
- Are there any signs of insects, particularly termites? When was the last termite inspection?
- If the home does not come with a washer and dryer, is there a laundry room in the building?
- Outside, do you feel comfortable? Will you feel safe here at night?
- Is there secure parking? Is there enough? Where do guests park? Does the driveway accommodate two cars side by side, or only with one car blocking the other? Does parking cost extra?
- Is there convenient access to public transportation and shopping? How late do the buses run, and do they run on weekends?

The Savvy Renter's Kit by Ed Sacks (Dearborn Publishing, 1998) includes a thorough renter's checklist, useful anywhere in the country; in D.C., a checklist in the *Tenant's Guide to Safe and Decent Housing* includes relevant legal information about housing codes and leases. (See the section on **Leases & Tenant/Landlord Problems** below.) If you've given the place a thorough inspection, gotten satisfactory answers to all your questions, and everything passes muster, be prepared to stake your claim without delay—before someone else does.

STAKING A CLAIM

True story: A newcomer went for a morning walk before an appointment with a rental agent, and didn't have time to change out of her sweat suit before looking at luxury apartments. She was given the cold shoulder and grudging service—until, when probed, she stated her income bracket. Suddenly she got red-carpet treatment. Unbeknownst to the rental agent, the newcomer was the new editor of an influential local newspaper. The rental agent's judgmental attitude was the subject of a column a few days later.

Most of us don't write a weekly column in an influential newspaper, so it pays to be aware that landlords and property managers are human, and will make judgments based upon your appearance and demeanor. Yes, such discrimination is illegal—but an experienced landlord can always find a watertight reason to turn you down. The impression you want to make is that of a responsible and conscientious tenant who will pay the rent on time. With that in mind, also come prepared with checkbook (often it is the first person to come with a deposit who gets the apartment), and have ready access to your references—both credit and personal—and your bank account information.

Almost all landlords or property managers will require a security deposit, usually equal to a month's rent which, less any damages, will be refunded to you, with interest, when you move. Most landlords require an additional deposit from tenants with pets—often a nonrefundable deposit (a polite way to say "fee") anywhere from $50 to $200. Also, application fees of $10 to $25 are sometimes charged as a way to discourage frivolous rental applications. The fee is usually credited to your deposit if your application is approved.

Some landlords—especially individuals who own only one or two rental properties, as opposed to full-time professional property managers—will ask for personal references, and most will want to check with your bank or your employer. If you've just arrived and you have few local contacts, explain your situation and offer references from your hometown; it's not unusual. In larger apartment buildings, the application process is likely to be simpler and more objective: you'll have to show that the rent is no more than a certain fraction of your income, usually one-third.

LEASES & TENANT/LANDLORD PROBLEMS

The standard one-year lease in D.C. and most surrounding jurisdictions is a renewable contract that, at the end of the term, automatically reverts to a month-to-month lease unless renewed for a definite period. A month-to-month lease remains in effect until the landlord or tenant gives 30 days' notice of termination.

Typically, lease details focus on: the address to which rent should be mailed or delivered, late payment penalties, terms of the security deposit, including interest, rules and deposits regarding pets, policy on subletting, maintenance and repairs, right of entry for the landlord and contractors, and mandatory tenant's insurance. Read carefully for these details, and remember that the lease is most likely a standard form; you and your landlord can make any agreed upon changes. Just be sure you both initial any handwritten changes and you both possess signed copies of exactly the same agreement.

Be sure to do a "walkthrough" with the landlord to inspect the property for any pre-existing damage that should not be blamed on the new tenant. You and the landlord should both sign a list of all existing damages and keep a copy.

Federal law requires the owner of rental housing to disclose any lead-based paint hazards to all tenants, and to provide an approved pamphlet explaining that housing built before 1978 may contain lead-based paint. Lead in dust and chips from such paint can be a health hazard, especially to young children. In the District, if you want to have your child tested for lead poisoning, call the Childhood Lead Poisoning Prevention Program at 202-535-2690. If test results warrant, the HRA will inspect the property for lead-based paint and order abatement measures.

Rental housing codes are fairly uniform throughout the Washington area, but here's the deal in the District: The law requires landlords to maintain rental properties in "clean, safe, and sanitary condition, in good repair, and free from rodents or vermin." (However, if those rodents or vermin show up after you move into a rented single-family home, they're legally your problem, not the landlord's.) If you bring a problem to the landlord's attention and repairs do not get under way within a reasonable time, you can ask the Housing Regulation Administration (HRA) to intervene—call 202-442-4610. Of course, "reasonable" means one thing when the problem is a broken furnace in the winter and another thing when it's a hole in a window screen.

If the heating and air conditioning are not under the tenant's control, the landlord is required to maintain a temperature of 68°F from 6:30 a.m. to 11 p.m. and 65°F at night. There are no exceptions; even if a tenant fails to pay rent or utility bills, the landlord cannot turn off the heat in an occupied unit during the winter.

If a D.C. landlord threatens you with the "E" word, you can usually be sure it's an empty threat. Eviction is a rare and extreme remedy in the tenant-friendly District. With legal counsel, almost any tenant can tie an eviction proceeding up for months or years. Many small-time landlords neglect the provision of D.C. Code Section 45-1406 that requires eviction notices to be served in English and Spanish, even if the tenant only speaks Farsi. Once the authorities show up to execute an eviction order, however, the only way to stop the eviction is to pay the full amount of rent or damages due in cash or by money order. In the suburbs, courts tend to look more favorably on owners' rights, and you'll need to get legal aid as soon as you receive a "notice to quit."

The informative 35-page *Tenant's Guide to Safe and Decent Housing* is available from the HRA—pick up a free copy at 941 North Capitol Street NE or download the PDF version at http://dcra.dc.gov. In addition to details about landlord and tenant rights and responsibilities, the booklet includes a checklist for prospective homes; a detailed explanation of grievance and hearing procedures; and a list of low-cost legal aid services.

Contact the landlord-tenant affairs agency in your jurisdiction if you have any questions about the terms of the lease and your rights and responsibilities. The following agencies can answer your questions and mediate landlord/tenant disputes:

- **D.C. Department of Consumer & Regulatory Affairs**, Housing Regulation Administration, 202-442-4620, http://dcra.dc.gov
- **Alexandria Office of Housing**, Landlord-Tenant Relations Division, 703-838-4545, www.ci.alexandria.va.us/city/housing
- **Arlington County Housing Information Center & Tenant Landlord Commission**, 703-228-3765, www.co.arlington.va.us/cphd
- **Fairfax County Tenant-Landlord Commission**, Department of Telecommunications & Consumer Services, 703-222-8435, www.co.fairfax.va.us/dtcs
- **Montgomery County Commission on Tenant-Landlord Affairs**, 240-777-3670, www.co.mo.md.us/services/hca
- **Prince George's County Department of Housing & Community Development**, 301-883-5500, www.goprincegeorgescounty.com/Government/HCD

For more information about landlord and tenant rights and responsibilities, visit the online legal resources **www.nolo.com** or **www.rentlaw.com**. These sites include statutes and case citations from D.C. and every state, and Nolo sells a number of plain-English legal handbooks for tenants— notably *Every Tenant's Legal Guide* and *Renter's Rights: The Basics,* both by Attorney Janet Portman & Marcia Stewart.

If you must break a lease (for reasons you can't blame on the landlord), you should expect to take a financial hit. At a minimum, you will lose your security deposit. Depending on the amount of rent at stake—the time remaining in the lease and the amount per month—your landlord might not bother to sue, especially if it's a good time of year to put a unit on the rental market (ideally, late spring or late summer). You could, in theory, be sued for the full amount of rent you would pay throughout the remainder of the lease, but in practice, it's a lively rental market and landlords seldom bother chasing down a leasebreaker for more than one or two months' rent. Keep in mind, though, your next rental application will ask for contact information for your most recent landlord—so you will be much better off if you get a lawyer's advice and negotiate an amicable deal. (One way to placate a jilted landlord is to recruit a new tenant yourself, to save on the cost of advertising the vacancy.) At www.nolo.com, you can download a kit for $3.99 entitled "Break Your Lease without Breaking the Law."

RENTER'S/HOMEOWNER'S INSURANCE

Upon signing a lease, your next step should be to get renter's insurance; in fact, most leases here require it. Depending on your possessions, renter's insurance won't likely cost more than $150 a year. Fine jewelry, electronics, or other special items will require additional coverage. A renter's insurance policy typically covers damages to your belongings and personal liability in the event of theft, fire, water damage, or injury. Structural damage to the property is not covered. (Note that most leases become null and void if a fire or other catastrophe makes the home uninhabitable.)

The ideal renter's or homeowner's policy provides "replacement value" coverage, but inflation has made replacement value policies hard to find in recent years; instead, many insurance companies offer coverage for 120% to 125% of the face value of your house and belongings. If disaster strikes, you will be glad you shopped around for a replacement value policy. Visit these web sites to shop for insurance:

- **www.insure.com**, a comprehensive guide for consumers and insurance professionals, with detailed information about policies and coverage, tips on making a claim, and a listing of complaints filed against insurance companies
- **Quotesmith**, www.quotesmith.com, offering instant quotes from more than 300 companies
- **QuickenInsurance**, www.insuremarket.com, ranked No. 1 in the *Smart Money* 2000 Internet Guide for finding inexpensive insurance rates online.

To find an insurance agent in your neighborhood, check the Yellow Pages, where agencies are listed by town, or contact one of these national companies:

- **Allstate**, 703-385-6600, www.allstate.com
- **Hartford**, 800-624-5578, www.thehartford.com
- **Nationwide**, 800-882-2822, www.nationwide.com,
- **State Farm**, 301-620-5000, D.C. and Maryland; 804-972-5000, Virginia; www.statefarm.com
- **Travelers**, 866-428-2374, www.travelerspc.com\

BUYING

Buying a house, condo, or co-op is a complex and time-consuming process, but the resources listed here—and the professionals in the community—can help you at every step: calculating your budget, choosing the right home in the right neighborhood, finding and obtaining a mortgage, protecting your investment with adequate insurance, moving in, and making repairs and improvements. To get a sense of the current real estate market, study the Real Estate section of Saturday's *Washington Post*—and not just the classified ads. Every week, the *Post* features an in-depth profile of a different neighborhood; a chart showing, by zip code, the number and median price of home sales in a local jurisdiction in the past year; current mortgage rates at area lenders; and a Q&A column. Also, in the "Business

Leads" section of the weekly *Washington Business Journal*, you can peruse a list of every real estate transaction in the Washington area valued at $200,000 or more and every building permit issued for a new home.

Of course, finding the perfect home is just the beginning of the process. Your purchase will cost more than the price of the home. Add up the fees for the title search, title insurance, and other legal services; the inspection and land survey; recording tax; mortgage origination (points). Then add the property tax payment and homeowner's insurance premiums you'll be required to place in an escrow account. In all, expect to pay five to eight percent more than the purchase price. Assuming you are not paying cash, but seeking a mortgage from a bank, you can usually figure on borrowing up to three or four times your annual income, no more. Be prepared for a thorough examination of your credit history, finances, and employment status. The required down payment is usually 20% of the purchase price, though it can be as low as 10% if you pay higher origination fees. The lender is required to give you a good-faith estimate of closing costs.

The search for a house or condo begins in the same place, whether you're buying or renting: word of mouth, legwork, and the classified ads listed above. Most people in the market for a house enlist the services of a real estate broker—a buyer's agent who knows the market and the neighborhood. And you might benefit from the services of a mortgage broker—a financial advisor who helps you get the best possible mortgage. At no charge to you, a broker will examine your financial situation (age, income, assets, debt load, etc.), and the property you want to buy and recommend the most appropriate lender and the best type of mortgage for your needs. A good broker knows the local banks and can guide you at every step in the process. For a list of mortgage brokers serving the Washington area, visit www.dcpages.com/Real_Estate. Also, if you are purchasing an older home, consider hiring a real estate lawyer who can help you with the special hurdles involved in buying a home that is, or could be, declared historic.

Lenders suggest that you "pre-qualify" for a loan—in other words, meet with your potential lender to determine a realistic range of financing. Go prepared with documentation of your financial history, and contact the three major credit bureaus listed below to make sure your credit history is accurate. (You will need to provide your name, address, previous address, and Social Security number with your request. Contact each company for specific instructions, or visit www.icreditreport.com for online access to all three. You can obtain a free report if you've been denied credit within the last 30 days; otherwise, you may be charged up to $8.) For more information about credit, see "Banking & Credit Resources" in the **Money Matters** chapter.

The major credit bureaus are:

- **Experian** (formerly TRW), P.O. Box 2104, Allen, TX 75002-2104, 888-397-3742

- **TransUnion Corporation**, P.O. Box 390, Springfield, PA 19064-0390, 800-916-8800
- **Equifax**, P.O. Box 105873, Atlanta, GA 30348, 800-685-1111

Before a home sale can be completed, termite inspection is mandatory, and most prospective homeowners will hire a building engineer to make a thorough inspection of the structure, heating and cooling systems, plumbing, roof, and major appliances. Should an inspector's report find that major repairs will be likely within a few years, you may be able to negotiate thousands of dollars off the purchase price—or you might decide to keep looking.

The purchase of a condo is a bit simpler. Here, you are buying a unit in a larger complex; the unit is yours to use, rent, or sell. Annual or monthly condo fees cover the expenses of a condo association, which takes care of the building and grounds, laundry room, parking lots or garages, swimming pool, and any other shared amenities. Condo fees can be steep, and when looking at prospective units, it's not enough to have the annual fee quoted. Check past records to find out how often the fees have been raised and by how much. You will also want a lawyer, or a real estate agent specializing in condos, to examine the condominium's prospectus and financial statement, so you don't buy into a financially unstable property.

There are a few cooperative apartment buildings (co-ops) in D.C. and scattered around the suburbs, especially in Takoma Park. Buying into a co-op means purchasing a share in a building—the share allows you the exclusive use of a particular unit, but you do not own that unit outright. Prospective buyers must be approved by the existing shareholders (or their board, in a larger building). If you wish to sell or rent your apartment, the buyer or tenant must be approved by the same process. It may be difficult to get a mortgage for a small co-op, since a small number of shareholders collectively posses a relatively high risk of default. Also, keep in mind that co-op maintenance fees, which pay for upkeep of the building and common areas, can be steep, and only the portion of such fees earmarked for property tax payments is tax-deductible.

ASSISTANCE FOR FIRST–TIME HOMEBUYERS

Many major lenders offer special rates for first-time homebuyers below a certain income level—often $60,000 a year. Ask your lender or mortgage broker whether you might qualify for a reduced down payment or below-market interest rate.

If you have not owned a home in D.C. at any time during the past year, you're considered a first-time homebuyer for the purposes of the **D.C. Homebuyer Tax Credit**. If you're a single taxpayer earning no more than

$70,000 a year, you get a $5,000 tax break when you buy a home in D.C. for your primary residence; likewise if your tax status is "married filing jointly" and you and your spouse have a combined income of no more than $110,000 a year. A partial credit is available up to the income limits of $90,000 for single taxpayers and $130,000 for joint taxpayers. Each January this tax credit legislation has to be reauthorized. To claim the credit, download IRS Form 8859, "D.C. Homebuyer," or request it by phone at 800-829-3676.

The **Home Purchase Assistance Program**, a project of the Greater Washington Urban League, provides interest breaks on mortgages for low- and moderate-income homebuyers in the District. A family of four can qualify for some assistance if household income is $79,500 or less; for a couple, the income limit is $63,600. Depending on household size and income, participants may borrow up to $20,000 interest-free. You'll need to rent a home in D.C. before you apply—the program is open to District residents meeting the income guidelines. For details, call the program office nearest you:

- **Greater Washington Urban League**, 3501 14th Street NW, 202-265-8200, www.gwul.org
- **Housing Counseling Services**, 2430 Ontario Road NW, 202-667-5331
- **University Legal Services**, 300 I Street NE, Suite 202, 202-547-4747
- **Marshall Heights Community Development Corp.**, 3917 Minnesota Avenue NE, 202-396-1200
- **University Legal Services**, 3101 Martin Luther King Jr. Avenue SE, 202-645-7088

For information about similar opportunities in the suburbs, contact the **Maryland Department of Housing & Community Development** at www.dhcd.state.md.us, 410-514-7700, or the **Virginia Housing Development Authority**, www.vhda.com, 800-968-7837 or 804-782-1986. In Maryland, you can also browse promotional mortgage rates at **www.marylandmortgageshop.com**.

HomeFree USA is a non-profit organization providing evening and weekend classes for homebuyers and new homeowners. Topics include "Finding a Home/Working With a Realtor," "Home Inspections," "Closing & Settlement," "Life as a New Homeowner," "Down Payment & Closing Cost Assistance," "Credit Enhancement," "Buying a Home on a Shoestring Budget," and "Homeowner's Insurance & Security." Most classes are open to members only; a free class, "10 Homebuying Secrets Everyone Ought to Know," is offered every Thursday from 6:30 to 8 p.m. at 318 Riggs Road NE. With your $45 membership fee, you get a one-hour counseling session to help you find (and get) the best mortgage. For more information, call 202-526-2000 or 800-289-4632 or visit www.homefreeusa.org.

Finally, check out these helpful publications:

- *10 Steps To Homeownership: A Workbook for First-Time Buyers* by

Ilyce R. Glink, Times Books, 2001; a manual by the author of *100 Questions Every First-Time Homebuyer Should Ask,* Times Books, 2000
- ***Your New House****: the Alert Consumer's Guide to Buying and Building a Quality New Home* by Alan and Denise Fields, Windsor Peak Press (800-888-0385 or www.windsorpeak.com), 1999; rated by the *San Francisco Chronicle* as one of the ten "Best Real Estate Books"
- ***Opening the Door to a Home of Your Own****,* a free pamphlet by the Fannie Mae Foundation; call 800-834-3377

REAL ESTATE BROKERS

There is no substitute for the advice of a local real estate broker. Brokers are trained, licensed professionals who keep a close eye on the neighborhoods they serve. A knowledgeable broker may know the average SAT scores at the local high school, the crime rate in the local police beat, how many minutes it takes to drive to the Beltway, and—most important—the long-term and recent trends in property values right down to a given block. A good broker will also interview you in detail about your needs and inter-ests—not just your preferred price range, but every detail of your lifestyle. Are you planning to have any more children? Do you need space in the basement to set up your electric trains? Do you want to plant a garden, or would you prefer an ivy-covered lawn that needs no maintenance? Will you ride a bike to the Metro station every day? The more information you pro-vide, the better your broker can match you with a home.

So how do you find a broker who knows the neighborhood where you want to live? Most real estate agencies claim to serve the entire Washington area, and indeed, most agencies can offer at least some valuable assistance with any home on the market. Naturally, however, an agency is best quali-fied to show you homes in the neighborhood where it is located—so the agencies listed below, and in the Yellow Pages, are organized by neighbor-hood. Also, most neighborhood newspapers carry lots of advertising from individual brokers boasting their intimate knowledge of the community.

To find a broker online, **www.realtor.com** and **http://home-loca-tor.com** provide links to specific real estate brokers serving the neighbor-hoods or cities you select.

DISTRICT OF COLUMBIA

CAPITOL HILL
- **Century 21 Ashby & Associates**, www.century21.com, 202-543-8060
- **John C. Formant Real Estate**, www.johncformant.com, 202-544-3900
- **Pardoe**, www.pardoe.com, 202-547-3525

- **Re/Max Capital Realtors**, www.remaxdc.com, 877-947-5600 or 202-547-5600

CHEVY CHASE
- **Long & Foster**, www.longandfoster.com, 800-762-0782 or 202-363-9700
- **Pardoe**, www.pardoe.com, 202-362-5800
- **W.C. & A.N. Miller**, http://millernet.com, 202-966-1400
- **Weichert**, www.weichert.com, 202-326-1300

CLEVELAND PARK
- **Weichert**, www.weichert.com, 202-326-1100

DOWNTOWN
- **Federal City/Mowbray**, Logan Circle, 202-483-5035
- **Tutt, Taylor & Rankin**, www.tutttaylorrankin.com, 202-234-3344

DUPONT CIRCLE
- **Federal City/Mowbray**, Dupont Circle, 202-745-0700
- **McClain, Dewey & Mounts**, 202-332-3131
- **Randall H. Hagner & Co.**, www.hagner.com, 202-857-4300
- **Weichert**, www.weichert.com, 202-326-1010

FOXHALL/SPRING VALLEY
- **Cathie Gill**, www.cathiegill.com, 202-364-3066
- **W.C. & A.N. Miller**, http://millernet.com, 202-362-1300

FRIENDSHIP HEIGHTS
- **Evers & Co.**, www.eversco.com, 202-364-1700

GEORGETOWN
- **Long & Foster**, www.georgetowndchomes.com, 202-944-8400
- **Pardoe**, www.pardoe.com, 202-333-6100
- **Re/Max Capital Realtors**, www.remaxdc.com, 877-398-8900 or 202-338-8900
- **Rod Johnston Real Estate**, www.georgetownrealty.com, 202-333-6749
- **Tutt, Taylor & Rankin**, www.tutttaylorrankin.com, 202-333-1212

TENLEYTOWN
- **Coldwell Banker Stevens**, Washington, www.northernva.com/cbsweb, 202-686-5000
- **Re/Max Capital Realtors**, www.remaxdc.com, 877-963-9800 or 202-363-9800

MARYLAND

ANDREWS AIR FORCE BASE
- **Century 21 Advantage**, www.century21.com, 800-221-8054 or 301-449-9100
- **Coldwell Banker Stevens, Camp Springs**, www.northernva.com/cbsweb, 301-899-7100
- **Coldwell Banker Stevens, Oxon Hill**, www.northernva.com/cbsweb, 301-839-4100
- **Long & Foster**, Fort Washington, www.fortwashingtonmd.com, 301-292-0700
- **Weichert**, Andrews, www.weichert.com, 301-423-9200

BETHESDA
- **The Buyer's Edge**, www.buyersagent.com, 800-207-6810
- **Long & Foster, Elm Street** (Downtown), www.bethesda-md.com, 866-215-6444
- **Long & Foster, One Democracy Center** (North Bethesda), www.bethesdahouses.com, 301-654-4900
- **Luxury Homes**, Montgomery, luxuryhomes-md-va.com, 800-711-7988
- **The Mattingly Group**, www.mattinglygroup.com, 301-652-1868
- **Pardoe**, www.pardoe.com, 301-718-0010
- **Prestige Properties**, www.prestigepropertiesintl.com, 301-320-4002
- **W.C. & A.N. Miller**, http://millernet.com, 301-229-4000
- **Weichert**, www.weichert.com, 301-656-2500

BOWIE
- **Coldwell Banker Stevens**, www.northernva.com/cbsweb, 301-262-6800
- **Long & Foster**, Bowie, www.bowiehomes.com, 301-262-6900
- **Weichert**, www.weichert.com, 301-262-3100

CHEVY CHASE
- **Gerlach Real Estate**, 301-656-8686
- **Realty Network**, www.realtynetwork.com, 888-765-3148 or 301-951-0581
- **Weichert**, www.weichert.com, 301-718-4000

COLLEGE PARK
- **Long & Foster**, www.collegeparkhomes.com, 800-446-9498

GAITHERSBURG
- **Avery-Hess**, www.averyhess.com, 888-402-7200 or 301-948-7200
- **Coldwell Banker Stevens**, www.northernva.com/cbsweb, 301-921-1040
- **Long & Foster**, www.gaithersburghomes.com, 800-341-7355 or 301-975-9500
- **Weichert**, www.weichert.com, 301-417-7700

GREENBELT
- **Coldwell Banker Stevens**, Lanham, www.cbstevens.com, 301-474-5700
- **Weichert**, www.weichert.com, 301-345-7600

LAUREL
- **Century 21 H.T. Brown**, www.htbrown.com, 800-368-2551
- **Coldwell Banker Stevens**, www.northernva.com/cbsweb, 800-673-2433 or 301-725-5278
- **Prince George's County Realtors**, www.homes-prince-georges-maryland.com, 800-711-7988

POTOMAC
- **Long & Foster**, www.potomacvillagemd.com, 888-899-2218 or 301-983-0060
- **Pardoe**, www.pardoe.com, 301-983-020
- **W.C. & A.N. Miller**, http://millernet.com, 301-299-6000
- **Weichert**, www.weichert.com, 301-718-4100

ROCKVILLE
- **Avery-Hess**, www.averyhess.com, 800-927-0425 or 301-984-9700
- **Century 21 All Properties**, www.c21all.com, 301-294-0990
- **Llewellyn**, www.llewellynrealtors.com, 800-729-7355 or 301-424-0900
- **Metro Realty Group**, www.metrorealtygroup.com, 301-946-9600
- **Weichert**, www.weichert.com, 301-468-1600

SILVER SPRING
- **Weichert**, **Burtonsville**, www.weichert.com, 301-681-0444
- **Weichert**, **White Oak**, www.weichert.com, 301-681-0400

WHEATON
- **Weichert**, **Aspen Hill**, www.weichert.com, 301-681-0550
- **Weichert**, **Wheaton**, www.weichert.com, 301-681-0500

VIRGINIA

ALEXANDRIA

- **Century 21 New Millennium**, www.century21.com, 800-708-7085 or 703-549-0600
- **Coldwell Banker Stevens**, www.northernva.com/cbsweb, 703-212-8000
- **Long & Foster**, www.mtvernonhomes.com, 800-336-6164 or 703-960-8900
- **Luxury Homes**, Alexandria, www.luxuryhomes-md-va.com/alexandria, 800-711-7988
- **McEnearney Associates**, www.mcenearney.com, 703-549-9292
- **Pardoe**, www.pardoe.com, 703-518-8300
- **Re/Max Horizons, Seminary Road**, www.remaxhorizons.com, 800-736-6645 or 703-824-4800
- **Re/Max Horizons, Old Town**, www.remaxhorizons.com, 703-549-9200
- **Weichert, Belle View**, www.weichert.com, 703-765-4000
- **Weichert, Old Town**, www.weichert.com, 703-549-8700

ANNANDALE

- **Century 21 Howell & Associates**, www.century21.com, 800-422-2556 or 703-941-1300
- **Coldwell Banker Stevens**, www.northernva.com/cbsweb, 703-941-1600
- **EJ Properties**, www.ejproperties.com, 703-323-7966
- **Re/Max Horizons**, www.remaxhorizons.com, 703-354-9800
- **Weichert**, www.weichert.com, 703-941-0100

ARLINGTON

- **Buck & Associates**, www.adpages.com/qd2000/wbuckusa, 703-528-2288
- **Coldwell Banker Stevens**, www.northernva.com/cbsweb, 703-524-2100
- **Long & Foster**, www.arlingtonvahomes.com, 800-760-7282 or 703-522-0500
- **McEnearney Associates**, www.mcenearney.com, 703-525-1900
- **Weichert**, www.weichert.com, 703-527-3300

FAIRFAX

- **Better Homes**, www.betterhomesva.com, 703-385-3003
- **Blue Heron**, www.blueheronrealty.com, 703-451-6670

- **Buyer's Agents Fairfax County**, www.buyers-agents-fairfax-county.mp2.homes.com, 800-903-2997
- **Coldwell Banker Stevens, Fairfax**, www.northernva.com/cbsweb, 703-691-1400
- **Coldwell Banker Stevens, Fairfax Station**, www.northernva.com/cbsweb, 800-431-4663 or 703-250-1000
- **ERA Elite Group**, www.eraelitegroup.com, 800-441-5420, 703-359-7800
- **The Nellis Group, Re/Max**, www.nellisgroup.com, 800-344-7253 or 703-503-4375
- **Pardoe**, www.pardoe.com, 703-921-0600
- **Re/Max Premier**, www.dulleshomes.com, 800-297-8382 or 703-818-9603
- **Weichert, Burke**, www.weichert.com, 703-569-7870
- **Weichert, Fairfax**, www.weichert.com, 703-691-0555
- **Weichert, Fair Oaks**, www.weichert.com, 703-934-0400

FALLS CHURCH
- **Times Realty**, www.timesrealty.com, 703-533-8100

GREAT FALLS
- **Coldwell Banker Stevens**, www.northernva.com/cbsweb, 800-368-3465 or 703-759-4202
- **Weichert**, www.weichert.com, 703-759-6300

HERNDON
- **New Homes Realty**, www.newhomesrealty.com, 703-709-8288
- **Weichert**, www.weichert.com, 703-709-0101

MCLEAN
- **The Buyer Brokerage**, www.thebuyerbrokerage.com, 800-903-2297
- **Century 21 Laughlin Realty**, www.century21laughlin.com, 800-638-0021 or 703-356-0100
- **Coldwell Banker Stevens**, www.northernva.com/cbsweb, 800-555-3095 or 703-356-7000
- **Long & Foster**, www.longandfoster.com, 800-819-9971
- **McEnearney Associates**, www.mcenearney.com, 703-790-9090
- **Pardoe**, www.pardoe.com, 703-734-7020
- **Weichert, McLean Center**, www.weichert.com, 301-893-1500
- **Weichert, Dolley Madison Boulevard**, www.weichert.com, 703-760-8880
- **Weichert, Old Dominion Drive**, www.weichert.com, 703-821-8300

RESTON

- **Coldwell Banker Stevens**, www.northernva.com/cbsweb, 800-856-8440 or 703-476-8440
- **Long & Foster**, www.restonvirginia.com, 800-316-7355 or 703-437-3800
- **Pardoe**, www.pardoe.com, 703-471-7220
- **Weichert**, www.weichert.com, 703-264-0000

SPRINGFIELD

- **Avery-Hess**, www.averyhess.com, 800-220-9797 or 703-451-9797
- **Coldwell Banker Stevens**, Burke, www.northernva.com/cbsweb, 703-451-2500
- **Re/Max Metro 100**, www.remax-metro100.com, 703-642-3380
- **Weichert**, www.weichert.com, 703-569-9700

TYSONS CORNER

- **Avery-Hess**, www.averyhess.com, 800-659-0729 or 703-821-5005
- **Weichert**, www.weichert.com, 703-893-2510

VIENNA

- **Coldwell Banker Stevens**, www.northernva.com/cbsweb, 703-938-5600
- **Fairfax County Real Estate**, www.homes-fairfax-county.com, 800-711-7988
- **Long & Foster**, Lilian Jorgenson, www.lilian.com, 703-790-1990
- **Luxury Homes**, Fairfax, www.luxuryhomes-md-va.com/fairfax, 800-711-7988
- **Re/Max Preferred Properties**, www.remax-preferred-vienna-va.com, 800-828-9698 or 703-255-9700
- **Summerwood Realtors**, 888-917-9191 or 703-255-6500
- **Vienna Real Estate**, 703- 242-1460, www.viennarealestate.com
- **Weichert**, www.weichert.com, 703-938-6070

FOR SALE BY OWNER

When you buy a home directly from the owner, you can negotiate for a portion of the savings on the agent's commission. **EconoBroker**, www.econobroker.com or 888-989-4657, lists such homes on the Multiple Listing Service used by real estate agents nationwide. Other sites listing homes for sale by owner include:
- **www.4salebyowner.com**
- **FiSBO Registry**, www.fisbos.com
- **FSBO Network**, www.FSBOnetwork.com (Maryland and Virginia)
- **www.homesbyowner.com**

ADDITIONAL RESOURCES

HOUSE-HUNTING

In addition to sources listed under "Real Estate Classifieds" above, the following web sites and free publications available around town are devoted to listings of homes for sale in the Washington area:

- *Homes & Land*, 800-277-7800, www.homesandland.com
- *The Real Estate Book*, 800-841-3401, www.realestatebook.com
- *Washington, D.C. Homebuyer's Journal*, 800-344-1052, www.homebuyersjournal.com
- The **US Department of Housing & Urban Development** lists properties for sale due to foreclosure on government-backed mortgages. Visit www.hud-va-foreclosures-maryland.com or call 800-711-7988

Among nationwide resources, the **National Association of Realtors**, www.realtor.com, should be your first stop on the web. This extensive site features nationwide property listings, neighborhood profiles and statistics, virtual tours, loan calculators, and extensive information about mortgage lenders, relocation, contractors and, of course, real estate agents.

The following web sites list homes for sale nationwide and provide extensive information about moving, mortgages, real estate agents, neighborhoods, home improvement, and more:

- **www.cyberhomes.com**
- **www.homeadvisor.com**
- **www.homeseekers.com**
- **www.homestore.com**
- **www.jobrelocation.com**
- **www.realtylocator.com**

Check www.scorecard.org to find out about toxic waste issues in or near your prospective neighborhood. This site, sponsored by the Environmental Defense Fund, is a database of polluters by zip code; the Washington area has practically no heavy industry, but plenty of trash incinerators and waste transfer stations—and anything the Potomac brings down from the paper mills and coal mines of Western Maryland.

To determine how your cost of living will change when you move to Washington, check out the online salary calculators at **www.jobrelocation.com** or **www.homefair.com**. A similar tool on the **Coldwell Banker** web site, www.coldwellbanker.com, compares the cost of similar homes in different cities.

See **Moving and Storage** for more relocation tips and tools.

MORTGAGES

In addition to the loan resources listed in the **Money Matters** chapter and the housing resources listed above, check out these helpful web sites:

- **BankRate.com,** www.bankrate.com, as its name suggests, it offers everything about mortgages and interest rates.
- **Countrywide Home Loans**, www.countrywide.com, offers moving services, branch locators, mortgage rates and calculators, credit evaluations, and more.
- **Freddie Mac**, www.freddiemac.com, provides information on low-cost loans, a home inspection kit, and tips to help avoid unfair lending practices.
- **iOwn**, www.iown.com, claims to provide the best mortgage deals online, plus information about buying and selling a home and relocating.
- **The Mortgage Professor**, www.mtgprofessor.com, offers Q&A service and archives of advice about shopping for a mortgage—plus critical reviews of other online resources.
- **www.owners.com** offers loan status, mortgage rates, credit evaluations, mortgage tools, and virtual tours of homes for sale.

BEFORE YOU START YOUR NEW LIFE INSIDE THE BELTWAY, YOU AND your worldly possessions have to get here. That can be expensive and complicated or cheap and simple, depending on how much stuff you've accumulated, where you're coming from, and how much of the heavy lifting you plan to do. If you're traveling light or you already have friends or family in Washington, you can save a lot of money by driving your own rented moving van; if you're moving everything but the kitchen sink and there are no extra hands waiting on this end of the trip, you'll need to hire movers—chosen carefully on the basis of reputation.

TRUCK RENTALS

If you plan to doing everything yourself or bribe a few friends with pizza, you can simply rent a vehicle and head for the open road. Look in the Yellow Pages under "Truck Rental" or online at www.vanlines.com, and then call around for quotes—making sure to mention your AAA membership, military or veteran's ID, or anything else that might be good for a discount. Even if you're dealing with a nationwide company, call the location nearest you. If you need a truck between May and September—peak moving season—be sure to reserve one at least a month in advance, especially for one-way rentals.

Here are the major national van lines:

- **Budget**, 800-527-0700, www.budgetdc.com
- **Hertz**, 888-999-5500, www.hertztrucks.com
- **National**, 888-628-5826, www.nationalvanlines.com
- **Penske**, 800-222-0277, www.pensketruckleasing.com
- **Ryder**, 800-297-9337, www.ryder.com
- **U-Haul**, 800-468-4285, www.uhaul.com

Once you're on the road, keep in mind that your rental truck may be a tempting target for thieves. If you must park it overnight or for more than a couple of hours, try to find a well-lit place where you can keep an eye on it, and don't leave anything valuable in the cab.

If you just need a minivan or a small trailer, get quotes from the car rental companies listed in the **Transportation** chapter. If you don't want to hire movers or drive a truck, there's an in-between option: you can hire a commercial freight carrier to bring a truck or trailer to your house and then drive it to your destination after you load it. Usually they provide a bigger vehicle than you need, so they can haul some commercial freight in the left-over space. Contact **CF Moves U** at 800-419-7395, www.cfmovesu.com, or **ABF U-Pack Moving** at 800-355-1696, www.upack.com.

MOVERS

Start with the Yellow Pages and ask around for recommendations. For long-distance moves, the **American Moving and Storage Association** web site, www.moving.org, features a good directory; also check out the most recent *Consumer Reports* index at a public library or www.consumerre-ports.org to find any helpful articles or surveys. If you belong to **AAA**, you can call their local office and receive discounts and advice through the AAA Consumer Relocation Service.

Interstate movers are licensed by the **Federal Motor Carrier Safety Administration (FMCSA)**, 202-358-7028 or www.fmcsa.dot.gov. As the agency's chief safety officer testified to Congress in 2001, "Consumers are well served by registered, legitimate, safe, and efficient household goods carriers. However, we receive letters and complaints from distraught consumers who have their household possessions held hostage for exorbitant, unexpected fees. ... A Brooklyn moving company's practice was to accept shipments under non-binding estimates and then, after the furniture and possessions were loaded on a truck and driven away, call cus-tomers and tell them the cost of delivery had increased, sometimes as much as 400%." Since 1998, the agency has disciplined 30 carriers, levying fines up to $45,000 and, in a few cases, pressing criminal charges. If you do your homework on a moving company before signing a contract, you can make sure you're one of the consumers "well served."

First, look for the federal motor carrier (MC) number on the compa-ny's advertising and promotional literature. Every federally licensed mover has such a number, three to six digits. Contact the FMCSA to verify that the number matches the company, the license is current, and the carrier is properly insured. Second, go to the "State Government" link on the FMCSA web site and find the transportation agency for your state. See whether motor carriers in your state are subject to additional licensing and insurance requirements at the state level, and make sure your prospective movers are in compliance. Be familiar with the consumer protection agencies listed in the **Helpful Services** chapter in case disputes do arise. But most important, be aware of these tips and precautions to help ensure a hassle-free moving experience:

- Once you've narrowed your search down to two or three companies, ask each company for references, particularly from customers who made moves similar to yours. If a moving company is unable or unwilling to provide such information or tells you that they can't give out names because their customers are all in the federal Witness Protection Program ... perhaps you should consider another company. You can get a second opinion about a prospective mover from your local Better Business Bureau, www.bbb.org, or from www.epinions.com. For **local movers** within the Washington area, visit www.checkbook.org to download a *Washington Consumers' Checkbook* article for $10 (free to subscribers), providing detailed ratings of 30 moving companies based on customer satisfaction, price, complaints registered with government agencies, and the availability of extra services such as moving consultants.

- If someone recommends a mover to you, get names, and keep a record of them—from the sales rep or estimator, to the drivers and movers. To paraphrase the NRA, companies don't move your stuff, people do.

- Take inventory. Even though movers will put numbered labels on everything, you should still make your own list of every box and item being loaded and hauled by the moving company. No shortcuts here—list the contents of each box, and photograph anything valuable, especially if it's fragile. Don't sign anything releasing the movers until you've checked everything off the list at your destination, and even then, keep the list until you're absolutely sure nothing was damaged. (It's a good idea to keep this list for your new insurance agent to see what policy riders you'll need for your new home.)

- Be aware that during the busy season (May through September), demand for moving services can exceed supply, and moving may be more difficult and expensive than during the rest of the year. If you must relocate during the peak moving months, arrange for service well in advance—a month at least. If you can reserve service way in advance, say four to six months early, you may be able to lock in a lower winter rate for your summer move.

- *Never* mislead a salesperson about how much and what you are moving. And make sure you tell a prospective mover about how far they'll have to transport your stuff to and from the truck as well as any stairs, driveways, obstacles or difficult vegetation, long paths or sidewalks, etc. The more information you give, the better your mover will be able to serve you.

- You should never have to pay for an estimate. Ask for a "not to exceed" price—a guaranteed maximum. If your shipment is lighter than estimated, you will be charged less. Some carriers, especially interstate movers, give "fixed price" quotes (the price you pay regardless of weight and labor) or non-binding estimates. Even fixed-price charges can be adjusted if the estimated weight is *way* off; the driver may protest and require an additional charge. The prospect of such last-minute surprises is yet another reason to give the estimator clear and accurate information up front.

- Remember that price, while important, isn't everything, especially when you're entrusting all of your worldly possessions to strangers. Choose a mover you feel comfortable with.

- Be ready for the truck on both ends of the trip—don't make the movers wait. Not only will it irritate them, it may cost you. Understand, too, that things can happen on the road that are beyond a carrier's control (weather, accidents, etc.) and your belongings may not get to you at the time or on the day promised.

- Ask about insurance—the standard coverage, 60 cents per pound, is not enough. If you have homeowner or renter's insurance, check to see if it will cover your belongings during transit. If not, consider purchasing "full replacement" or "full value" coverage from the carrier for the estimated value of your shipment. Though it's the most expensive type of coverage offered, it's probably worth it. Trucks get into accidents, they catch fire, they get stolen. If full coverage seems too expensive, ask about a $250 or $500 deductible. This can reduce your cost substantially while still giving you much better protection in the event of a catastrophic loss. Of course, transport irreplaceable items—such as jewelry, photographs or important papers—yourself.

- Be prepared to pay the full moving bill upon delivery. You may be required to pay in cash or with a cashier's check, money order, or traveler's checks. Some carriers will take credit cards, but it is a good idea to get it in writing—the delivering driver may not be aware that credit cards are accepted and may demand cash. Unless you have thousands of greenbacks on you, you could have a problem getting your stuff off the truck.

- If you have a dog or cat, attach a collar tag with your new address *before* you move in case your pet accidentally wanders off in the confusion of moving.

- Treat your movers well, especially the ones loading your stuff on and off the truck. Offer to buy them lunch, and tip them if they do a good job.

- Above all, ask questions and if you're concerned about something, ask for an explanation in writing. And listen to your movers; they are professionals and can give you expert advice about packing and preparing.

PACKING & ORGANIZING

Don't wait until the last minute to think about packing. You'll need plenty of boxes, tape, and packing material. Moving companies offer sturdy boxes in convenient sizes—but, at several dollars each, new boxes can add a lot to the cost of a big move. Sometimes a mover will give a customer free used boxes; it doesn't hurt to ask. Look in the Yellow Pages under "Packaging Materials" (and, if you don't have time or a steady hand with fragile items, look under "Packaging Service"); or, to save money, starting well in advance, save newspapers and foam peanuts, and ask grocery stores and liquor stores for their discarded boxes.

If you have a lot of stuff and don't know what to jettison, call a moving consultant. These experts help you sort through your belongings and decide what to keep; in addition, they can help you consign or donate unwanted items; unpack; arrange the furniture; and handle change-of-address paperwork. The **National Association of Professional Organizers** makes referrals at 202-362-6276 or www.napo.net. If you're moving within the Washington area, or you need help mainly on the unpacking end, contact one of the following companies (listed in *Washingtonian* magazine's 2001 guide to special services, available at www.washingtonian.com):

- **Amazing Space**, 202-625-1414, www.amazingspc.com
- **Art of Moving**, 301-320-0888, www.artofmoving.com
- **Busy Buddies**, 703-422-0797, www.busybuddiesinc.com
- **Clearly Organized**, 703-471-6085, www.clearly-organized.com

STORAGE

If you find your new pad is too small for all of your belongings, or you need a temporary place to store your stuff while you find a new home, contact **Storage Locator** at 800-301-8655, www.storagelocator.com, or look in the Yellow Pages under "Storage - Household & Commercial." If you would like to arrange for storage before you arrive, check with your local public library for D.C., suburban Maryland, and Northern Virginia Yellow Pages or try www.bigyellow.com.

When shopping for storage facilities, security, climate control, and fire protection are a given; beyond that, look at price, convenience, and accessibility. Some storage facilities only allow daytime access. Others have gates that only open when a car or truck triggers a weight-sensitive lock, which can be a problem if you don't own a car. If you plan to open your storage locker just twice—the day you fill it and the day you empty it—then you should consider choosing a remote suburban location that will be cheaper than facilities downtown. If you plan to keep things in storage for several months and you might need occasional access to your locker, location will matter and so will access fees—be sure to ask whether there's a fee each time you open your locker. Ask about billing and security deposits, too, and don't be late with payments: if you fall behind, the storage company will not dump your stuff on your doorstep—they'll auction it off.

More convenient, and more expensive, than self-storage is "mobile" or "modular" storage. The company delivers a large container to your door, you load it, and the company hauls it away until you call for it. This can save you a lot of time and effort (it's one less round of unpacking and re-packing), but it's not good for easy access.

The biggest storage company in the Washington area is **Public Storage**, with about 50 locations plus modular service. Call 800-447-8673 or visit www.publicstorage.com for locations and quotes. Here are some other storage companies that have convenient locations in the city and inner suburbs:

- **Capital Self Storage**, 202-543-1400, www.storagefinder.com
- **Downtown Storage Center**, 202-635-0714
- **National Self Storage**, 202-636-8282, www.storagefinder.com
- **Shurgard Storage**, 301-568-7656, www.shurgard.com
- **Storage USA**, 800-786-7872, www.sus.com
- **The Storage Place**, 202-232-0400, www.storageplace.baweb.com
- **Store to Door** (modular), 888-867-2800, www.storetodoor.com
- **U-Haul Self Storage**, 202-269-1200
- **U-Store**, 202-783-2990, www.u-store.com

CHILDREN

Studies show that moving, especially frequent moving, can be hard on children. Children moving to a new and faraway city are suddenly isolated from their friends and have to start over in an unfamiliar school and community. According to an American Medical Association study, children who move often are more likely to suffer from such problems as depression, aggression, and feelings of worthlessness. Often their academic performance suffers as well. Aside from avoiding unnecessary moves, there are a few things you can do to help your children cope with these stressful upheavals:

- Talk about the move with your kids. Be honest but positive. Listen to their concerns. Involve them in the process as fully as possible.
- Make sure the children have their favorite possessions with them on the trip; don't pack "blankey" in the moving van.
- Have some fun activities planned on the other end. Your children may feel lonely in their new surroundings, and some ready-made activities

can ease the transition.
- Keep in touch with family and loved ones as much as possible. Photos, phone calls, and e-mail are important ways to maintain links to the important people you have left behind.
- If your children are of school age, take the time to involve yourself in their new school and in their academic life. Don't let them get lost in the shuffle.

For younger children, there are dozens of good books on the topic. Just a few perennial favorites:
- *Alexander, Who's Not (Do You Hear Me? I Mean It!) Going to Move* by Judith Viorst (Aladdin)
- *The Leaving Morning* by Angela Johnson (Orchard Books)
- *Little Monster's Moving Day* by Mercer Mayer (Cartwheel Books)

For older children, try:
- *Amber Brown is Not a Crayon* by Paula Danziger (Scholastic Books)
- *The Kid in the Red Jacket* by Barbara Park (Random House)
- *Hold Fast to Dreams* by Andrea Davis Pinkney (Hyperion Press)
- *Flip-Flop Girl* by Katherine Paterson (Puffin)
- *My Fabulous New Life* by Sheila Greenwald (Browndeer Press)

Finally, because kids aren't the only ones who can get stressed out and apprehensive about moving, read *Smart Moves: Your Guide through the Emotional Maze of Relocation* by Nadia Jensen, Audrey McCollum and Stuart Copans (Smith & Krauss).

These resources and more are available from First Books at www. firstbooks.com.

TAXES

If your move is work-related, some or all of your moving expenses may be tax-deductible—so keep those receipts. Generally, the cost of moving yourself, your family and your belongings is tax-deductible, even if you don't itemize. In order to take the deduction, your move must be job-related; your new job must be more than 50 miles away from your current residence; and you must be here for at least 39 weeks during the first 12 months after your move. If you take the deduction and then fail to meet the requirements, you will have to pay the money back—unless you were laid off or transferred again by your employer. It's probably a good idea to consult a tax expert, but if you are a confident soul, you can file for the deduction yourself—get a copy of IRS Form 3903 at www.irs.gov or the public library.

ONLINE RESOURCES

These sites feature moving tips and links to movers, real estate leads, and other relocation resources:

- **American Moving and Storage Association**, www.moving.org: referrals to interstate movers, local movers, storage companies, and packing and moving consultants
- **Employee Relocation Council**, www.erc.org: if your employer is a member of this professional organization, you may have access to specialized reports and services. Non-members can use the online database of real estate agents and related services.
- **First Books**, www.firstbooks.com: relocation resources and information on moving to Atlanta, Boston, Chicago, Los Angeles, Minneapolis-St. Paul, New York City, San Francisco and San Jose, Seattle, and Washington, D.C., as well as London, England.
- **HomeFair**, www.homefair.com: realty listings, moving tips, cost-of-living calculators, and more
- **Home Store**, www.springstreet.com: apartment rentals, moving tips, movers, and more
- **Monster Moving**, www.monstermoving.com: comprehensive web portal featuring a tool that lets you compare movers' rate quotes online.
- **www.moverquotes.com**: comparison shopping site for mover quotes
- **www.moving.com**: packing tips, mover estimates, and more
- **http://realestate.yahoo.com/realestate**: national real estate and rentals listings; relocation advice
- **RentNet**, www.rent.net: apartment rentals, movers, relocation advice and more
- **United Rentals**, www.unitedrentals.com: referrals to van lines
- **US Postal Service Relocation Guide**, www.usps.com/moversnet: includes a detailed checklist and tips to make sure you avoid common mistakes that can delay your mail.

A S SOON AS YOU FIND A PLACE TO HANG YOUR HAT, YOU WILL want to find a home for your money. For major deposits, shop around for interest rates, but for routine checking and savings, you'll be more interested in ATM fees, online banking options, and direct deposit services—an increasingly common alternative to getting a paycheck in the mail or on your desk. Remember that a bank in the Maryland or Virginia suburbs might not have branches in the District; if you do most of your banking at lunchtime or on the way to work, this might be a concern.

BANK ACCOUNTS & SERVICES

In the 1990s, dozens of local banks were acquired by regional or national giants, so it's possible that your old bank has a branch in your new neighborhood. All major banks offer a variety of checking accounts to fit a variety of personal banking habits: if you write a lot of checks and keep a low average balance, you will want to pay attention to per-check fees and service charges that kick in when your balance drops below a certain minimum; if you only use your checking account to pay your monthly bills, you might want an interest bearing checking account with some fees instead of a non-interest bearing free checking account. Be sure to ask about ATM fees—at your own bank's automated teller machines and at network ATMs owned by other banks—and overdraft insurance. Also inquire about the average and maximum time between a deposit and the availability of funds.

All major banks also offer money market accounts and certificates of deposit, with terms and interest rates displayed in the lobby or the window, as well as regular passbook savings accounts.

Here are some of the largest banks in the Washington area; if you prefer a smaller community bank, check out **City First**, 202-332-5002; **Adams**,

202-466-4090, www.adamsbank.com; or **Industrial**, 202-722-2000.

- **Allfirst**, 800-842-BANK, www.allfirst.com
- **Bank of America**, 800-932-2265, www.bankofamerica.com
- **BB&T**, 202-835-9215, www.bbandt.com
- **Chevy Chase**, 800-987-BANK, www.chevychasebank.com
- **Citibank**, 800-446-5331, www.citibank.com
- **Riggs**, 800-368-5800, www.riggsbank.com
- **First Virginia**, 800-223-2891, www.firstvirginia.com
- **Mellon**, 800-635-5662, www.mellon.com
- **Sandy Spring**, 301-774-6400, www.ssnb.com
- **SunTrust**, 888-786-8787, www.suntrust.com
- **Wachovia**, 800-922-4684, www.wachovia.com

CHECKING ACCOUNTS

A typical checking account application will ask the name and address of your employer, two forms of current government-issued ID, proof of address, and an opening deposit. This amount will usually be debited for the cost of your first order of checks, but some checking accounts with a monthly fee or a high minimum balance include free checks. Be sure to ask for enough starter checks to get you through the two weeks or more it will take to get your new checkbook—but note, too, that some merchants will not accept starter checks and you may need to buy money orders.

Most banks now issue **debit cards**, usually at no cost, which electronically deduct money from your checking account. They are accepted just about anywhere credit cards are accepted, and—unlike checks—they can be used for internet transactions.

SAVINGS ACCOUNTS

Opening an ordinary savings account is as simple as opening a checking account, and most banks allow you to link it to your checking account so you can transfer funds between checking and savings instantly, by ATM or touch-tone phone, and track both accounts on a combined statement. Usually, all of your accounts at a particular bank—passbook savings, CDs, money market funds, individual retirement accounts, medical savings accounts, and checking—can be combined to determine your eligibility for discounts and special services offered to customers with a certain total balance on deposit. Note that most savings accounts charge monthly fees if the balance falls below a certain minimum.

CREDIT UNIONS

Credit unions provide an inexpensive alternative to consumer banking. Compared to many large banks, credit unions offer lower fees and more personalized service, and they keep your assets "in the family," so to speak, enhancing the collective economic security of their members. In an era when many community banks have been absorbed by regional banks, and many regional banks are being taken over by national giants, you can be sure a credit union will stay close to its roots.

Most government agencies, public school districts, and counties and municipalities provide credit unions for their employees, as do many large companies such as Marriott and Lockheed Martin. Employees of smaller companies might be eligible to join a regional credit union serving a select group of public, private, and non-profit employers; ask your supervisor or benefits administrator. Here are some local credit unions that have a broad "field of membership"—see whether your employer is on their list. In most cases, if you or a member of your immediate family can show eligibility, you can join for a $5 fee and a $5 opening deposit.

- **Apple Federal Credit Union**, 800-666-7996 or 703-323-0246, www.applefcu.org
- **Lafayette Federal Credit Union**, 800-888-6560 or 301-929-7993, www.lfcu.org, (open to all residents of Potomac, MD)
- **Mid-Atlantic Federal Credit Union**, 800-95-MAFCU or 301-921-3500, www.mafcu.org (open to all residents of northern Montgomery County)
- **Money One Federal Credit Union**, 800-638-0232 or 301-925-4600, www.moneyonefcu.org
- **National Capital Federal Credit Union**, 800-245-3805 or 301-918-3991, http://ncfcu.cuwebs.com

CREDIT CARDS

Washingtonians rely so heavily on plastic—and not just for online, phone, and mail-order shopping—that one regional chain of furniture stores no longer accepts cash! You might insist that it's illegal to refuse cash, the only "legal tender for all debts, public and private," but if a sales clerk stands frozen and dumbfounded at the sight of green paper and gray metal, you'll just have to reach for the more familiar 3" x 2" card.

- **American Express**, 800-528-4800, www.americanexpress.com; once famous for issuing charge cards that must be paid off every month, American Express now offers nearly two dozen different cards, including credit cards and airline affinity cards that help you accumulate frequent-flyer miles. With the exception of a student card, all Amex cards have minimum income requirements, and all but the Optima True Grace Card charge annual fees.

- **Diner's Club**, 800-234-6377, www.dinersclub.com; with annual fees and income requirements, the Diner's Club card is accepted mainly in travel and hospitality circles; cardholders have access to special amenities at most major airports.
- **Discover/Novus**, 800-347-2683, www.discovercard.com; Discover cards and affiliated Novus/Private Issue cards give you an annual rebate based on the amount you charge, and some plans let you accumulate credit at various hotels or retail chains.
- **VISA**, www.visa.com; **MasterCard**, www.mastercard.com; almost all banks issue VISA and MasterCard credit cards, but so do airlines, long distance companies, magazines, car manufacturers, professional associations, charities, and retailers. Competition is fierce not just for interest rates or low fees, but for fringe benefits, from long distance minutes to dollars donated to charity in your name—so it pays to shop around, especially if you don't pay off your balance every month. Most purchases made with these cards are automatically insured against loss or damage. You can also buy prepaid **VISABuxx** cards that work like cash but give you the convenience of a credit card number, useful for online and phone purchases.
- **Department stores**: most department stores and other major retail chains issue charge cards, sometimes with lines of credit. Usually these accounts are issued automatically and instantly if you already have a VISA or MasterCard account. Store charge accounts may have lower fees, or none, and lower interest rates than major credit cards; and perks may include advance notice of sales, access to special services, and cardholder discounts.

BANKING & CREDIT RESOURCES

For a list of articles about trends in banking, and links to the Federal Trade Commission and other consumer protection agencies, visit the **National Institute for Consumer Education** web site at www.nice.emich.edu. To look up current interest rates on deposits, check out **www.rate.net** or **www.bankrate.com**. **CardWeb**, www.cardweb.com, is an online directory of credit cards; search or browse by interest rates, fees, special offers, or affinity features such as frequent-flyer miles or charity donations based on the amount you charge. The same information can be retrieved by phone at 800-344-7714.

If you're buying a car or boat, renovating your new fixer-upper, or sending the kids to college, you can still shop for loans the old-fashioned way, using the Yellow Pages and the financial section of the newspaper, but the internet can make the job a lot easier. Online loan calculators let you experiment with different payment plans—check out **www.loanlizzard.com**, **www.411-loans.com**, **www.eloan.com**, and **http://financialpowertools.com**, just for example. You can also find the current interest rates at dozens of local financial institutions at a glance using **www.interest.com/washington_dc**.

Visit the personal finance section of **www.epinions.com** for customer reviews of specific institutions' credit cards. You can obtain copies of your credit report from the three major credit bureaus at **www.icreditreport.com** for a small fee. Avoid ordering your credit report more than once a year, though—frequent requests could negatively affect your credit rating.

TAXES

SALES TAX

The D.C. sales tax is 5.75% on consumer goods and 14.5% on hotel bills—a surtax to pay for the MCI Center and the new Washington Convention Center under construction as this book goes to press. Groceries are not taxed. The sales tax on restaurant bills is 10%.

In Maryland, the sales tax is 5%, with no tax on groceries other than snack foods (a gray area, perhaps, but generally it's a chips-and-pretzels tax). In Montgomery County, soft drinks are subject to sales tax, and some soda bottles are labeled "$.99, $1.03 in Mont. Co." Virginia sales tax is 4.5% in most jurisdictions, 4.4% in Arlington County and 4.75% in Alexandria. The sales tax on hotel bills varies from 9% to 12% by county.

Many local jurisdictions are experimenting with a designated "Back to School Week," suspending the sales tax for up to nine days in August. Since these are pilot programs, watch your local newspaper for details.

FEDERAL INCOME TAX

D.C. license plates bear the sarcastic motto "Taxation Without Representation," a reminder that District residents pay federal income tax but do not have a vote in the Congress that levies the income tax and decides how to spend it. While some residents would be more than willing to pay their fair share in exchange for equal representation, others would gladly do without representation in exchange for tax breaks.

Federal, District, and state tax forms are available at any library or post office, but don't wait until April 14—indeed, such places may run out of the more common forms by early March, and may not have more esoteric forms at all. Most libraries do have a book of tax forms available for photocopying. Fortunately, you now live in the same city as the IRS, and you can always drop by and pick up tax forms from the belly of the beast: IRS headquarters at 1111 Constitution Avenue NW. You can also **download tax forms** at www.irs.gov, order them by mail at 800-829-3676, or have them faxed to you by calling 703-368-9694.

Don't be afraid to call the IRS and ask for help. You may be placed on hold for a long time, but you will get your questions answered by a real person. The IRS Tax Help Line is 800-829-1040, and at 800-829-4477, you can hear a variety of recordings to help you. Of course, there are plenty of accountants listed in the Yellow Pages and, under "Tax Return Preparation," you'll find dozens of firms, including the giants: H&R Block, www.hrblock.com, and Jackson Hewitt, www.jacksonhewitt.com, specializing in federal tax filings and high-interest instant cash advances against your expected tax refund.

STATE INCOME TAX

The Chief Financial Officer of the District of Columbia issues an annual report on tax rates and tax burdens, comparing the District to the largest cities in each state. The 1999 report showed D.C.'s taxes to be the 13th highest of the 51 cities profiled, and 6.6% above the national average.

Most cities this size—the District's population is around 572,000—have a reciprocal tax agreement with the state, allowing the city to collect income tax from suburbanites who work in the city, but the D.C. Home Rule Charter, granted by Congress in 1973, expressly prohibits any form of "commuter tax." So if you live in one jurisdiction and work in another, your employer is required to withhold income taxes for the state or territory where you live.

As with federal tax forms, most of the filing materials you'll need are available at your local library or government office. In addition, the District and both neighboring states offer online tax filing options, electronic transfer of tax payments and refunds, forms by mail or download, and extensive taxpayer assistance on the web.

- **D.C. Chief Financial Officer**, 202-727-2476, www.cfo.washingtondc.gov
- **Maryland Comptroller of the Treasury**, 800-MD-TAXES, http://individuals.marylandtaxes.com
- **Virginia Department of Taxation**, 804-367-8031 (information), 888-268-2829 (forms), www.tax.state.va.us

ONLINE FILING & ASSISTANCE

Filing your taxes online can save you time, especially if you already keep your personal financial records software such as TurboTax or MacInTax.

Visit www.irs.gov/elec_svs for details, including a list of companies that make tax software.

If your taxable income is $50,000 or less and you are not self-employed, you may be eligible to file your federal taxes by touch-tone phone—visit www.irs.gov/elec_svs or call 800-829-1040 to find out.

Visit **www.taxhelponline.com**, **www.taxresources.com**, or **www.taxlinks.com** for answers to practically any question about federal taxes—or go straight to the extensive **IRS help page** at www.irs.gov/tax_edu. From instructions for filing federal Form 1040EZ to the minutiae of Executive Order 13084, "Consultation and Coordination with Indian Tribal Governments," this site probably has the answer.

STARTING OR MOVING A BUSINESS

Washington is, let's face it, the world's leading manufacturer of red tape, and it's no surprise that the city government has a long and justified reputation as a bureaucratic labyrinth. The permits and fees involved in setting up a business in D.C. are enough to keep a special breed of lawyers busy: "expediters" are educated errand runners who know their way around the D.C. Department of Consumer & Regulatory Affairs (DCRA). In recent years, the District has made a conscious effort to streamline the DCRA experience. Unless you're trying to build an eight-story hotel, you won't need to hire an expediter. If you start a small business, just go to the DCRA office at 941 North Capitol Street NE and plan to spend a few hours there. Business license applications can be downloaded from the DCRA site, www.dcra.org.

INCORPORATION

- **D.C. Department of Consumer & Regulatory Affairs**, 202-727-1000, www.dcra.org
- **Maryland Department of Assessments & Taxation**, 888-246-5941 or 410-767-1340, www.dat.state.md.us
- **Virginia State Corporation Commission**, 800-552-7945 or 804-371-9967, www.state.va.us/scc
- **Internal Revenue Service**, 800-829-1040, www.irs.gov (for employer ID number)

BUSINESS & PROFESSIONAL LICENSING

- **D.C. Department of Consumer & Regulatory Affairs**, 202-727-1000, www.dcra.org
- **Maryland Department of Labor, Licensing & Regulation**, 888-218-5925 or 410-230-6231, www.dllr.state.md.us

- **Virginia Department of Professional & Occupational Regulation**, 804-367-8500

ECONOMIC DEVELOPMENT AGENCIES

- **D.C. Office of the Deputy Mayor for Planning & Economic Development**, 202-727-6365, www.dcbiz.dc.gov
- **Maryland Business Information Network**, 800-541-8549, www.mdbusiness.state.md.us
- **Virginia Economic Development Partnership**, 804-371-8100, www.yesvirginia.org
- **Small Business Administration**, US Department of Commerce, www.sba.gov

CHAMBERS OF COMMERCE

County and municipal chambers of commerce are listed in the *Washington Business Journal Book of Lists*, available at most public libraries or for sale at www.bizjournals.com/washington, 703-875-2200. The *Business Journal* also publishes an annual supplement dedicated to corporate relocation and market statistics.

NOW THAT YOU'VE FOUND THE HOME OF YOUR DREAMS, OR AT least a place to hang your hat, you'll need to get your utility accounts arranged, including phone, electricity, water, and perhaps gas. If you have a car, you'll need to get it registered and apply for a new driver's license. Other items of business may include getting an internet service provider and a library card, finding a physician, hooking up cable or satellite TV, subscribing to a newspaper; and, if you've brought Fido, getting a dog license and finding a vet. Read on.

UTILITIES

ELECTRICITY

Two public electric utility companies serve the Washington area, and private competition is on its way. The public utilities don't charge hookup fees, and unless your home is brand new and barely finished, you can have your power turned on almost immediately when you call to set up your account.

In D.C. and suburban Maryland, the public utility is the **Potomac Electric Power Company**, Pepco for short. Call 202-833-7500 or visit www.pepco.com. In Virginia, the local utility is **Dominion Virginia Power**, 703-934-9660 or www.dom.com.

In the District and Maryland, residents are now allowed to choose an electric power producer; Virginia will finish phasing in a similar policy by 2004. Pepco will still be the sole distributor supplying power to homes and maintaining power lines, but residents can purchase electricity—delivered through the common grid—from a growing number of licensed energy producers. The electric industry expects that consumers will have a choice of power companies that offer cheap energy, energy from renewable sources, or the opportunity to save money through a community purchasing co-op or "aggregator." At the time of publication, the only electricity producer competing with Pepco was **Washington Gas Energy Services**, 888-236-9437 or www.wges.com.

As with long distance carriers, you have legal protection if your electric company is changed without your consent. If a private electric company fails to deliver, the public utility will automatically supply your power without interruption.

Check with your public service commission, listed below, for the current list of licensed electric companies. In Virginia, visit www.yesvachoice.com for updates on utility deregulation.

NATURAL GAS

Many houses and apartments in Washington do not use gas at all; some have a gas stove but an electric water heater and electric heat. At the other extreme, a few townhouses in Georgetown and off Dupont Circle still have working gaslights, gas heat, and clothes dryers. As with electricity, natural gas deregulation in the late 1990s opened the door to private competition, providing alternatives to consumers. The public utility, which serves the entire Washington area, is **Washington Gas**, www.washgas.com. Call 703-750-1000 to have gas service activated. There are no hookup fees, unless you are converting electric amenities to gas—in which case you will need to have a serviceman come to your house. Natural gas deregulation is a few years ahead of electricity, and there are several alternative gas companies doing business in the District and suburbs including **PowerChoice/Pepco Energy Services**, 800-ENERGY-9, www.powerchoice.com/residential, and **Washington Gas Energy Services**, 888-236-9437, www.wges.com.

Before you do any digging or building on your property, call the **"Miss Utility" hotline** at 800-257-7777 to have the gas company mark the location of buried gas lines.

TELEPHONE

Verizon, formerly known as Bell Atlantic, provides most of D.C.'s local phone service, although Starpower, Qwest, and a growing array of newcomers are in the local market as well. Verizon, www.verizon.com, provides basic residential phone service for about $20 a month including taxes. The company also offers optional services, for a fee, such as call waiting, caller ID, voice-mail, and call forwarding. All features are explained in the Customer Guide section of the local White Pages. Verizon requires first-time customers to pay a $50 security deposit, refunded with interest (or credited to your account) after one year. If your home is already wired to suit your needs, you'll only need to call to have service activated; if you need a Verizon technician to do any wiring, you will be charged for the time and labor.

To start or stop Verizon service, be prepared to spend about 20 minutes with an agent when you call:

- **D.C.**, 202-346-1000
- **Maryland**, 301-954-6260
- **Virginia**, 703-876-7000

Competition in the local phone service market is aimed mostly at business customers, but a few companies provide residential lines; look in the Yellow Pages under "Telecommunications Companies" or check the Public Service Commission's web site, www.dcpsc.org. Companies providing residential phone service in the Washington area include:

- **Capital Telecom**, 800-673-2400, www.captel.com
- **Close Call America**, 800-845-2215, www.closecallamerica.com
- **Qwest**, 800-860-2255, www.qwest.net
- **RCN**, 888-782-7313, www.rcn.com
- **Verizon Avenue**, 866-892-8368, www.onepointcom.com

AREA CODES

There are certain complications that come with a territory that spans two states and a federal colony. If you come from a place where phone numbers have only seven digits, you'll need to get used to area codes: even local calls require an area code here.

The District has only one area code, **202**. In Maryland, area codes **301** and **240** are both used in areas west of the Patuxent River, from the Washington suburbs to the mountains of Western Maryland, and the area code alone does not reveal whether a Maryland number is a long-distance call from Washington. Gaithersburg to the north and Waldorf to the south are the approximate limits of the local calling area, although some residents and most businesses throughout neighboring counties pay extra to have a metro-area phone number. In Virginia, area code **703** covers the suburbs and not much else. Beyond the suburbs, Virginia uses area codes **540** to the west and **804** to the south; in Maryland, area codes **410** and **443** are found to the east.

Within the Washington area, you must always dial the area code if it is different from your own, even if it's a local call. (In some parts of Maryland, but not yet in the immediate suburbs, you have to dial the area code for all calls, period.)

LONG DISTANCE CARRIERS

The competition among major long distance companies is so intense that some industrious consumers have actually made money by changing carriers every few weeks, taking advantage of the latest rebates, incentives, and bonuses. If you don't plan to make a hobby of juggling long distance promotions, though, you'll want to read the fine print and choose your service carefully. For a helpful comparison of long distance and wireless services, from an independent clearinghouse not funded by the telecommunications industry, contact the **Telecommunications Research and Action Center** at 202-263-2950 or www.trac.org.

The major long-distance players in the Washington market include:

- **AT&T**, 800-222-0300, www.att.com
- **MCI WorldCom**, 800-950-5555, www.mci.com
- **Cable & Wireless**, 888-454-4264, www.cw.com
- **Sprint**, 800-877-7746, www.sprint.com
- **Verizon**, 800-343-2092, www.verizon.net
- **Winstar**, 888-WINSTAR, www.winstar.com

Working Assets Long Distance, 800-788-0898, www.workingfor-change.com, donates a percentage of your long distance bill to environmental and human rights groups and, although you won't be needing it here, the company gives free long distance time to customers calling their federal lawmakers.

Every convenience store and corner market sells **prepaid calling cards** in denominations of $5 to $25, some claiming rates of 1.2 cents a minute. These rates apply to actual talking time, though—with dialing charges and a surcharge for using a pay phone, a lot of short calls will deplete the card quickly. Still, it's cheaper than most long distance carriers, and the only catch is that the local number you dial to access your prepaid long distance account might give you an occasional busy signal.

You can also make domestic long distance calls for free using your computer through www.dialpad.com. The sound quality is generally not as good as a phone, but hey, it's free. And you can compare long distance plans and rates online at http://abtolls.com, www.e-wizdom.com, or www.saveonphone.com.

Occasionally, you may find that your long distance carrier has been changed without your consent—an illegal, but common, practice known as slamming. Or you might suspect that your chosen long distance company has been cramming your bill with charges for special features you did not order or calls you did not make. You are not liable for these charges, but cases of slamming or cramming can be difficult to straighten out; try to protect yourself before it happens. Ask your local phone company to "freeze" your chosen long distance carrier so it cannot be changed without your authorization. If you are slammed by a carrier that has a billing agreement with your local phone company, usually the phone company will back you up and refuse to collect the disputed amount from you. Read the Customer Guide section of the White Pages and understand what features you have requested and which you have declined; if you're billed for additional features, such as voice mail or caller ID, call the customer service number on your phone bill. If a problem persists, contact the appropriate agency listed in the Utility Complaints section of this chapter.

WIRELESS PHONES AND PAGING SERVICES

A modern convenience, considered a necessity by many, some people never turn off their cell phones; even state dinners at the White House have been interrupted by the familiar chirp. A few area restaurants are trying to enforce a "no cell phones" policy, but it's almost like asking people to check their left arm at the door.

"Cell phone" has become a casual term that encompasses satellite-based digital wireless phones as well as true cellular phones whose radio signals are relayed from one local antenna to the next. As with long distance service, competition is fierce and promotional deals vary every week. Check the ads in the *Washington City Paper* or the Sunday advertising supplement to the *Washington Post,* or visit www.point.com, an online retailer of wireless phones and service. Most plans include a certain amount of airtime each month and charge by the minute if you exceed that time; some offer free long distance or free airtime at night and on weekends. Beware of "roaming" charges that add up quickly if you use your phone outside a designated home calling area. Long-term contracts often offer the best rates, but have hefty cancellation fees if you change services before your contract expires. If you want to avoid long contracts, deposits, and credit checks, you can get prepaid wireless service from one of the regular wireless companies or by buying prepaid cellular calling cards, available at many convenience stores and drugstores. However, in addition to paying slightly higher rates with a prepaid calling card, you don't get a permanent wireless phone number.

- **AT&T Wireless Service**, 800-IMAGINE, www.attws.com
- **Cingular**, 866-CINGULAR, www.cingular.com
- **Metrocall**, 703-660-6677, http://storefront.metrocall.com
- **Nextel**, 800-NEXTEL9, www.nextel.com
- **Verizon Wireless**, retail stores at 1304 G Street NW, 202-624-0072; 1744 L Street NW, 202-296-4400; for other locations and online shopping, see www.verizonwireless.com.
- **VMC Communications**, 301-261-2165 or 703-532-9100
- **VoiceStream Wireless** (prepaid plans only), 800-937-8997, www.voicestream.com

- **Sprint PCS**, retail store at 1208 18th Street NW, 202-496-9400, for other locations and online shopping, see www.sprintpcs.com.

INTERNET SERVICE PROVIDERS

Exploring your new environs can be much easier with the help of the web. You can track down store hours, learn about community organizations, manage your financial accounts, and shop at midnight, all from the convenience of your own home. And keeping in touch with friends and family via e-mail is easy and less expensive than using the phone for long-distance calls. Here are some of the major internet service providers in the area:

- **America Online**, 800-827-6364, www.aol.com
- **AT&T WorldNet**, 800-967-5363, www.att.net
- **Earthlink**, 800-EARTHLINK, www.earthlink.net
- **Erol's**, 888-GO-EROLS, www.erols.com
- **Juno Online Services**, 800-879-5866, www.juno.com
- **Microsoft Network**, 800-426-9400, www.msn.com
- **RCN**, 888-782-7313, www.rcn.com
- **SmartNet Internet Services**, 301-470-3400, www.smart.net
- **Verizon Internet**, 800-NET-2026, www.bellatlantic.net

Also, you can surf for free (in 15-minute time slots) at most public libraries, at Kramerbooks & Afterwords (see **Cultural Life**), or Lakeforest Mall's Internet Room (see **Shopping for the Home**). Or you can rent computer time at one of the following:

- **Atomic Grounds**, 1555 Wilson Boulevard, Arlington, 703-524-2157
- **CyberStop Cafe**, 1513 17th Street NW, 202-234-2470
- **Interactive Cybercafe US**, 1217 22nd Street NW, 202-861-5858
- **Kinko's**, dozens of locations, 888-457-4357, www.kinkos.com

WATER

In the District, water and sewer bills are addressed to "occupant"—so you don't need to set up an account, just make sure service is turned on. The **D.C. Water & Sewer Authority** distributes water from Army Corps of Engineers reservoirs—mainly the Dalecarlia Reservoir near the western tip of the District, fed by an underground aqueduct from the Potomac River. The McMillan Reservoir, near Howard University, and the Georgetown Reservoir provide backup during dry spells.

Most residents of suburban Maryland get their water from the Triadelphia Reservoir, impounded by Brighton Dam, and the T. Howard Duckett Reservoir, impounded by Rocky Gorge Dam, both on the Patuxent River. The Virginia suburbs draw their water from the Potomac and

Occoquan rivers—except Arlington, which buys water from the same Corps of Engineers division that supplies water to the District.

The dry summer of 1999 caught the Washington area off guard, and local jurisdictions have developed contingency plans for water restrictions in the event of a drought. During a moderate dry spell, authorities will call for voluntary limits on the use of water for lawn care and car washing; if conditions get worse, such activities might be limited to certain days or even prohibited.

Call the local water utility to start service:

- **District of Columbia**: D.C. Water & Sewer Authority, 202-354-3600, www.dcwasa.com
- **Maryland**: Washington Suburban Sanitary Commission, 301-206-4001 or 800-634-8400, www.wssc.dst.md.us
- **Arlington County**: Department of Public Works, 703-228-3636, www.co.arlington.va.us/dpw
- **Fairfax County**: Fairfax County Water Authority, 703-698-5800, www.fcwa.org
- **Alexandria**: Virginia-American Water Co., 703-549-7080; www.vawc.com/alex
- **Falls Church**: Public Utilities Division, 703-248-5071, www.ci.falls-church.va.us

Each of these utilities issues an annual report on water quality, available online or by mail. Tap water in D.C. is always nasty tasting and occasionally dangerous—in the late 1990s, the EPA issued several "boil water" alerts, fearing unlawfully high levels of cryptosporidium. The official advisories have been lifted, but many residents—especially those with young children, the elderly, or those with compromised immune systems—rely on bottled water or water filters. In the suburbs, the tap water is generally better, though Brita filters are popular throughout the region. These inexpensive filters remove the taste and odor of chlorine, which can be strong at times, but they don't eliminate most pollutants.

Heavy-duty water filters that remove almost all microbes, lead, chlorine, and other toxic trace elements from tap water are available by mail from Gaiam, 800-869-3446 or www.gaiam.com, or Real Goods, 800-762-7325 or www.realgoods.com, and area department stores carry a few models.

For information about local water utilities, including a record of violations and enforcement actions, call the Safe Drinking Water Hotline, a joint project of the EPA and the Centers for Disease Control, at 800-426-4791 or visit www.epa.gov/safewater. The office also publishes consumer pamphlets and factsheets on home filtration systems, home water testing, conservation tips, and the Safe Drinking Water Act of 1974.

If you have doubts about the quality of your tap water, you can buy testing kits at large hardware stores or look in the Yellow Pages under "Laboratories-Testing." Test kits—and advice for improving test results—are also available from the non-profit **Water Quality Association**, 800-749-0234 or www.wqa.org.

If you prefer to have bottled water delivered on a weekly or monthly basis, call:

- **Aqua Cool**, 800-649-PURE, www.ionics.com
- **Crystal Spring**, 800-444-PURE, www.crystalspringswater.com
- **Culligan**, 800-626-3942, www.culligan.com
- **Deer Park**, 800-759-7375, www.deerparkwater.com
- **Snow Valley**, 800-766-9426, www.snowh20.com

CONSUMER PROTECTION–UTILITY COMPLAINTS

Public utility companies providing electricity, natural gas, water, and local telephone service are regulated by the state or D.C. public service commission. These commissions set maximum rates, investigate consumer complaints, and license alternative service providers setting up to compete with public utilities. If you have a question or concern that the utility company cannot resolve, contact:

- **Public Service Commission of the District of Columbia**, 202-626-5100, www.dcpsc.org
- **Maryland Public Service Commission**, 410-767-8028 or 800-492-0474, www.psc.state.md.us/psc
- **Virginia State Corporations Commission**, 804-371-9141 or 800-552-7945, www.state.va.us/scc

The **D.C. Office of People's Counsel**, 202-727-3071 or www.dcpsc.org, handles consumer complaints about proposed rate increases and other changes in utility service.

If you have a billing dispute with your **long distance provider**, and your local phone company cannot help, the next step is to file a complaint with the **Federal Communications Commission** at 888-225-5322, www.fcc.gov, or the **Federal Trade Commission** at 202-382-4357, www.ftc.gov.

The following agencies oversee **cable TV providers**:

- **D.C. Office of Cable Television & Telecommunications**, 202-671-0066
- **Montgomery County Office of Cable Communications**, 240-777-3636; e-mail preferred, catv.complaints@co.mo.md.us
- **Prince George's County Cable Television Commission**, 301-952-3990
- **Arlington County Cable Administrator**, 703-228-3969

- **Fairfax County Department of Telecommunications & Consumer Services**, 703-222-8435
- **Alexandria Cable TV complaints line**, 703-838-4533

If you have a problem with a local business, see the **Consumer Resources** section in the **Shopping for the Home** chapter and **Consumer Protection** in **Helpful Services**; for landlord or property issues, check the chapter on **Finding a Place to Live**.

GARBAGE, RECYCLING, COMPOSTING

Except in a few outlying suburbs where you actually take your trash to a local dump, Washington area trash collection is a county or city service. If you live in an apartment, your landlord or condo association will arrange for trash and recycling pickup. In most D.C. neighborhoods, each house is issued a sturdy plastic "Supercan"—a big trashcan on wheels—owned by the Department of Public Works. In some neighborhoods, trash and recycling are collected in a back alley, and in others at the front curb; just ask a neighbor, or see where people keep their trashcans and recycling bins.

In some suburban cities and towns, trash and recycling are collected by a municipal service rather than the county agency; to find out, call the municipal phone number listed in the **Useful Phone Numbers and Web Sites** chapter. Some suburban jurisdictions provide trashcans; in others you'll need to buy a trashcan with a lid to keep out rats and raccoons as well as neighborhood dogs. Most jurisdictions provide plastic bins or color-coded plastic bags for recyclables.

Unfortunately the Washington area is not one of the parts of the country where households are charged by the bag or the pound for trash pickup. Here homeowners pay for waste management as a percentage of their property taxes, regardless of their efforts to reduce, reuse, and recycle. However, almost all jurisdictions in the Washington area have mandatory curbside recycling, and provide bins for your glass, cans, and plastic containers. These may be commingled in the same bin, and you do not need to sort glass by color. Newspapers are collected separately, and must be bundled with twine or in paper grocery bags; in some jurisdictions, cardboard, magazines, junk mail, and other mixed paper are also collected at curbside.

Call the following agencies for details about recyclables, and to find out when trash and recyclables are collected in your neighborhood:

- **D.C. Department of Public Works**, 202-727-1000, www.washingtondc.gov
- **Montgomery County Solid Waste Services Division**, 240-777-6410, www.dpwt.com/SolWstSvcDiv

- **Prince George's County Department of Environmental Resources**, 301-952-7630, www.goprincegeorgescounty.com; recycling: 301-883-5045
- **Arlington County Department of Environmental Services**, 703-228-6570, www.co.arlington.va.us/des
- **Fairfax County Department of Public Works & Environmental Services**, 703-550-3481, www.co.fairfax.va.us/dpwes; recycling: 703-324-5052
- **Alexandria Division of Solid Waste**, 703-751-5130, www.ci.alex-andria.va.us/solidwaste

The same solid waste agencies collect raked leaves in the fall. In some areas, leaves must be bagged; in others, vacuum trucks sweep up the piles raked to the curb. Christmas trees are collected at curbside in early January in most jurisdictions. Montgomery County encourages you to compost lawn clippings—for information about the "grasscycling" program, call the County Department of Environmental Protection at 240-777-7700 or visit www.co.mo.md.us/services/dep. Call your solid waste agency to arrange special trash pickups for unusually large quantities or bulky items that cannot be recycled.

In all jurisdictions, backyard composting of kitchen scraps (vegetable matter only) is allowed, as long as neighbors don't complain of a nuisance. A properly managed compost pile does not smell bad or attract pests, but the compost pile must be properly aerated and maintained—as with yard waste composting, the Montgomery County DEP web site is a good source of advice. Helpful tools and ready-made compost bins are available at larger hardware stores, or by mail from Gaiam and Real Goods (see the section on **Water** above). City dwellers without yards might consider indoor composting, letting worms turn kitchen scraps into soil in a specially designed bin. Instructional booklets, bins, and industrious worms are available by mail from Gardens Alive, 812-537-8651, www.gardensalive.com.

DRIVER'S LICENSE, NON-DRIVER'S ID

If you expect the Department of Motor Vehicles to greet you with long lines and inefficient, complicated paperwork, you won't be disappointed. However, D.C. residents are finding DMV lines moving faster than they once did, and in Maryland express offices handle routine license renewals, so you only need to go to a full-service office for a new license or vehicle registration. DMV offices also issue official photo ID cards ("non-driver's ID") for residents not licensed to drive. These IDs are not mandatory, but they are universally accepted as a substitute for a driver's license for identification and proof of age.

New residents of D.C., Maryland, and Virginia have 30 days to obtain a local driver's license and vehicle registration. If your current out-of-state or foreign driver's license has not expired, you can get a local license without taking a road test or a written test if your previous state or country offers registration reciprocity with your new jurisdiction. Just bring your current license and proof of residence, such as a recent utility bill, voter registration card, or a copy of your lease or mortgage statement; in Maryland and Virginia, you will also need to bring an official copy of your birth certificate. In the District, if you have any unpaid parking tickets or other administrative debts of more than $100, you will have to pay them in order to get a driver's license. Then you just take an eye test and pay a fee. If your previous state or country does not have reciprocity with your new jurisdiction, you may have to take a road test, a written test, or both. All area DMV offices provide free booklets covering local traffic laws.

If you do not have a current driver's license, you will have to get a learner's permit and schedule a road test at a later date. To obtain a learner's permit bring an official photo ID or your embossed birth certificate, proof of residence, and your original social security card; a bank statement, IRS document, or pay stub bearing your social security number will suffice in place of your social security card. You must also pass a written test and eye test, and pay the fee. And you provide your own vehicle for the road test; the learner's permit does not allow you to drive alone, so you will need to be accompanied by a licensed driver.

To obtain an ID card, you'll need to show proof of identity—a comparable card from another state, a birth certificate, a passport, or military ID—and pay a small fee.

In D.C., the fee for a driver's license is $30; a learner's permit or non-driver's ID is $15. In Maryland, the fee is $30 for a license, $45 for a learner's permit, and $10 for ID. In Virginia, the driver's license fee is $2.50 per year (your license will expire on your birthday the next time your age is divisible by 5), $3 for a learner's permit, and $5 for ID.

DRIVER'S LICENSE OFFICES

- **D.C. Department of Motor Vehicles**, 202-727-5000, http://dmv.washingtondc.gov:
    - 301 C Street NW, Room 1157, open weekdays 8:15 a.m. to 4 p.m., Wednesdays until 7 p.m. (least crowded before 10 a.m. and between 2 and 4 p.m.)
    - RFK Stadium Lot 8, 1910 Independence Avenue SE, weekdays, 8:15 a.m. to 4 p.m.
    - 616 H Street NE (license renewals and vehicle registration only), weekdays 11 a.m. to 4 p.m., Wednesdays until 7 p.m., Saturdays 8:15 a.m. to 3:30 p.m.

- **Maryland Motor Vehicle Administration**, 800-950-1682, www.mva.state.md.us; offices are open weekdays 8:30 a.m. to 4:30 p.m. and, for driver's license services only, Saturdays 8:30 a.m. to noon:
  - 15 Metropolitan Grove Road, Gaithersburg
  - 11760 Baltimore Avenue, Beltsville
  - 10251 Central Avenue, Largo
- **Virginia Department of Motor Vehicles**, 866-DMV-LINE, www.dmv.state.va.us; offices are open weekdays 8:30 a.m. to 5:30 p.m.; Saturdays, 8:30 a.m. to 12:30 p.m.:
  - 2681 Mill Road, Alexandria
  - 6306 Grovedale Drive, Alexandria
  - 4150 South Four Mile Run Drive, Arlington
  - 1968 Gallows Road, Vienna
  - 14950 Northridge Drive, Chantilly

OWNING A CAR

AUTOMOBILE REGISTRATION

Visit the same DMV office you used to register your vehicle within 30 days after your arrival. You will need to show the title, proof of insurance, and proof of a safety inspection; you'll be charged a registration fee, and a one-time excise tax based on the vehicle's book value.

In **D.C.**, there is only one inspection facility, and lines are long. It's located at 1001 Half Street SW, open weekdays 6 a.m. to 7 p.m. (8 p.m. in the summer), and Saturdays, 7 a.m. to 3 p.m. It's least crowded weekdays, 4 to 7 p.m. (Certain lanes are reserved for senior citizens on the third Tuesday of each month from 7 to 11 a.m.) The excise tax is six percent of the book value for vehicles weighing under 3,500 pounds, and seven percent for those weighing more. Vehicle weight also determines the registration fee: $55 for vehicles under 3,500 pounds; $88 for vehicles of 3,500 pounds or more. Along with the registration fee, you will be charged $10 for the inspection and $10 for a residential parking permit. You may choose to register your vehicle for two years—doubling each of these amounts. Minimum insurance coverage is $50,000 for bodily injury, $10,000 for property damage, and $25,000 for third-party and uninsured motorist liability. Note: You must convert your old driver's license to a D.C. license before you register a vehicle in the District. For more information, call the DMV at 202-727-5000.

The excise tax in **Maryland** is five percent of the vehicle's book value. Safety inspections are performed at service stations or repair shops displaying a state-issued sign marking it as an authorized inspection station; in addition, your car will need to pass an emissions test. **Emissions test stations** are open weekdays, 7 a.m. to 7 p.m., Saturdays, 7 a.m. to 1 p.m. Locations are:

- 2121 Industrial Parkway, White Oak (off US Route 29 near New Hampshire Avenue)
- 7407 Lindbergh Drive, Gaithersburg (central Montgomery County)
- 15910 Chieftain Avenue, Derwood (northern Montgomery County)
- 7213 Old Alexandria Ferry Road, Clinton (near Andrews Air Force Base)
- 7401 Jefferson Avenue, Glenarden (near the Beltway and US Route 50)

In Maryland, minimum insurance coverage is $20,000 for bodily injury (one person), $40,000 for bodily injury (two or more people), and $15,000 for property damage; personal injury, $2,500. For more information, call the MVA at 301-948-3177.

In **Virginia**, any authorized service station can perform an emissions test; call 703-583-3900 or 800-275-3844 for locations. Testing fees vary, but the DMV says they "should not" exceed $20. The excise tax is three percent of the sale price of the car or $35, whichever is greater, and there is a $10 registration fee. Minimum insurance coverage: $25,000 for bodily injury or death of one person; $50,000 for bodily injury or death of two or more persons; and $20,000 for property damage. For more information, call the DMV at 703-761-4655.

Don't have time to stand in line? See **Automobiles** in **Helpful Services** for a list of companies that, for a fee, will send someone to the DMV in your stead.

LOCAL REGISTRATION & PARKING PERMITS

And you thought you were done! In Virginia, you have to register your vehicle with the county as well as the state, and some municipalities in Maryland require you to buy a residential parking decal. (See the **Useful Phone Numbers and Web Sites** chapter for county and municipal government phone numbers.) If you live in a subdivision, condominium or apartment complex, check with the property manager about parking permits for yourself and your guests.

In Virginia, you will receive a local registration decal as a receipt for payment of the tax on your car. Contact the local tax authority to pay for your registration decals in person or by mail—or, if you're on active duty in the armed services, to get your tax-exempt decals:

- **Arlington County** vehicle registration decals cost $24/year, payable to the Treasurer of Arlington County at 2100 Clarendon Boulevard, Suite 200. You can register by mail if you do not have any unpaid parking tickets or property tax bills, and if you are not a diplomat or NATO staff member. Vehicles owned solely by US military personnel on active duty are exempt; you will need to mail in photocopies of your military ID and transfer orders. Call 703-228-3135 or download a form at www.co.arlington.va.us/cor/register.

- **Fairfax County** vehicle registration decals cost $25/year for most passenger vehicles, payable to Fairfax County, Department of Tax Administration, 12000 Government Center Parkway, Suite 223, Fairfax, VA 22035. You must register your vehicle within 60 days after moving into the county. Vehicles owned by military or diplomatic personnel are exempt, and decals are free (with payment of property tax) for certain categories of veterans and police, fire and rescue personnel, and for antique cars. Call 703-222-8234 or download a form at www.co.fairfax.va.us/dta.
- **Alexandria** vehicle registration decals cost $25/year for most passenger vehicles, payable to the Alexandria Department of Finance, Revenue Division, P.O. Box 178, Alexandria, VA 22313. You must register your vehicle within 30 days after moving into the city. You can register in person at City Hall, Room 1410; bring your state registration, the title or bill of sale, and your driver's license. To register by mail, call 703-838-4560 or download a form at www.ci.alexandria.va.us/finance/ppapp2.

PARKING

In D.C. and some suburban municipalities, parking tickets are an important source of public revenue. After a bizarre crime wave in the mid-1990s in which hundreds of D.C. parking meters were stolen, the city decided to get out of the meter business, and awarded a contract to Lockheed Martin to replace and maintain the city's parking meters. (Just the meters themselves—tickets are still issued by the Metropolitan Police Department, http://mpdc.dc.gov.) While thousands of D.C. residents have diplomatic immunity and can park wherever they like, the city doesn't miss any opportunity to ticket those who don't have magic "DPL" tags.

If you park at a meter that is malfunctioning, call 202-541-6030 to report the number of the meter. Your license tag number will be recorded, and you will be allowed to remain parked at the broken meter for the maximum amount of time the meter would normally allow. (In such a scenario you might still get a ticket, but by reporting the meter broken you will have a valid defense against it.)

The procedures for paying or contesting a ticket are printed on the back of the citation. You have 15 days to pay or demand a hearing; after that the fine is doubled. After 30 days, the ticket is considered delinquent and you lose the right to contest it; if you have two or more delinquent tickets at any time, your car may be booted, and you will have to pay $50 plus all outstanding tickets in order to get the boot removed.

For more information about parking tickets and paying fines, contact the DMV at 202-727-5000 or http://dmv.washingtondc.gov. In the suburbs, follow the instructions on the ticket if you choose to pay by mail or in person, or if you want to contest the citation. The following jurisdictions also accept payments by phone or online using a credit or debit card:

- **Montgomery County**, www.emontgomery.org
- **Arlington County**, 888-272-9829, www.co.arlington.va.us/treas
- **Alexandria**, 888-872-9829, http://ci.alexandria.va.us/city/tax_guide

PARKING GARAGES & LOTS

Parking in downtown D.C. is an expensive and often difficult proposition, and a compelling incentive to use Metrorail and buses. If you must commute by car, monthly passes are available from parking garages—daily rates can easily run $10, and the "daily" rate can apply to anything longer than two or three hours. If you drive downtown in the evening, skip the commercial lots and look for parking meters—most metered parking spaces are free after 6 p.m. and on weekends.

In D.C., public parking garages are located every few blocks. Here are some major chains—call for locations and monthly rates:

- **Central Parking System**, 202-496-4200
- **Colonial Parking**, 202-295-8100
- **InterParking**, 202-466-4300
- **PMI**, 202-785-9191

TOWING

If your vehicle is towed in D.C., call 202-727-5000 to find its location—usually the Brentwood Impoundment Lot on Brentwood Road off Rhode Island Avenue NE. Before you can retrieve your car, you must pay all outstanding fines plus a towing fee of $75 and a storage fee of $10 per day. Go to the DMV Adjudication Services office, 65 K Street NE, four blocks from Union Station. The office is open weekdays 8:30 a.m. to 6:45 p.m., and until 7:45 p.m. Wednesdays.

The Brentwood lot is open weekdays from 7 a.m. to 8 p.m. Take Metrobus route D8 from Rhode Island Avenue or Union Station, or walk from Rhode Island Avenue Metro station through a desolate industrial park. If your car is registered in the name of your spouse, parent, employer, etc., you must show a notarized statement from the owner authorizing you to pick it up; if the vehicle is leased, you must show the lease.

In the suburbs, call these numbers for instructions:

- **Alexandria Code Enforcement Bureau**, 703-838-4360
- **Arlington County Police**, 703-228-4040
- **Fairfax County Police Traffic Division**, 703-280-0587
- **Montgomery County Police**, 301-840-2454 or 301-279-8000
- **Prince George's County Police**, 301-772-4740

AUTOMOBILE SAFETY

Drunk drivers in D.C., Maryland, and Virginia killed 521 people in 1999. And, according to the National Highway Traffic Safety Administration, in D.C. more than half of all traffic-related deaths in 1999 involved alcohol.

In the District, if convicted of driving while intoxicated (DWI) or driving under the influence of alcohol (DUI), your license will be revoked for at least six months. In Maryland, a first conviction for DWI can result in revocation of your license, fines up to $1,000, and up to a year in jail; a DUI can result in suspension of your license, fines up to $500, and up to 60 days in jail. In Virginia, if you're convicted of an alcohol-related driving offense, you may be ordered to have your vehicle equipped with a special lock that only opens when you pass a Breathalyzer test. Maryland prosecutors are allowed to notify a jury if you refuse to take a Breathalyzer test. And in all three jurisdictions, the DMV can suspend your license through administrative hearings even if you are not convicted in court. The legal threshold for DWI is a blood alcohol content of 0.08 in D.C. and both neighboring states.

All three jurisdictions require federally approved car seats for children, birth to age 4, and the National Safe Kids Campaign recommends using booster seats up to age 8. All drivers and front seat passengers are required to wear seatbelts at all times, and D.C. and Maryland are two of the nation's 11 jurisdictions where seatbelt laws are enforced even in the absence of other violations. Contact the Safe Kids Campaign at 202-662-0600, www.safekids.org, or the National Highway Traffic Safety Administration at www.nhtsa.dot.gov for details about the proper use of passenger restraints.

BUYING AN AUTOMOBILE

The Sunday **Car Pages** in the *Washington Post* are the biggest traditional source for car ads placed by individuals and dealers. The online editions of the *Post*, www.washingtonpost.com, and the *City Paper*, www.washingtoncitypaper.com, are accessible earlier—and searchable by price range and other criteria. Dealers also run photo classifieds in free booklets such as **Harmon Autos** and the **Washington Post AutoBuyers Guide**—look for them in the clusters of newspaper vending boxes at Metro stations and on downtown street corners. The *Washington Consumers' Checkbook* web site, www.checkbook.org, features a biweekly newsletter, **Car Deals**, describing current rebates and incentive programs at area dealerships. If you subscribe to the *Checkbook* (see **Shopping for the Home**), you can download *Car Deals* for free; otherwise, it's $7—a small price to pay to save hundreds, possibly thousands, of dollars on a new vehicle. The web site also offers free tips about auto buying and leasing, mechanics, body shops, and insurance.

Those looking at used cars should call the US Department of Transportation's **Auto Safety Hotline**, 800-424-9393, for information about vehicle recalls. Go to the **Kelley Blue Book** site, www.kbb.com, to check the fair market value of used automobiles. **Autosite**, www.autosite.com, offers up-to-date details about dealer incentives and rebate programs, as well as car specs and book values. For general information about new and used cars, visit **www.edmunds.com** or **www.intellichoice.com**.

See the **Money Matters** chapter for online finance calculators and web sites that list current lending rates at area financial institutions.

VOTER REGISTRATION

Voter register deadlines in the District, Maryland, and Virginia are 30 days prior to any general or primary election. D.C. and Maryland hold closed primaries—in order to vote in a party's primary election, you must be a registered member of that party. In Virginia, voters with no party affiliation may vote in the Democratic or Republican primary.

In each jurisdiction, mail-in voter registration forms are available at libraries, community centers, and other public buildings. You can also register to vote at DMV offices or with your state or local board of elections:

- **D.C. Board of Elections & Ethics**, 202-727-2525, www.dcboee.org
- **Maryland State Board of Elections**, 800-222-8683, www.elections.state.md.us
- **Montgomery County Board of Elections**, 240-777-8500, www.co.mo.md.us/services/elections; 24-hour information line, 240-777-VOTE
- **Prince George's County Board of Elections**, 301-952-3270, www.co.pg.md.us; 24-hour information line, 301-627-2814
- **Virginia State Board of Elections**, 800-552-9745, www.sbe.state.va.us
- **Alexandria Office of Voter Registration**, 703-838-4050, www.alexandriavoter.org
- **Arlington County Registrar of Voters**, 703-228-3456, www.co.arlington.va.us/voters
- **Fairfax County Electoral Board & General Registrar**, 703-222-0776, www.co.fairfax.va.us/eb; 24-hour information line, 703-324-4700

POLITICAL PARTIES

In D.C., there are 38 political parties recognized by the Board of Elections & Ethics; three are officially considered "major" parties and are entitled to hold primaries—the Democratic, Republican, and D.C. Statehood Green parties. (The D.C. Statehood Party and the D.C. Green Party merged in 1999.) In addition, the Umoja, Socialist Workers, and Libertarian parties have placed candidates on the ballot in recent years. In Maryland and Virginia, state election authorities recognize several major and minor parties.

DISTRICT OF COLUMBIA
- **Democratic Party**, 202-554-8790, www.dcdemocrats.org
- **Republican Party**, 202-608-1407, www.dcgop.org
- **D.C. Statehood Green Party**, 202-546-0940, www.dcstatehoodgreen.org
- **Libertarian Party**, 202-636-4277, www.lp-dc.org
- **Socialist Workers Party**, 202-722-6221, www.militant.com
- **Umoja Party**, 202-234-1016

MARYLAND
- **Democratic Party**, 301- 858-8818, www.mddems.org
- **Republican Party**, 410-269-0113, www.mdgop.org
- **Constitution Party**, 877-4TRUTHS, www.goldensquare.net/mdconstitutionparty
- **Green Party**, 301-474-1998, www.enviroweb.org/mdgreens
- **Libertarian Party**, 800-MLP-1776, www.md.lp.org
- **Reform Party**, 301-469-8001

VIRGINIA
- **Democratic Party**, 804-644-1966, www.vademocrats.org
- **Republican Party**, 804-780-0111, www.rpv.org
- **Constitution Party**, 877-4TRUTHS, www.inetresults.com/ustp-va
- **Green Party**, http://organizations.rockbridge.net/greens
- **Libertarian Party**, 800-619-1776, www.lpva.com
- **Natural Law Party**, 703-823-6933, www.va-natural-law.org
- **Reform Party**, 804-780-0111, virginia.reformparty.org

Project Vote Smart tracks the voting records and positions of federal, state, and local officials nationwide. Call 888-VOTE SMART or visit www.votesmart.org. Other web sites useful in comparing candidates include:
- **D.C. Watch**, www.dcwatch.com
- **Center for Responsive Politics**, www.opensecrets.org
- **C-SPAN Online**, www.cspan.org
- **InPolitics**, www.inpolitics.com
- **League of Women Voters**, www.lwv.org
- **www.politics1.com**

Also, since you happen to live in the nation's capital, you can stop by the storefront reading room at Federal Election Commission headquarters,

999 E Street NW, on any business day, and browse campaign finance records on every presidential and congressional candidate, as well as every PAC that gives them money. For more information, call 202-694-1120 or visit www.fec.gov.

PASSPORTS

A routine application for a US passport takes about six weeks. If you are leaving the country within three weeks or you need foreign visas, make an appointment at the **Washington Passport Agency,** 202-647-0518, for special processing. Routine applications are accepted in D.C. at:

- The **Old Post Office** (Ben Franklin Station), 1200 Pennsylvania Avenue NW (weekdays 10 a.m. to 4 p.m.)
- **Friendship Heights Post Office**, 4005 Wisconsin Avenue NW (weekdays 10 a.m. to noon and 1:30 to 6 p.m.)
- **Lamond-Riggs Public Library**, 5401 South Dakota Avenue NE (call for hours: 202-541-6255)
- **Southeast Public Library**, 7th and D streets SE (call for hours: 202-698-3377)
- **West End Public Library**, 24th and L streets NW (call for hours: 202-724-8707)

In the suburbs, most post offices handle routine applications—contact the **Bureau of Consular Affairs** at http://travel.state.gov to find the nearest location. (The bureau no longer accepts phone calls about routine passport procedures. For information by phone, call the **National Passport Information Center** at 888-362-8668 or 900-225-5674. You will be charged $4.95 per call to the 888 number, and the 900 number is 35 cents per minute for recorded information and $1.05 per minute for operator assistance.)

You will need to show proof of citizenship (old US passport, birth certificate, naturalization certificate) and proof of identity (driver's license or other government-issued photo ID). The fee for routine processing is $60 for a new passport ($40 for persons under 16) or $40 for a renewal; for expedited service, the Washington Passport Agency charges an additional $35. You also need to provide two identical photos, 1 3/8" x 1 3/4." For this purpose, practically every camera store, travel agency, and copy shop offers "passport photos"—twin Polaroid pictures taken with a two-chambered camera—for about $10.

In most cases, you can renew a passport by mail—download the application forms and instructions from the Bureau of Consular Affairs site.

LIBRARIES

Library cards are issued free with proof of residence (a current utility bill, a copy of a lease or insurance policy, voter registration card, or ID bearing your address). In some jurisdictions, a parental consent form is required for children obtaining their own cards. The main library in each jurisdiction is listed in the **Literary Life** section of **Cultural Life**, along with private and special-interest libraries; branch locations are included in the neighborhood profiles. If you want to borrow materials from another jurisdiction's library system, your neighborhood librarian can arrange an inter-library loan.

MEDIA

TELEVISION

Many Washingtonians would be lost without CNN and C-SPAN; others are content to watch "The West Wing" and Jim Lehrer for free. In addition to the national broadcast networks, there are several public television stations here, and many residents on high ground or with good antennas can pick up Baltimore and Annapolis broadcasts as well.

LOCAL BROADCAST STATIONS
- **Channel 4**   WRC/NBC
- **Channel 5**   WTTG/FOX
- **Channel 7**   WJLA/ABC
- **Channel 9**   WUSA/CBS
- **Channel 20**   WDCA/UPN
- **Channel 26**   WETA/PBS
- **Channel 32**   WHUT/PBS
- **Channel 50**   WBFF/WB

In the outer suburbs in Maryland, you might also receive Baltimore and Annapolis signals: ABC on Channel 2, NBC on 11, CBS on 13, Maryland Public Television on 32, Fox on 45, and UPN on 54.

CABLE & SATELLITE TV SERVICE
- **District Cablevision**, 202-635-5100
- **Comcast Cable–Montgomery**, 301-424-4400
- **Comcast Cable–Arlington**, 703-841-7700
- **Cox Communications–Fairfax**, 703-378-8400
- **Comcast Cable–Alexandria**, 703-823-3000
- **Jones Communications–Alexandria**, 703-823-3000
- **Starpower Communications** (regional), 703-321-8000

For satellite TV service, call **DirecTV**, 800-237-5988, or **Dish Network**, 800-333-DISH.

Problems with your cable provider? See **Consumer Protection** in this chapter.

RADIO STATIONS

From Amy Goodman to G. Gordon Liddy, and from Chuck D to Berlioz to the Dixie Chicks, there isn't much missing from the radio dial in the Washington area. (With at least 21 hours of bluegrass programming every week, promoting live bluegrass at several acoustic clubs in the area, Washington might actually be the bluegrass capital of the world.) Soon, XM Satellite Radio, with its national headquarters on Eckington Place NE, will sell equipment and services that make it possible to receive hundreds of radio stations from anywhere, by satellite, with consistent CD sound quality—but Washington already has plenty of stations you can hear now, for free, on a $5 radio.

ALTERNATIVE ROCK
- WMUC-FM 88.1
- WHFS-FM 99.1

CHRISTIAN/GOSPEL
- WABS-AM 780
- WAVA-FM 105.1
- WCTN-AM 950
- WFAX-AM 1220
- WFSI-FM 107.9
- WGTS-FM 91.9
- WWGB-AM 1030
- WYCB-AM 1340

CLASSIC ROCK
- WARW-FM 94.7
- WKIK-AM 1560
- WWDC-FM 101.1

CLASSICAL
- WGMS-FM 103.5

CONTEMPORARY POP/TOP 40
- WJMO-FM 99.5
- WRQX-FM 107.3
- WWVZ-FM 103.9
- WWZZ-FM 104.1

COUNTRY
- WFRE-FM 99.9
- WMZQ-FM 98.7
- WXTR-AM 820

ETHNIC
- WACA-AM 1540, Latino
- WBZS-AM 730, Latino
- WDCT-AM 1310, Korean
- WILC-AM 900, Latino
- WKDL-AM 1050, Latino
- WKDM-AM 1600, Latino
- WKDV-AM 1460, Asian
- WUST-AM 1120, international
- WZHF-AM, Chinese

NEWS/TALK
- WWRC-AM 570
- WMAL-AM 630
- WMET-AM 1150
- WOL-AM 1450
- WTOP-AM 1500/FM 107.7

OLDIES
- WBIG-FM 100.3

PUBLIC/NONCOMMERCIAL
- WAMU-FM 88.5, NPR, talk, bluegrass
- WCSP-FM 90.1, C-SPAN
- WETA-FM 90.9, NPR, classical
- WPFW-FM 89.3, Pacifica, jazz

SOFT ROCK/EASY LISTENING
- WJZW-FM 105.9, smooth jazz
- WASH-FM 97.1, soft rock
- WGAY-AM 1260, nostalgia

SPORTS
- WJFK-FM 106.7
- WTEM-AM 980

URBAN CONTEMPORARY
- WHUR-FM 96.3
- WKYS-FM 93.9

- WMMJ-FM 102.3
- WPGC-FM 95.5

NEWSPAPERS & MAGAZINES

Few would dispute that Washington is the news capital of the world, and it's no accident that the Freedom Forum's museum of journalism, the Newseum, is moving from its Rosslyn headquarters to a place of honor between the Capitol and the White House. Indeed, the new site is just a few doors down from the National Archives, where you can go see the First Amendment itself. Naturally, Washingtonians are news junkies—practically everybody reads the *Post* and the free weekly *City Paper*, and many homes and most offices subscribe to more than one newspaper.

- The **Washington Post**, 202-334-6100, www.washingtonpost.com; a necessity, even though many find its local news coverage leaves a lot to be desired. If you're looking for a home, job, car, movie review, restaurant review, or practically any kind of consumer news, the *Post* and the *City Paper* are your two essential stops. The *Post* also offers plenty of original (not canned) coverage of national and world affairs; big, intelligent literary, arts, and opinion sections on Sunday; and four pages of daily comics. Folksy hometown columnist Bob Levey, in the weekday comics pages, is a Washington institution. Conservatives say the *Post* has a liberal bias and liberals say it has a conservative bias, so journalists believe it must be doing something right.

- **Washington City Paper**, 202-332-2100, www.washingtoncitypaper. com; essentially an arts and entertainment guide, with lots of advertising including a huge and useful classified section. The free *City Paper* does run some ambitious feature stories, and the weekly "Loose Lips" column packs into one page more knowledge of D.C. politics than the *Post* demonstrates in a week. For a real overview of Washington culture, read the personal ads in the *City Paper*, even if you're not looking for a date. Generally available by Thursday evening rush hour; the classified ads are posted on the web site on Tuesday, at least 48 hours before they hit the streets.

- The **Washington Times**, 202-636-3333, www.washtimes.com; not officially a partisan paper, but the *Times* is the preferred paper among conservatives. The *Times* devoted a daily section to Whitewater and other investigations throughout President Clinton's two terms. Its owner, Rev. Syn Myung Moon, says he is not involved in editorial decisions. Daily

- The **Common Denominator**, 202-635-6397, www.thecommondenominator.com; the only local newspaper serving all of the District and just the District, this little biweekly offers solid coverage of D.C. politics and its communities, offering consumer news aimed at an economically diverse audience. Includes homegrown editorial cartoons and a thorough calendar of civic meetings and D.C. government hearings. Published alternate Mondays.

- **Journal Newspapers**, 703-846-8500, www.jrnl.com; this regional chain of county newspapers offers thorough coverage of state and local politics, high school sports, and suburban communities and civic life. Indispensable if you plan to buy or rent a home in the suburbs. The *Montgomery Journal, Prince George's Journal, Arlington Journal, Fairfax Journal*, and *Alexandria Journal* are archived online and share a central subscription number. Weekly
- **Gazette Newspapers**, 301-607-1015, www.gazette.net; Maryland's oldest newspaper, the *Gaithersburg Gazette*, is now part of a regional chain of community papers owned by The Washington Post Company. The Montgomery, Prince George's, and Frederick *Gazettes* still provide in-depth coverage of local news and civic life.
- **Times Community Newspapers**, 703-437-5400, www.timescommunity.com; these local papers serve a dozen suburban communities in Virginia, from Arlington to Chantilly.

NEIGHBORHOOD NEWSPAPERS

These biweekly or monthly papers are available free at Metro stations, bookstores, libraries, restaurants, bars, and other neighborhood establishments. This is the best way to follow real estate markets, zoning and development issues, and politics as they relate to a specific section of D.C.

- The *Georgetowner*, 202-338-4833, www.georgetowner.com
- *Hill Rag*, 202-543-8300, www.hillrag.com
- The *InTowner* serves Adams Morgan, Cleveland Park, Columbia Heights, Dupont Circle, Mt. Pleasant, Shaw, and Woodley Park. 202-234-1717, www.intowner.com
- *Montgomery Sentinel*, 301-838-0788, www.thesentinel.com/mcfolder
- The *Northwest Current* serves D.C. neighborhoods west of Connecticut Avenue NW; in some neighborhoods, it's the *Rock Creek Current*, with some zoned articles. 202-244-7223
- *Prince George's Sentinel*, 301-306-9500, www.thesentinel.com/pgfolder
- The *Takoma Voice* mainly serves Takoma Park, MD, but also covers the adjacent Takoma neighborhood in D.C. 301-891-6744, www.takoma.com
- *Voice of the Hill*, 202-544-0703, www.voiceofthehill.com

SPECIAL-INTEREST WEEKLY NEWSPAPERS

- *Afro-American*, 202-332-0080, www.afro.com
- *Catholic Standard*, 202-281-2410, www.cathstan.org
- *El Pregonero*, 202-281-2440
- *The Hill* (covering Congress), 202-628-8500, www.hillnews.com

- *Legal Times*, 202-457-0686
- *Progressive Review*, 202-835-0770, http://emporium.turnpike.net/P/ProRev
- *Roll Call* (covering Congress), 202-824-6800, www.rollcall.com
- *Tiempo Latino*, 703-527-7860
- *Washington Blade* (GLBT interests), 202-797-7000, www.washblade.com
- *Washington Business Journal*, 703-875-2200, www.bizjournals. com/washington
- *Washington Diplomat* (covering D.C.'s international community), 301-933-3552, www.washdiplomat.com
- *Washington Informer* (African-American interests), 202-561-4100, www.usbol.com/informer
- *Washington Jewish Week*, 301-360-2222, www.washingtonjew-ishweek.com

MAGAZINES

- *Washingtonian*, 202-331-0715, www.washingtonian.com; combines society pages and consumer news to cover the movers and shakers in Washington and the places where they dine, shop, live, go to school, and go on vacation. Annual features include "Cheap Eats," "Best & Worst of Everything," and "10 Charities That Deserve Your Money."
- *Capital Style*, 202-824-9950, www.rollcall.com/capstyle; professing to cover "the art of political living," this smaller, younger alternative to the *Washingtonian* features more articles about people in the Washington spotlight and not as much consumer-oriented "news you can use."

FINDING A PHYSICIAN

If you have a job that includes health benefits, your insurance plan or HMO will provide you with a list of participating doctors. If you're self-employed, self-insured, or a member of Washington's growing ranks of "career temps," you will need to shop around for a doctor.

Ideally, get a referral from a friend or trusted co-worker. Also check out the **Washington Consumers' Checkbook** web site, www.checkbook.org, for ratings of local doctors and dentists, hospitals, health plans, and pharmacies, along with general advice about choosing health services. Or you can call **800-DOCTORS** (in D.C., 202-DOCTORS) for a referral; to find a dentist, call 202-547-7613. The **American Board of Medical Specialties** can tell you whether a particular doctor is board certified—call 866-275-2267 or visit www.abms.org.

In 1999, *Washingtonian* magazine asked 5,000 Washington-area physicians to name the top specialists in 31 medical fields—the doctors to whom they would refer their own families. The resulting list is available at www.washingtonian.com.

To check a doctor's credentials and history of lawsuits or professional sanctions, or to make a formal complaint about a doctor or other medical professional, call:

- **D.C. Board of Medicine**, 202-442-9200
- **Maryland Board of Physician Quality Assurance**, 800-492-6836 (for information about professional records)
- **Maryland Health Claims Arbitration Office**, 410-767-8200 (for information about malpractice cases)
- **Virginia Board of Medicine**, 804-662-9908

A database of doctors licensed in Maryland is available at www.bpqa. state.md.us. Virginia doctors are listed at www.dhp.state.va.us/medicine.

For alternative health care practitioners—acupuncture, ayurveda, Feldenkrais, herbalism, macrobiotics, reflexology, yoga, and other holistic disciplines—check out *Pathways* magazine, available free at libraries and heath food stores, or visit www.pathwaysmag.org.

PET LAWS AND SERVICES

Washington is a great walking city, and walking a well-behaved dog is an easy way to meet people—and to feel safe if you're not accustomed to a big city. Busy Washingtonians support a huge industry of pet sitters, dog-walking services, and even doggie day care. If your neighbors have pets, ask them for recommendations—especially for a good veterinarian and pet food store.

LICENSING

The District and all neighboring counties require dogs to be licensed after the age of four months. A rabies certificate from a vet or shelter must be presented along with the license fee. In most cases you can apply by mail—ask the vet or shelter for an application, or contact your local licensing agency:

- **D.C. Animal Control Shelter**, 202-576-6664
- **Montgomery County Police, Division of Animal Control & Humane Treatment**, 301-279-1249, www.co.mo.md.us/services/police
- **Prince George's County Animal Control Commission**, 301-883-6009
- **Arlington County Office of the Treasurer**, 703-228-3255, www.co. arlington.va.us/treas
- **Fairfax County Department of Tax Administration**, 703-222-8234, www.co.fairfax.va.us/dta
- **Alexandria Police—Animal Control/Protection Service**, 703-838-4774

VETERINARIANS

While it's no substitute for a personal referral, the **American Veterinary Medical Association's** web site, www.avma.org, offers advice on finding and choosing a vet. Also visit the health care section of the **Washington Consumers' Checkbook** web site, www.checkbook.org.

There are at least 20 veterinary clinics in D.C. and the inner suburbs. Most have 24-hour emergency service, or at least a recording with a vet's pager or emergency phone number. Get to know a local vet promptly, so you won't need to shop around in an emergency:

DISTRICT OF COLUMBIA
- **Adams Morgan Animal Clinic**, 2112 18th Street NW, 202-638-7470
- **Animal Clinic of Anacostia**, 2210 Martin Luther King Jr. Avenue SE, 202-889-8900
- **Animal Clinic of Capitol Hill**, 1240 Pennsylvania Avenue SE, 202-543-2288
- **Collins Hospital for Animals**, 1808 Wisconsin Avenue NW, 202-659-8830
- **Dupont Veterinary Clinic**, 2022 P Street NW, 202-466-2211
- **Friendship Hospital for Animals**, 4105 Brandywine Street NW, 202-363-7300
- **Kindcare Animal Hospital**, 3622 12th Street NE, 202-635-3622
- **Petworth Animal Hospital**, 4012 Georgia Avenue NW, 202-723-7142
- **Southeast Animal Hospital**, 2309 Pennsylvania Avenue SE, 202-584-2125
- **VCA MacArthur Animal Hospital**, 4832 MacArthur Boulevard NW, 202-337-0120

MARYLAND
- **Ambassador Animal Hospital**, 7979 Georgia Avenue, Silver Spring, 301-589-1344
- **Brentwood Animal Hospital**, 3900 Rhode Island Avenue, Brentwood, 301-864-3164
- **Cat Medical Center**, 12601 New Hampshire Avenue, Silver Spring, 301-680-0800
- **Chevy Chase Veterinary Clinic**, 8815 Connecticut Avenue, Chevy Chase, 301-656-6655
- **Del Ray Animal Hospital**, 9301 Old Georgetown Road, Bethesda, 301-564-1923
- **Kenilworth Avenue Medical Center**, 5702 Riverdale Road, Hyattsville, 301-277-5408

VIRGINIA
- **Alexandria Veterinary Emergency Service**, 2660 Duke Street, Alexandria, 703-823-3601
- **Arlington Animal Hospital**, 2624 Columbia Pike, Arlington, 703-920-5300
- **Cherrydale Veterinary Clinic**, 4038 Lee Highway, Arlington, 703-528-9001
- **Suburban Animal Hospital**, 6879 Lee Highway, Arlington, 703-532-4043

You can even enroll your pet in an animal HMO, Pet Assure, and receive 25% off medical care and supplies from participating veterinarians and 10% to 50% off pet food, supplies, training, grooming and boarding at participating establishments. Call 888-789-PETS or visit www.petassure.com. Straight medical coverage is available from Veterinary Pet Insurance, 800-872-7387.

WALKING YOUR DOG

Most neighborhoods in the city and inner suburbs are dog-friendly. Every local jurisdiction requires leashes and scoops. In the outer suburbs, most homes have generous yards or wide, grassy medians on subdivision streets.

In the District, **parks** favored by dogs and their owners include Rose Park, 26th & P streets NW; Battery Kemble Park, off Loughboro Road; Stanton Square, on C Street NE between 4th & 6th; Lincoln Park, on East Capitol Street between 11th & 13th; Malcolm X Park, on 16th Street NW between W and Euclid streets; and the green wedge bounded by New Hampshire Avenue, 17th Street, and T Street NW. If you have to work long hours, look in the Yellow Pages under "Pet Sitting Services" for midday dog walkers.

Well-behaved dogs are allowed off leash at several **official dog parks** in the suburbs:
- In **Arlington County** seven parks have designated dog exercise areas: Benjamin Banneker Park, Fort Ethan Allen Park, Allie S. Freed Park, Glencarlyn Park, Shirlington Park, Towers Park, and Utah Park. For directions and rules, contact the Department of Parks, Recreation & Community Resources, 703-228-6525 or www.co.arlington.va.us/prcr.
- In **Fairfax County** try Blake Lane Park in Oakton at Blake Lane and Bushman Drive. For more information contact the Park Authority, 703-324-8702 or www.co.fairfax.va.us/parks.
- In **Alexandria** there are fenced dog parks at Ben Brenman Park, Chetworth Park, Montgomery Park, Simpson Stadium Park, and the 5000 block of Duke Street, east of Charles E. Beatley Jr. Library In addi-

tion, there are 14 designated dog parks without fences. Contact the Department of Recreation, Parks & Cultural Activities, 703-638-4345 or www.ci.alexandria.va.us/rpca.

ADOPTING A PET

Local animal shelters always have dogs and cats in need of loving homes. At some shelters, staff will interview everyone in your household and visit your home to make sure you are indeed capable of taking proper care of a companion animal. Also, in the classified ads in the *Washington Post* and *Washington City Paper*, pet owners who are moving into apartments or out of town are constantly seeking good homes for animals who cannot go along. Here are the city and county animal shelters:

- **Washington Humane Society**, 7319 Georgia Avenue NW, 202-723-5730; 1201 New York Avenue NE, 202-576-6664; www.washhumane.org
- **Washington Animal Rescue League**, 71 Oglethorpe Street NW, 202-726-2556; www.warl.org
- **Montgomery County Humane Society**, 14645 Rothgeb Drive, Rockville, 240-773-5054, www.mchumane.org
- **Humane Society of Southern Maryland** (foster placements—no shelter), 301-630-6110, www.dogrescue.org
- **Animal Welfare League of Arlington**, 703-931-9241; www.awla.org
- **Fairfax County Animal Shelter**, 4500 West Ox Road, 703-830-1100; www.co.fairfax.va.us/ps/ac
- **Alexandria Animal Shelter**, 910 South Payne Street, 703-838-4775; www.adoptapet.com/adoptapet

PET CARE SERVICES

If you can find a friend or trusted neighbor to look after your pets while you're out of town, it's probably easier on your pets than a boarding kennel. Several companies provide licensed and bonded in-house pet sitters and midday dog walkers, and many animal hospitals offer boarding. "Doggie day care" centers became popular in the late 1990s. These facilities are not kennels, but well-appointed recreational facilities for dogs, with optional grooming services. You can even get organic pet food and all-natural grooming products—call Pet Essentials at 202-986-7907 or visit www.greenpets.com.

Pet sitters, dog walkers, day care centers, pet food stores and grooming salons are listed in the Yellow Pages under "Pet."

On your way to Washington, or on vacation, look for pet-friendly hotels and resorts at www.travelpet.com. For more advice about four-legged passengers, check out *Vacationing With Your Pet* by Eileen Barish, published by Pet Friendly Publications.

CRIME & SAFETY

Every major city in the US has its "good" and "bad" sections, and every major city has street gangs. Here in D.C., "bad" neighborhoods are those with a concentration of gang-related shootings, and they tend to be highly localized—often a single block or intersection. Statistically, you aren't likely ever to experience violent crime in the Washington area. Most long-time residents know one or two people who have been mugged—in a metropolis approaching 7 million residents and commuters. If you live here long enough, eventually a case of car theft or a "smash-and-grab" (theft of articles from parked cars) may hit close to home.

Panhandling, or begging, is not a crime unless it's done "aggressively" or on private property. In D.C., the only place where panhandling is consistently discouraged is within designated Business Improvement Districts, where business owners collectively hire private security guards and cleaning crews for their section of downtown.

Bicycle theft is a serious concern for those who rely on a bike for urban transportation. If you're new to a big city, have a bike salesperson give you a few tips on the proper use of U-locks and cables. You'll see people carrying bike seats around all day—which is a deterrent: even if a thief can break a lock, a bike without a seat isn't likely to be taken very far. Call your local police department (see **Useful Phone Numbers and Web Sites**) to register your serial number. CityBikes, 202-265-1564, keeps a registry of stolen bikes.

Finally, Washington has a special place in the history of the world's oldest profession: during the Civil War, a Washington garrison commander rounded up the city's prostitutes and marched them across the Potomac into Virginia. They came back, and they're mostly in the same place—east of Logan Circle—but today they bear the name of that hapless officer, Major General Hooker.

CRIME PREVENTION

As in any big city, pay attention to your surroundings—avoid poorly lit streets and deserted areas, and don't walk alone late at night. Remember that large bills, jewelry, and even maps can attract the wrong kind of attention. Know roughly what time it is—if a stranger asks, you can answer without showing off your watch. And, no, you *don't* have a cigarette. On a crowded bus or train, watch out for pickpockets and purse-snatchers.

Two common scams to watch out for: at public phones, if you use a calling card, make sure no one can see you dial—someone could steal your account number. And if you pull into a parking space and someone offers to "watch your car" for $5, park somewhere else—the offer could be a thinly veiled threat to vandalize your vehicle.

Call your local police non-emergency number for information about neighborhood watch groups (also known as "Citizens On Patrol" groups or "Orange Hat Patrols") in your area. The police department can also provide pamphlets and workshops on crime prevention.

Here are the home burglar alarm dealers with the highest rating from *Washington Consumers' Checkbook* in 1999; this is by no means a complete list of reputable dealers—see the Yellow Pages under "Burglar Alarm Systems."

- **Allied Alarm Specialists**, 703-329-8660
- **Cain Security Systems**, 703-360-1900
- **Interamerican Security**, 301-840-0004
- **N&D Security**, 703-243-0499
- **National Security**, 703-273-5555
- **Potomac Security Systems**, 301-983-0907
- **Satellite Industries**, 301-840-5420
- **Vector Security**, 800-688-0150

WHETHER YOU REALLY ARE A SUPER-BUSY WASHINGTON VIP OR just think you are, time is money here, and it may pay to hire somebody to take care of some time-consuming chores and errands. You can hire someone to stand in line for theater tickets, organize your closet, auction off your old furniture, renovate your house, or get your license tags renewed—do practically anything, for a fee. Mechanics, manicurists, yard workers, housekeepers, caterers, grocers, and other helpful people will come to you, with goods and services in hand, and the meter running.

PERSONAL ASSISTANTS

If you're just plain busy and you need a personal assistant or concierge—a 21st-century Jeeves—to take care of assorted chores and errands, start by looking at *Washingtonian* magazine's annual review of companies providing custom personal services. Look for bonded and insured professionals to run errands, wait for deliveries, take care of repair calls, shop for gifts, take the dog to the vet, get the car inspected, and pay the bills. Usually the only thing these agencies won't do is transport people—only a licensed taxi service can do that. With fees ranging from $30 to $100 an hour, you probably won't want to hire someone to run out for sandwiches, but sometimes it's worth the expense to have someone else run a few errands. Check the latest list under "Shopping & Services" at www.washingtonian.com or contact:

- **Concierge America**, 301-986-0418, www.conciergeamerica.com
- **Custom Assignments**, 301-962-5797, www.customassignments.com
- **The Runaround**, 301-922-0196, www.runaround.com

Couriers are listed in the Yellow Pages under "Delivery Service." Most courier services offer "placeholder" service, too: for about $20 an hour, you can hire someone to stand in line for you. This service caters mainly to lob-byists and junior federal officials who need to attend crowded hearings on the Hill, where seating is scare and cannot be reserved.

RENTAL SERVICES

If you need to furnish a home right away and you don't have time to shop for the perfect furniture and appliances, or if you won't be in town for more than a couple months, you can rent practically anything you need. Be care-ful, though: if you rent household items for more than a few months, you will almost always end up paying more than if you had bought new furni-ture—even credit purchases are usually cheaper in the long run than "rent-to-own" plans. Use these services sparingly.

FURNITURE

For a wide selection of new furniture available for short-term rental, lease, or rent-to-own, check out:

- **Aaron Rents & Sells**, 52 Derwood Circle, Rockville, 301-424-3922; 11714 Baltimore Avenue, Beltsville, 301-210-0120; 5720 General Washington Drive, Alexandria, 703-941-7195; 4124-A Walney Road, Chantilly, 703-378-0080; www.aaronrents.com
- **Alperstein's**, 1015 7th Street NW, 202-783-0100, www.alpersteins.com
- **Cort Furniture Rental**, 1100 New York Avenue NW, 202-223-9241; 11711 Parklawn Drive, Rockville, 301-881-7388; 3101 Park Center Drive, Alexandria, 703-379-8846; 8500 Leesburg Pike, Tysons Corner, 703-790-8338; 14130 Sullyfield Circle, Chantilly, 703-818-2660; 800-669-2678, www.cort1.com
- **Scherr Furniture Rental**, 12340 Parklawn Drive, Rockville, 301-881-8960

These are established rental outfits, and most offer free next-day deliv-ery on orders above a certain minimum, if the items you need are in stock.

Special needs can be met as well. Let's say you need to host an elegant reception at your gas-lighted Capitol Hill townhouse and you don't even own a punchbowl. You can rent such niceties, including antiques, from **Antique & Contemporary Leasing**, 709 12th Street SE, 202-547-3030, www.antiqueleasing.com. You can also hire their interior design and installa-tion staff for an hourly fee.

APPLIANCES

Most of the appliance showrooms listed in **Shopping for the Home** aren't in the rental business, but many offer financing plans that enable you to defer payment for several months. A few rental outfits handle major appliances:

- **King Rent-A-Fridge**, 9519 Georgia Avenue, Silver Spring, 301-565-8035
- **Rent-A-Center**, 2845 Alabama Avenue SE, 202-583-2052; 621 Georgia Avenue NW, 202-722-1070; 807 H Street NE, 202-543-1280; 628 Rhode Island Avenue NE, 202-526-6891

COMPUTERS

Most of these companies deliver within 24 hours and offer weekly and monthly rentals and longer leases:

- **ABT Micro**, 800-727-4768 or 301-840-0809, www.computerrents.com
- **Computerent.com**, 888-666-3579, www.computerent.com
- **Any Hour Computing**, 800-972-0950, www.anyhourcomputing. baweb.com
- **Electro Rent**, 800-688-1111, www.electrorent.com
- **Fox Computer Rentals**, 202-582-0900, www.foxcomp.com
- **Item Inc.**, 703-971-5700, www.iteminc.com
- **National MicroRentals**, 800-637-2496 or 202-628-2364, www.nmr-rents.com
- **Personal Computer Rentals**, 800-473-6872 or 703-393-0200, www.pcrrent.com
- **RAC Solutions**, 202-628-3639, www.racsolutions.com
- **Rent-A-PC**, 202-775-0666, www.rentapc.com
- **Rush Computer Rentals**, 800-922-0708 or 301-490-7411, www.rushcomputer.com
- **USRental.com**, 800-877-3682, www.usrental.com
- **Vernon Technology Solutions**, 800-347-7333, www.vernontech.com

DOMESTIC SERVICES

Cabinet nominees aren't the only people in Washington who hire domestic help. Plenty of people chose not to spend a lot of time doing housework or yard maintenance.

DIAPER SERVICES

There aren't many diaper services left, but the last holdouts in this quaint industry have generations of good reputation. Call **Dy-Dee** at 202-832-1112 or **Modern Diaper Service**, 703-823-3993.

DRY CLEANING & LAUNDRY

Following the example of the Bergmann's chain, in business since 1917, most dry cleaners in the Washington area offer pickup and delivery service; check the Yellow Pages. For regular laundry pickup and delivery, contact **Mom's Laundry**, 202-686-1300 or www.momslaundrydc.com, or in Fairfax County, the **Laundry Club**, 703-771-8283 or www.thelaundryclub.com.

HOME IMPROVEMENT

For free referrals to licensed repair services with good references, contact:
- **Home Connections**, 888-POINT ME or 301-565-5902, www.homecon-nections.com
- **Home USA**, 800-466-3872
- **Independent Home Inspection**, 703-836-6121

If you own a home but would like the convenience of having a property manager, **Delbe Home Services** will manage your home repairs and maintenance, working on your behalf with contractors and suppliers; call 202-237-0187 or visit www.delbe.com.

HOUSE CLEANING SERVICES

Maid services are listed in the Yellow Pages under "House Cleaning." Agencies employing bonded and insured maids usually say so in display ads. As domestic labor is often a first stop for new immigrants entering the workforce, you may find *Spanish-English Housekeeping* by Ruth M. Dietz, a phrasebook for employers of Latino domestic workers, helpful.

For serious cleaning—after accidents, fires, or other disasters—call **Special Forces** at 202-289-6501 or 703-560-2151. Some of the larger agencies dispatching domestic workers for occasional or scheduled cleaning include:
- **A to Z Cleaning Service**, 202-319-8243
- **Chase Cleaning Service**, 202-347-3188 or 301-431-2929
- **Dial-A-Maid**, 800-950-MAID
- **DomestiCall**, 703-534-1100
- **Dyna-Clean**, 202-332-2331
- **Empire Maintenance**, 301-654-4444 or 703-534-2323
- **Jiffy Maids**, 202-638-7703 or 301-431-1970
- **Maid Brigade**, 800-515-MAID
- **Maid Magic**, 301-434-1400
- **Maid to Order**, 301-593-8982
- **Maid to Perfection**, 202-783-1821 or 301-891-2800

- **Naudus Window & House Cleaning Service**, 703-820-3660
- **New World Cleaning Services**, 703-237-7617
- **Ragin Cleaning Services**, 888-517-2446 or 301-725-6088

PEST CONTROL

Roaches love Washington in the summer. On the sidewalk in the evening, under the cheery light of fireflies, you will see dozens of big Asian cockroaches. The best way to keep them outside is to keep your home, especially the kitchen, scrupulously clean and to keep baseboards and kitchen fixtures painted or caulked. Even then, don't be surprised by the occasional six-legged visitor. If you have an infestation, reach for the Yellow Pages to look up "Hardware Stores," for traps, or "Pest Control Services" for chemicals. If you're trying to prevent an infestation, though, little plastic "bait stations" available at any drugstore or hardware store are generally effective. The Gardens Alive catalog sells nontoxic pest control supplies such as pantry moth traps, old-fashioned flypaper strips, and natural chemicals that repel or kill ants and roaches. Call 812-537-8651 or visit www.gardensalive.com.

Rats abound here too—as one local politician put it, the four-legged kind as well as the two-legged kind. And don't assume rats stick to unsavory neighborhoods; they're egalitarian pests, just as likely to turn up in elite zip codes. The best deterrent is to keep your trash and recycling areas clean and avoid putting your trash out more than 12 hours before pickup; or get a cat. (It doesn't matter whether your cat will actually chase rodents—the rodents will smell cat.) As with other pests, your best resources for rat control are hardware stores and exterminators listed in the Yellow Pages.

If you have small children, chemical sensitivities, an impaired immune system, or just an aversion to harsh chemicals, visit www.pestweb.com for information about natural pest control products and integrated pest management (ecological controls, such as attracting ladybugs to eat aphids or keeping a cat to repel mice). It's an industry site and some of the information is fairly technical, but it's a comprehensive source of good advice.

LAWN CARE

For routine cutting and clipping, there's always an enterprising teenager down the block (in the suburbs) or a neighborhood jack-of-all-trades (in the District). The going rate depends on the neighborhood, but expect to pay $10 to $20 for an average lawn. For comprehensive lawn maintenance, look in the Yellow Pages under "Lawn Maintenance"—or just find a neighbor with a nice lawn and ask for a referral. Natural Lawns, 703-204-9000, www.natlawns.com, provides organic lawn care, and Fairway Lawn Care, 301-681-3708 or www.fairwaylawncare.com, offers pesticide-free service.

No matter where you live, visit the Montgomery County Department of Environmental Protection web site at www.co.mo.md.us/services/dep for advice about composting yard waste.

POSTAL & SHIPPING SERVICES

MAIL DELIVERY

Mail delivery in D.C. is erratic—if you mail ten letters to local addresses all at once, nine will arrive the next day and the tenth might take a week. Your mail at home might be delivered at 4 p.m. one day and 10 a.m. the next, with no apparent pattern. But the problems are easy to exaggerate—the mail is generally so reliable we can take it for granted, and when it disappoints, it really disappoints.

The simplest way to help ensure fast delivery is to use the nine-digit zip code. Call 202-635-5300, 800-ASK-USPS, or visit www.usps.com for zip codes, postal rates and other general information.

JUNK MAIL & TELEMARKETING

You've just moved to one of the most affluent cities and, quite possibly, one of the most affluent neighborhoods in the world. You most certainly will be inundated with junk mail and pestered almost every day by telephone solicitors. Most companies will take you off their own lists if you ask them to, but it would be a full-time job to contact every outfit that sends you unsolicited mail or to speak to the supervisor of every telemarketer who interrupts your dinner.

You can curtail junk mail and telemarketers to some extent: first, write a note to the Direct Marketing Association, P.O. Box 9008, Farmingdale, NY 11735, requesting that your address be listed with the Mail Preference Service and your phone number listed with the Phone Preference Service. Most—not all—business and charities sending junk mail will exclude addresses and phone numbers registered with these services. It will not deter companies that do not buy the preference lists.

The four major credit bureaus—Experian, Equifax, Innovis, and TransUnion—share an "automated opt-out" line, 888-567-8688; call to have your name removed from any lists these bureaus sell to direct mail companies.

If all else fails, remember, junk mail is recyclable.

MAIL RECEIVING

A post office box might be convenient if you're in a short-term rental or sublet or if you're staying with friends. Also, if you expect to move around a few times while looking for the perfect home, a box will spare you the hassle of changing your address repeatedly. Most post offices have boxes for rent, though there may be a waiting list at busy downtown locations. You can also have mail delivered to Mail Boxes Etc., which has 14 locations in D.C., 800-789-4623 or 202-686-2100, www.mbe.com, or Vantas, with 20 locations in D.C. and the suburbs, 800-356-9543, www.vantasinc.com. Or you can arrange to receive mail at any of the "office clubs" listed in the **Temporary Lodgings** chapter that provide office space and clerical services on a short-term basis.

SHIPPING

For bulky or heavy items, **Craters & Freighters**, 301-926-7166, www.cratersandfreighters.com, advertises: "Too large for UPS? Too small for movers? We'll ship it!" For conventional packages, the nationwide parcel services are all familiar names:

- **Airborne Express**, 800-247-2676, www.airborne.com
- **DHL Worldwide Express**, 800-225-5345, www.dhl-usa.com
- **FedEx**, 800-238-5355, www.fedex.com/us
- **FedEx Ground**, (formerly RPS), 800-238-5355, www.fedex.com/us
- **UPS**, 800-742-5877, www.ups.com
- **US Postal Service Express Mail**, 800-222-1811, www.usps.com

AUTOMOBILES

Nearly a quarter of a million commuters in the Washington area spend more than two hours a day behind the wheel; for more than a million commuters, it's at least an hour a day. Bumper-to-bumper traffic on the Beltway puts a lot of wear on your brake pads. In the winter, salt and slush leave their mark on your paint job. One resident of downtown D.C. found that his ignition wires had been gnawed apart by rats—on several occasions. And then there's parking, one of the city's most treasured commodities.

REPAIRS & MAINTENANCE

By far, the best way to find a trustworthy mechanic is to get recommendations from friends, neighbors, or co-workers, preferably from those with the same make of car. The consumer resources listed in **Shopping for the Home**: *Washington Consumers' Checkbook*, the Better Business Bureau, *Washingtonian* magazine, Themail at www.dcwatch.com, and www.epinions.com, can help if you need to start from scratch. It's a good idea to shop around for a mechanic before you need one; when your car is in urgent need of repairs, you may be tempted to go to the nearest hack shop down the street.

Auto dealerships are generally reliable, if pricey, but at least they definitely have the parts, equipment, and expertise to deal with the models they sell. The Yellow Pages list more than 300 dealerships, so you don't have to go far afield to get expert service for your Volkswagen, Lamborghini, or Hummer.

Many auto repair shops offer pickup and delivery, but several make house calls for minor repairs and maintenance—usually at rates not much higher than shops you drive to:

- **Auto Repair Anywhere**, 301-595-1155
- **Brake Masters**, 703-385-3453, www.brakemasters.net
- **William Ivins Automotive**, 301-585-8268

For a free second opinion about car repairs, you can always call "Click" and "Clack," the guys on National Public Radio's "Car Talk," which airs on Saturday mornings, 9 to 10 a.m. on WAMU-FM 88.5, and 10 to 11 a.m. on WETA-FM 90.9, or visit http://cartalk.cars.com.

Some **auto clubs** provide seals of approval or will rate certain local repair shops, but it's a good idea to read the fine print to see whether the shops pay a fee or are listed based on the quality of provided services. The most comprehensive auto club, in terms of services and coverage area, is AAA (contact AAA Mid-Atlantic at 888-859-5161 or go to www.aaamidatlantic.com). The lesser-known Auto Club of America, 800-411-2007, www.autoclubofamerica.com, offers similar services. In addition, many national service station chains and some insurance carriers, such as Allstate and GEICO, offer road service plans. (See **Getting Settled** for more information about auto insurance companies.)

REGISTRATION, INSPECTION & TICKETS

Several companies help you navigate the Department of Motor Vehicles and traffic court. For fees many consider modest compared to the time and hassle involved with the DMV, you can hire an experienced bureaucracy-buster to handle your paperwork, get your car inspected, arrange for the release of booted or towed vehicles, and counsel you in the process of contesting a ticket or appearing at an administrative hearing. Contact:

- **Dorsey & Associates**, 202-434-8189, www.parkingviolations.com
- **Parking Tickets 2 Us**, 202-546-5544
- **US Vehicle Registration Service**, 202-342-2558 or www.usvrs.com

FOOD

GROCERIES

Several online grocers deliver orders at prices competitive with bricks-and-mortar grocery stores, with reasonable delivery fees. For a minimum order of $50, www.peapod.com will deliver your groceries the next day, within a two-hour period you select. Bulk quantities of premium items, such as free-range organic meat, are available from www.horizonfoods.com, and ww3.kingarthurflour.com delivers top-quality baking ingredients. Most of the gourmet stores listed in the **Food** section of the **Shopping for the Home** chapter also deliver grocery orders and prepared foods.

TAKEOUT/DELIVERY

The following delivery companies will pick up your restaurant order and deliver it by car or bike to your home or office. Pricing can be complicated, and usually varies according to distance. Pick up a booklet at any participating restaurant, which will include a map of the delivery area and restaurant menus. If you're not sure which delivery service to use, call the restaurant and ask, or check the restaurant database at http://dc.diningweb.com. You can also order online from hundreds of restaurants at www.food.com.

- **A La Carte Express**, 202-232-8646, www.alacart.com
- **Takeout Taxi**, 202-986-0111, 301-565-3030, 703-578-3663
- **Restaurants on the Run**, 703-820-1000
- **Waiter on the Way**, 301-869-0300, www.waierontheway.com

PREPARED MEALS

- **The US Personal Chefs Association** provides referrals to local chefs who prepare meals in your home, typically for $10 to $20 per person including ingredients. 800-747-2433, www.hireachef.com
- **Diet-to-Go** prepares low-calorie meals twice a week and delivers them to your home, office, or a central distribution point in your neighborhood; call 301-951-3438, 703-550-3438 or 800-743-7546, www.diettogo.com.

CAREER SERVICES

"Welcome to Washington. What do you do for a living?" Get used to it—and to the more perfunctory "Who are you with?" (meaning your firm, not your date). In a city where people are largely defined by their careers, it's no surprise that a whole industry emerged in the late 20th century to provide services to people seeking to advance their careers.

There are dozens of agencies and solo consultants specializing in resumes and SF-171s, the standard application form for federal jobs. And many executive and management jobs in private companies are filled with the assistance of outplacement and recruiting agencies. These services can make your career, but be sure you know what you're buying: some head-hunters and resume consultants do little more than scan your previous job titles and generate a list of job openings with matching keywords. Anyone serious about helping you advance in a challenging career will start with a personal, in-depth interview.

To find an agency, check the Yellow Pages under "Resumes" and "Employment Agencies," and look in the employment classifieds in Sunday's *Washington Post*. Smaller resume shops, which may offer more personalized service, advertise in the *Washington City Paper* classifieds too.

If you move here without a job lined up, you might join the vast ranks of Washingtonians who have taken at least a few assignments through temp agencies. The 20 biggest temporary placement firms alone send more than 5,000 people into hundreds of offices every day—not just secretaries and data entry clerks, but paralegals; writers and editors; computer network administrators; even lawyers and legislative analysts. Temp placement in the Washington area, which is a $300 million industry, can be a good way to get the feel of a company or industry. All kinds of employers use temps—law firms, federal contractors, nonprofits, trade associations, newspapers and magazines, even presidential campaigns. Just make sure you communicate your interests clearly to the agency—some agencies offer lots of short-term assignments, and some prefer to make "temp-to-perm" assignments.

Temp agencies are listed in the Yellow Pages under "Employment Contractors - Temporary Help" and in the Employment section of the *Washington Post* on Sundays. A more detailed listing of the largest temp agencies, with some information about their specialties, is published in the *Washington Business Journal Book of Lists*, along with a list of the top head-hunters, politely called "executive search firms."

MISCELLANEOUS SERVICES

Here is a sampling of the chores you can pay someone to do for you (from the *Washingtonian* magazine review of services):

- **Set up your computer**: for referrals, contact Capital PC User Group, 301-762-9372, www.cpcug.org or Washington Apple Pi, 301-984-0300, www.wap.org.
- **Process your health insurance paperwork**: Medical Bill Management, 703-933-7580 or 800-234-4454, www.medicalbillhelp.com
- **Ghostwrite complaint letters**: Ellen's Poison Pen, 703-781-0077, www.ellenspoisonpen.com

- **Give you a manicure at your office**: PersoNAILities, 410-523-3146
- **Clean up after your pet**: Doggie-Doo Dog Waste Removal Service, 301-391-6706

CONSUMER PROTECTION—RIP-OFF RECOURSE

You're a savvy consumer: you read all the fine print, you save receipts and canceled checks, you always write down the name of the customer service rep who answers your call, you make sure contractors are licensed by the **Department of Consumer & Regulatory Affairs**, 202-442-4320, and have clean files with the Better Business Bureau. You even order free pamphlets about industries from the **Federal Consumer Information Center** at 800-688-9889 or www.pueblo.gsa.gov, and you stay up-to-date on the latest tricks at www.scambusters.org. But you've been ripped off. You negotiate, calmly but firmly, with documents in hand, but to no avail. What can you do?

First, contact the **Better Business Bureau of Metro Washington D.C.** at 202-393-8000 or www.dc.bbb.org. Though this agency will keep a permanent record of unresolved complaints, its first priority is to encourage its affiliated businesses to address all reasonable complaints promptly and thoroughly. The BBB will not get involved until you have exhausted the usual channels of complaint—contacting the supervisor of your sales representative, for example, or the manager or owner. You can also file a complaint with the **Federal Trade Commission** at 202-382-4357 or www.ftc.gov, or the agency responsible for consumer protection where the offending business is located:

- **D.C. Office of the Corporation Counsel**, 202-442-9828
- **Maryland Office of the Attorney General**, Consumer Protection Division, 410-528-8662 (complaint hotline), 410-576-6550 (consumer information)
- **Virginia Department of Agriculture and Consumer Services**, Office of Consumer Affairs, 804-786-2042 or 800-552-9963

Finally, if all else fails, you can go to court. The D.C., Maryland, and Virginia court systems each have offices that provide referrals to court-approved alternative dispute resolution (ADR) agencies, offering legally binding mediation, arbitration, and other out-of-court negotiation services. Both parties must agree to use ADR, and it works best when the dispute is mostly about fault and there is no major disagreement about the underlying facts. The result, in most cases, is a negotiated agreement acceptable to both sides and much less time and hassle than a trial, even in small claims court.

If ADR won't work—for instance, if there is substantial disagreement about facts—or if someone violates the terms of an agreement reached by

ADR, you can take the case to small claims court without a lawyer. Call the clerk of the court in the appropriate jurisdiction for details, or download an informational pamphlet at:

- **D.C. Superior Court,** 202-879-1120 or 202-879-1037 (recorded information), www.dcbar.org; the Small Claims & Conciliation Division hears cases regarding damages or property valued up to $5,000.
- **Maryland District Court**, Montgomery County, 301-279-1500; Prince George's County, 301-952-4240, www.courts.state.md.us/district; the Small Claims Division hears cases regarding damages or property valued up to $2,500 plus interest and court costs.
- **Virginia General District Court**, Arlington County, 703-228-4590; Fairfax County, 703-691-7320; Alexandria, 703-838-4010, www.courts.state.va.us; the Small Claims Division hears cases regarding damages or property valued up to $1,000.

SERVICES FOR PEOPLE WITH DISABILITIES

Among cities its size, Washington is on the leading edge of accessibility. After all, it has more than the usual share of public buildings subject to the Americans with Disabilities Act. Government buildings, museums, monuments, and the Metro system are all fully accessible, and the government and most major private employers make substantial efforts to hire and accommodate workers with disabilities.

Stores and restaurants are not as universally accessible. The Washington D.C. Convention & Visitors Association offers a free fact sheet on the accessibility of area hotels, restaurants, shopping centers, and tourist sites—call 202-789-7093 or visit www.washington.org. Another good web site is www.wiredonwheels.org, which rates restaurants for wheelchair access.

Just north of Capitol Hill, between Florida and New York avenues NE, is Gallaudet University, the nation's only university for the deaf and hearing impaired. In addition to a complete and academically respected university curriculum, Gallaudet features a model high school, a conference center, its own cable TV programming, and athletic programs. Gallaudet's football team invented the huddle—to hide its sign-language "audibles" from the other team.

GETTING AROUND

PUBLIC TRANSPORTATION
Given at least 24 hours notice, most local and national passenger carriers will make any needed accommodations for passengers with special needs. Guide dogs are welcome practically everywhere, but call to make sure.

Metrorail is fully accessible and most Metrobus coaches on major routes are equipped with lifts. Metro stations have Braille signage, and train operators announce each stop; on the newer buses, computerized recordings announce each stop. When a Metro station elevator is out of service, loudspeakers and electronic signs announce that free shuttle service is available from a nearby station. For information about:

- Metro system accessibility in general, call 202-962-0128 or TDD 202-638-3780.
- Specific amenities at Metro stations and on Metro vehicles, call 202-962-6464 or TDD 202-638-3780.
- Disabled Passenger ID card (for fare discounts), call 202-962-1245 or TDD 202-628-8973.
- MetroAccess paratransit service for eligible disabled passengers outside regular bus and rail routes, call 301-562-5360 or TDD 301-588-7535.

COMMUTER TRAINS
Call these numbers for details about accessibility:
- **MARC**, 800-325-7245 or TDD 410-539-3497
- **Virginia Railway Express**, 703-684-0400 or TDD 703-684-0551

CARS
- **Rentals**: the car rental companies listed in **Getting Settled** can accommodate special needs with 48 to 72 hours' notice. **Wheelchair Getaways**, 800-873-4973, www.blvd.com, specializes in renting lift-equipped vehicles.
- **Taxis**: the **Project Action** database at www.projectaction.org/paweb lists taxi companies and hotel and airport shuttles with accessible vehicles. Generally, according to this database, Montgomery County is the only jurisdiction where most taxi companies offer vans.
- **Parking**: for information about handicapped license plates and parking permits, contact the appropriate DMV listed in **Getting Settled**.

AIRLINES
The **US Department of Transportation** publishes a free pamphlet on "Air Transportation of Handicapped Persons." For a copy, write to Free Advisory Circular No. AC12032, Distribution Unit, US Department of Transportation, Publications Division, M-4332, Washington, D.C. 20590.

RAIL & BUS LINES
- **Amtrak** is fully accessible. Call 800-USA-RAIL or TDD 800-523-6590 for details and to arrange for special accommodations.
- **Greyhound** offers free travel for companions attending passengers with special needs; call 800-231-2222 for details. To arrange for special accommodations, call 800-752-4841 or TDD 800-345-3109.

TRAVEL RESOURCES

Travelocity.com lists resources and important phone numbers for disabled travelers. Also consider:

- **Mobility International USA**, 541-343-1284 (voice and TDD), www.miusa.org; publishes *A World of Options*, a 658-page book available for $35
- **Moss Rehab Hospital Travel Information Service**, 215-456-9603, www.mossresourcenet.org
- **Project Action Accessible Travel Database**, 202-347-3066, www.projectaction.org/paweb
- **Society for the Advancement of Travel for the Handicapped**, 212-447-7284, www.sath.org

COMMUNICATION

- **Recording for the Blind**, 202-244-8900, provides books on tape, including academic textbooks.
- **Washington Ear**, 301-681-6636, provides newspapers and magazines on tape.
- **Telecommunications Relay Service** allows deaf and hearing persons to communicate with each other by phone through a trained operator using text telephones. The relay operator translates both parties' words verbatim and is required by law to keep all conversations strictly confidential. The service is free.
  - **D.C. Relay**, 202-885-1000 or TDD 202-855-1234
  - **Maryland Relay**, 800-735-2258
  - **Virginia Relay**, 800-828-1140 or TDD 800-828-1120
  - **Spanish Relay**, 800-546-5111 or TDD 800-546-7111

HOUSING

Centers for Independent Living can help you find accessible housing or contractors who specialize in making homes accessible. Contact:

- **D.C. Center for Independent Living**, 202-388-0033
- **Independence Now**, 301-587-4162
- **Endependence Center of Northern Virginia**, 703-525-3268 or TTD 703-525-3553, www.ecnv.org

ADDITIONAL RESOURCES

The most comprehensive sources of information for people with special needs are **www.disAbility.gov**, a portal to hundreds of federal government sites and related links, and the **International Center for**

Disability Resources on the Internet, www.icdri.org. Other good resources include:

- **Columbia Lighthouse for the Blind**, 202-454-6400 or 877-324-5252, www.clb.org, offers employment training, vocational rehabilitation, and placement services, and runs an Assistive Technology Center providing access to the latest devices aiding blind and visually impaired readers and computer users.
- **Davis Memorial Goodwill Industries**, 202-636-4225, www.dcgoodwill.org, provides rehabilitation, job placement, and employment for people with disabilities.
- **The Disability Resource**, 800-695-4042, www.disabilityresource.com, is an online store specializing in books and accessories for independent living.
- **National Council on Independent Living**, 703-525-3406, TTY 703-525-4153, is an advocacy group for accessible housing, public spaces, and technology, provides dozens of useful links at www.ncil.org.

GAY & LESBIAN LIFE

The free weekly *Washington Blade* and the bulletin board at Lambda Rising, 1625 Connecticut Avenue NW, are the two indispensable sources of information about the large and prominent gay, lesbian, bisexual and transgender community in Washington. The Dupont Circle neighborhood is famous as one of the capitals of gay and lesbian culture in the United States, and businesses along Connecticut Avenue north of the circle and along 17th Street between P and R streets NW cater to "the sexual minority"—as well as plenty of straight folks attracted to the thriving nightlife. But there are rainbow flags and "Queer Nation" bumper stickers throughout residential Washington, and in the suburbs—especially in Takoma Park; so, no matter where you live in Washington, unless you moved here from San Francisco or New York City, you're likely to encounter more gay and lesbian culture than you did before.

D.C. voters elected their first openly gay city council member in 1997—David Catania, then a 29-year-old Republican, was elected to fill a vacant at-large seat. In 1998, gay Democrat Jim Graham, longtime executive director of the Whitman-Walker Clinic, was elected to represent Adams Morgan, Columbia Heights, Kalorama, Mt. Pleasant, and upper Shaw. Many private employers here recognize domestic partnership for insurance purposes, and housing discrimination based on sexual orientation is rare. The District and Montgomery County extend spouse benefits to the domestic partners of local government employees, and in 2001, the Maryland legislature outlawed discrimination based on sexual orientation.

THE WASHINGTON AREA CAN BE AN EXCELLENT PLACE TO RAISE A family—in addition to good schools, the area offers countless opportunities to explore the arts and culture, the great outdoors, history, sports, and science, mostly for free. Some children who grow up here are astonished to learn that there are cities where you have to pay to get into a museum. As in any city, however, you will want to take care in choosing the right school and childcare programs, public or private, keeping in mind that even institutions with the best reputations many not be suited to your child's individual needs. Get comfy with the phone book and the web—a lot of research is in order.

CHILDCARE

The Washington area has one of the highest percentages of two-career couples in the country, making childcare a major concern and a major industry. At many government agencies, large companies, and organizations in large office buildings, onsite childcare is a coveted employee benefit. Professional and family childcare facilities—large and small, licensed and unlicensed— abound in the District and suburbs, and they're as diverse in character and price as the city itself. In addition, most public and private schools have after-school programs. Before you entrust your child to a daycare facility, you will want to research your options, talk to co-workers or neighbors with children, visit facilities and meet with staff, and familiarize yourself with the local regulatory agencies, and area parenting publications.

REFERRAL & RESOURCES

In D.C., daycare facilities must be licensed except for those providing "occasional babysitting in the babysitter's home, informal parent-supervised neighborhood playgroups, care furnished in places of worship during religious services, or child development centers providing only a before- or after-school child-development program." The regulations set the maximum size of daycare enrollment in each age group (from eight for toddlers to 30 for pre-teens), the maximum ratio of children to adults (4 to 1 for toddlers, 15 to 1 for pre-teens), and standards for physical facilities, safety, snacks, and government inspections.

When visiting prospective daycare centers—and you should visit, at least a couple of times—look for a clean, safe, calm environment, and then start asking questions: what degrees or training do the employees have? Is the center licensed? How frequent is staff turnover? What is the ratio of children to adults? How much time is spent outdoors? Are teachers or other experts involved in designing activities and programs? And pay attention to your gut feeling—the "vibe" you pick up is just as important as the certifications and curriculum.

These government offices and programs offer listings of licensed providers:

- **D.C. Office of Early Childhood Development**, 202-397-3800
- **Maryland Child Care Resource Network** "LOCATE" program, 301-279-1773 (Montgomery County), 301-772-8400 (Prince George's County)
- **Montgomery County Child Care Resource Center**, 301-279-1811
- **Prince George's Child Resource Center**, 301-772-8420
- **Arlington County Child Care Office**, 703-228-1685
- **Fairfax County Office for Children**, 703-449-9555 or www.co.fairfax.va.us/service/ofc
- **Alexandria Department of Social Services**, 703-338-0700

You can call these local regulatory agencies with questions about licensing:

- **D.C. Health Regulation Administration**, 202-442-5888
- **Maryland Office of Licensing**, Child Care Administration, 410-767-7805
- **Virginia Department of Social Services**, Division of Licensing Programs, 804-692-1776

These agencies regulate licensed childcare programs and provide consumer advice and referrals:

- **D.C. Department of Human Services**, Office of Early Childhood Development, 202-727-1839, www.dhs.washington.dc.us (select "OECD")
- **Maryland Department of Human Resources**, Child Care Administration, 410-767-7805, www.dhr.state.md.us/cca
- **Virginia Department of Social Services**, 804-692-1900, www.dss.state.va.us/family/childcare

NANNIES

Hiring a nanny is generally the most expensive childcare option, but it can be a very rewarding arrangement for everyone involved. A day nanny can easily cost $1,200 a month, and for a live-in nanny, room and board expenses are an additional factor. If you hire a nanny directly (not through an agency), you will need to cover payroll taxes and social security, Medicare, and possibly unemployment insurance. For tax questions about employing domestic childcare, contact **Nanitax**, 800-NANITAX, www.4nannytaxes.com, or **GTM Associates**, 888-432-7972, www.4easypay.com. Also, keep in mind that most nannies are recent immigrants and you will need to make sure they can legally work in the US and communicate fluently with you and your family.

Visit **Nanny Network**, www.nannynetwork.com, for a national database of nanny agencies, tax and background check services, training materials, and other resources to help you find and employ the right caregiver.

Excel Domestics, 703-823-8645, and **Helping Hands**, 301-251-1475, place all kinds of domestic help including nannies, maids, butlers, cooks, and drivers. **Teacher Care**, 888-832-2407, www.teachercare.com, places retired or part-time schoolteachers as nannies, especially for summer help. Other nanny agencies include:

- **A Choice Nanny**, 301-652-2229
- **American Nannies**, 301-588-7066
- **American Registry for Nannies & Sitters**, 800-240-1820 or www.american-registry.com
- **Doctor Care Nanny Services**, 703-799-7852
- **Home Care Services**, 703-391-2721, www.firsthomecare.baweb.com
- **Kinder Contractor**, 202-508-3786
- **Monday Morning Moms**, 301-384-1212 (Montgomery County only)
- **Mothers' Aides**, 703-250-0700, www.mothersaides.com
- **Nanny Dimensions**, 800-691-1669, www.nannydimensions.com
- **Nannies Inc.**, 301-718-0100 (Maryland), 703-255-5312 (Virginia)
- **Nanny Link**, 202-543-0259
- **Nanny Match**, 301-365-7078
- **Potomac Nannies**, 301-986-0048
- **Quality Care Alternatives**, 888-838-5810
- **White House Nannies**, 301-654-1242

Most agencies run their own background checks, but if you have any doubts or you want a second opinion, you can check online for various services. Type "employment screening" into your search engine for links. Likely services include criminal and driving records and credit information. **Eisenberg Associates**, 800-777-5765, www.eisenbergassociates.com, provides health insurance and other fringe benefits for nannies.

AU PAIRS

Au pairs are young adults, usually college-age women, visiting the United States with a special visa status that allows them to provide childcare and light housekeeping services in exchange for room and board, airfare, and a stipend (usually $240 per week). The host family benefits from the cultural exchange as well as the relatively inexpensive child care—but the placement only lasts one year, and an au pair might not offer the same level of maturity and experience as a career nanny. Be realistic, though, as one Potomac family told *Washingtonian* magazine when childcare duties cut into their au pair's free time, "What you have is a teenager who sulks in two languages."

Au pair placement agencies are regulated by the US Information Agency, and these national agencies will connect you with a local placement coordinator:

- **Au Pair in America**, 800-928-7247
- **Au Pair Programme & Childcrest**, 800-937-6264, www.aupairprogrammeusa.com
- **AuPairCare**, 800-428-7247 or 703-502-9511, www.aupaircare.com
- **Au Pair USA/InterExchange**, 800-AU-PAIRS or 301-434-7646, www.interexchange.org
- **EF Au Pair**, 800-333-6056, www.efaupair.org
- **EurAu Pair**, 800-618-2002 or 703-968-2691

BABYSITTING

The perfect babysitter is usually the responsible high school or college student whose parents are your friends, neighbors, or co-workers. Ask around about the going rate, and be prepared to pay more when giving short notice or on holidays. (Of course, you might also be charged extra based on your child's reputation among neighborhood sitters.)

If you don't know any suitable young people, you might try classified ads or the bulletin board at a local supermarket or coffeehouse. Many places of worship run day care programs or provide good referrals, and they are happy to help regardless of your religious affiliation or faith.

If your sitter calls in sick at the last minute, or you haven't yet found a reliable sitter, most of the agencies listed above—notably American Nannies, Mothers' Aides, Nanny Dimensions, and White House Nannies—provide sitters on short notice, at a premium.

Most colleges and universities post job listings for students interested in babysitting on an occasional or scheduled basis. Fax your job listing to the student employment office at the institution nearest you:

- **American University**, 202-885-1861; for a list of students available for babysitting, send $1 and a self-addressed stamped envelope to Job

Corps List, AU Career Center, 4400 Massachusetts Avenue NW, Washington, D.C. 20016

- **Catholic University**, 202-319-4480
- **George Mason University**, 703-993-2361
- **Georgetown University**, 202-687-6542, or call 202-687-4187 for a list
- **Howard University**, 202-806-2818
- **Montgomery College**, 301-279-5089
- **University of Maryland**, 301-314-9919, or call 301-314-8324

Private **babysitter agencies** include:
- **Chevy Chase Babysitters**, 301-916-2964
- **Mothers-in-Deed**, 703-920-2454
- **Weesit**, 703-764-1542

PARENTING & CHILD SAFETY RESOURCES

- *Washington Parent* is a monthly tabloid whose ads are just as helpful as the articles. Available free at libraries, or online (with archives and resource listings) at www.washingtonparent.com.
- *The Parent Pages* is a phone directory of family resources—childcare providers, pediatricians, children's clothing stores, athletic and arts programs, even adoption agencies and teacher certification courses. $8.75 by mail, including postage, from 703-698-8066 or www.parentpagesmetro.com, but sometimes available for free at public libraries.
- **The Family Works** is Maryland's official state "Parent Information & Resource Center," which provides advice and referrals online at www.thefamilyworks.org or by phone at 877-937-3659 or 301-608-8173.
- **National Safe Kids Campaign** provides information about auto safety devices, bike helmets, and product recalls. Visit www.safekids.org or call 202-662-0600.
- The National Capital Chapter of the **American Red Cross** offers basic and advanced courses in first aid, CPR, and rescue, including special courses for babysitters and lifeguards. Call 202-728-6531 or visit www.redcrossdc.org.

SCHOOLS

There are approximately 1,200 public and private schools in the Washington area, making the decision about where to send your child to school less than simple. Matters such as personal finances, the location and reputation of a school, a students' academic strengths, and religious or secular beliefs all will factor into the process. The public school systems in the District and most neighboring jurisdictions offer a growing range of choices, with a proliferation of magnet programs and public charter schools.

The *Washington Post* publishes a quarterly **education review** in January, April, July, and October, replete with ratings of area public schools and ads for private schools. Articles from the education review and regular news sections are specially archived on the "Schools" page at www.washingtonpost.com. Also on the web, the *American School Directory* offers general information about each of the country's 108,000 K-12 schools at www.asd.com; D.C. public schools are profiled at www.dcschoolsearch.com. *The Washington School & Daycare Guide* by Andrew Fogaty lists over 300 private schools in the Washington area; it's available at local bookstores, or send $11.95 to P.O. Box 114658, Chicago, IL 60614. *Washingtonian* magazine's annual directory of area private schools is published in November and archived at www.washingtonian.com/schools. In addition to the listings, the online edition provides links to each school's web site. Finally, visit the education page at www.checkbook.org for advice from *Washington Consumers' Checkbook* about choosing a school, public or private.

In the city and suburbs alike, a key to students' prospects for success is the level of parent and community involvement in the school. Dropout rates, truancy, and disciplinary problems are all consistently lower in schools with active PTAs and accessible, responsive teachers and principals. So perhaps the most important step in choosing a school is to talk to parents, teachers, neighbors, school district officials, and the principal; find out whether parents play an active role in efforts to improve the school.

Visit a prospective school—public or private—and ask yourself:
- Am I comfortable here? Will my child be comfortable here?
- Does the school feel safe? Are the bathrooms clean and free of graffiti?
- Do the students seem to be engaged? Is student work on display?
- Are adults present throughout the building and grounds? Are parents encouraged to volunteer?
- Are classrooms crowded? Do teachers appear to be overworked?
- Are instructional materials, desks, and computers plentiful and new?
- Does the school offer academic and extracurricular opportunities for students to explore their own special interests (such as art, music, sports, or science)?
- Does the school have a clear mission statement? Do teachers seem to teach with that mission in mind? Can teachers articulate the school's educational philosophy?
- In an elementary school, pay attention to the way children are moving around—are they interacting naturally, but staying on task? In a secondary school, notice how students interact with each other and with teachers at the beginning and end of class, and in the halls.

Pay attention to your gut feeling about a school, as well as to the wealth of perspectives you can get from parents and teachers. And, to paraphrase JFK, ask not only what the school can do for your child, but what you can do for your child's school.

PUBLIC SCHOOLS

In the Washington area, you will find some of the finest public schools in the country, and some of the most desperate. As in many big cities, inner-city schools here have metal detectors at the doors and uniformed security guards patrolling the halls. Most high schools—in the suburbs as well as the city—have at least a few gangs ("crews"), whose activities vary from teenage mischief to serious involvement with drugs and weapons. Still, the District and surrounding counties produce a consistently large number of National Merit Scholars, Advanced Placement graduates, and high SAT scores.

DISTRICT OF COLUMBIA

D.C. public schools have a per-pupil budget that is much higher than the national average, yet the schools are struggling; many have chronic short-ages of desks, books, and other basic materials—teachers have been known to reach into their own pockets to buy supplies. The main culprit is the cost of maintaining the city's aging school buildings, most of which were built in the first half of the 20th century—some even earlier. In 1997, a court order delayed the start of the school year because too many school build-ings were in hazardous condition, and a judge ordered major repairs to be completed within three weeks. Congress stepped in and placed an emer-gency school oversight board in charge of the District's schools for four years, returning power to local elected officials in 2001.

Not surprisingly, the school system has been plagued with blame games and nasty politics. Parents were starkly divided over a referendum in 2000 that changed the structure of the D.C. school board, replacing some elected seats with mayoral appointees and changing the geographic constituencies of the remaining elected seats. The close vote underscored the city's economic divide, with the more affluent precincts west of Rock Creek approving the changes and the precincts east of Rock Creek voting to preserve the fully elect-ed board. Supporters of the reform hoped the new structure would result in a board with fewer politicos and more blue-ribbon experts; opponents argued that it would make the school system less accountable to the community.

Despite chronic political struggles over management, there are plenty of good educational opportunities available to D.C. students. The city has a prestigious fine arts magnet, the Duke Ellington School in Georgetown, 202-282-0123, and an academic magnet, Benjamin Banneker High School near Howard University, 202-673-7322. School Without Walls in Foggy Bottom, 202-724-4889, emphasizes experiential learning, taking advantage of the city's cultural resources; like a magnet, "Walls" requires an entrance application. The District is also experimenting with public charter schools—public schools run autonomously by a board of trustees approved by the government, outside the jurisdiction of the superintendent of schools. Some charter schools offer a regular curriculum, but promise closer oversight and smaller classes than regular public schools; others offer specialized curricula, such as the Cesar Chavez Public Charter School for Public Policy or the Marriott Hospitality High School. Contact the **D.C. Public Charter School Board** at 202-328-2660 or www.dcpubliccharter.com for more information about charter schools.

Even regular public schools vary in character from one neighborhood to another. Some schools have adopted mandatory school uniforms, especially in neighborhoods with large numbers of low-income households; school officials hope children will be relieved of peer pressure to keep up with fashion. Some neighborhoods have middle schools, grades 6-8; others have junior high schools, grades 7-9. And many schools have had their budgets for athletics, arts, and extracurricular activities drastically cut since the mid-1990s, and the range and quality of extracurricular activities often depends on the ability of concerned individuals to buy enough baked goods and M&Ms to fund band uniforms or soccer cleats.

Your child has a right to attend your neighborhood school. If you can provide the transportation, however, your child may attend any public school in the District, if space permits. Many parents wait in long lines for "out-of-boundary" applications to enroll their kids in schools with well-funded extracurricular programs.

For more information about the Board of Education, school boundaries, special programs, and policies and reforms, contact D.C. Public Schools at 202-724-4222 or visit www.k12.dc.us. The main offices are located at 825 North Capitol Street NE.

HOW TO ENROLL IN D.C. PUBLIC SCHOOLS

Schooling is compulsory for D.C. residents from age 5 to 18. Children should be enrolled in kindergarten in the fall of the calendar year in which they turn 5, and may be enrolled in pre-K in the fall of the calendar year in which they turn 4.

To register your children, go to the school you want them to attend; if you want to enroll a child in an "out-of-boundary" school, you need permission from the principal of that school. Generally, principals accept out-of-boundary requests in late January and February for the following school year, and allow enrollment as space permits. Call the school district or ask your local school for the exact dates each year.

Once you have chosen your neighborhood school or secured space in an out-of-boundary school, you must provide proof of residence and, for each child, proof of age and immunization records.

- **Proof of residence**: you must provide three documents showing that you currently live in D.C. One of these documents must also show your tax status—you can provide a current tax withholding statement or proof of payment of D.C. personal income tax, or ask the school for a release you can sign to authorize the school to verify your tax status. For the other two documents, you can use a driver's license or non-driver's ID, your vehicle registration, the deed or lease to your home, your voter registration card, or utility bills with receipts or canceled checks showing payment within the past two months. For more information, call the Office of Tuition Enforcement at 202-442-5215. If you are registering more than one child, you only need to show proof of residency once at each school. Also, the school is not permitted to ask you any questions about your citizenship or immigration status when you register.
- **Proof of age**: show an embossed copy of the child's birth certificate or copy of official records from your old school district.
- **Immunization records**: your child must be immunized against diphtheria/pertussis/tetanus; oral polio vaccine; measles/mumps/rubella; hemophilus influenza type B; hepatitis B; and, for children who have not had chicken pox, varicella. A tuberculosis screening is also required, and students entering grade 5 or above should have a diphtheria/tetanus booster if they have not been immunized within the past five years. For a list of clinics providing free and low-cost immunizations, call 202-576-7130.
- Students entering middle school, junior high school, or senior high school at the beginning of the school year must attend an orientation program in late August. Orientation schedules will be mailed to registered students.

The D.C. school day is 8:45 a.m. to 3:15 p.m. at all grade levels.

THE SUBURBS

Suburban school districts generally have one huge advantage over D.C. schools: in the suburbs, local government isn't a novelty. Because the District has had a school board since only 1973 and a legislature since 1974, the D.C. school board still attracts a lot of ambitious politicos who use it as a stepping-stone to a more prestigious office in the neighboring counties; in the suburbs it's more likely that the average school board member is dedicated first and foremost to education.

Of course, the suburbs present their own challenges. After two decades of sprawl and population boom, with no end in sight, many schools are overcrowded and capital budgets are strained by frantic construction of new schools. And even in affluent suburban neighborhoods, high schools are hardly immune to the nationwide problems of gangs and drugs. However, county schools in the area have dropout rates 50% to 75% lower than D.C.'s, and despite crowding, most school districts manage to keep the average class size below a respectable 20.

Each local jurisdiction has several magnet schools offering a special curriculum to students who have demonstrated a particular aptitude—in math and science, the arts, vocational skills, and other areas of emphasis. Also, every local jurisdiction allows students from other jurisdictions to attend public school by paying non-resident tuition. This little-known option enables all students to take advantage of the region's best public schools.

HOW TO ENROLL IN COUNTY OR CITY PUBLIC SCHOOLS

In every jurisdiction in suburban Maryland and Northern Virginia, schooling is compulsory for ages 5-16. As in D.C., most students should be enrolled in the school closest to home. Contact the local school district at the phone number or web site below for details about school boundaries and magnet schools. Each jurisdiction has its own rules and procedures for out-of-boundary admissions, and such arrangements aren't in as much demand in the suburbs as in the District—the quality of schools within any given county is much more consistent.

Registration procedures are fairly uniform throughout the Washington area—go to the appropriate school and present proof of residence (usually a lease, deed, property tax bill, or current utility bill); proof of age (birth certificate, passport, or affidavit); school transcript, unless your child is enrolling in kindergarten for the first time; and immunization records. Contact the school district for the exact list of required immunizations and other documents to bring. Also request, or download, an academic calendar. If you move here during the summer, note that most schools have an August registration fair for new students. Finally, contact the school district for instructions if you need to register a child whose primary language is not English or who has other special needs.

The school day in most jurisdictions is 9 a.m. to 3 p.m. for elementary and 8 a.m. to 3:15 p.m. for high schools. Middle schools, junior high schools and intermediate schools (grades 7-8) may vary, but generally, students have to get up earlier as they get older.

- **Montgomery County Public Schools**, 850 Hungerford Drive, Rockville; 301-279-3331; www.mcps.k12.md.us
- **Prince George's County Public Schools**, 14201 School Lane, Upper Marlboro; 301-952-6001; www.pgcps.pg.k12.md.us
- **Arlington County Public Schools**, 1426 North Quincy Street, Arlington; 703-228-6000; www.arlington.k12.va.us

- **Fairfax County Public Schools**, 10700 Page Avenue, Fairfax; 703-246-2502, www.fcps.k12.va.us
- **Alexandria Public Schools**, 2000 North Beauregard Street, Alexandria; 703-824-6600; www.acps.k12.va.us
- **Falls Church Public Schools**, 803 West Broad Street, Falls Church; 703-248-5600; www.fccps.k12.va.us

PARENT ORGANIZATIONS

To find your local PTA and regional council of PTAs, contact:
- **D.C. Congress of PTAs**, 202-543-0333
- **Maryland PTA**, 410-235-7290, www.mdpta.org
- **Virginia PTA**, 804-264-1234, www.vapta.org
- **National PTA**, 800-307-4PTA, www.pta.org

Other organizations working to improve students' D.C. public school experience include:
- **D.C. Action for Children**, 202-234-9404, www.dckids.org
- **D.C. Voice**, 202-986-8535, www.dcvoice.org
- **Parents United for the D.C. Public Schools**, 202-518-3667, www.dcwatch.com/parents
- **Communities In Schools of Washington, D.C.**, 202-610-3316, www.cisdc.org

PUBLIC SCHOOL EVALUATIONS

D.C. schools are evaluated by the Stanford-9 Achievement Test, and average test scores at each school are used to calculate funding and staffing priorities. For information about each school's Stanford-9 scores, visit www.k12.dc.us/dcps and select Stanford-9 Tests under "Curriculum." The annual Maryland School Performance Report is available from the State Department of Education at www.msp.msde.state.md.us, or by calling 888-246-0016 or 410-767-0600. In Virginia, controversial high-stakes Standards of Learning tests can determine the future not only of schools, but of individual students and teachers. For more information, go to www.pen.k12.va.us and select SOL Testing under "Most Requested Information."

PRIVATE AND PAROCHIAL SCHOOLS

Every jurisdiction in the Washington area has a range of private elementary and secondary schools, both religious and secular. Many parents, religious or not, prefer the academic and disciplinary rigor of Catholic, Jewish, and other parochial schools. Others seek alternative secular approaches to education, including Waldorf and Montessori methods, the International Baccalaureate program recognized throughout Europe, or a bilingual or multicultural setting.

Private school tuition ranges from $1,000 to $15,000 a year, depending on a school's academic reputation and social prestige—Sidwell Friends School in Tenleytown was commanding more than $12,000 a year even before Chelsea Clinton enrolled there. Most private schools offer some need-based scholarships, but get in line and don't count on it. In D.C., a controversial pilot program awards tuition vouchers to a few needy families, and the credit is good toward tuition at any accredited private school, but it doesn't take a huge bite out of the tuition at the best schools.

For the text of state and local regulations governing academic and safety standards for private schools, visit the US Department of Education web site at www.ed.gov/pubs, or call the National Library of Education at 202-219-6018. For more information about private schools, contact:

- **Association of Independent Schools of Greater Washington**, 202-625-9223
- **Association of Independent Maryland Schools**, 410-761-3700, www.aimsmd.org
- **Virginia Association of Independent Schools**, 804-282-3592, www.vais.org
- **National Association of Independent Schools**, 202-973-9700, www.nais-schools.org

Parents Council of Washington, 301-365-3843, www.parentscouncil.org, is the private-school equivalent of a regional council of PTAs.

HOME SCHOOLING

Parents who have misgivings about urban public schools have the right to take their children's education into their own hands. Many parents believe that they are best suited to design an educational program that will engage and challenge their children, responding to each child's unique psychological and intellectual traits. Home schooling is especially popular among strongly religious parents who object to the secular nature of public schools, and among liberal parents who object to the public schools' increasing reliance on educational materials provided by corporate sponsors.

Teaching is not easy—you will need a lot of time and energy to plan and execute a study program that will enable your children to earn a high school diploma at home—but there are plenty of organizations and resources to help you. Check out **Homeschooling Today** magazine online at www.homeschooltoday.com for dozens of useful links.

TUTORS

For a referral to after-school tutors, contact your local school district at the number or web site above. In D.C., the direct number for tutor referrals is 202-442-5155. Your child's teacher should also be able to recommend appropriate tutors for specific skills. Private tutoring services are listed in the Yellow Pages and *Parent Pages*. **TutorFind**, www.tutorfind.com, represents hundreds of tutors at a standard rate of $45 per hour, regardless of subject or grade level. Call 301-585-0650 in D.C. or Maryland, 703-368-6275 in Virginia.

APART FROM METRO STATIONS, THE LEADING HUBS OF TRAFFIC and development in the Washington area are shopping malls. Tysons Corner, a busy cluster of office high-rises in Northern Virginia, was originally a shopping mall and a cluster of car dealerships; today, it's grown into a recognized suburb in its own right. Likewise, you might hear people say they live in White Flint or Seven Corners or Pentagon City—all neighborhoods that grew up around malls of the same name. The vast Potomac Mills discount mall in Woodbridge, VA, draws more visitors than any tourist attraction in the Washington area.

While area malls have lost some traffic, in recent years, to "big-box" stores—destination stores like Wal-Mart, Target, Best Buy, Sports Authority, Borders Books & Music, and Barnes & Noble—Washingtonians still spend $4 billion a year at the area's 10 largest malls. And then there are the ubiquitous strip malls in the suburbs, which typically include a grocery store and a big-box outlet. Rockville Pike, between North Bethesda and downtown Rockville, is practically a two-mile-long strip mall.

In downtown D.C., all but one of the big, elegant, free-standing department stores closed in the early 1990s—many after a century or more. The last holdout is the Hecht Company, whose six-story emporium stands above the Metrorail hub station at Metro Center. Stores today are smaller and more specialized—furniture boutiques abound in Adams Morgan and along U Street NW, and clothing stores line Connecticut Avenue NW between Dupont Circle and the White House. You can find just about anything in Georgetown, along Wisconsin Avenue and M Street NW, from distinctive local shops to popular national chains.

Retail hours here cater to a workaholic climate and busy two-career couples. Almost all stores are open seven days a week, and many—especially in malls—are open until 10 p.m. six days a week and 6 p.m. on Sundays.

Although consumer prices are high, Washington is fertile ground for bargain hunters. There are always people coming and going here, not just after an election—military and diplomatic families get deployed, college students head off to school, graduates move here to launch careers—all contributing to an endless supply of inventory for thrift stores, consignment shops and yard sales. Classified ads, too, are replete with $50 sofas and $100 stereos in good condition.

Unless otherwise noted, stores listed here are in D.C.

SHOPPING MALLS

The handful of malls in the District are fashionable, pricey, and relatively small. Suburban malls range from upscale fashion meccas to utilitarian discount centers. At most of the larger malls, you'll find a good mix of the luxurious and the practical; for a general idea of a mall's character, though, check the list of the major department stores at each mall against the descriptions under **Department Stores** below.

DISTRICT OF COLUMBIA

- **Chevy Chase Pavilion**, 5335 Wisconsin Avenue NW (Metro: Friendship Heights), 202-686-5335; 30 stores including The Cheesecake Factory and Linens 'n' Things
- **Mazza Gallerie**, 5300 Wisconsin Avenue NW (Metro: Friendship Heights), 202-966-6114, www.mazzagallerie.net; 60 stores including Filene's, Neiman Marcus, Williams-Sonoma
- **Shops at Georgetown Park**, 3222 M Street NW (Metrobus: routes 30-36 from Farragut West), 202-342-8190, www.shopsatgeorgetownpark.com; 105 stores including F.A.O. Schwartz, J. Crew
- **The Shops at National Place**, 1331 Pennsylvania Avenue NW (Metro: Metro Center), 202-393-1999; 85 specialty stores and restaurants
- **Union Station**, 50 Massachusetts Avenue NE (Metro: Union Station), 202-289-1908, www.unionstationdc.com; 130 specialty stores and restaurants

MARYLAND

- **Beltway Plaza**, 6000 Greenbelt Road, Greenbelt (Metrobus: routes T15-T17 from Greenbelt), 301-345-1500, http://beltwayplazacenter.com; 120 stores including Burlington Coat Factory, Giant Food, Marshall's, PetSmart, Sports Authority
- **Capitol Plaza Mall**, 6200 Annapolis Road, Landover Hills (Metrobus: routes A11-A15 from Landover), 301-773-6611; 65 stores including Montgomery Ward
- **City Place**, 8661 Colesville Road, Silver Spring (Metro: Silver Spring),

301-589-1091; 65 stores including Burlington Coat Factory, Marshall's, Nordstrom Rack, Ross

- **Congressional Plaza**, 1300 Rockville Pike, Rockville (Metro: Twinbrook); no customer information number; 25 stores including Fresh Fields, Tower Records, Zany Brainy
- **Iverson Mall**, 3737 Branch Avenue, Marlow Heights (Metrobus: route P12 from Addison Road), 301-423-7400, www.iversonmall.com; 70 stores including Montgomery Ward, Value City
- **Lakeforest Mall**, Route 355 & Montgomery Village Avenue, Gaithersburg (Ride-On: routes 57-58 from Shady Grove), 301-670-0599; 160 stores including Hecht's, JC Penney, Lord & Taylor, Sears
- **Landover Mall,** 2103 Brightseat Road, Landover (Metrobus: routes A11-A15 from Landover), 301-341-3200; 110 stores including Hecht's, JC Penney, Sears
- **Laurel Mall**, 14828 Baltimore Avenue, Laurel (Metrobus: route 89 from Greenbelt), 301-953-3300; 105 stores including Hecht's, JC Penney, Montgomery Ward
- **Milestone Center**, Route 355 & Shakespeare Boulevard, Germantown (Ride-On: route 79 from Shady Grove), 301-631-7510; 10 stores including Giant Food, Kohl's, PetSmart, Target, Wal-Mart
- **Montgomery Mall**, Democracy Boulevard & Westlake Drive, Bethesda (Metrobus: routes J1-J3 from Silver Spring), 301-469-6025, www.montgomerymall.shoppingtown.com; 200 stores including Hecht's, JC Penney, Nordstrom, Sears
- **Prince George's Plaza**, 3500 East-West Highway, Hyattsville (Metro: Prince George's Plaza), 301-559-8844, www.princegeorgesplaza.com; 120 stores including Hecht's, JC Penney; farmer's market Tuesdays, in season
- **Westfields Wheaton Plaza**, 11160 Veirs Mill Road, Wheaton (Metro: Wheaton), 301-942-3200, www.wheaton.shoppingtown.com; 140 stores including Giant Food, Hecht's, JC Penney, Montgomery Ward
- **White Flint**, 11301 Rockville Pike, North Bethesda (Metro: White Flint), 301-468-5777, www.shopwhiteflint.com; 125 stores including Borders Books & Music, Bloomingdale's, Dave & Buster's, Lord & Taylor

VIRGINIA

- **Ballston Common Mall**, 4238 Wilson Boulevard, Arlington, 703-243-8088, www.ballston-common.com; 100 stores including Hecht's, JC Penney
- **Dulles Town Center**, Routes 7 and 28, Dulles, 703-404-7120, www.shopdullestowncenter.com; 170 stores including Hecht's, JC Penney, Lord & Taylor, Sears

- **Fair Lakes Center**, 6 Fair Lakes Parkway, Fairfax (Metrobus: route 12S from Vienna), 703-227-0883; 50 stores including Best Buy, Wal-Mart
- **Fair Oaks Mall**, I-66 and US Route 50, Fairfax (Metrobus: route 2G from Vienna), 703-359-8302; 180 stores including Hecht's, JC Penney, Lord & Taylor, Macy's, Sears
- **Fashion Centre at Pentagon City**, 1100 South Hayes Street, Arlington, (Metro: Pentagon City) 703-415-2400, www.fashioncentrepentagon.com; 160 stores including Macy's, Nordstrom
- **Landmark Mall**, 5801 Duke Street, Alexandria (Metrobus: routes 29K-29N from King Street), 703-354-8405; 150 stores including Hecht's, JC Penney, Sears
- **Potomac Yard Center**, Jefferson Davis Highway & Reed Avenue, Alexandria (Metrobus: routes 9A, 9E from Pentagon), 703-548-9770; 15 stores including Barnes & Noble, Shoppers Food Warehouse, Target, T.J. Maxx
- **Seven Corners Center**, 6201 Arlington Boulevard, Falls Church (Metrobus: routes 4B, 4H from Rosslyn), 703-986-2200; 40 stores including Barnes & Noble, Best Buy, Home Depot, JoAnn's Fabrics
- **Tysons Corner Center**, 703-893-9400, www.shoptysons.com and **Tysons Galleria**, 703-827-7700, www.tysons-galleria.com, Dolley Madison Boulevard and International Drive, McLean (Metrobus: routes 3W, 3Z from West Falls Church); 340 stores including Bloomingdale's, Hecht's, JC Penney, Lord & Taylor, Macy's, Neiman Marcus, Nordstrom, Saks Fifth Avenue
- **Springfield Mall**, I-95 and Franconia Road, Springfield (Fairfax Connector: route 401 from Franconia-Springfield), 703-971-3600, www.springfieldmall.com; 230 stores including JC Penney, Macy's, Montgomery Ward

OUTLYING AREAS

These malls are outside the area covered in this book, but their huge selections or discount outlets draw thousands of Washingtonians on weekends:
- **Annapolis Mall**, 2002 Annapolis Mall, Annapolis, MD, 410-266-5432, http://annapolis.shoppingtown.com; 160 stores including Hecht's, JC Penney, Lord & Taylor, Montgomery Ward, Nordstrom
- **Arundel Mills**, Route 100 & Route 713, Baltimore/Washington International Airport Business District, MD, 410-580-9050, www.millscorp.com/arundel; 200 discount stores including Burlington Coat Factory, Old Navy, Saks Fifth Avenue outlet, T.J. Maxx
- **Columbia Mall**, 10300 Little Patuxent Parkway, Columbia, MD, 410-730-3300, www.themallincolumbia.com; 190 stores including Hecht's, JC Penney, Lord & Taylor, Sears

- **Leesburg Corner Premium Outlets**, Route 7 & Fort Evans Road, Leesburg, VA, 703-737-3071, www.chelseagca.com; 60 discount stores including Liz Claiborne outlet, Saks Fifth Avenue outlet
- **Manassas Mall**, 8300 Sudley Road, Manassas, VA, 703-368-7232, www.manassasmall.com; 120 stores including Hecht's, JC Penney, Montgomery Ward, Sears, Target
- **Potomac Mills**, 2700 Potomac Mills Circle, Woodbridge, VA, 703-643-1855, www.millscorp.com/potomac; 230 discount stores including Saks Fifth Avenue Outlet, Nordstrom Rack, IKEA, Marshall's
- **Prime Outlets at Hagerstown**, I-70 in Hagerstown, MD, 888-883-6288, www.primeoutlets.com; over 90 discount stores including Brooks Brothers, J. Crew and Tommy Hilfiger outlets
- **Prime Outlets at Queenstown**, US Route 50 & US Route 301 in Queenstown, MD, 410-827-8699, www.primeoutlets.com; over 60 discount stores including Bass, J. Crew and Liz Claiborne outlets
- **St. Charles Towne Center**, US Route 301 in Waldorf, MD, 301-870-6997; 130 stores including Hecht's, JC Penney, Kohl's, Montgomery Ward, Sears

DEPARTMENT STORES

- **Bloomingdale's**: renowned for its furniture collections and model rooms, "Bloomies" stores are great for browsers looking for decorating ideas. Tysons Corner Center, White Flint
- **The Hecht Company**: "Hecht's" sells clothing, appliances, furniture, toiletries, electronics, linens and housewares. Stand-alone locations: Metro Center, 12th and G streets NW, Washington, 202-628-6661, and 701 North Glebe Road, Arlington, 703-524-5100; mall locations: Montgomery Mall, Lakeforest Mall, Wheaton Plaza, Prince George's Plaza, Landover Mall, Laurel Mall, Tysons Corner Center, Fair Oaks Mall, Landmark Mall, Ballston Common Mall, Dulles Town Center
- **JC Penney**: has taken over most of the space vacated by the Woodward & Lothrop department store chain that went out of business in the late 1990s, and is now all over town, selling everything from washing machines and lawnmowers to jewelry and cosmetics. Locations: Montgomery Mall, Lakeforest Mall, Wheaton Plaza, Prince George's Plaza, Landover Mall, Laurel Mall, Tysons Corner Center, Springfield Mall, Fair Oaks Mall, Landmark Mall, Ballston Common Mall, Dulles Town Center
- **Lord & Taylor**: this "white glove" store still carries clothing and accessories for the traditional set, and small, select gift items. Locations: 5255 Western Avenue NW, Washington, 202-362-9600; Lakeforest Mall, White Flint, Tysons Corner Center, Fair Oaks Mall, Dulles Town Center

- **Macy's**: attracts fashion-conscious men and women, and it's also attractive to gourmet cooks looking for fine housewares and delicacies. Locations: Tysons Galleria, Fair Oaks Mall, Pentagon City
- **Neiman Marcus**: extravagant and eccentric gift items, from the chocolate Monopoly set to the private submarine, made Neiman Marcus famous, but most come here for the elegant, designer clothing. Locations: Tysons Galleria, Mazza Gallerie
- **Nordstrom**: this West Coast retailer is known for superlative service, knowledgeably selling well-made clothing, cosmetics, toiletries and accessories. Locations: Montgomery Mall, Tysons Corner Center, Pentagon City
- **Saks Fifth Avenue**: carries top-of-the-line clothing and accessories for men, women, and children; its extensive lines of evening wear attract the charity ball crowd. Locations: 5555 Wisconsin Avenue, Chevy Chase, 301-657-9000; Tysons Galleria
- **Sears**: known for Craftsman brand power tools, Sears is also a mainstay for family clothing, appliances and home electronics. Locations: Montgomery Mall, Lakeforest Mall, Landover Mall, Fair Oaks Mall, Landmark Mall, Dulles Town Center

DISCOUNT DEPARTMENT STORES

Many upscale department stores have their own outlets where they sell discontinued, overstocked, or slightly irregular merchandise at reduced prices. Such goods are also sold through discount outlets such as Marshall's, Ross, and T.J. Maxx. Other discount chains—Ames, Caldor, Kmart, and Target—carry name-brand goods, but not the designer labels available at upscale department stores.

- **Ames**, various locations; call 800-746-7263 or see www.amesstores.com
- **Caldor**, 8041 Kennett Street, Silver Spring, 301-496-9545
- **Filene's Basement**, 11840 Rockville Pike, 301-881-7830
- **Kmart/Big K/Super K**, various locations; call 866-562-7848 or see www.bluelight.com
- **Marshall's**, various locations; call 301-495-9566
- **Nordstrom Rack**, City Place, 301-608-8118; 15760 Shady Grove Road, Gaithersburg, 301-527-1133
- **Ross**, various locations; call 301-588-7993
- **Syms**, 100 East Broad Street, Falls Church, 703-241-8500
- **Target**, various locations; call 800-800-8800 or see www.target.com
- **T.J. Maxx**, various locations; call 301-464-6334
- **Today's Man**, 7475 Greenbelt Road, Greenbelt, 301-220-3811; 5220 Randolph Road, Rockville
- **Tuesday Morning**, various locations; call 202-942-1884

- **Wal-Mart**, 20910 Frederick Road, Germantown, 301-515-6700; 3330 North Crain Highway, Bowie, 301-805-8850

And don't forget the membership warehouse giants Costco and Sam's Club. They offer low prices on food, electronics, cameras, small appliances, housewares, automotive supplies, sporting goods, even eyeglasses; membership fees apply, and you don't get—or pay for—the level of service you expect from a regular department store. See the **Food** section for locations.

APPLIANCES, ELECTRONICS, COMPUTERS, SOFTWARE

For computer experts, the best deals on hardware may be found in classified ads in the Business section of the *Washington Post* on Mondays, or in *Computer User,* a monthly tabloid distributed in newspaper boxes at Metro stations. If you don't need the latest technology, the classified ads in the Washington City Paper are bursting with bargains on used computers. Savings can also be found at the MarketPro Computer Show & Sale, a consumer-oriented trade show held almost every weekend, rotating through a series of suburban venues. Dealers sell clearance items for less than half the retail price, and if you find what you want, the savings will certainly cover the $7 admission. See www.marketproshows.com for dates and locations.

For computer stores, check the Yellow Pages under "Computers"; look for other home electronics under "Appliances," "Stereo," and "Television," or try these electronics dealers and appliance stores:

- **Belmont TV**, 9101 Marshall Avenue, Laurel, 301-498-5600; 12500 Layhill Road, Wheaton, 301-942-1300; 4723 King Street, Arlington, 703-671-8500; www.belmonttv.com; mostly TVs, VCRs and DVD players
- **Best Buy**, over a dozen locations—see www.bestbuy.com—sells computers, home electronics, small appliances and housewares.
- **Circuit City**, two dozen locations; call 301-386-6120 or 877-932-2225 or go to www.circuitcity.com; carries a huge selection of TVs, VCRs, stereos and multimedia equipment.
- **CompUSA**, 5901 Stevenson Avenue, Alexandria, 703-212-6610; 8357 Leesburg Pike, Vienna, 703-821-7700; 1776 East Jefferson Street, Rockville, 301-816-8963; www.compusa.com; the area's largest retailer of home computer hardware and software.
- **Graffiti Audio/Video**, 1219 Connecticut Avenue NW, 202-296-8412; 4914 Wisconsin Avenue NW, 202-244-9643; 7810 Old Georgetown Road, Bethesda, 301-907-3660; a local chain carrying TVs, VCRs, and stereo components.
- **Murrell's Electronics**, 2140 Wisconsin Avenue NW, 202-338-7730; sells discount TVs and stereos—not top brands, but cheap.
- **Office Depot**, over a dozen locations; call 888-GO-DEPOT or see

www.officedepot.com; sells computers, software, and supplies such as printer cartridges.

- **Radio Shack**, dozens of locations, mostly in shopping malls; call 800-843-7422; remains the definitive source of parts for do-it-yourself electronics, and a reputable dealer of radio and phone equipment.
- **Staples**, over a dozen locations; call 301-251-8640 or 800-3-STAPLE, or see www.staples.com; sells computers, software, and related supplies.

MAJOR APPLIANCES

- **ABD Appliance Distributors**, 7406-A Lockport Place, Lorton, 703-550-8585; 300 D Street SW, Suite 319, 202-488-1000, www.abdappliancedistrib.com; boasts the area's largest appliance showroom at its Virginia location.
- **Appliance Distributors Unlimited**, 729 Erie Avenue, Takoma Park, 301-608-2600, www.adu.com
- **ApplianceLand, Etc.**, 10801 Baltimore Avenue, Beltsville, 301-595-7360; 866 Rockville Pike, Rockville, 301-762-5544; carries Amana, Whirlpool and other name-brand appliances.
- **Bray & Scarff**, seven area locations; see the Yellow Pages or check www.brayscarff.com; offers next-day delivery.
- **DAD's Discount Appliance Distributors**, 12200 Distribution Place, Beltsville, 301-937-0222, www.dadsappliance.com; carries kitchen appliances.

FUTONS & MATTRESSES

- **Atlantic Futon**, 7501 Leesburg Pike, Tysons Corner, 703-893-9125
- **Bedroom Factory Outlet**, 9445 US Route 1, Laurel, 800-800-2378; 515 Baltimore Pike, Bel Air, 888-888-5376; www.bfo.com
- **Custom Fit Foam & Futon**, 15809 Frederick Road, Rockville, 301-670-9090
- **Dial-A-Mattress**, 10235 Southard Drive, Beltsville, 301-937-0800
- **Ellen's Futon Wholesalers**, 516-D South Van Dorn Street, Alexandria, 703-823-8127; 11106 Lee Highway, Fairfax, 703-352-5111, www.ellensfuton.com
- **Futons & Furniture Outlet**, 2130 P Street NW, 202-833-3717; 5620 General Washington Drive, 703-941-5042
- **The Market Home Furnishings**, 3229 M Street NW, 202-333-1234; Fair Lakes Center, 703-222-1200, www.markethomefurnishings.com
- **Mattress Discounters**, dozens of locations; call 202-244-3905 or see www.mattressdiscounters.com

- **Mattress Warehouse**, more than 20 locations; call 301-230-BEDS or see www.sleephappens.com
- **Urban Accents**, 3111 Duke Street, Alexandria, 703-370-1211
- **United Futons**, 13929 Baltimore Avenue, Laurel, 301-776-0006; 819 Hungerford Drive, Rockville, 301-315-0222

CARPETS, RUGS & TILE

If you don't have time to go to a carpet showroom, **Carpet Discounters**, 301-568-5900, will bring samples to your home. Most carpet dealers will make free house calls to provide estimates, and most offer their own financing plans.

- **Best Buy Carpet**, 1401 Chain Bridge Road, McLean 703-749-0700, www.bestbuycarpet.com
- **Bill's Carpet Warehouse**, 3914 Bexley Place, Marlow Heights, 301-423-4060; 10980 Lee Highway, Fairfax, 703-691-1664; Amherst Avenue & Old Keene Mill Road, Springfield, 703-569-8020
- **Custom Carpet Shop**, 5414 Randolph Road, Rockville, 301-881-7322
- **Georgetown Carpet**, 2208 Wisconsin Avenue NW, 202-342-2262; 7828 Wisconsin Avenue, Bethesda, 301-654-0202; 2976 Gallows Road, Falls Church, 703-207-0006; 10708 Lee Highway, Fairfax, 703-273-2500
- **Georgetown Floorcoverings**, 3233 K Street NW, 202-965-3200, www.georgetownfloorcoverings.baweb.com
- **J&J Oriental Rug Gallery**, 1200 King Street, Alexandria, 703-548-0000
- **Kemper Carpet**, 12145 Rockville Pike, 301-231-6300; 7501 Leesburg Pike, Tysons Corner, 703-734-0300; 3895 Pickett Road, Fairfax, 703-978-9001
- **Ken's Carpet Corner**, 2662 University Boulevard, Wheaton, 301-949-0550
- **Manoukian Brothers**, 1862 Columbia Road NW, 202-332-0700, www.manoukianbrothers.com
- **Mark Keshishian & Sons**, 4505 Stanford Street, Chevy Chase, 301-654-4044
- **Mill Direct Floor Coverings**, 7508 Richmond Highway, Alexandria, 703-765-1900; 8446 Lee Highway, Merrifield, 703-698-0002
- **Parivizian**, 7034 Wisconsin Avenue, Bethesda, 301-654-8989; 8065 Leesburg Pike, Tysons Corner, 703-749-9090; Landmark Mall, 703-750-0404
- **Park Carpet**, 8433 Lee Highway, Fairfax, 703-560-5100; Lee Highway & Glebe Road, Arlington, 703-524-7275, www.parkcarpet.baweb.com
- **Tile & Carpetland**, 11414 Georgia Avenue, Wheaton, 301-942-6050; 12516 Parklawn Drive, Rockville, 301-984-6222, www.tileandcarpetland.baweb.com

FURNITURE

Retailers of traditional fine furniture advertise in the *Washington Post* Sunday magazine and the *Washingtonian*. For vintage, funky or avant-garde styles check out the Adams Morgan and U Street boutiques, which advertise in the *Washington City Paper*.

- **Apartment Zero**, 406 7th Street NW, 202-628-4067, http://apartmentzero.com; sells sleek, artistic modern furniture.
- **Carolina Furniture Gallery**, Georgia and Missouri avenues NW, 202-722-1900, offers modern styles at moderate prices.
- **Crate & Barrel**, 703-847-8555, www.crateandbarrel.com; mainly known for housewares, the Tysons Corner store carries modern and country traditional furniture.
- **Danker Furniture**: 120 Halpine Road, Rockville, 301-881-6010; 1211 South Fern Street, Arlington, 703-416-0200; Danker Office Furniture, 10670 Lee Highway, Fairfax, 703-691-4333; sells elegant contemporary designs.
- **Ethan Allen Gallery**: 4473 Connecticut Avenue NW, 202-364-2301; 1800 Rockville Pike, 301-984-4360; 8520-A Leesburg Pike, Vienna, 703-356-6405; Springfield Mall, 703-971-4504; known for its selection of early American furniture.
- **Good Wood**, 1428 U Street NW, 202-986-3640; sells select vintage and restored wooden furniture.
- **Home Elements**, half a dozen locations in the suburbs; see the Yellow Pages or www.homelements.com; carries contemporary pieces.
- **Home Rule**, 1807 14th Street NW, 202-797-5544; helps trendy Logan Circle residents outfit vintage downtown homes.
- **The Hub**, six locations, call 301-762-6164; sells traditional and contemporary discount room sets.
- **IKEA**, Potomac Mills, 703-494-4532; 800-434-IKEA, www.ikea-usa.com; offers a huge selection of inexpensive, stylish, sturdy, mostly wood furniture to be assembled from simple kits.
- **Jennifer Convertibles**: 11520 Rockville Pike, 301-984-3490; 18306 Contour Road, Gaithersburg, 301-670-0793; 8849 Greenbelt Road, Greenbelt; 301-552-4144, sells modular pieces that can be arranged to fit any living room.
- **LA-Z-BOY Furniture Galleries**, eight locations; see the Yellow Pages or call 301-770-1658; specializes in recliners, sofas and sleep sofas.
- **The Market Home Furnishings**, 3229 M Street NW, 202-333-1234; Fair Lakes Center, 703-222-1200, www.markethomefurnishings.com; offers a good selection of futons, sofas, lamps, bookcases and accent pieces in classic and modern styles.

- **Marlo**, six locations, 202-842-0100; sells traditional and contemporary discount room sets.
- **Reincarnations Furnishings**, 1606 17th Street NW, 202-319-1606; 917 King Street, Alexandria, 703-838-9217; sells carefully restored antique pieces.
- **SCAN**, six locations, 301-656-2900, www.scanfurniture.com; sells modern wood furniture in Scandinavian styles.
- **Saah**, 811 Hungerford Drive, Rockville, 301-424-6911; 2330 Columbia Pike, Arlington, 703-920-1500; 5641-F General Washington Drive, 703-256-4315; 14802 Build America Drive, Woodbridge, 703-494-4167; specializes in unfinished wood pieces awaiting custom stains and treatments.
- **Skynear & Co.**, 18th Street & Wyoming Avenue NW, 202-797-7160; 3301 New Mexico Avenue NW, 202-362-5523, www.skynearonline.com; carries an eclectic array of funky and elegant modern furnishings, including direct imports at bargain prices.
- **Storehouse**, five locations, 301-231-7310, www.storehousefurniture.com
- **Theodore's**, 2233 Wisconsin Avenue NW, 202-333-2300, www.theodores.com; sells sleek, modern designer pieces.
- **Zfutons+Furniture**, 2130 P Street NW, 202-833-3717; 5620 General Washington Drive, Alexandria, 703-941-5042; claims to offer the largest selection of futon frames and covers in the area. Also carries beds and other furniture.

HOUSEWARES & LINENS

If the department stores don't have just what you're looking for, these specialty stores might:
- **Anthropologie**, 11500 Rockville Pike, North Bethesda, 301-230-6520; sells ornamental pieces and furnishings with a Southwestern flair.
- **Appalachian Spring**, 1415 Wisconsin Avenue NW, 202-337-5780; Union Station, 202-682-0505; 1641 Rockville Pike, 301-230-1380; fine pottery and wood accessories.
- **April Cornell**, 3278 M Street NW, 202-625-7887; linens and ornamental pieces.
- **The Container Store**, Congressional Plaza, 301-770-4800; 8508 Leesburg Pike, Vienna, 703-833-2122; sells... guess what?
- **Chesapeake Knife & Tool**, Montgomery Mall, 301-365-3440; Wheaton Plaza, 301-946-7971; Lakeforest Mall, 301-258-0450; sells and sharpens fine cutlery.

- **Crate & Barrel**, Montgomery Mall, 301-365-2600; Tysons Corner, 703-847-8555; outlet, 1700 Prince Street, Alexandria, 703-739-8800, www.crateandbarrel.com; home accessories, from giant candles to wrought-iron wine racks to beach umbrellas to cheese graters.
- **Dean & DeLuca**, 3276 M Street NW, 202-342-2500; the gourmet food store has a good kitchenware department at its Georgetown location.
- **Finewares**, 7042 Carroll Avenue, Takoma Park, 301-270-3138, sells pottery and craft pieces by local artisans on consignment.
- **Hecht's Clearance Center**, 6200 Little River Turnpike, Alexandria, 703-354-9542, sells discontinued or overstocked housewares.
- **Hinckley Pottery**, 1707 Kalorama Road NW, 202-745-7055, www. hinckleypottery.com; sells fine handmade pottery—and offers classes.
- **Linens 'n' Things**, eight locations; check the business section of the White Pages or see www.linensnthings.com; sells a huge line of housewares and accessories at moderate prices.
- **Pier One Imports**, 12 locations; 301-657-9196, 800-245-4595, www.pier1.com; sells a wide range of housewares and linens.
- **Platypus**, Georgetown Park, 202-338-7680; elegant accent pieces including wine racks and fine glassware
- **Pottery Barn**, White Flint, 301-230-0020; comfortable and well-made home furnishings and kitchenware.
- **Reed Electric Co**. 1611 Wisconsin Avenue NW, 202-338-7500, carries practically every kind of lighting imaginable—even ballroom chandeliers.
- **Restoration Hardware**, 1222 Wisconsin Avenue NW, 202-625-2771; 614 King Street, Alexandria, 703-299-6220; Tysons Corner Center, 703-821-9655, www.restorationhardware.com; sells ornamental fixtures and knick knacks as well as old-fashioned tools.
- **Rodman's**, 5100 Wisconsin Avenue NW, 202-363-3466; Veirs Mill & Randolph roads, Wheaton, 301-946-3100; sells housewares, small appliances, and groceries under one roof.
- **Williams-Sonoma,** eight locations, mostly in shopping malls; call 800-541-1262 or see www.williams-sonoma.com. Sells high-end cookware and hard-to-find utensils.

For home trimmings such as towel racks, doorknobs, switch plates, curtain rods, and doors, check out **The Brass Knob**, which sells salvaged antique architectural elements at 2311 18th Street NW, 202-332-3370. And **Rugs to Riches** sells high-end vintage home furnishings at 116 King Street, Alexandria, 703-739-4662.

HARDWARE & GARDEN CENTERS

With the demise of local hardware giant Hechinger, other hardware and garden superstores, such as Home Depot and Lowe's, have stepped up and filled the void. But, don't forget about the many neighborhood hardware stores scattered about Washington, where the lights are dim and you'll find more nails and hammers than decorator accessories. **Carl's** at 5700 Georgia Avenue NW, and **Adams Morgan Hardware** at 2200 18th Street NW are veritable neighborhood institutions—just for example. Check the Yellow Pages or go for a walk to find a gem near you. Here are the major regional home and garden stores:

- **Behnke Nurseries**, 11300 Baltimore Avenue, Beltsville, 301-656-3311; 7405 River Road, Bethesda, 301-469-7690; 700 Watkins Park Drive, Largo, 301-249-2492
- **Fischer's**, 6129 Backlick Road, Springfield, 703-451-3700
- **Frank's Nursery & Crafts**, six locations; call 703-591-6851 or see www.franks.com.
- **Hardware City**, 10504 Connecticut Avenue, Kensington, 301-933-2027; 11105 New Hampshire Avenue, Silver Spring, 301-593-3200; 13711 Annapolis Road, Bowie, 301-464-9030
- **Home Depot**, seven locations; see the Yellow Pages or call 301-680-3500
- **J.H. Burton & Sons Nurseries**, 5950 Ager Road, Hyattsville, 301-559-1100
- **Johnson's Flower & Garden Center**, 4200 Wisconsin Avenue NW, 202-244-6100; 10313 Kensington Parkway, Kensington, 301-946-6700; Route 28 and Quince Orchard Road, Gaithersburg, 301-948-5650; 5011 Laytonsville Road, Olney, 301-987-1940
- **Lowe's**, 205 Kentlands Boulevard, Gaithersburg, 301-208-0400; 16301 Heritage Boulevard, Bowie, 301-805-8000; 10440 Campus Way S, Upper Marlboro, 301-350-6777; 6750 Richmond Highway, Alexandria, 703-765-8011; www.lowes.com
- **Merrifield Garden Center**, 8132 Lee Highway, Merrifield, 703-560-6222; 12101 Lee Highway, Fairfax, 703-968-9600
- **Roozen Nursery & Garden Center**, 9513 Georgia Avenue, Silver Spring, 301-565-9544; 8009 Allentown Road, Fort Washington; 7610 Little River Turnpike, Annandale, 301-941-2900
- **Smith & Hawken**, 3077 M Street NW, 202-965-2680
- **Strosnider's**, 6930 Arlington Road, Bethesda, 301-654-5688; 10110 River Road, Potomac, 301-299-6333

Contact **Garden Resources of Washington (GROW)** at 202-234-0591 for information about local garden clubs. Also, the **National Arboretum** sponsors gardening classes and plant sales—call 202-245-2726.

SPORTING GOODS

Discount chain department stores and The Sports Authority superstores attract a lot of weekend athletes, offering good selections of recreational equipment and discount prices. For enthusiasts, there are specialty stores for almost every sport. Along with the new L.L. Bean retail stores in Tysons Corner and Columbia Mall, the REI co-op offers offer the biggest selection of camping, climbing, and cycling gear. REI stores are open to everyone, but members get discounts and dividends.

- **Bikes USA**, nine locations; call 301-590-3000
- **The Dive Shop**, 3013 Nutley Street, Fairfax, 703-698-7220
- **Fitness Resource**, 2946-I Chain Bridge Road, Oakton, 703-938-1400
- **Fleet Feet**, 1841 Columbia Road NW, 202-387-3888
- **The Hockey Stop**, 5544 Nicholson Lane, Rockville, 301-770-4500
- **Hudson Trail Outfitters**, nine locations; see the Yellow Pages or call 202-363-9810
- **L.L. Bean**, Tysons Corner, 703-288-4466; Columbia Mall, 800-341-4341; www.llbean.com
- **Modell's**, 10 locations; see the Yellow Pages or www.modellssavings.com
- **Potomac Ski & Sail**, 3610 University Boulevard W, Kensington, 301-949-7575
- **REI**, 9801 Rhode Island Avenue, College Park, 301-982-9681; 3509 Carlin Springs Road, Baileys Crossroads, 703-379-9400
- **Rugby & Soccer Supply**, 2744 Gallows Road, Vienna, 703-280-5540
- **Ski Center**, 49th Street and Massachusetts Avenue NW, 202-966-4474
- **Soccer American**, 3835 Plyers Mill Road, Kensington, 301-942-9010
- **Sports Authority**, 12055 Rockville Pike, Rockville, 301-231-8650; 110 Odendhal Avenue, Gaithersburg, 301-926-3445
- **Tennis Factory**, 2500 Wilson Boulevard, Arlington, 703-522-2700
- **Washington Golf Center**, eight locations; see the Yellow Pages or call 202-728-0088

SECONDHAND SHOPPING

ANTIQUE DEALERS

"Antiqueing" is a favorite weekend pastime in Washington, especially among Georgetown and Northern Virginia homeowners looking to fill their 19th-century homes with period pieces. Antique stores abound in pedigreed neighborhoods like Georgetown and Old Town Alexandria, and prices reflect the refined surroundings. For more affordable antique dealers, head toward Howard Avenue in Kensington and East Diamond Avenue in

Gaithersburg—or, for the real troves of antique furniture and decor, go to the old town sections of Ellicott City, Frederick, and Waldorf in Maryland; to Baltimore's Antique Row on North Howard Street; or to the villages of Sperryville and New Market in Virginia.

For vintage clothing, 1950s funk, conversation pieces, and old glassware and housewares, there are a number of vintage shops on 18th Street NW in Adams Morgan and Carroll Avenue in Takoma Park.

Watch the Weekend section of the *Washington Post* on Fridays for listings of antique shows, and the classified ads in the *Post* and *Washington City Paper* for estate sales.

THRIFT & CONSIGNMENT SHOPS

Almost every neighborhood has at least one resale shop. Some are thrift stores, whose merchandise is donated and whose profits benefit a charitable organization; others are consignment shops.

Small resale shops offer bargains on clothing and housewares in particular, and patient scavengers browse forgotten stacks of books and records. The larger shops listed here also handle furniture and small appliances:

- **Amvets**, 6101 Georgia Avenue NW, 202-291-4013
- **Arlington Resale Thrift Shoppe**, 2919 Columbia Pike, Arlington, 703-486-2362
- **Goodwill Industries** runs more than a dozen thrift stores in the area. Call 202-636-4225 or look in the business section of the White Pages for locations.
- **The Salvation Army** runs 11 thrift stores in the suburbs and one in D.C. Call 202-783-9085 or look in the business section of the White Pages for locations.
- **Rainbow Christian Services Thrift Shop**, 2620 Wilson Boulevard, Arlington, 703-243-0239

For a complete directory of Washington-area resale shops, order a copy of *A Guide to Washington's Thrift & Consignment Shops* by William West Hopper, available for $9 from Washington's Thrift & Consignment Publications, P.O. Box 42712, Northwest Station, Washington, D.C. 20015-6112.

Pawn shops, which sell forfeited collateral from cash loans, can be a source of good deals on cameras, jewelry, musical instruments, and home electronics. Look in the Yellow Pages under "Pawn." Check to make sure a pawnbroker is licensed and bonded; in the District, look for members of the industry's self-monitoring group, the Pawnbrokers Association of D.C.

YARD SALES & FLEA MARKETS

Every weekend, from April through October, telephone poles are festooned with hand-lettered signs pointing to yard sales. These aren't necessarily junk sales—remember, a lot of government families live here and move around as careers unfold. Some yard sales are listed in the classifieds, especially in the local Journal or Gazette newspapers; devotees scour these ads and get to the sales early. Furniture, musical instruments, cameras, and other prize items are often sold within the first few minutes of a yard sale.

Community flea markets, church bazaars, and multi-family yard sales are listed in the Weekend section of the *Washington Post*; also, there are permanent flea markets in the spring and summer across from Eastern Market, 7th & C streets SE, and in Georgetown, across from the Safeway at 1855 Wisconsin Avenue NW.

CONSUMER RESOURCES—SHOPPING

Before you shop for a houseful of furniture, appliances, and electronics, check out the reviews local businesses have earned for the quality and the price of their goods and services.

- **Washington Consumers' Checkbook**, www.checkbook.org, 202-347-7283; the regional edition of *Consumers' Checkbook*, a publication of the non-profit Center for the Study of Services, is a magazine that rates everything from retail stores and restaurants to HMOs and insurance plans. The companion *Bargains* newsletter lists the best prices in town on specific models of appliances and electronics. Findings are sometimes reported in the Style section of the *Washington Post.* Subscribers can take part in consumer-to-consumer message boards; read the online *Guide to Washington Area Restaurants*, with more than 22,000 customer ratings of hundreds of restaurants; read the biweekly newsletter *CarDeals*, which lists car manufacturers' rebates and incentives; and receive discounts on car-shopping services and publications including *Guide to Top Doctors, Hospital Guide,* and *Federal Employees Guide to Health Insurance.* A two-year subscription is $30 for four issues of *Checkbook* magazine, the *Bargains* newsletter, and access to the online resources. Online access only is $25 for two years. For an additional one-time fee of $25, you can view all archived *Checkbook* reports and ratings online as long as you maintain a subscription.
- **Brandwise.com** offers online product reviews based on testing by the Good Housekeeping Institute. Categories include electronics, lawn and garden, small appliances, baby products, home gyms, and power tools.

- ***Washingtonian* Online**, www.washingtonian.com, offers recent articles and annual features online, including the latest guide to "Cheap Eats," "100 Very Best Restaurants," "Top Doctors," and "Weekend Getaways."
- **Better Business Bureau of Metro Washington D.C**. is a membership association whose goal is to hold the business community to high ethical standards. You can view an online database at www.dc.bbb.org that shows a "satisfactory" rating for companies that do not have an unusual volume or pattern of customer complaints, are not facing serious legal action, and meet certain standards of conduct in responding to customer complaints referred by the organization. Automated help is available 24 hours a day at 202-393-8000.
- Local **referrals**—there is no substitute for a personal review, positive or negative, of a specific business. In the District, the online newsletter ***Themail*** is read by hundreds of residents who know the city well and care about their neighborhoods. For a virtual earful about the best and worst places to buy a futon, fresh bagels, a car, or a pet guinea pig, send an e-mail message to themail@dcwatch.com asking for recommendations. (Messages to *Themail* are compiled and distributed to subscribers on Sunday and Wednesday nights.) Also check out **www.epinions.com**, a national service which offers hundreds of consumer reviews of products and companies.

FOOD

Washington isn't exactly famous for its restaurant scene, but the city deserves more credit than it gets. The District and, increasingly, the suburbs offer enough culinary choices to please any connoisseur exploring cuisines from all over the world. Individual restaurants come and go, but there's always a new bistro or Thai noodle house or vegetarian Tandoori place stepping up to face the *Washington Post's* food critic, Tom Sietsema.

Neighborhoods like Adams Morgan, Bethesda, Dupont Circle, Wheaton, Woodley Park, and Capitol Hill can keep the most avid restaurant-hopper busy for years, and there are plenty of downtown residents who dine out twice a day, every day, and never get bored.

Zagat's Restaurant Survey, available at www.firstbooks.com, compiles consumer ratings, while the restaurant reviews in the ***Washington Post*** (in the Food section on Wednesday and in the Sunday magazine) offer more detailed opinions of new restaurants, or old favorites with new chefs. Also, you can search a database of restaurants by neighborhood, cuisine, delivery service, and other features at http://dc.diningweb.com. The ***Washington Consumers' Checkbook*** web site, www.checkbook.org, also offers restaurant ratings. For a directory of vegetarian restaurants and grocers, contact the **Vegetarian Society of D.C.** at 202-362-8349. And don't forget the Yellow Pages, where restaurants are listed by cuisine.

Even if you like to dine out a lot, you will, at some point, need to buy some groceries. Hardly any home in the Washington area is more than a mile or two from a major supermarket, but there are dozens of neighborhood markets and specialty stores catering to gourmet, ethnic, or health-conscious shoppers. And, when you don't have time to cook *or* go out, there are delivery services that will pick up your takeout order from any restaurant in your neighborhood and deliver it to your door. (See the **Helpful Services** chapter.)

For a directory of farmers' markets, community gardens, community-supported agriculture or "farm-share" programs, and other ways to "think globally, eat locally," visit www.goodfooddc.net. The informative web site is maintained by Community Harvest, a local nonprofit that promotes locally-grown food with an emphasis on organic and sustainable production. Dozens of neighborhoods have little farmers' markets once or twice a week, but two big markets remain from the bygone days of cavernous market halls: **Eastern Market** on Capitol Hill, and **Montgomery County Farm Women's Co-op** in Bethesda. (See **Farmers' Markets** below for locations and hours.) From organic peaches and corn to free-range beef and Chesapeake Bay fish, the stalls of these old-fashioned markets are a kaleidoscope of the region's purest tastes and aromas.

Finally, in an international city of 3.5 million people, it's no surprise that it's hard to identify a unique local cuisine. New Orleans has its Cajun food and Baltimore has Chesapeake Bay seafood; Philadelphia has its signature dish, cheesesteaks, and Boston has baked beans. In 2000, *Washington Post* readers were invited to nominate a culinary symbol for the city. Inspired by a favorite dish at Ben's Chili Bowl, 1213 U Street NW, the winner was the Washington half-smoke, a grilled kosher sausage served like a hot dog, topped with sauerkraut if you like. Sure enough, in downtown D.C. and along the Mall, ubiquitous vending trucks do a lively business in half-smokes.

SUPERMARKETS

Giant Food and Safeway supermarkets have dozens of locations in the Washington area, and two big Southern chains, Food Lion and Harris Teeter, are making inroads in Virginia. Fresh Fields/Whole Foods Market stores, specializing in natural and organic foods, serve Northwest D.C., Montgomery County, and Northern Virginia. Shopper's Food Warehouse supermarkets offer slight discounts in a no-frills, no-nonsense shopping environment. Check the Yellow Pages or the advertising supplements to the *Washington Post* on Sundays and Wednesdays.

Some supermarkets in D.C. have earned nicknames: the "Social Safeway" at 1855 Wisconsin Avenue NW, which has a legendary reputation among Georgetown singles, and the "Soviet Safeway" at 17th and Corcoran streets NW, which is notorious for its long lines.

In addition to the major chains, there are plenty of local and independent grocery stores, including countless little markets in apartment buildings or office complexes. Here are some of the larger independent stores:

- **Best Supermarket**, 1507 U Street NW, 202-265-9110
- **Brookville Supermarket**, 3427 Connecticut Avenue NW, 202-244-9114
- **Eighth Street Market**, 419 8th Street SE, 202-548-4919
- **Food Barn**, 6205 Georgia Avenue NW, 202-726-4350
- **Greenbelt Co-op** (worker-owned), 121 Center Way, Greenbelt, 301-474-0522
- **Grosvenor Market**, 10401 Grosvenor Place, Bethesda, 301-493-6217
- **Magruder's**, 5626 Connecticut Avenue NW, 202-244-7800; 3501 Connecticut Avenue NW, 202-237-2531
- **Rodman's Discount Gourmet & Wine**, 5100 Wisconsin Avenue NW, 202-363-3466; Veirs Mill and Randolph roads, Wheaton, 301-946-3100; 5130 Nicholson Lane, Kensington, 301-881-6253
- **Roland's of Capitol Hill**, 333 Pennsylvania Avenue SE, 202-546-9592
- **Snider's**, 1936 Seminary Road, Silver Spring, 301-589-3240

WAREHOUSE STORES

These membership warehouses have low prices on groceries and other household goods, but only in much larger volumes than you would buy at an ordinary grocery store. Don't expect much service, either—part of the savings comes from the fact that there are no baggers, loaders or delivery people.

You'll need a membership card to shop here. Household memberships are available for a fee if you can't get a free card through an employer, union, military base or other institution that has a group membership.

- **Costco**, 10925 Baltimore Avenue, Beltsville, 301-902-2643; 880 Russell Avenue, Gaithersburg, 301-417-1503; 1200 South Fern Street, Arlington, 703-413-2324; 4725 West Ox Road, Fairfax, 703-802-0372; 7373 Boston Boulevard, Springfield, 703-912-1203, www.costco.com
- **Sam's Club**, 8500 Landover Road, Landover, 301-386-5577; 610 North Frederick Avenue, Gaithersburg, 301-216-2550, www.samsclub.com

SPECIALTY FOODS

In the heart of D.C., from Shaw to Mt. Pleasant, corner grocery stores carry good selections of Asian, Mexican, Salvadoran, and Caribbean items. Other ethnic goods may require a trip to a specialty store. With more Fresh

Fields/Whole Foods Markets opening in the area, traditional supermarkets have been forced to expand their offerings of natural and organic foods, though probably not enough for shoppers who put a premium on organic items. If your local supermarket doesn't have everything you need, try these specialty shops.

HEALTH FOOD AND PRODUCE

- **Becraft's Farm Produce**, 14722 New Hampshire Avenue, Silver Spring, 301-236-4545; sells local produce and honey.
- **Bethesda Co-op**, 6500 Seven Locks Road, Bethesda, 301-320-2530; member-owned vegetarian market with extensive bulk selections.
- **Cash Grocer Natural Foods**, 1315 King Street, Alexandria, 703-549-9544; carries bulk goods and organic produce.
- **Country Boy**, 2211 Randolph Road, Glenmont, 301-942-6355; specializes in fresh local produce.
- **DeBaggio Herbs**, 923 North Ivy Street, Arlington, 703-243-2498; sells fresh herbs and live plants.
- **Ecology Mart**, 8200 Fenton Street, Silver Spring, 301-589-8474; has a huge selection of herbal teas and nutritional supplements as well as health food.
- **Everlasting Life**, 2928 Georgia Avenue NW, 202-232-1700; worker-owned co-op near Howard University
- **Glut Food Co-op**, 4005 34th Street (under the sign of the giant carrot), Mt. Rainier, 301-779-1978, advertises that it hasn't changed much since the 1960s: "Still cheap! Still funky!"
- **Good Health Natural Foods**, 325 Pennsylvania Avenue SE, 202-543-2266; neighborhood store and deli off Capitol Hill.
- **The Greenhouse at Washington National Cathedral**, Wisconsin and Massachusetts avenues NW, 202-537-6263; sells fresh herbs grown on the premises.
- **Heyser's**, 14526 New Hampshire Avenue, Colesville, 301-384-7859; this farm and apple orchard has its own shop, in season.
- **Maryland Food Co-op**, Stamp Student Union Building, University of Maryland, College Park, 301-314-8089; student-owned grocery store and deli on the University of Maryland campus.
- **MOM's (My Organic Market)**, 12050 Parklawn Drive, Rockville, 301-816-4944; Rhode Island Avenue and Edgewood Road, College Park, 301-220-1100; medium-sized grocery stores with an emphasis on fresh organic produce.
- **Potomac Adventist Book & Health Food Store**, 8400 Carroll Avenue, Takoma Park, 301-572-0700; caters to the Seventh Day Adventist community—strictly vegetarian.

- **Senbeb Natural Foods**, 5922 Georgia Avenue NW, 202-723-5566; worker-owned co-op in Brightwood
- **Smile Herb Shop**, 4908 Berwyn Road, College Park, 301-474-8791; specializes in herbs, teas and nutritional supplements.
- **Takoma Park-Silver Spring Co-op**, 201 Ethan Allan Avenue (Route 410), Takoma Park, 301-891-2667; 8309 Grubb Road, Silver Spring, 240-247-2667; this member-owned vegetarian market does enough business every year to be classified by the grocery industry as a supermarket.
- **The Uncommon Market**, 1041 South Edgewood Street, Arlington, 703-521-2667; Arlington's member-owned food co-op.
- **Yes! Natural Foods**, 1825 Columbia Road NW, 202-462-5150; 3425 Connecticut Avenue NW, 202-363-1559; 658 Pennsylvania Avenue SE, 202-546-9850; local chain of health food stores features extensive bulk sections.

ETHNIC FOOD, SEAFOOD MARKETS
- **Addisu Gebeya**, 2202 18th Street NW, 202-986-6013; the place to buy *tef* to make your own Ethiopian *injera*.
- **Chevy Chase Seafood Market**, 5509 Connecticut Avenue NW, 202-686-1068; the definitive uptown source of fresh seafood.
- **Chinese Dragon**, 103 Rhode Island Avenue NW, 202-234-4640; carries Asian spices, noodles and more.
- **Katz's**, 4860 Boiling brook Parkway, Rockville, 301-468-0400; a full-scale kosher supermarket off Rockville Pike.
- **Maine Avenue Seafood Market**, 1100 Maine Avenue SW, 202-479-4188; waterfront source of fish and crabs fresh off the boat.
- **Marchone's**, 11224 Triangle Lane, Wheaton, 301-949-4150; an authentic family-owned Italian market and deli.
- **Middle East Market**, 7006 Carroll Avenue, Takoma Park, 301-270-5154; your headquarters for hummus, tabouleh, baba ghanouj, and falafel.
- **Muskan**, 685 Thayer Avenue, Silver Spring, 301-588-0331; sells Indian spices, vegetarian foods and Ayurvedic health products.
- **Polonez Gourmet Delicatessen & Bakery**, 8113 Georgia Avenue, Silver Spring, 301-495-2650; carries Polish deli specialties.
- **Via Reggio's Italian Grocery & Deli**, 1727 Connecticut Avenue NW, 202-332-9100; sells a vast array of meats, cheeses and packaged goods.

GOURMET FOOD
- **Calvert-Woodley Liquors**, 4339 Connecticut Avenue NW, 202-966-4400; has an extensive deli section with one of the area's best selections of gourmet cheeses.

- **Dean & DeLuca**, 3276 M Street NW, 202-342-2500; 1299 Pennsylvania Avenue NW, 202-628-8155; sells gourmet groceries, prepared foods, wine and kitchenware.
- **Dupont Market**, 1807 18th Street NW, 202-797-0222; neighborhood gourmet shop.
- **Everyday Gourmet**, 6923 Laurel Avenue, Takoma Park, 301-270-2270; mainly a sandwich shop, also sells bread, cheese and packaged goods.
- **Lawson's Gourmet Provisions**, five locations; see the Yellow Pages under "Gourmet Shops"; a local chain selling packaged goods, wine, and prepared foods.
- **Neam's Market**, 3217 P Street NW, 202-338-4694; a neighborhood gourmet shop in Georgetown.
- **Sutton Place Gourmet**, six locations; see the Yellow Pages under "Gourmet Shops"; the oldest gourmet grocer in the area.
- **Trader Joe's**, seven locations, 800-746-7857, www.traderjoes.com; this West Coast chain of budget gourmet shops arrived here in the late 1990s.

BAKERIES

Most of these bakeries have their own sandwich shops or cafes; the giant Eatzi's is actually an emporium of prepared foods for takeout.
- **A. & W. Van Tol**, 2516 University Boulevard W, Wheaton, 301-933-1517
- **Bread & Chocolate**, 2301 M Street NW, 202-833-8360; 5542 Connecticut Avenue NW, 202-966-7413; 666 Pennsylvania Avenue SE, 202-547-2875
- **The Dessert Committee**, 1904 18th Street NW, 202-986-3350
- **Eatzi's Market & Bakery**, 11503 Rockville Pike, North Bethesda, 301-816-2020
- **Firehook Bakery**, 3411 Connecticut Avenue NW, 202-362-2253; 1909 Q Street NW, 202-588-9296; 912 17th Street NW, 202-429-2253
- **Heller's**, 3221 Mt. Pleasant Street NW, 202-265-1190; 4220 Fessenden Street NW, 202-363-9291
- **La Madeleine French Bakery & Cafe**, 3000 M Street NW, 202-337-6975; 7607 Old Georgetown Road, Bethesda, 301-215-9142; 11858 Rockville Pike, Rockville, 301-984-2270
- **Marvelous Market**, eight locations; see the Yellow Pages under "Bakers" or call 301-656-2700
- **Rolling Pin Bakery**, 4916 Annapolis Road, Bladensburg, 301-699-9119
- **Uptown Bakers**, 3313 Connecticut Avenue NW, 202-362-6262
- **Vie de France Bakery & Café**: 1725 K Street NW, 202-775-9193; 600 Maryland Avenue SW, 202-554-7870

For big discounts—often 50% or more—on Wonder and Hostess brand products, and a variety of grocery items from peanut butter and jelly to rice and pasta mixes, check out the **Wonder Bread & Hostess Cakes** outlet store at 3110 Hamilton Street, Hyattsville, 301-853-2180.

FARMERS' MARKETS

Farmers' markets enable you to skip the middleman and buy fresh produce from the people who grew it. It's all locally produced, a lot of it is organic, and usually much less expensive than comparable goods in stores. Most farmers' markets in the D.C. area run from May through November, depending on the harvest.

DISTRICT OF COLUMBIA
- **Adams Morgan**, Saturday, 8 a.m. to 1 p.m. at 18th Street and Columbia Road NW
- **Anacostia**, Friday, 4 p.m. to 6:30 p.m. at Union Temple Baptist Church, 1225 W Street SE
- **Anacostia-Congress Heights**, Saturdays 10 a.m. to 2 p.m. at Congress Heights School, Martin Luther King Jr. and Alabama avenues SE
- **Burleith**, Tuesday, 7 p.m. to 8 p.m., 37th Street and Whitehaven Parkway NW.
- **Capital City Market** (open all year), Tuesday-Thursday, 7 a.m. to 5:30 p.m.; Friday and Saturday, 7 a.m. to 6:30 p.m.; Sunday, 7 a.m. to 2 p.m.; Florida Avenue and 5th Street NE
- **Capitol Hill Eastern Market** (open all year), Saturdays and Sundays all day, 225 7th Street SE, 202-546-2698, www.easternmarket.net
- **Cleveland Park**, Saturday, 11:30 a.m. to 1:30 p.m., 35th and Newark streets NW
- **Columbia Heights**, Wednesday, 4:30 p.m. to 7:30 p.m. at the Josephine Butler Parks Center, 2437 15th Street NW; Saturday, 9 a.m. to noon, at 14th and Irving streets NW (Columbia Heights Metro station)
- **Dupont Circle**, Saturday and Sunday, 9 a.m. to 1 p.m., 20th and Q streets NW (at the Q Street entrance to the Dupont Circle Metro station)
- **Howard University**, Saturday, 11 a.m. to 3 p.m. at Everlasting Life Community Co-op, 2928 Georgia Avenue NW
- **RFK Stadium**, Thursday and Saturday (all year) and Tuesday (summer), 7 a.m. to 5 p.m. in the north parking lot at Oklahoma Avenue and Benning Road NE
- **Shaw**, Saturday, 9 a.m. to 1 p.m. at Bread for the City, 1525 7th Street NW; Shaw Eco-Village Project, Saturday, 9 a.m. to 1 p.m. at 13th and U streets NW

- **Southern Marketplace Shopping Center**, Saturday, 9 a.m. to 6 p.m., 800 Southern Avenue
- **Tenleytown**, Tuesday, 4:30 to 6:30 p.m. at Reno Road and Warren Street NW; Sheridan School, Saturday, 8 a.m. to 11 a.m. at 36th Street and Alton Place NW
- **US Department of Agriculture**, Friday, 10 a.m. to 2 p.m., 12th Street and Independence Avenue SW
- **US Department of Labor**, alternate Tuesdays, 10 a.m. to 2 p.m., 200 Constitution Avenue NW
- **US Department of Transportation**, Tuesday, 10 a.m. to 2 p.m., 400 Seventh Street NW
- **Woodley Park**, Saturday, 9 a.m. to 1 p.m. at All Souls Episcopal Church, Woodley Road and Cathedral Avenue NW

MARYLAND
- **Beltsville**, Thursdays, 10 a.m. to 2 p.m., 5601 Sunnyside Avenue
- **Bethesda**, Montgomery County Farm Women's Cooperative Market, Wednesdays and Saturdays (open all year), 7 a.m. to 3 p.m., 7155 Wisconsin Avenue; National Institutes of Health, Tuesday, 2 p.m. to 6 p.m. at Parking Lot 41B, 9000 Wisconsin Avenue; River Road, Wednesday, 10 a.m. to 2 p.m. at Concord St. Andrews United Methodist Church, River and Goldsboro roads; Bethesda United Church of Christ, Saturday (all year) and Thursday (summer and fall), 10 a.m. to 2 p.m. at Fernwood Drive and Democracy Boulevard; Bethesda-Chevy Chase YMCA, Tuesday, 10 a.m. to 2 p.m., 9401 Old Georgetown Road
- **Bowie**, Sunday, 9 a.m. to noon at Gallant Fox Lane and Route 197
- **College Park**, Saturday, 7 a.m. to noon at Linson Pool, 5211 Paint Branch Parkway
- **Chevy Chase**, Saturday, 9 a.m. to 2 p.m. at Friendship Heights Village Center, 4433 South Park Avenue
- **Gaithersburg**, Thursday, 1 p.m. to 6 p.m. at East Cedar and South Frederick avenues
- **Garrett Park**, Saturday, 9 a.m. to 1 p.m. at the post office, 4600 Waverly Avenue
- **Hyattsville**, Prince George's Plaza, Tuesday, 3 p.m. to 6 p.m. at 3500 East-West Highway
- **Kensington**, Saturday, 8 a.m. to noon at the train station, Howard Avenue off Connecticut Avenue
- **Laurel**, Thursday, 11:30 a.m. to 3 p.m., in the 300 block of Main Street
- **Potomac**, Thursday, 1 p.m. to 4:30 p.m. at Potomac Presbyterian Church, 10301 River Road

- **Riverdale**, Thursday, 3 p.m. to 7 p.m. on Queensbury Road at the train station
- **Rockville**, Wednesday, 11 a.m. to 2 p.m., and Saturdays, 9 a.m. to 1 p.m. at Rockville Town Center (across from the Metro station)
- **Silver Spring**, Saturday, 7 a.m. to 1 p.m. at Fenton Street Village parking lot
- **Takoma Park**, Sunday, 10 a.m. to 2 p.m. at Laurel and Carroll avenues
- **Wheaton**, Sunday, 8 a.m. to 1:30 p.m. on Reedie Drive between Georgia Avenue and Veirs Mill Road

VIRGINIA
- **Annandale**, Thursday, 8 a.m. to 12:30 p.m. at Mason District Park, 6621 Columbia Pike
- **Arlington**: Saturday, 8 a.m. to noon at the Courthouse Square, North 14th Street and North Courthouse Road; Sunday, 10 a.m. to 2 p.m. at Columbia Pike and South Walter Reed Drive
- **Alexandria**: Alexandria City Hall, Saturday (open all year), 5 a.m. to 10 a.m., 301 King Street; Friday, 8:30 a.m. to 12:30 p.m. at Lee District Park, 6601 Telegraph Road; Saturday, 8 a.m. to noon at Mt. Vernon and Oxford avenues
- **Burke Centre**, Saturday, 8 a.m. to noon at the train station, 5671 Roberts Parkway
- **Clifton**, Sunday, 8 a.m. to noon at the post office, Chapel Road
- **Fairfax**, Tuesday, 8 a.m. to 12:30 p.m. at 10480 Main Street
- **Falls Church**, Saturday, 8 a.m. to noon at City Hall, 300 Park Avenue
- **Frying Pan Park**, Wednesday, 8 a.m. to 12:30 p.m., 2709 West Ox Road
- **Herndon**, Thursday, 8:30 a.m. to 12:30 p.m. at Eldon and Spring streets
- **McLean**, Friday, 8:30 a.m. to 12:30 p.m. at Lewinsville Park, 1659 Chain Bridge Road
- **Mt. Vernon**, Tuesday, 8:30 a.m. to 12:30 p.m. at the Mt. Vernon Government Center, 2511 Parkers Lane
- **Reston**, Saturday, 8 a.m. to noon at Lake Anne Plaza, North Shore Drive
- **Vienna**, Wednesday, 8:30 a.m. to 12:30 p.m. at Nottoway Park, 9601 Courthouse Road

COMMUNITY GARDENS

If your yard is too small for a vegetable patch, you can sign up for a plot at a community garden. Some offer community-owned tools and some are bring-your-own. Many vacant lots are being converted into shared gardens; contact Garden Resources of Washington (GROW) at 202-234-0591 for a list or to find out if any new sites are available near you.

COMMUNITY-SUPPORTED AGRICULTURE

In a Community Supported Agriculture (CSA) program, consumers buy shares of a year's harvest directly from the farmer. You pay a fee in the spring, and throughout the harvest season, you'll receive a certain volume of just-picked produce every week. In some CSAs, consumers go to the farm to pick up weekly crates; in others, farmers will make drop-offs at central locations in the city or suburbs. Most CSAs sell shares by the bushel, and only the largest households can use a whole bushel of fruits and vegetables every week. If you split a share with a few neighbors or co-workers, however, this can be an inexpensive and healthy way to get fresh produce. Community Harvest, 202-667-8875, offers smaller CSA shares on a pay-by-the-crate basis instead of seasonal subscriptions. The following farms have CSA programs with distribution points less than an hour from D.C.:

- **Ecosystem Farm** (organic), 301-283-2113 ext. 906, www.accokeek.org; serves Accokeek
- **From the Ground Up**, 202-526-5344, www.clagettfarm.org; serves Anacostia, Brookland, Dupont Circle, Bethesda
- **Maryland Certified Organic Growers Co-op**, 410-472-6764, www.mcogc.pair.com; makes UPS shipments to Maryland and D.C. addresses
- **Planet Veg**, 301-963-3979; serves sites in Montgomery County and selected D.C. office buildings
- **Red Wiggler Foundation**, 301-916-4133, www.redwiggler.org; serves Gaithersburg and Clarksburg
- **Shaw Farms**, 410-531-9577, www.shawfarms.com; serves Columbia, MD
- **Bull Run Mountain Organic Farm**, 703-754-4005, www.bullrun-farm.com; serves Northern Virginia
- **Great Country Farms**, 540-554-2073, www.greatcountryfarms.com; serves Northern Virginia
- **Potomac Vegetable Farms**, 703-759-2119; serves Arlington and Falls Church
- **Waterpenny Farms**, 540-987-8567; serves Northern Virginia

WASHINGTON D.C.'S DIVERSITY IS CLEARLY REFLECTED IN THE vast number of exciting cultural opportunities available. Year round, there is a wide-ranging selection of performances, touring shows, exhibits, and events in which to take part. Many of the events in the District are free or inexpensive, making them easy to take advantage of. In addition to traditional performances or art exhibits, there are endless activities unique to the D.C. area, including events in historic locations—see a play in Ford's Theatre and sit where Lincoln sat, or eat lunch in the National Building Museum where decades of Inaugural Balls have been held. Make sure you visit at least one embassy—D.C. has the highest concentration of embassies in the US, and all of them host events that are open to the public. Some people even make a hobby of embassy hopping; if this looks interesting check www.embassy.org/embassies for a link to the country that interests you.

Most of the following listings are in D.C. That is not to imply that cultural opportunities are limited to the District. In fact, there are loads of events, venues, and performances taking place in the suburbs that should not be missed, and those listed here are just a sample. For more information about cultural events in your own community, check in your local paper's weekly events section or the arts and entertainment guide.

Area-wide publications include:
- **The Washington Post**, www.washingtonpost.com
- **Washington City Paper**, www.washingtoncitypaper.com
- **Washingtonian Magazine**, www.washingtonian.com

Neighborhood and regional newspapers that offer area-specific listings include:
- **Georgetowner** www.georgetowner.com
- **Intowner**, www.intowner.com
- **Northwest Current**, 202-244-7223

- **_Baltimore Sun_**, www.sunspot.net
- **_Montgomery County Sentinel_** and **_Prince George's Sentinel_** www.thesentinel.com (both in Virginia)
- **_Fairfax Times_** (serving the entire Fairfax County) www.fairfaxtimes.com
- **_Eastern Loudon Times_** 703-430-5900

TICKETS

If you go directly to the box office to buy your tickets, you'll save some money on pesky handling fees, but if you want the convenience of buying tickets over the phone or online, there are a few options. **TicketMaster** sells tickets to almost every event in town. Call 703-573-7328 or visit www.ticketmaster.com and have your credit card ready. The half-price, same day ticket sales at **Ticketplace** in the Old Post Office Pavilion, 1100 Pennsylvania Avenue NW, are a great deal if you're flexible and don't mind making last-minute plans. Call 202-842-5387 or log onto www.cultural-alliance.org to see if they have anything you're interested in. Keep in mind that you can only buy tickets in person. Ticketplace is open Tuesday-Saturday from 11 a.m. to 6 p.m. (Sunday tickets are sold on Saturdays, when available). **Tickets.com** (formerly Protix) also serves the D.C. area.

Unless otherwise noted, venues listed below are in Washington D.C.

PERFORMING ARTS

Washington provides its residents with some of the finest performance choices available. Many nationally run shows make an appearance in D.C., while shows of international acclaim often make it their only US stop. In some cases the theaters themselves are of interest. Stories abound of presidents and dignitaries who sat where you sat, etc. Most of the larger performance houses are located near excellent restaurants, and the combination of a show and dinner is a wonderful night out. A lot of people buy season tickets with good friends, thus ensuring that at least six times a year they can all sit down together.

There are also a great many community-based arts organizations that also host high-quality performances. Looking at the list one would think that almost everyone in the greater Washington area has a talent that they enjoy sharing with the community—lucky for the rest of us! These shows are well run and quite approachable. And, if you've got that secret talent hidden away that you're aching to share, this is the place to do it. Many of the groups are quite welcoming to newcomers. Another great aspect of the community performance arena is that during intermission you can usually meet some other people who live in your neighborhood.

Don't rule out the contemporary music and dance scene as a way to meet new people, though. Washingtonians work hard, so when the day is done huge flocks of people head out to clubs to relax and leave their worries behind. Whatever your music tastes, you can find a great place in the city to make friends, unwind and forget about work for a while.

CLASSICAL MUSIC, BALLET

PROFESSIONAL

The **Washington Performing Arts Society**, 202-785-WPAS, www.wpas.org, is a unique society that allows you to design a personalized series from performances showing all around the city. Call or check their site for a schedule.

Professional classical music and ballet venues in the D.C. area include:

- **George Mason University Center for the Arts**, George Mason University Fairfax Campus, Fairfax, VA, 703-993-ARTS, www.gmu.edu/cfa; known around D.C. for its wide range of quality music and dance performances, including a series of "family friendly" performances. Discounts offered to students.
- **The Kennedy Center for the Performing Arts**, New Hampshire Avenue and Rock Creek Parkway NW, 800-444-1324, www.kennedy-center.org; home of the National Symphony Orchestra, The Washington Chorus (www.thewashingtonchorus.org), and the Choral Arts Society of Washington (www.choralarts.org), welcomes a multitude of unique musical presentations. Student, senior, military personnel and persons with disabilities discounts, and discounted day of show tickets when available.
- **Library of Congress**, 101 Independence Avenue SE, 202-707-5502, www.loc.gov; schedule not posted on the web, must call for information.
- **Master Chorale of Washington**, 202-966-3869, www.masterchorale.org; performances are mainly at the Kennedy Center, although the chorale tours throughout America and Europe.
- **Millennium Stage** (located at the Kennedy Center), New Hampshire Avenue and Rock Creek Parkway NW, 800-444-1324, www.kennedy-center.org/programs/millennium; free music, dance and special interest performances offered every evening at 6 p.m. All performances are catalogued in their entirety on the web site.
- **National Museum of Women in the Arts**, 1250 New York Avenue NW, 202-783-5000, www.nmwa.org, features the Women in Music Concert Series and special events throughout the year ranging from the pricey to the reasonable. Discounts offered for students and seniors.
- **Phillips Collection**, 1600 21st Street NW, 202-387-2151, www.phillipscollection.org, offers two concert venues for classical music and jazz: the

Sunday Concert Series, running from September through May at 5 p.m. (tickets included in the price of admission), and Artful Evenings on Thursdays from 6 p.m. to 8 p.m. Cost $5. Thursday performances offer a cash bar w/light refreshments and discounted parking.

- **Smithsonian Institution**, www.si.edu; many of the museums on The Mall have concert series. Check the main calendar for the schedule of events. Free
- **Washington Chamber Symphony**, 202-452-1321, www.wcsymphony.org, performs at either the Kennedy Center or the Corcoran Gallery of Art.
- **The Washington Revels**, (located on the campus of The George Washington University) Lisner Auditorium, 21st & H streets NW, 202-723-7528, www.revelsdc.org; currently featuring Christmas and May Day revels, although there is talk of expansion.
- **Wolf Trap Farm Park for the Performing Arts**, 1624 Trap Road, Vienna, VA, 703-255-1860, www.wolftrap.org; this large outdoor National Park hosts performing artists, featuring touring classical, jazz and popular music concerts, plays and dance performances. Picnicking encouraged! Bring sweaters and umbrellas as concerts go on rain or shine. There are also undercover arenas that hold events year round, including the Barns of Wolf Trap and the Filene Center.

COMMUNITY

- **Alexandria Choral Society**, 703-548-4734, www.alexchoralsociety.org; performs at different locations throughout Alexandria, VA.
- **Alexandria Harmonizers** (barbershop quartet), 703-922-0962, www.harmonizers.org; performances are scattered throughout the mid-Atlantic region.
- **Alexandria Symphony Orchestra**, 703-845-8005, www.alexsym.org; performances are held in various locations in Alexandria, VA, although the symphony plans to move to a permanent home in 2002.
- **Arlington Symphony Orchestra**, Bishop O'Connell High School Auditorium, 6600 Little Falls Street, Arlington, VA, 703-528-1817; www.arlingtonsymphony.org
- **Cathedral Choral Society** (located at the National Cathedral), Massachusetts and Wisconsin Avenues NW, 202-537-8980, www.cathedralchoralsociety.org
- **Fairfax Choral Society**, 703-642-0862, www.fairfaxchoralsociety.org; performances are at various locations throughout Northern Virginia.
- **Fairfax Symphony Orchestra**, 703-642-7200, www.fairfaxsymphony.org; concerts take place at various locations on the George Mason University campus.

- **Gay Men's Chorus**, 202-338-SING, www.gmcw.org; performances are at a variety of locations throughout D.C.
- **Lesbian and Gay Chorus of Washington**, 202-546-1549, www.lgcw.org; performances are at a number of different locations both in and around D.C.
- **Mt**. **Vernon Orchestra**, 703-799-8229, www.hometown.aol. com/mvorch; performs at various locations in the town of Mt. Vernon.
- **National Chamber Orchestra**, F. Scott Fitzgerald Theatre, Rockville Civic Center Park, Rockville, MD, 301-762-8580, www.nationalchamberorch.org
- **The Washington Ballet**, 202-362-3606, www.washingtonballet.org, performances are at different sites around the city and in VA, call or visit the web site for information.
- **Washington Men's Camerata**, 202-363-1064, www.camerata.com; the chorus performs at various locations throughout D.C. including the Kennedy Center.

OPERA

- **Baltimore Opera Company**, Lyric Opera House, 110 West Mt. Royal Avenue, Baltimore, MD, 410-727-6000, www.baltimoreopera.com; student discount package available.
- **Opera Camerata of Washington** (on the campus of The George Washington University), Lisner Auditorium, 21st & H streets NW, 202-887-5654, www.operabase.com
- **Opera Theatre of Northern Virginia**, 4736 Lee Highway, Arlington, VA, 703-528-1433, www.operabase.com
- **Summer Opera Theatre Company**, 620 Michigan Avenue NE, 202-526-1669, http://dc.on-stage.com
- **Washington Concert Opera**, 3509 Connecticut Avenue NW, 202-333-1768, http://dc.on-stage.com
- **The Washington Opera** (at The Kennedy Center Opera House), New Hampshire Avenue and Rock Creek Parkway NW, 202-467-4600, www.dc-opera.org

THEATER

PROFESSIONAL

- **Arena Stage**, 1101 6th Street SW, 202-488-3300, www.arenastage.org; season is always exciting and diverse, including dramas, musicals and comedies. Special college night promotions, student, senior and persons with disabilities discounts.

- **The Folger Shakespeare Library Elizabethan Theatre**, 201 East Capitol Street NE, 202-544-7077, www.folger.edu/public/theater, presents an all Shakespeare program. Student, teacher, senior, military personnel and group discounts.
- **Ford's Theatre**, 511 10th Street NW, 202-347-4833, www.fordstheatre.org; historical theatre and museum act as a tribute to President Lincoln. Their annual production of "A Christmas Carol" is a D.C. tradition. Group rates available.
- **GALA Hispanic Theatre**, 1625 Park Road NW, 202-234-7174, www.galatheatre.org; established to preserve and promote Hispanic culture in the US, award-winning company performs in D.C. and around the world. Student and senior discounts.
- **The Kennedy Center for the Performing Arts**, New Hampshire Avenue and Rock Creek Parkway NW, 202-467-4600, www.kennedy-center.org; a stunning arts center located on the Potomac River, it is the premier performance venue of D.C., featuring nationally run plays, concerts, and dance performances, in addition to fine dining. Student, senior, military personnel and persons with disabilities discounts, and discounted day of show tickets when available.
- **Lincoln Theatre**, 1215 U Street NW, 202-328-6000; this early "movie palace" has been fully restored to a 1,300 seat theatre that hosts premiere multicultural performances.
- **The National Theatre**, 1321 Pennsylvania Avenue NW, 202-628-6161, www.nationaltheatre.org; the oldest cultural organization in the District, hosts nationally run plays. Beware: may have to share seat with theatre ghost! Student, senior and military personnel discount.
- **The Shakespeare Theatre**, 450 7th Street NW, 202-547-1122, www.shakespearedc.org; offers a mixed program of Shakespeare and other established playwrights, including Tennessee Williams and the occasional Greek Tragedy. Student and senior discounts. Standing room tickets available.
- **The Source Theatre Company**, 14th Street NW, 202-462-1073, www.dcmdva-arts.org/sourceth; a non-profit organization showcasing local artists in a forum for contemporary work, or contemporary interpretations of established works. Student and senior discounts.
- **Studio Theatre**, 1333 P Street NW, 202-332-3300, www.studiotheatre.org; highly praised, award-winning theatre presents contemporary productions.
- **The Warner Theatre**, 13th & E streets NW, 202-783-4000, www.warnertheatre.com; recently renovated playhouse hosts nationally run productions, including Broadway shows, popular music concerts, recitals, dance and comedy shows.
- **Woolly Mammoth Theatre Company**, Kennedy Center, 202-393-

3939, www.woollymammoth.net, offers "daring" theater; nationally renowned for its creative performances. Discount tickets available to those under the age of 25. (Woolly Mammoth will be moving to its new home on 7th & D streets NW in late 2003.)

COMMUNITY

- **Actors' Theatre of Washington**, 1734 V Street NW, 202-319-1919
- **Church Street Theater**, 1742 Church Street NW, 202-265-3748
- **Dominion Stage**, Gunston Arts Center, 2700 South Lang Street, Arlington, VA, 703-683-0502, www.dominionstage.org
- **Fitzgerald Theatre**, Rockville Civic Center Park, Rockville, MD, 301-251-5766
- **Horizons Theater**, 1041 Wisconsin Avenue NW, 202-342-7706
- **Jefferson Theater**, 125 South Glebe Road, Arlington, VA, 703-548-1154
- **Little Theatre of Alexandria**, 600 Wolfe Street, Alexandria, VA, 703-683-0496
- **Olney Theatre Center for the Arts**, Mulitz-Gudelsky Theatre Lab, 2001 Olney-Sandy Spring Road, Olney, MD, 301-924-3400, www.olneytheatre.org
- **Silver Spring Stage**, 10145 Colesville Road, Silver Spring, MD, 301-593-6036, www.ssstage.dancinman.com
- **Theater J**, District of Columbia Jewish Community Center, 1529 16th Street NW, 800-494-8497, www.dcjcc.org
- **Theatre Conspiracy**, D.C. Arts Center, 2438 18th Street NW, 202-462-7833, www.theatreconspiracy.org
- **Warehouse Theater**, 1021 7th Street NW, 202-745-3662

DINNER

- **Blair Mansion Inn Restaurant Murder Mystery Dinner Theatre**, 7711 Eastern Avenue, Silver Spring, MD, 301-588-1688
- **Burn Brae Dinner Theatre**, 3811 Blackburn Lane, Burtonsville, MD, 301-384-5800
- **Capitol Steps Political Satire** (appearing at Chelsea's in Georgetown), call for show times: 703-683-8330, www.capsteps.com
- **Toby's—The Dinner Theatre of Columbia Inc.**, South Entrance Road, Columbia, MD, 301-596-6161
- **West End Dinner Theatre**, 4615 Duke Street, Alexandria, VA, 703-370-2500, www.wedt.com

COMEDY

- **Headliners**, 8120 Wisconsin Avenue, Bethesda, MD, 301-942-4242
- **Improv**, 1140 Connecticut Avenue NW, 202-296-7008, www.dcimprov.com
- **Metro Cafe**, 1522 14th Street NW, 202-518-7900
- **Mr. Henry's**, 1836 Columbia Road NW, 202-773-1294

CONTEMPORARY MUSIC AND DANCE

LARGE CONCERT VENUES

- **Carter Barron Amphitheater**, 4850 Colorado Avenue NW, 202-426-6837
- **MCI Center**, 601 F Street NW, 202-628-3200, www.mcicenter.com
- **Merriweather Post Pavilion**, Columbia, MD, 301-982-1800, www.mppconcerts.com
- **Nissan Pavilion**, 7800 Cellar Door Drive, Barstow, VA, 703-754-6400
- **Patriot Center**, 4400 University Drive, Fairfax, VA, 703-993-3000

NIGHT CLUBS

ALTERNATIVE/ROCK
- **Black Cat**, 1831 14th Street NW, 202-667-7960, www.blackcatdc.com
- **Cowboy Cafe North**, 4792 Lee Highway, Arlington, VA, 703-243-8010
- **Evening Star Cafe**, 2000 Mt. Vernon Avenue, Alexandria, VA, 703-549-5051
- **Fast Eddie's**, 9687 Lee Highway, Arlington, VA, 703-385-7529, www.fasteddies.com
- **Galaxy Hut**, 2711 Wilson Boulevard, Arlington, VA, 703-525-8646, www.galaxyhut.com
- **Garage**, 1214 B 18th Street NW, 202-331-7123
- **Iota**, 2832 Wilson Boulevard, Arlington, VA, 703-522-8340
- **Jaxx**, 6355 Rolling Road, West Springfield, VA, 703-569-5940, www.jaxxroxx.com
- **Metro Cafe**, 1522 14th Street NW, 202-518-7900
- **9:30 Club**, 815 V Street NW, 202-393-0930, www.930.com
- **Politiki**, 319 Pennsylvania Avenue SE, 202-546-1001
- **Velvet Lounge**, 915 U Street NW, 202-462-ROCK
- **Whitlow's on Wilson**, 2854 Wilson Boulevard, Arlington, VA, 703-276-9693, www.whitlows.com
- **Zig's Bar & Grille**, 4531 Duke Street, Alexandria, VA, 703-823-2777

FOLK/COUNTRY

- **Birchmere**, 3701 Mt. Vernon Avenue, Alexandria, VA, 703-549-7500, www.birchmere.com
- **Fado**, 808 7th Street NW, 202-789-0066, www.fadoirishpub.com
- **Irish Times**, 14 F Street NW, 202-543-5433
- **Pat Troy's**, 111 North Pitt Street, Alexandria, VA, 703-549-3309
- **Soho Tea & Coffee**, 2150 P Street NW, 202-463-7646, www.sohot-nc.com

JAZZ/BLUES

- **Black's Bar & Kitchen**, 7750 Woodmont Avenue, Bethesda, MD, 301-652-6278
- **Blues Alley**, 1073 Wisconsin Avenue NW, 202-337-4141, www.bluesalley.com
- **Bohemian Caverns**, 2001 11th Street NW, 202-299-0800
- **Cafe La Ruche**, 1039 31st Street NW, 202-965-2684
- **Cate's Bistro**, 715 King Street, Alexandria, VA, 703-549-0533
- **Colonel Brooks' Tavern**, 901 Monroe Street NE, 202-529-4002, www.colbrooks.com
- **Columbia Station**, 2325 18th Street NW, 202-462-6040
- **Cowboy Cafe South**, 2421 Columbia Pike, Arlington, VA, 703-486-3467
- **Ellington's**, 424 8th Street SE, 202-546-8308
- **Felix**, 2406 18th Street NW, 202-483-3549, www.thefelix.com
- **Fino's**, 3033 M Street NW, 202-337-4500
- **Laportas**, 1600 Duke Street, Alexandria, VA, 703-683-6313
- **Madam's Organ Soul Food Restaurant & Blues Bar**, 2461 18th Street NW, 202-667-5370, www.madamsorgan.com
- **New Vegas Lounge**, 1415 P Street NW, 202-483-3971
- **One Step Down**, 2517 Pennsylvania Avenue NW, 202-331-8863
- **St. Elmo's Coffee Pub**, 2300 Mt. Vernon Avenue, Alexandria, VA, 703-739-9268
- **Saloun**, 3239 M Street NW, 202-965-4900
- **Smokeless Blues Room**, 617 I Street NW, 202-589-0089
- **Tabard Inn Restaurant**, 1739 N Street NW, 202-331-8528
- **Town & Country Lounge** (located in the Mayflower Hotel), 1127 Connecticut Avenue NW, 202-347-3000
- **Twins Lounge**, 1344 U Street NW, 202-234-0072, www.twinsjazz.com
- **Utopia**, 1418 U Street NW, 202-483-7669
- **Zanzibar on the Waterfront**, 700 Water Street SW, 202-554-9100, www.zanzibar-otw.com
- **Zoo Bar**, 3000 Connecticut Avenue NW, 202-232-4225

POP/DANCE

- **Chief Ike's Mambo Room**, 1725 Columbia Road NW, 202-332-2211, www.greatidea.com/chiefike
- **Club Asylum**, 2471 18th Street NW, 202-319-9353
- **Club Heaven & Hell**, 2327 18th Street NW, 202-667-HELL
- **Crush**, 2323 18th Street NW, 202-319-1111
- **Nation**, 1015 Half Street SE, 202-554-1500
- **Platinum**, 915 F Street NW, 202-393-3555, www.platinumclubdc.com
- **Polly Esther's**, 605 12th Street NW, 202-737-1970, www.pollyesthers.com
- **Zei Club**, 1415 Zei Alley NW, 202-842-2445, www.zeiclub.com

WORLD

- **Cafe Mozart**, 1331 H Street NW, 202-347-5732
- **Casablanca**, 1504 King Street, Alexandria, VA, 703-549-6464
- **Chi-Cha Lounge**, 1624 U Street NW, 202-234-8400, www.chi-cha.com
- **Rumba Cafe**, 2443 18th Street NW, 202-588-5501
- **Tel Aviv Cafe**, 4867 Cordell Avenue, Bethesda, MD, 301-718-9068

KARAOKE

- **Cafe Japone**, 2032 P Street NW, 202-223-1573, www.cafejapone.com
- **New Shiroya Restaurant**, 2512 L Street NW, 202-659-9449

FILM

Washington has a thriving film community, consisting of nationally released films, smaller cinemas that show limited-distribution, art and independent films, and a number of wonderful film festivals throughout the year. Bear in mind that not all cinemas show all films, and during prime viewing times (weekends and evening shows later in the week) new releases often sell out.

CINEMAS

- **American Film Institute Theater** (located at the Kennedy Center) New Hampshire Avenue and Rock Creek Parkway NW, 202-785-4600, www.afionline.org; focusing primarily on films of great cultural significance. (*The AFI will move to the Silver Theater in Silver Spring, MD, in the autumn of 2002.*)
- **Arlington Cinema 'N' Drafthouse**, 2903 Columbia Pike, Arlington, VA, 703-486-2345; a good place to unwind and watch a movie.
- **The Foundry**, 1055 Thomas Jefferson Street NW, 202-333-8613; cinema shows second run films on the big screen for a discounted rate.
- **The Outer Circle**, 4849 Wisconsin Avenue NW, 202-244-3116; features independent, foreign, and art films.

- **The Smithsonian**, www.si.edu/activity/events; several of the museums, both on and off the Mall, include films as part of their public programming, including the summer "Screen on the Green" outdoor film festival. Most of these events are free.
- **The Uptown Theatre**, 3426 Connecticut Avenue NW, 202-966-5400; beautiful "movie palace" cinema with a wrap-around screen and balcony seating.

FESTIVALS

- **Environmental Film Fest**, 202-342-2564, www.dcenvironmental-filmfest.org; all environmental films. Annually, usually in March, call for more information.
- **Filmfest D.C.: Washington D.C. International Film Festival**, 202-724-5613, www.filmfestdc.org; a celebration of the best world film has to offer. Annually, usually in April, call for more information.
- **Johns Hopkins Film Festival**, 410-889-9596, www.jhu.edu; showcases independent films. Annually, usually in April, call for more information.
- **Microcine Fest**, 410-243-5307, www.microcinefest.org; showcase for low-budget underground films. Annually, usually in November, call for more information.
- **Reel Affirmation: Washington, D.C.'s International Gay and Lesbian Film Festival**, 202-986-1119, www.reelaffirmations.org; films by, for and about the gay experience. Annually, usually in October, call for more information.
- **Washington Jewish Film Festival**, 202-518-9400, www.dcjcc.org; annually, usually in December, call for more information.

LITERARY LIFE

Famous for endless speeches, memos, and political reports, it's no surprise that, per capita, Washington D.C.'s population is one of the most literate in the world. And Washingtonians' literary appetites are served by dozens of special interest libraries and hundreds of bookstores, from familiar national chains to an interesting array of independent and specialty bookstores, and plenty of used book dealers as well.

Washington is a stop on every author's book tour. Large and small bookstores alike host book signings several nights a week, often drawing tightly-packed crowds. The "Book World" section of Sunday's *Washington Post* features a calendar of author nights at area bookstores. Check here for announcements of annual used book sales, including the Davis Memorial Goodwill Industries, which sells over 200,000 used books every November.

Most public and private museums have bookstores reflecting the subject matter of their collections; the National Air & Space Museum, the National Museum of Natural History, the National Gallery of Art and the National Building Museum have particularly good selections. So do the National Cathedral, the National Shrine and the Washington Islamic Center, as well as area colleges and universities.

BOOKSTORES

GENERAL INTEREST

- **B. Dalton** stores carry current bestsellers and coffee-table books, and have sections devoted to books of regional interest. 12 locations; see the Yellow Pages
- **Barnes & Noble** superstores offer vast selections of literary, reference, trade, and children's books, plus magazines on every subject and newspapers from around the world. Hosts author readings and events, including an annual wine tasting, plus reading groups and workshops. Most locations have in-store cafes. Locations in Georgetown, Bethesda, Rockville, Falls Church, Alexandria; see the Yellow Pages or check www.barnesandnoble.com.
- **Books-A-Million** is a growing chain of discount bookstores making inroads to fill the gap left by the defunct Crown books chain. 10 locations; 800-201-3550, www.bamm.com
- **Borders Books & Music**, many locations throughout the region, offer a wide range of events from readings to book groups to actual writing classes, all of which are free and open to the public. Check www.borders.com for a location near you.
- **Bridge Street Books**, 2814 Pennsylvania Avenue NW, 202-965-5200; an independent shop in Georgetown specializing in politics, literature, history, philosophy, Judaica, and film.
- **Chapters Literary Bookstore**, 1512 K Street NW, 202-347-5495, www.chaptersliterary.com; an independent, in the heart of downtown D.C.
- **Chuck & Dave's Books**, 7001 Carroll Avenue, Takoma Park, 301-891-2665, www.chuckanddaves.com; has an extensive science section, bargain prices on last year's bestsellers, and a toy department with creative playthings for all ages.
- **Cleveland Park Bookshop**, 3416 Wisconsin Avenue NW, 202-363-1112; www.clevelandparkbooks.com; offers a good selection of books, cards and stationery.
- **Drum & Spear Books**, 556 Varnum Street NW, 202-722-4758, www.drumandspear.com, a general bookstore specializing in African-American interests

- **Kramerbooks & Afterwords**, 1517 Connecticut Avenue NW, 202-387-1400; http://kramers.com; was Washington's first bookstore/cafe and is still a hip nightspot; open late every night and 24 hours on weekends.
- **Olsson's Books & Music**; a local chain known for its superior customer service and a thoughtful, if not huge, selection of books and CDs. 10 locations including one just opened at Reagan National Airport; see the Yellow Pages or call 202-338-9544.
- **Politics & Prose**, 5015 Connecticut Avenue NW, 202-364-1919; www.politics-prose.com; this bookstore and cafe is often packed with crowds anxious to meet visiting authors, especially Washington luminaries from Sunday morning talk shows. Honored by the industry as Bookseller of the Year in 1999.
- **Reprint Book Shop**, 455 L'Enfant Plaza SW, 202-554-5070, www.reprintbookshop.com; an independent shop just off Capitol Hill— good selection of business titles.
- **Tower Books**, a division of Tower Records, specializes in books and magazines about music, but also carries a large selection of hard-to-find titles about alternative politics and lifestyles. Five locations; call 202-331-2400 or check www.towerrecords.com
- **Trover Shop**, 221 Pennsylvania Avenue SE, 202-547-BOOK; 1031 Connecticut Avenue NW, 202-659-8138; www.trover.com; a local chain with an extensive selection of political books and magazines, as well as greeting cards, fine pens, and stationery.
- **Vertigo Books**, 7346 Baltimore Avenue, College Park, 301-779-9300, once a Dupont Circle institution, has moved to the suburbs; it continues to stock books devoted to politics, African-American topics, and local authors, also offers a good general selection of fiction and children's books.
- **Waldenbooks**, nine locations; check the Yellow Pages or call 202-333-8033.

SPECIAL INTEREST

- **Blue Nile Books**, 2828 Georgia Avenue NW, 202-232-2583, www.nilevalleyassn.org; specializes in health, metaphysical and Afro-centric titles, and gifts.
- **Dale Music**, 8240 Georgia Avenue, Silver Spring, 301-589-1459, sells sheet music collections, symphony and opera scores, and music instruction books.
- **Franz Bader Bookstore**, 1911 I Street NW, 202-337-5440, specializes in art, architecture, and photography.
- **Lado International Books**, 2233 Wisconsin Avenue NW, 202-338-3133; large selection of foreign language titles

- **Lambda Rising**, 1625 Connecticut Avenue NW, 202-462-6969; one of the country's oldest and largest bookstores catering to the gay, lesbian, bisexual and transgender communities.
- **Luna Books**, 1633 P Street NW, third floor, 202-332-2543, www.skewers-cafeluna.com; tucked into the upstairs dining room shared by Skewers restaurant and Café Luna, sells a small assortment of hard-to-find titles on politics and citizen activism, and it doubles as a meeting space for community organizations.
- **Maryland Book Exchange**, 4500 College Avenue, College Park, 301-927-2510; www.marylandbook.com, is a huge retailer of new and used scholarly books and textbooks as well as general-interest titles
- **MysteryBooks**, 1715 Connecticut Avenue NW, 202-483-1600, www.killerbooks.com
- **Olde Soldier Books**, 18779-B North Frederick Avenue, Gaithersburg, 301-963-2929, www.oldesoldierbooks.com, sells new and used books on American military history.
- **The Newsroom & International Learning Center**, Connecticut and Florida avenues NW, 202-332-1489, www.foreignmedia.com; carries hundreds of magazines and newspapers from all over the world.
- **Pathfinder Bookstore**, 3437 14th Street NW, 202-387-1590; the die-hard source of socialist and communist titles. Limited hours, call ahead.
- **Reiter's Scientific & Professional Books**, 2021 K Street NW, 202-223-3327; www.reiters.com, carries over 60,000 titles in math, science, engineering, medicine and philosophy.
- **Sisterspace & Books**, 1515 U Street NW, 202-332-3433, www.sisterspace.com; specializes in books by and about African-American women.
- **The US Government Bookstore**, 710 North Capitol Street NW, 202-512-0132, www.gpo.gov; the retail outlet for the Government Printing Office, which prints all federal publications and documents. If you want your very own copy of the North American Free Trade Agreement, this is the place.
- **Washington Law & Professional Books**, 1900 G Street NW, 202-223-5543, www.washingtonlawbooks.com; caters to lawyers, students, policy wonks and accountants.
- **The Writer's Center Book Gallery**, 4508 Walsh Street, Bethesda, MD, 301-654-8664; www.writer.org, carries local poetry, small-press titles, and resources for local authors.
- **The World Bank InfoShop**, 18th Street and Pennsylvania Avenue NW, 202-458-5454, www.worldbank.org/infoshop, sells books and reports on international development.

USED BOOKSTORES

- **All Books Considered**, 10408 Montgomery Avenue, Kensington, 301-929-0036
- **Atticus Books & Music**, 2308 Mt. Vernon Avenue, Alexandria, 703-548-7580; www.atticusbooks.com
- **Barbarian Book Shop**, 11234 Grandview Avenue, Wheaton, 301-946-4184
- **Bartleby's Books**, 3034 M Street NW, 202-298-0486
- **Bonifant Books**, 11240 Georgia Avenue, Wheaton, 301-946-1526
- **Book Alcove**: Shady Grove and Gaither Roads, Gaithersburg, 301-977-9166; 706 Rockville Pike, Rockville, 301-309-1231
- **BookMarkIt**, 3507 12th Street NE, 202-529-2360
- **Books Etc.**, in the lobby of Martin Luther King Memorial Library, 9th and G streets NW, 202-727-1111
- **Capitol Hill Books**, 657 C Street SE, 202-544-1621
- **Friends of the Library Bookstore**, Wheaton Plaza, 301-946-9711
- **Georgetown Book Shop**, 7770 Woodmont Avenue, Bethesda, 301-907-6923
- **Idle Time Books**, 2410 18th Street NW, 202-232-4774
- **Imagination Books**, 946 Sligo Avenue, Silver Spring, 301-589-2223; www.imaginationbooks.com
- **Kulturas**, 1608 20th Street NW, 202-462-2541
- **The Old Forest Book Shop**, 3145 Dumbarton Street NW, 202-965-3842
- **Rainbow Books & Thrift Shop**, 2620 Wilson Boulevard, Arlington, 703-243-0239
- **Science Books**, 1531 33rd Street NW, 202-337-0945; www.thesciencebookstore.com
- **Second Story Books**, 2000 P Street NW, 202-659-8884; 12160 Parklawn Drive, Rockville, 301-770-0477; 4836 Bethesda Avenue, Bethesda, 301-656-0170; www.secondstorybooks.com
- **Takoma Book Exchange**, Carroll and Westmoreland avenues, Takoma Park, 301-891-4656; www.takkybooks.com
- **Washington Used Book Center**, 11910 Parklawn Drive, Rockville, 301-984-7358

LIBRARIES

In addition to the specialty bookshops mentioned above, D.C. has national and international treasures—including rare editions of scholarly works, and historic archives and documents—tucked away in its library shelves, stacks, and tomes.

PUBLIC LIBRARIES

Check the listings at the end of the **Neighborhood Profiles** for a branch library near you. Or visit one of the main county libraries listed here.

- **District of Columbia**, 202-727-0321, http://dclibrary.org; Martin Luther King Jr. Memorial Library, the District's main library, is located at 901 G Street NW. Dr. King is commemorated in a mural overlooking the lobby. The library has three floors of open stacks, special collections for the visually impaired, and the best single source of information about D.C. history: the Washingtoniana Division, which includes a reading room with reference and local history books, old and current city directories, local government archives, real estate plats, old newspapers on microfilm, and thousands of files of photos.
- **Montgomery County**, 240-777-0002, www.montgomerylibrary.org, has three regional libraries, instead of a single flagship, and there are separate facilities for special format collections and the county archives.
- **Gaithersburg Regional Library**, 18330 Montgomery Village Avenue, 301-840-2515
- **Rockville Regional Library**, 99 Maryland Avenue, 240-777-0140
- **Wheaton Regional Library**, 11701 Georgia Avenue, 301-929-5520
- **Special Needs Library**, 6400 Democracy Boulevard, Bethesda, 301-897-2212; TTY, 301-897-2217
- **Montgomery County Archives**, 29 Courthouse Square, Room G09, Rockville, 301-279-1218; www.montgomeryarchives.org
- **Prince George's County**, 301-699-3500, www.prge.lib.md.us; the Hyattsville branch library at 6532 Adelphi Road, 301-985-4690, shares a building with the Prince George's County library system's offices. The branch includes the Maryland Room collection of state and county records and historical volumes, the Audio-Visual Division of the library system, and a bookstore. The county Public Documents Library is at 14741 Governor Oden Bowie Drive, Upper Marlboro, 301-952-3904.
- **Arlington County**, 703-823-5295, www.co.arlington.va.us; Arlington County Central Library at 1015 North Quincy Street, 703-228-5990, includes the Virginia Room collection of Northern Virginia historical information, oral histories, and the county archives.
- **Fairfax County**, 703-324-3100, www.co.fairfax.va.us/library; Fairfax City Regional Library at 3915 Chain Bridge Road, 703-246-2281, includes the Virginia Room collection of historical materials and the county archives.
- **Alexandria**, 703-519-5900, www.alexandria.lib.va.us; The Charles E. Beatley Jr. Central Library at 5005 Duke Street, 703-519-5900, is the

flagship library with the largest collections. Special cc
to local history and records, genealogy, the Civil Wa
dating from the original Alexandria Library Compan)
1790s are located at the Kate Waller Barrett Branch, ;
703-838-4577 ext. 213.

LIBRARY OF CONGRESS

It's all here, including one of the first books ever printed on a press, a
Gutenberg Bible. Under US copyright law, two copies of every work copy-
righted in the United States must be given to the Library of Congress—
which doesn't quite keep everything, but is by far the largest library in the
world. The historic Main Reading Room will look familiar if you remember
Robert Redford and Dustin Hoffman squinting over library records in *All the
President's Men;* but if you're here to do research, you'll probably spend
more time in several of the 19 special reading rooms, from the Law Library
or Manuscript Reading Room to the collections of film, audio recordings
dating back to wax cylinders cut by Thomas Edison, or the library's 4.5 million maps and 13.6 million photos and prints. Only members of Congress
have borrowing privileges here, but adults with photo ID may use materials
in the reading rooms and make photocopies for scholarly purposes permitted by copyright law. The Jefferson Building is the main section, with special reading rooms in the Adams and Madison buildings next door: 101
Independence Avenue SE. Call 202-707-5000 or visit www.loc.gov.

NATIONAL ARCHIVES

The Smithsonian Institution is often described as "the nation's attic." If so,
the National Archives can be considered the nation's safe deposit box. This
is where we keep the Constitution and the Declaration of Independence,
for starters; flanking their permanent displays, rotating exhibits might show
the Louisiana Purchase, or the letter from General Cornwallis to General
Washington surrendering King George's colonies, or the Emancipation
Proclamation. There is also a reading room for genealogical research,
where you can retrieve an ancestor's military records or immigration
papers. A growing collection of historic recordings is open by appointment,
and you can listen to President Nixon's secret tapes without the expletives
deleted. The entrance to the genealogy and federal records offices is at 700
Pennsylvania Avenue NW; the Charters of Freedom exhibit hall is on the
Constitution Avenue side, facing the Mall at 7th Street NW. Call 202-501-
5000 or 800-234-8861, or visit www.nara.gov.

SPECIAL LIBRARIES

Students, researchers, policy wonks, and inquisitive citizens have access to dozens of special-interest libraries in Washington. The Business & Professional Women's Foundation, the Environmental Law Institute, the National Association of Broadcasters, the Population Reference Bureau, and the Urban Institute are just a few of the national organizations that have reference and lending libraries in the area. So do the colleges and universities listed in the **Higher Education** chapter, and many museums, including the National Arboretum, Dumbarton Oaks, and the Discovery Creek Children's Museum (see **Greenspace**) and the Phillips Collection, the Anacostia Museum, and the Textile Museum (see below under **Museums**). Cabinet departments and many "alphabet soup" agencies—EPA, FBI, GSA, and dozens more—have libraries or information centers; for links, visit http://lcweb.loc.gov/flicc.

The libraries listed here, which are only some of the most significant collections, are open to the public, but may require an appointment or registration for a library card, and some charge a small fee. Call for policies and hours.

Since many smaller libraries are housed in old mansions or English basements near Dupont Circle, the online neighborhood directory "Dupont Circle on the Web" includes a list of some 60 special libraries: www.dupont-circle.com/libraries.

- **Arthur R. Ashe Jr. Foreign Policy Library**, 1774 R Street NW, 202-797-2304, www.transafricaforum.org/ashe, has 10,000 scholarly volumes on Africa and the Caribbean.
- **American Institute of Architects Information Center**, 1735 New York Avenue NW, www.e-architect.com/reference/library, is open to the public with a $5 admission fee for non-members.
- **Daughters of the American Revolution Library**, 1776 D Street NW, 202-628-1776, http://dar.org/library, has 160,000 books on American history and genealogy, and many genealogical records dating from colonial times.
- **Federal Election Commission**, 999 E Street NW, 202-694-1120, www.fec.gov, has a reading room where you can "follow the money" from PACs to federal lawmakers, and find out just who owns whom on the Hill.
- **Folger Shakespeare Library**, 201 East Capitol Street SE, 202-544-4600, www.folger.edu; www.penfaulkner.org, is where the nation's collection of original Renaissance English volumes and related scholarly work is held; it includes some original Shakespeare folios. Hosts the esteemed PEN/Faulkner Reading Series each year. Events are open to the public, but there is an admission fee.

- **The Foundation Center**, 1001 Connecticut Avenue NW, 202-331-1400, www.foundationcenter.org, this library contains directories, periodicals, and other reference materials and guides to philanthropy and fundraising, including the tax records and annual reports of most grant making foundations and many charities.
- **Historical Society of Washington, D.C.**, 1301 New Hampshire Avenue NW, 202-785-2068, www.hswdc.org, has a collection of local history books, archives, correspondence, photos, prints, and slides. Admission is $3 for nonmembers, $1.50 for students.
- **The Middle East Institute**, 1761 N Street NW, 202-785-0183, www.mideasti.org, has 25,000 books in Western languages and more than 300 periodicals—the largest US collection of materials on the Middle East except the Library of Congress.
- **National Agricultural Library**, 10301 Baltimore Avenue, Beltsville, 301-504-5755, www.nal.usda.gov, has 3.3 million works related to farming, food, nutrition, biotechnology, biology, animal welfare, international trade, and other topics of interest to the USDA.
- **National Library of Education**, 400 Maryland Avenue SW, 202-205-5015 or 800-424-1616, www.ed.gov, has 100,000 books, 850 journals, and 450,000 microfilmed materials on education theory, policy, and statistics.
- **National Library of Medicine**, 8600 Rockville Pike, Bethesda, 301-594-5983 or 888-346-3656, www.nlm.nih.gov, has 5 million books, journals, technical papers, and other materials in the field of health and medicine, including a significant collection of rare and antiquarian medical texts.
- **National Genealogical Society**, 4527 North 17th Street, Arlington, 703-525-0050 or 800-473-0060, www.ngsgenealogy.org; this library holds 30,000 reference books and files to assist amateur and professional genealogy researchers, and publishes a beginner's genealogy kit available in the library bookstore.
- **National Geographic Society**, 1145 17th Street NW, 202-857-7783, www.nationalgeographic.com/resources/ngs/library, has 50,000 books and 300 journals on geography, cartography, natural history, travel, art, science, photography, and more.
- **National Press Club**, 529 14th Street NW, http://npc.press.org; another D.C. exclusive that provides a fantastic environment for both lectures and readings.
- **Writer's Center**, 4508 Walsh Street, Bethesda, MD, 301-654-8664, www.writer.org; excellent opportunities to both study writing with master craftspeople at a reasonable price and to hear authors read their works.

MUSEUMS

There are so many museums in D.C. that making the decision of where to spend an afternoon can be an awesome prospect. The Smithsonian alone offers such a wide range of choices, including numerous performances, tours and lectures, that it's quite tempting to spend all your free time there. Don't overlook some of the less famous museums and historic homes, though.

BeyondGuide is a series of recorded tours of historic sites in D.C, available by wireless phone. Users can listen to recordings of historic speeches while standing at the sites where they were made; also, tours of historic hotels and churches are available. For $10 per 24 hours, you can listen to an unlimited number of recordings. Call 866-334-8533—for a free sample, select "preview."

ART MUSEUMS AND PUBLIC GALLERIES

- **Art Museum of the Americas**, 201 18th Street NW (directly behind the Organization of American States building), 202-458-6016; in-depth collection of contemporary Latin American and Caribbean art. Open Tuesday-Saturday, 10 a.m. to 5 p.m. Free
- **Arts and Industries Building** (Smithsonian), 900 Jefferson Drive SW, 202-357-4500, www.si.edu, is housed in an exquisite brick and tile Victorian building, showcases rotating exhibits. Open daily, 10 a.m. to 5:30 p.m. except December 25. Free
- **The Arts Club of Washington**, 2017 I Street NW, 202-331-7282; located on this site since 1916, the group shows local artists. Open Tuesday-Friday, 10 a.m. to 5 p.m. and Saturday, 10 a.m. to 2 p.m. Free
- **Black Fashion Museum**, 2007 Vermont Avenue NW, 202-667-0744, displays of garments designed, made or worn by African-Americans. By appointment only.
- **Corcoran Gallery of Art**, 1801 35th Street NW, 202-638-1700, www.corcoran.org; impressive collection of European art from the 17th to the 20th centuries, and American art from the 18th to the 20th centuries. Open Wednesday-Monday, 10 a.m. to 5 p.m. and Thursday, 10 a.m. to 9 p.m. Donations: $3 individuals, $5 families, $1 seniors and students.
- **District of Columbia Arts Center**, 2438 18th Street NW, 202-462-7833, www.dcartscenter.org; gallery and black box theater provides structured programs showcasing emerging artists. Open Wednesday-Sunday, 2 p.m. to 7 p.m. and Friday and Saturday, 2 p.m. to 10 p.m. The gallery is free, but there is a charge for events.
- **Dumbarton Oaks**, 1703 32nd Street NW, 202-339-6409, www.doaks.org; houses an exceptional collection of Byzantine and Pre-

Columbian art, and beautiful gardens where Washingtonians picnic weekends. Museum open Tuesday-Sunday, 2 p.m. to 5 p.m. Admission: $5 adults, $3 seniors and children. Gardens open, November-March, 2 p.m. to 5 p.m., April-October, 2 p.m. to 6 p.m. Free.

- **Fondo del sol Visual Arts Center**, 2112 R Street NW, 202-483-2777; museum of the arts and cultural heritage of the Americas. Open Wednesday-Saturday, 12:30 p.m. to 5:30 p.m. Free
- **Freer Gallery of Art** (Smithsonian), Jefferson Drive at 12th Street SW, 202-357-1300, www.si.edu/Asia; breathtaking collection of Asian art and rare works by James McNeill Whistler, including the famed "Peacock Room." Open daily, 10 a.m. to 5:30 p.m. except December 25. Free
- **Hirshhorn Museum and Sculpture Garden** (Smithsonian), 8th Street and Independence Avenue SW, 202-357-1300, www.si.edu; interesting round building with a brilliant modern art collection, shows by contemporary artists, and one of the best sculpture gardens in the country. Summertime outdoor cafe. Open daily, 10 a.m. to 5:30 p.m. except December 25. Free
- **The Kreeger Museum**, 2401 Foxhall Road NW, 202-337-3050, www.kreegermuseum.com; diverse museum covers art, architecture, education and music; especially nice collection of African art. Admission: $5 suggested donation.
- **Montpelier Cultural Arts Center**, Muirkirk Road, 301-953-1993, www.smart.net/~parksrec/montarts, features three galleries with changing exhibits and opportunities to watch artists at work. Open daily, 10 a.m. to 5 p.m. Free
- **National Gallery of Art and Sculpture Garden**, 600 Constitution Avenue NW, 202-737-4215, www.nga.gov; East Wing is architecturally splendid with a fantastic permanent collection of contemporary art, and West Wing has pre-20th century American and European art. Both wings have grand scale temporary exhibits. Food and refreshments are available at the cafeteria and three cafes. Sculpture Garden's fountain transforms to a public skating rink in the winter months, skates are available for rental. Open Monday-Saturday, 10 a.m. to 5 p.m. and Sunday, 11 a.m. to 6 p.m. Closed January 1 and December 25. Free
- **National Museum of African Art** (Smithsonian), 950 Independence Avenue SW, 202-357-2700, www.si.edu; stunning underground building with permanent and temporary exhibits focused on the traditional and cultural arts of Africa, film series and other performances. Open daily, 10 a.m. to 5:30 p.m. except December 25. Free
- **National Museum of American Art** (Smithsonian), 759 9th Street NW, 202-357-2700, www.nmaa.si.edu
- **National Museum of Women in the Arts**, 1250 New York Avenue NW, 202-783-5000, www.nmwa.org; permanent collections plus

shows and a unique annual bookbinding exhibit, in addition to a film and lecture series. Café open for lunch Monday-Friday. Open Monday-Saturday, 10 a.m. to 5 p.m. and Sunday, noon to 5 p.m. except January 1, Thanksgiving and December 25. Donations requested

- **National Portrait Gallery** (Smithsonian), 750 9th Street NW, 202-357-1300, www.si.edu
- **Phillips Collection**, 1600 21st Street NW, 202-387-2151, www.phillips-collection.org, houses a distinguished collection of 19th century and contemporary paintings, in addition to major traveling exhibits. Open Tuesday-Saturday, 10 a.m. to 5 p.m., until 8:30 p.m. on Thursday, Sunday noon to 7 p.m. Admission: adults $7.50, seniors and students $4.
- **Renwick Gallery** (Smithsonian), 17th Street and Pennsylvania Avenue NW, 202-357-2700, www.si.edu; lovely building designed in 1859, housing a permanent collection of crafts and decorative objects and featuring unusual temporary exhibits. Open daily 10 a.m. to 5:30 p.m. except December 25. Free
- **Rock Creek Gallery** (located in Rock Creek Park), across from Pierce Mill at Tilden Street, 202-244-2482; exhibiting ceramics, paintings and photographs done by local artists. Open Thursday-Sunday 11 a.m. to 4:30 p.m. except July 4. Free
- **Arthur M. Sackler Gallery** (Smithsonian), 1050 Independence Avenue NW, 202-357-2700, www.si.edu/Asia; beautiful contemporary building houses an impressive Asian art collection, shows of contemporary Asian art, a film series and special presentations, and one of the best gift stores in D.C. Open daily 10 a.m. to 5:30 p.m. except December 25. Free
- **Charles Sumner School Museum and Archives**, 1201 17th Street NW, 202-442-6060; local art and history exhibits. Open Monday-Saturday 9 a.m. to 6 p.m. Free
- **The Textile Museum**, 2320 S Street NW, 202-667-0441, www.textilemuseum.org; interesting temporary exhibits complement a substantial permanent collection and library. Monday-Saturday 10 a.m. to 5 p.m. except federal holidays and December 25. Donations requested
- **Torpedo Factory Art Center**, 105 North Union Street, Alexandria, VA, 703-838-4565, www.torpedofactory.org; former WW I and WW II torpedo factory, now outfitted as artist studios. All studios open to the public and all works for sale. Open daily 10 a.m. to 5 p.m. except January 1, Easter, July 4, Thanksgiving, and December 25. Free

SCIENCE MUSEUMS, PLANETARIUMS, AQUARIUMS

- **Arlington Planetarium**, 1426 North Quincy Street, Arlington, VA, 703-358-6070, presents several planned programs per year, call for dates.

- **Explorer's Hall, National Geographic Society**, 17th and M streets NW, 202-857-7700, www.nationalgeographic.com/society/ngo/ explorer; spectacular changing exhibits relating to current magazine topics, in addition to numerous films and lectures. Open Monday-Saturday 9 a.m. to 5p.m. and Sunday 10 a.m. to 5 p.m., except December 25. Free
- **H.B. Owens Science Center Planetarium**, 969 Greenbelt Road, Lanham, MD, 301-918-8750
- **NASA-Goddard Visitors' Center**, Soil Conservation Road, Greenbelt, MD, 301-286-8981, www.gsfc.nasa.gov, offers a rare opportunity to go behind the scenes of NASA with tours, exhibits, interactive presentations, and programs. Open daily 9 a.m. to 4 p.m. except January 1, Thanksgiving, and December 25. Free
- **National Air and Space Museum** (Smithsonian), 6th Street and Independence Avenue SW, 202-357-2700, www.nasm.edu; the most popular of all the Smithsonian museums is too large for just one visit. Exhibits range from a unique collection of world stamps commemorating the first manned space flight, to actual planes, including the Wright Brothers' *Flyer I*, the *Spirit of St. Louis* and the original Star Trek *Enterprise* model. Cafeteria and giant gift shop. Open daily 9:30 a.m. to 5:30 p.m. except December 25. Free
- **National Aquarium** (located in the Department of Commerce Building), 14th Street and Constitution Avenue NW, 202-482-2825, is the oldest public aquarium in the US. Displays more than 1,200 fish and sea creatures. Open daily 9 a.m. to 5 p.m. except December 25. Admission: $2 adults, $.75 children, two to ten.
- **National Building Museum**, 401 F Street NW, 202-272-2448, www.nbm.org; interesting changing exhibits relating to both D.C. history and the art of building itself. Nice carryout cafe with seating around an indoor fountain. Open Monday-Saturday and holidays, 10 a.m. to 4 p.m., Sunday noon to 4 p.m., except January 1, Thanksgiving, and December 25. Free
- **National Museum of Health and Medicine**, 6900 Georgia Avenue (on the Walter Reed Army Medical Center campus), 202-782-2200, www.natmedmuse.afip.org; established during the Civil War to collect "specimens," museum currently offers such opportunities as viewing Paul Revere's dental tools and touching an actual brain. Open daily 10 a.m. to 5 p.m. except December 25. Free
- **National Museum of Natural History** (Smithsonian), 10th Street and Constitution Avenue NW, 202-357-2700, www.nmnh.si.edu; home of such treasures as the Hope Diamond, the Hall of Minerals and the O. Orkin Insect Zoo. Best cafe on the Mall! Open daily 10 a.m. to 5:30 p.m. except December 25. Free

- **National Zoological Park** (Smithsonian), 3001 Connecticut Avenue NW, 202-673-4800, http://natzoo.si.edu; great zoo with many unusual animals and educational displays including an orangutan intelligence center, a bat cave and a rain forest center. Cafeterias and gift shops. Buildings open daily 10 a.m. to 6 p.m., May 1 through September 15. Free
- **Paul E. Garber Preservation, Restoration and Storage Facility** (Smithsonian), Suitland, MD, 202-357-1400, www.nasm.edu, offers tours of preserved and restored air and spacecraft. Three-hour guided tours only; you must call for reservations two weeks ahead of time. Tours are Monday-Friday at 10 a.m., Saturday and Sunday at 10 a.m. and 1 p.m. Cameras allowed. Free (Scheduled to move in 2003 to Washington Dulles International Airport.)
- **The Radio-Television Museum**; run by the Radio History Society; 2608 Mitchellville Road, 301-390-1020, www.radiohistory.org; open Saturday and Sunday, 1 p.m. to 4 p.m. and by appointment. Donations encouraged.

HISTORY AND MILITARY MUSEUMS

- **Alexandria Archeology Museum and Laboratory** (located in the Torpedo Factory Art Center), 105 North Union Street, Alexandria, VA 703-838-4399, www.ci.alexandria.va.us/oha; small museum which focuses on archeological methods and local finds. Offers interesting opportunities for all age groups to participate in local digs. Open Tuesday-Friday 10 a.m. to 3 p.m. Saturday 10 a.m. to 5 p.m. and Sunday 1 p.m. to 5 p.m. except January 1, Easter, July 4, Thanksgiving, and December 25. Free
- **Anacostia Museum** (Smithsonian), 1901 Fort Place SE, 202-357-2700, www.si.edu/anacostia, is dedicated to the documentation and preservation of African-American heritage. Changing exhibits, workshops, lectures and performances scheduled regularly. Open daily 10 a.m. to 5 p.m. except December 25. Free
- **B'nai B'rith Klutznick National Jewish Museum** (located in the B'nai B'rith Building), 1640 Rhode Island Avenue NW, 202-857-6583, www.bnaibrith.org/musuem; permanent collection of religious and fine art works, in addition to traveling exhibits. Open Sunday-Friday 10 a.m. to 5 p.m. Closed some federal and most Jewish holidays. Donations requested.
- **Collingwood Library and Museum on Americanism**, 8301 East Boulevard Drive, Alexandria, VA, 703-765-1652, www.collingwoodlibrary.com; the house dates from 1783, library can be used for research on American history, museum has an interesting collection of historical

artifacts. Open Monday, and Wednesday-Saturday 10 a.m. to 4 p.m., Sunday 1 p.m. to 4 p.m. Closed December 18 through January 2. Free

- **DAR Museum and Constitution Hall**, 1776 D Street NW, 202-879-3241, www.dar.org/museums; headquarters for the Daughters of the American Revolution, features permanent exhibits of period rooms and changing shows in its main gallery. Open Monday-Friday 8:30 a.m. to 4 p.m. and Sunday 1 p.m. to 5 p.m. Free

- **The Folger Shakespeare Library**, 201 East Capitol Streets SE, 202-544-7077, www.folger.edu; impressive changing exhibits relating to either Shakespeare or Elizabethan England, annual celebration of Shakespeare's birthday, includes many child-friendly activities. Library is for scholars' usage only. Open Monday-Saturday 10 a.m. to 4 p.m. Free

- **Ford's Theatre Museum**, 511 10th Street NW, 202-426-6924, www.fordstheatre.org; depicts the assassination of Lincoln and displays John Wilkes Booth's gun. Open daily 9 a.m. to 5 p.m. except December 25. Free

- **Fort Ward Museum and Historic Site**, 4301 West Braddock Road, Alexandria, VA, 703-838-4848, www.ci.alexandria.va.us/oha; Civil War fort was part of the defense system surrounding D.C. Interactive programs are presented throughout the year. Open Tuesday-Saturday 9 a.m. to 5 p.m. and Sunday noon to 5 p.m., except major holidays. Picnicking is permitted. Free

- **The Lyceum**, 201 South Washington Street, Alexandria, VA, 703-838-4994, www.ci.alexandria.va.us/oha; built in 1839 as the city's first cultural center, the museum of city history currently sponsors exhibits lectures, concerts and educational programs. Open Monday-Saturday 10 a.m. to 5 p.m. and Sunday 1 p.m. to 5 p.m., except January 1, Thanksgiving, and December 25. Free

- **Marine Corps Air-Ground Museum**, off US 1 & I-95, Quantico, VA, 703-784-2606; restored military aircraft and equipment from WW I and WW II and the Korean War. Open April 1 through November 15, except Easter, Tuesday-Saturday 10 a.m. to 5 p.m. and Sunday noon to 5 p.m. Free

- **National Museum of American History** (Smithsonian), 14th Street and Constitution Avenue NW, 202-357-2700, www.si.edu; this is the Smithsonian museum you've dreamed about your whole life. Home of the Star-Spangled Banner, Mr. Rogers' sweater, the Fonz's leather jacket, Dorothy's ruby slippers and much more, including changing exhibits relating to American heritage. Several cafeterias and an old-fashioned ice cream parlor. Open daily 10 a.m. to 5:30 p.m. except December 25. Free

- **National Museum of American Jewish Military History**, 1811 R Street NW, 202-265-6280, www.nmajmh.org; a collection of documents and exhibits relating to the contributions of American Jews to military endeavors. Open Monday-Friday 9 a.m. to 5 p.m. and Sunday 1 p.m. to 5 p.m. except federal and Jewish holidays. Donations requested.

- **National Postal Museum** (Smithsonian), 2 Massachusetts Avenue NE, 202-357-2700, www.si.edu; housed in the 1914 Old City Post Office building, the museum is hands-on with historical exhibits and great gift shops for philatelists. Open daily 10 a.m. to 5 p.m. except December 25. Free
- **Newseum**, 1101 Wilson Boulevard, Arlington, VA, 703-284-3544, www.newseum.org; fantastic, high-tech interactive news museum with many exciting opportunities to experience what it's like to deliver the news, plus permanent and changing exhibits, lectures and films. Open Wednesday-Sunday 10 a.m. to 5 p.m. except January 1, Thanksgiving and December 25. Free
- **Lillian and Albert Small Museum of Jewish History and the Jewish Historical Society**, 701 3rd Street NW, 202-789-0900, www.jewishculture.org/jewishmuseums; depicts Jewish lifestyles and contributions to the area. Open Sunday-Thursday noon to 4 p.m. except major federal and Jewish holidays. Donations requested.
- **US Holocaust Memorial Museum**, 100 Raoul Wallenberg Place SW, 202-488-0400, www.ushmm.org; offers powerful history of those who died in the Holocaust told through three floors of permanent exhibits, films and interactive displays. Open daily 10:30 a.m. to 5:30 p.m. with last admission to exhibits at 3:30 p.m. Closed Yom Kippur and December 25. Free, but tickets are necessary. Arrive early or call 800-400-9373 for advance tickets.
- **US Chess Hall of Fame and Museum**, 1501 M Street NW, 202-857-8333, www.chessctr.org; offers chess related displays and a unique opportunity for classes and matches. Open Monday-Thursday 6 p.m. to 11 p.m., Saturday noon to 6 p.m. and Sunday noon to 6 p.m., except January 1, Memorial Day, July 4, Thanksgiving, and December 25. Free
- **Washington Navy Yard**, 9th and M streets SE, 202-433-8697, www.history.navy.mil; established in 1799, the Navy Yard has nine sites open to the public including buildings from the early 19th century. Open March 21 to July 4, Monday-Friday 9 a.m. to 4 p.m. and Saturday, Sunday and holidays 10 a.m. to 5 p.m., the rest of the year, open daily, 10 a.m. to 5 p.m. except January 1, Thanksgiving, and December 25. Free

HISTORIC HOUSES

- **Mary McLeod Bethune Council House National Historic Site**, 1318 Vermont Avenue NW, 202-673-2404, www.nps.gov/mamc; a stately mansion, home of the founder of the National Council of Negro Women and advisor to four Presidents. Open Monday-Saturday 10 a.m. to 4 p.m. Free

- **Carlyle House**, 121 North Fairfax Street, Alexandria, VA, 703-549-2997, www.alexandriacity.com/carlylehouse, is a 1752 Georgian stone mansion. First campaigns of the French and Indian War were planned here. Open Tuesday-Sunday 10 a.m. to 4:30 p.m., Sunday noon to 4:30 p.m. Tours every half-hour. Admission: $3 adults, $2 under 17, free under 11.
- **Cedar Hill, Frederick Douglass National Historic Site**, 1411 W Street SE, 202-426-5960, www.nps.gov/frdo; this 21-room Victorian mansion was the last home of Douglass. Retains many original furnishings. Open daily 9 a.m. to 4 p.m. Tours 9 a.m. to 3 p.m. except noon. Admission: $3.
- **Decatur House**, 748 Jackson Place NW, 202-842-0920, www.decaturhouse.org; one of three remaining buildings designed by Benjamin Henry Latrobe. This 1818 neo-classical house was home to many prominent political figures, including Martin Van Buren. Open Tuesday-Friday 10 a.m. to 3 p.m. Saturday and Sunday noon to 4 p.m. Tours every hour, special programs offered. Admission: $4 adults, $2.50 students and seniors.
- **Dumbarton House Museum**, 2715 Q Street NW, 202-337-2288, www.doaks.org; Federal-style home featuring period furniture and decorations, and a collection of historical documents. Open Tuesday-Saturday 10 a.m. to 1 p.m. Closed August through Labor Day. Donations: $3, students free.
- **Lloyd House**, 220 North Washington Street, Alexandria, VA, 703-838-4577, www.alexandria.lib.va.us/lloyd; 1797 Georgian-style home, houses the Virginia Research Collection (materials about Virginia history and genealogy). Open Monday-Saturday 9 a.m. to 5 p.m. Free
- **The Heurich House Museum and The Historical Society of Washington, D.C.**, 1307 New Hampshire Avenue NW, 202-785-2068, www.hswdc.org; former home of Christian Heurich, beer baron of D.C. Romanesque Revival brownstone furnished with its original Victorian pieces. Hosts annual Oktoberfest. Open Monday-Saturday 10 a.m. to 4 p.m. Admission: $3.
- **Hillwood Museum and Gardens**, 4155 Linnean Avenue NW, 202-686-5807, www.hillwoodmuseum.org; epitome of the American country house tradition, its museum includes the greatest collection of Russian Imperial objects outside of Russia. Open Tuesday-Saturday, 9 a.m. to 5 p.m. Reservations required.
- **Mt**. **Vernon**, south end of the George Washington Memorial Parkway, 703-780-2000, www.mountvernon.org; home of George Washington, contains many of its original furnishings. Open daily, April-August, 8

a.m. to 5 p.m.; March, September, and October, 9 a.m. to 5 p.m. The remainder of the year 9 a.m. to 4 p.m. Admission: adults $8, seniors $7.50, children six to eleven, $4, children under six free.

- **The Octagon**, 1799 New York Avenue NW, 202-638-3221; 1801 Federal-style townhouse, was home to President Madison after the White House burned in the War of 1812. Reputed to be haunted by a number of its previous occupants, the building currently houses the museum of the American Architectural Foundation. Open Tuesday-Sunday, 10 a.m. to 4 p.m. Tours on the hour and half-hour. Admission: $5 adults, $3 students and seniors.

- **Old Stone House**, 3051 M Street NW, 202-426-6851; built in 1765, this is the oldest house in the District, dates from the pre-Revolutionary era. Open Wednesday-Sunday noon to 5 p.m. Free

- **Peterson House**, (The House Where Lincoln Died), 516 10th Street NW, 202-426-6924, across the street from Ford's Theatre, www.nps.gov/foth; built in 1849, the house has been restored to its 1860 appearance. Open daily, 9 a.m. to 5 p.m. Free

- **Pope-Leighey/Frank Lloyd Wright House**, (located on the Woodlawn Plantation, Route 1, Mt. Vernon, VA), 703-780-4000, www.nthp.org; this magnificent house exemplifies many of the techniques Wright contributed to modern architecture and contains original furnishings designed by the architect. Annual Christmas festival. Admission: adults $5 seniors and children 6 to 18, $3.

- **Sewall-Belmont House**, 144 Constitution Avenue NE, 202-546-3989; 1820 building, home to the National Women's Party since 1929, houses a museum dedicated to the suffrage movement. Open Tuesday-Friday, 11 a.m. to 2 p.m.; Saturday noon to 3 p.m. Tours on the hour. Donations requested.

- **The Society of the Cincinnati Museum at Anderson House**, 2118 Massachusetts Avenue NW, 202-785-2040; the society was founded in 1783 by General George Washington and the officers of the Continental Army and Navy. The 1905 Beaux-Arts mansion houses the society's collection of American Revolutionary artifacts. Open Tuesday-Saturday, 1 p.m. to 4 p.m. Free admission and concert series.

- **Surratt House and Museum**, 9118 Brandywine Road, Clinton, MD, 301-868-1121, www.surratt.org; John Wilkes Booth came here after his assassination of President Lincoln. Open March 1 through mid-December, Tuesday-Friday, 11 a.m. to 3 p.m.; Saturday and Sunday, noon to 4 p.m. Admission: $3 adults, $2 seniors, $1 ages 5 to 18, under 5 free.

- **Tudor Place Historic House and Garden**, 1644 31st Street NW, 202-965-0400 ext. 102, www.tudorplace.org; home to generations of Martha Washington's descendants, this 1812 Federal-style mansion holds an important collection of Mt. Vernon heirlooms. Tours Tuesday-

Friday, 10 a.m., 11:30 a.m., 1 p.m., and 2:30 p.m.; Saturday on the hour between 10 a.m. and 3 p.m. Donations requested.

- **Woodrow Wilson House**, 2340 S Street NW, 202-387-4062, www.nthp.org; this Georgian Revival townhouse is the only presidential museum in D.C. Open Tuesday-Sunday, 10 a.m. to 4 p.m. One-hour tours available. Admission: $5 adults, $4 seniors, $2.50 students.

CULTURE FOR KIDS

With so much emphasis on D.C.'s adult world, people often forget just how much there is for children to do here. Washington is a kid-friendly area, and it's important to remember that, in addition to the organizations listed below that are completely centered around children, many of the museums and cultural institutions listed above plan a wide variety of programs geared toward families. Start by looking at the Smithsonian's and the Kennedy Center's web sites for their child-friendly and educational programs. These cultural centers have monthly calendars of events geared specifically toward youngsters.

MUSEUMS

- **Capital Children's Museum**, 800 3rd Street NE, 202-543-8600, www.ccm.org; fosters a love of learning in children through the exploration of the five senses. Open daily, Easter through Labor Day, 10 a.m. to 6 p.m., and Labor Day through Easter 10 a.m. to 5 p.m. Admission: $6 adults, $4 seniors, children under 2 free. Half-price Sunday, before noon.
- **Discovery Creek Children's Museum**, 4954 MacArthur Boulevard, 202-364-3111, www.discoverycreek.org; designed to help children appreciate the natural world through science and the arts. Scheduled programs. Admission charged.
- **Discovery Room**, National Museum of Natural History (Smithsonian), 10th Street and Constitution Avenue NW, 202-357-2747, www.si.edu; encourages children to explore their world through sight, sound, and touch. Open Tuesday-Friday, noon to 2:30 p.m. and Saturday and Sunday 10:30 a.m. to 3:30 p.m. with special extended summer hours. Free
- **Dolls' House and Toy Museum**, 5236 44th Street NW, 202-244-0024; antique dollhouses, dolls, toys and games.
- **Hands On History Room**, National Museum of American History (Smithsonian), 14th Street and Constitution Avenue NW, www.si.edu; interesting room where children over the age of five can actually "play" with replicated artifacts. Free
- **Imagine That**, 1616 East Jefferson Street, Rockville, MD, 301-468-2101, is an interactive children's museum. Open daily, 10 a.m. to 6

p.m., Friday and Saturday until 8 p.m. Admission: children 18 months to 11 years $7.99, over age 11 $2.

- **National Capital Trolley Museum**, 1313 Bonifant Road, Silver Spring, MD, 301-384-6088, www.dctrolley.org; 17 streetcars on display, representing the history of the trolley in D.C. Rotating hours, call for information. Admission charged.
- **Samantha at the Heurich House Museum**, an American Girls Museum Program, 1307 New Hampshire Avenue NW, 202-887-8936, www.hswdc.org; the beloved American Girl series comes to life through a partnership between the Pleasant Company and the Historical Society of Washington. Two-hour programs include tours, activities and refreshments. Space is limited. Admission: $25 per person.

OUTDOOR

See the **Sports and Recreation** chapter for more outdoor opportunities.

- **Brookside Gardens and Nature Center**, 1400 Glenallan Avenue, Wheaton, MD, 301-946-9071
- **The Claude Moore Colonial Farm at Turkey Run**, 6310 Georgetown Pike, McLean, VA, 703-442-7557; www.cmcfatr.org; living history replicates life on a pre-Revolutionary War farm. Open April through mid-December, except in inclement weather. Admission: adults $2, seniors and children under 12, $1.
- **Kenilworth Aquatic Gardens**, Anacostia Avenue and Douglas Street NE, 202-426-6905; the only national park in the country devoted to aquatic plants, features over 1,000 different species. Open daily, 8 a.m. to 4 p.m. Free
- **National Colonial Farm**, Accokeek, MD, 301-283-2113, is a history museum that teaches about the rich agricultural heritage of Maryland, also displays contemporary farming science. Open Tuesday-Sunday, 10 a.m. to 4 p.m. except January 1, November 11, Thanksgiving, and December 25. Admission: adults $2, under 12 $.50, families $5.
- **National Zoological Park** (Smithsonian), 3001 Connecticut Avenue NW, 202-673-4800, www.si.edu; home to many unusual animals and educational displays including an orangutan intelligence center, a bat cave and a rain forest center. Cafeterias and gift shops. Buildings open daily, 10 a.m. to 6 p.m., May 1 through September 15. Free
- **Oxon Hill Farm**, Oxon Hill, MD, 301-839-1176, www.nps.gov/nace/oxhi; a working farm representative of the early 20th century. Open daily 8:30 a.m. to 4:30 p.m. except January 1, Thanksgiving, and December 25. Free
- **Reston Animal Park**, 1228 Hunter Mill Road, Vienna, VA, 703-759-3636; home to monkeys, llamas, zebras, bison and an elephant that can

be ridden. Many of the domesticated animals can be fed and petted. Varying hours and prices depending on the season. Call first.

- **Rock Creek Nature Center**, 5200 Glover Road NW, 202-426-6829, www.nps.gov/rocr/naturecenter; includes a hands-on discovery room. Open daily, 9 a.m. to 5 p.m. except January 1, July 4, Thanksgiving, and December 25. Free
- **US Botanic Gardens**, 1st Street and Maryland Avenue SW, 202-225-7099
- **US National Arboretum**, New York Avenue and R Street NE, 202-245-2726; a 444-acre arboretum includes pools stocked with fancy Japanese koi, the National Herb Garden, a formal European knot garden, the National Bonsai Collection, and a display of new plants recently bred. Open Monday-Friday, 8 a.m. to 4:30 p.m. Free

THEATER

- **Adventure Theater**, Old Arcade Building in Glen Echo Park, 7300 MacArthur Boulevard, Bethesda, MD, 301-320-5331, www.nps.gov/glec
- **Discovery Theater** (Smithsonian), Arts and Industries Building, 900 Jefferson Street SW, 202-357-1500, www.si.edu
- **Mt. Vernon Community Children's Theater**, 1900 Elkin Street, Alexandria, VA, 703-363-0686
- **Puppet Company Playhouse**, in the Spanish Ballroom in Glen Echo Park, Bethesda, MD, 301-320-6668, www.thepuppetco.org

H ERE IN ONE OF THE MOST HIGHLY EDUCATED CITIES IN THE world, you'll find it is quite common for grown and working adults to be studying for an advanced degree or a second bachelor's degree, either at night or full time. Even if you're not signing up for classes, the area's colleges and universities offer extensive libraries (see **Libraries** in the **Cultural Life** chapter) and a calendar crammed with distinguished lecturers, concerts, plays, sporting events, art exhibits, and more—often at bargain prices.

High schools maintain extensive collections of college and university literature: course catalogs, admissions information, scholarship bulletins, and more. Most high schools also employ guidance counselors with expertise in the complex process of choosing a college or university, getting admitted, and paying the bill. For adults returning to school, most of the same information is available in the reference section of the public library. For all prospective students, the **Greater Washington College Information Center** provides a wealth of free information at 202-393-1100 or www.collegeinfo.org.

TUITION ASSISTANCE

Students graduating from high school in D.C. get a consolation prize from Congress for not living in a state: they can, through the federal **D.C. Tuition Assistance Grant Program**, attend any state university in the country at the residential tuition rate. The program also provides up to $2,500 toward tuition at private institutions in the greater Washington area and at designated "Historically Black Colleges and Universities." To be eligible, students must: have lived in D.C. for at least a year; be admitted to a four-year degree or certificate program at an eligible college or university; be enrolled at least half time; and begin undergraduate studies within three years after graduating from high school. One bachelor's degree to a customer—no discount for students seeking a second degree. For more information, call the program office at 202-727-2824 or visit http://tuitiongrant.washingtondc.gov.

If you don't live in the District, look for the latest state financial aid programs offered through the **Maryland Higher Education Commission** at 800-974-0203 or www.mhec.state.md.us, or the **State Council of Higher Education for Virginia** at 804-225-2628 or www.schev.edu.

COLLEGES & UNIVERSITIES

Schools marked (**C**) are commuter schools with no student housing.

DISTRICT OF COLUMBIA

- **The American University**, 4400 Massachusetts Avenue NW, 202-885-1000, www.american.edu; private university known for international student body and WAMU public radio station. Kogod School of Business offers the MBA degree. 10,000 students
- **Catholic University of America**, 620 Michigan Avenue NE, 202-319-5000, www.cua.edu; owned and operated by the Catholic Church. Campus features impressive medieval and Renaissance styled architecture. 6,000 students
- **Gallaudet University**, 800 Florida Avenue NE, 202-651-5000 (TTY/voice), www.gallaudet.edu; academically prestigious school catering to deaf and hearing-impaired students. Chartered by President Lincoln. See "Services for People with Disabilities" in the **Helpful Services** chapter. 2,000 students
- **George Washington University**, 2121 I Street NW, 202-994-1000, www.gwu.edu; private university, teaching hospital and law school. Top international studies programs. 19,000 students
- **Georgetown University**, 37th and O streets NW, 202-687-4328, www.georgetown.edu; Jesuit school founded in 1789. Georgetown's law school and political science programs have produced many lawmakers, cabinet secretaries, and diplomats—and several presidents. 12,000 students
- **Howard University**, 2400 6th Street NW, 202-806-2250, www.howard.edu; historically black university with teaching hospital, business school, and law school. 10,000 students
- **Strayer University**, 1025 15th Street NW, 202-408-2400, www.strayer.edu; private business and technical school, popular with mid-career adults looking to expand or update skills. 10,500 students (C)

- **Trinity College**, 125 Michigan Avenue NE, 202-884-9050, www.trinitydc.edu; Catholic women's college. Satellite campus on Capitol Hill offers evening classes for working adults. 4,000 students
- **University of the District of Columbia**, 4200 Connecticut Avenue NW, www.udc.edu; public land-grant university. The David A. Clarke School of Law is a pioneering school emphasizing public-interest law and requiring every student to provide legal aid, under faculty supervision, to low-income clients. 5,300 students (C)
- **USDA Graduate School**, 600 Maryland Avenue SW, registrars office, 202-314-3320, www.grad.usda.gov; affordable evening and weekend continuing education courses. Ideal for working adults who need to expand their skills but don't need another degree. 37,500 students. (C)

MARYLAND

- **Bowie State University**, 14000 Jericho Park Road, Bowie, 301-464-3000, www.bowiestate.edu; part of the Maryland state university system. 5,000 students
- **Montgomery College**, 900 Hungerford Drive, Rockville, 301-279-5310, www.mc.cc.md.us; public two-year college with satellite campuses in Germantown and Takoma Park. Many students complete basic courses here and transfer to a four-year school for more specialized study. 20,000 students (C)
- **Prince George's Community College**, 301 Largo Road, Largo, 301-336-6000, http://pgweb.pg.cc.md.us; public two-year college similar to Montgomery County's. 12,000 students (C)
- **University of Maryland**, University Boulevard & Campus Drive, College Park, 301-405-1000, www.umd.edu; major state university with strong engineering, physics and journalism programs. Birthplace of Kermit the Frog; today, a scholarship endowed by alumnus Jim Henson promotes the study of puppetry. 33,000 students

VIRGINIA

- **George Mason University**, 4400 University Drive, Fairfax, 703-993-1000, www.gmu.edu; known especially for information technology programs and conservative scholars such as Robert Bork and Stephen Fuller. Many big-name entertainers perform at the Patriot Center on campus. 24,000 students
- **Marymount University**, 2807 North Glebe Road, Arlington, 703-284-1500, www.marymount.edu; Catholic school with strong business and nursing departments. Satellite campuses in Sterling and Ballston. Formerly a women's institution; went coed in 1986. 3,600 students

- **Northern Virginia Center**, 7054 Haycock Road, Falls Church, 703-358-1100; www.uvacc.virginia.edu or www.nvgc.vt.edu; continuing education campus shared by Virginia Tech and the University of Virginia. Emphasis on certificate programs in information technology. 7,500 students (C)
- **Northern Virginia Community College**, 4001 Wakefield Chapel Road, Annandale, 703-323-3000, www.nv.cc.va.us; public two-year college with additional campuses in Alexandria, Manasas, Sterling, and Woodbridge. 61,000 students (C)

I N A CITY FULL OF PEOPLE ACCUSTOMED TO TAKING SIDES ON political issues, it's only natural that the home team draws fiercely loyal fans—from, as Washingtonians say, "both sides of the aisle." The Washington Redskins hold the NFL record for consecutive sold-out home games, and since the Washington Wizards moved from the suburbs to the downtown MCI Center in 1998, so many fans clog the Metro stations on basketball nights that the Metro system was able to cancel a planned fare increase.

Of course, watching isn't everything. On summer weekends every public soccer field and tennis court in town is in use, and in-line skaters play street hockey in front of the White House. To accommodate cyclists, skaters, and scooters, Beach Drive in Rock Creek Park and Sligo Creek Parkway in Silver Spring are closed to motor traffic on Sundays. During the winter, high schools, condo associations, and church groups organize ski trips to Appalachian resorts. And runners have to register early to get a slot in the crowded annual Marine Corps Marathon.

Check the Sports sections of the *Washington Post* or *Washington Times* for thorough coverage of competitive sports—professional, collegiate, and even high school. Radio station WTEM-AM 980 specializes in sports coverage. Every local TV station carries sports talk shows, featuring interviews with coaches and players. And in the *Post*, Tony Kornheiser and Tom Boswell are the latest in a long line of great sports commentators.

In the Weekend section of Friday's *Post*, the "On the Move" pages list dozens of athletic clubs, classes, and events, covering opportunities to get involved in badminton, climbing, cycling, diving, equestrian, fencing, gymnastics, hiking, martial arts, rugby, running, skiing, volleyball, and more. And don't forget to visit the sporting goods stores listed in the **Shopping for the Home** chapter; in addition to good bulletin boards and stacks of brochures, these stores have knowledgeable and enthusiastic salespeople who will be happy to refer you to opportunities to practice your favorite sports.

PROFESSIONAL AND SCHOOL SPORTS

Several ticket agencies handle all professional games and venues in the Washington area. Ticketmaster is the standard vendor, but other agencies buy cancellations and may have seats after the box offices and Ticketmaster are sold out. Purchasing from a ticket agency will include a service charge.

- **Ticketmaster**, 202-432-SEAT or 800-551-SEAT, www.ticketmaster.com
- **All Sports & Concerts**, 301-595-4009 or 800-786-8425, www.ascticket.com
- **Encore Tickets**, 301-718-2525, www.encoretix.com

PROFESSIONAL SPORTS

BASEBALL

Washington hasn't had a baseball team on its soil since the Senators left town in the 1970s. Some residents are still bitter about it, but despite perennial efforts to bring a major-league team to D.C., most Washingtonians have adopted the Baltimore Orioles as their home team. Oriole Park at Camden Yards is a beautiful tribute to old-style ballparks, and there are no bad seats. However, with tickets, refreshments, and souvenirs, it can add up to an expensive outing for a family; some choose instead to watch the Bowie Baysox, Frederick Keys, and Potomac Cannons, minor-league teams close up and cheap.

- **Baltimore Orioles**, www.theorioles.com; Washington ticket office, 1666 K Street NW, 202-296-2473
- **Oriole Park at Camden Yards**, Pratt & Eutaw streets, Baltimore, 410-685-9800; MARC: Camden Station, Camden Line
- **Bowie Baysox**, 301-805-6000, www.baysox.com
- **Frederick Keys**, 301-662-0088, www.frederickkeys.com
- **Potomac Cannons**, 703-590-2311, www.potomaccannons.com

For Orioles home games on weekends, MARC commuter trains make special trips at the regular price of $10.75 round-trip. On weeknights, the last train from Baltimore to Washington leaves 20 minutes after the end of the game. See **Transportation**. By car or train, Oriole Park is about an hour from the District.

BASKETBALL

Washington has been a basketball town ever since a local gym teacher named Red Auerbach agreed to coach Washington's first NBA team. The old Capitols faced the Minneapolis Lakers in the 1949 championship series; three years later, Auerbach moved to Boston and became the most successful NBA coach in history. A more recent legend, Michael Jordan, arrived in D.C. in 2000 to take the reins of the Washington Wizards, and took to the court in 2001, hoping to make the MCI Center a venue for post-season play. Attendance doesn't seem to vary with the team's fortunes, though, and the Metro is consistently crowded on game nights. The devotion of Washington fans is even more evident with the Wizards' sister team, the Women's NBA Washington Mystics, who have the best attendance record and worst playing record in the WNBA.

- **Washington Wizards**, 202-661-5050, www.nba.com/wizards
- **Washington Mystics**, 202-661-5050, www.wnba.com/mystics
- **MCI Center**, 7th and F streets NW, www.mcicenter.com; Metro: Gallery Place-Chinatown (Red, Green, and Yellow lines)

FOOTBALL

The waiting list for tickets to a Washington Redskins home game is several years long, and every regular season game has been sold out since 1966. You can buy tickets from a scalper or from one of the "ticket agents" that advertise in the *Washington Post* classified ads; you can win tickets in a call-in contest on a local radio station; you can get friendly with someone who has season tickets or with a business associate whose firm has a stadium box to entertain clients; but you cannot just go buy a ticket to a Redskins game. (Well, maybe a pre-season exhibition.) The Redskins summer training camp is at Redskins Park in Ashburn, VA in late July through late August. During football season, city streets are quiet during game time, as hundreds of thousands of residents settle in front of the TV. Diehard fans mute the sound on the TV and watch the screen while they listen to Sonny Jurgensen and Sam Huff call the game on WJFK-FM 106.7.

Off the field, there is an ongoing controversy about the team's name. The first NFL team to win the Super Bowl under the leadership of an African-American quarterback (Doug Williams, 1988) faces perennial claims from Native American groups objecting to the name as a racial slur, and in 1999, the US Patent & Trademark Office agreed, revoking trademark protection of the team's name and logo. A tradition dating to 1937 is hard to abandon—the "Skins" were the first NFL team to have a marching band, and "Hail to the Redskins" is the oldest pro sports fight song in the nation—but, as the 1997 renaming of the Washington Bullets basketball team showed, loyal fans aren't deterred by politics.

The Redskins aren't the only pro football team in town. The D.C. Divas—women's professional football—made their debut in 2001. The National Women's Football League franchise plays at Eastern High School, across the street from RFK Stadium, from April through late June. Tickets are cheap and readily available, but it's real football.

If you do manage to get Redskins tickets, you can join the traffic jams on Route 202 or take a shuttle bus from the Metro to FedEx Field.

- **Redskins ticket office**, 202-546-2222, www.redskins.com
- **Divas ticket office**, 703-541-2247, www.dcdivas.com
- **FedEx Field**, directions, 301-276-6248; Metro: Landover (Orange Line) or Addison Road (Blue Line)
- **Redskins Park**, Route 28 & Waxpool Road, Ashburn; see www.redskins.com for details.

HOCKEY

During the winter and spring, the NHL Washington Capitals share the MCI Center with the men's and women's NBA teams, and you can readily spot the crowds of devoted "Caps" fans—a typical fan at a Capitals game is more likely to be wearing full team regalia than a Wizards or Mystics fan. Their team is more successful, usually making the division playoffs—but no Stanley Cup title yet. Contact the Washington Capitals at 202-661-5050 or www.washingtoncaps.com for more information.

SOCCER

Since 1994, when RFK Stadium hosted several World Cup matches, the first-ever MLS champions, the D.C. United, have adopted the former home field of the Redskins and Senators. Several United players have been tapped for the US Olympic team. Among Washington's international population and suburban "soccer mom" households, the team has a small but passionate following, and those who miss downtown baseball or football may find the United's first-rate soccer a welcome and inexpensive alternative.

In 2001, the D.C. United started sharing RFK Stadium with the Washington Freedom, a franchise of the Women's United Soccer Association. The Freedom roster includes Olympic gold medalist Mia Hamm, who has been featured in ads calling her "the best football player in the world." This is her home turf in more ways than one—she hails from Northern Virginia and attended Lake Braddock High School.

- **D.C. United**, 703-478-6600, www.dcunited.com
- **Washington Freedom**, 202-432-SEAT, www.washingtonfreedom.com
- **RFK Stadium**, 22nd & East Capitol streets, 202-547-9077; Metro: Stadium-Armory (Blue and Orange lines)

HORSE RACING

Pimlico Race Course, home of the Preakness Stakes and the Breeders' Cup, is an hour's drive from Washington in the northwest outskirts of Baltimore.

Closer to home, catch thoroughbred racing at Laurel Park and harness racing at Rosecroft Raceway.

- **Pimlico Race Course**, Northern Parkway and Pimlico Road, Baltimore, 410-542-9400, www.pimlico.com
- **Laurel Park**, Route 198 and Race Track Road, Laurel, MD, 301-725-0400, www.pimlico.com; MARC: Laurel Racetrack, Camden Line
- **Rosecroft Raceway**, Rosecroft Drive off Brinkey Road, Oxon Hill, MD, 301-567-4000, www.rosecroft.com

OTHER PROFESSIONAL SPORTS

- **The Kemper Open golf tournament** is held every May at Avenel Park in Potomac; see www.pgatour.com.
- **The Legg Mason Tennis Classic** is held every August at William H.G. Fitzgerald Tennis Stadium in Rock Creek Park; see www.leggmasontennisclassic.com.
- **Figure skating** and **gymnastics** meets and exhibitions are held occasionally at the MCI Center; check the arena's calendar at www.mcicenter.com.

COLLEGIATE SPORTS

The Washington area is home to a number of colleges and universities, offering plenty of exciting NCAA action. Several collegiate basketball and football teams in the area have attracted a following beyond the campus, and fill prominent regional venues; others draw less attention, but may be exciting and affordable alternatives to the pros. Some big names—including Patrick Ewing and Boomer Esaison—have been made in college games inside the Beltway.

- **Catholic University of America**: the Cardinals have been to the Orange Bowl and other bowl games, but not in recent decades; Catholic U's athletic strength lately is in swimming and track & field. Tickets and information, 202-319-5286 or http://athletics.cua.edu
- **George Mason University**: the Patriots play basketball at the Patriot Center, also a major concert venue. Tickets, 202-432-SEAT (Ticketmaster); information, www.gmusports.com
- **George Washington University**: the Colonials basketball packs the Smith Center in Foggy Bottom. Tickets, 202-994-6650; information, www.gwsports.com
- **Georgetown University**: the Hoyas are best known for men's basketball, though the legendary Coach John Thompson retired in the late 1990s. The Hoyas often play the best hoops in Washington. Their home games are at the MCI Center. Tickets, 202-687-4692; information, 202-687-7159, www.guhoyas.com

- **Howard University**: the Bison have been gaining strength in men's basketball in recent years, and football games at Greene Stadium are well attended. Tickets, 202-806-7198; information, www.bisonmania.com
- **Marymount University**: the Saints won the Capital Athletic Conference women's basketball tip-off championship in 1999. Information, 703-284-1619 or www.marymount.edu/ssa/athletic
- **University of Maryland**: the Terrapins ("Terps") basketball and football teams have a loyal following that has outgrown the home venues; Byrd Stadium and Cole Field House are both slated for major upgrades. Tickets, 301-314-8587 or www.umterps.fansonly.com; information, www.inform.umd.edu/athletics
- **US Naval Academy**: the Midshipmen take their college football seriously: when they score, especially in the annual Army-Navy game, cannons roar and plebes hit the deck for push-ups. Tickets, 800-US-4-NAVY; information, www.usna.edu.

HIGH SCHOOL SPORTS

For in-depth coverage of high school sports, pick up a copy of *SchoolSports* magazine, free in newspaper boxes at Metro stations. If you can't find it, call 877-776-7894 or visit http://schoolsports.com. Also, any high school newspaper or web site will include plenty of coverage of the home team, and community newspapers usually cover the local high school football and basketball teams. Soccer, baseball/softball, volleyball, lacrosse, wrestling, swimming, and other varsity sports usually make the box scores in Sunday's *Washington Post.*

PARTICIPANT SPORTS

The single best resource for participant sports activities, from charity 10K races to weekly 30-and-over flag football games, is the Weekend section of the *Washington Post*; also, *Metro Sports Washington* is a free monthly tabloid with articles about participant sports and lists of classes, sporting venues, ski resorts, and more. Pick it up at any sporting goods store or in newspaper boxes around town, or call 202-289-4551. The online edition, at www.metrosports.com, includes searchable archives.

Local recreation departments maintain parks, trails, beaches, tennis and basketball courts, baseball diamonds, soccer fields, pools, and other public amenities, and most offer lessons in a variety of sports.

- **D.C. Department of Parks & Recreation**, 202-673-7660, http://dpr. dc.gov
- **Montgomery County Department of Recreation**, 301-217-6790, www.mc-mncppc.org

- **Prince George's County Department of Parks & Recreation**, 301-699-2400, www.pgparks.com
- **Arlington County Department of Parks, Recreation & Community Resources**, 703-228-3338 (recreation), 703-228-4710 (sports), www.co.arlington.va.us/prcr
- **Fairfax County Park Authority**, 703-324-8702, www.co.fairfax.va.us/parks
- **Alexandria Department of Recreation, Parks & Cultural Activities**, 703-638-4345, www.ci.alexandria.va.us/rpca

BICYCLING

Whether you're in training for the annual 330-mile D.C. AIDS Ride or just enjoying the scenery and exercise, Washington offers plenty of first-rate cycling. The C&O Canal towpath, the Washington & Old Dominion Trail, the Rock Creek Park bike path, and others are detailed in the **Greenspace** chapter. In addition, the Capital Crescent Trail from Bethesda to Georgetown and the Metropolitan Branch Trail, under construction, from Silver Spring to Capitol Hill, are intended to serve bicycle commuters.

Note: in most jurisdictions, minors are required by law to wear approved helmets while riding; also, there are occasional outbreaks of muggings on various bike trails, and cyclists should not ride alone at night on area trails.

You can **rent bicycles** at:
- **Big Wheel Bikes**, 1034 33rd Street NW, 202-337-0254; Two Prince Street, Alexandria, 703-739-2300
- **City Bikes**, 2501 Champlain Street NW, 202-265-1564
- **Fletcher's Boat House**, 4940 Canal Road NW, 202-244-0461
- **Metropolis Bike & Scooter**, 709 8th Street SE, 202-543-8900
- **REI**, 9801 Rhode Island Avenue, College Park, MD, 301-982-9681; 3509 Carlin Springs Road, Baileys Crossroads, 703-379-9400
- **Washington Sailing Marina**, George Washington Parkway, Alexandria, VA, 703-548-9027

For **organized rides and touring**, contact:
- **Bike the Sites**, 202-966-8662 or www.bikethesites.com, leads guided tours promising "history, lore and scandal," covering "55 sites in three hours." Bikes and helmets provided, and the entire route is on bike paths.
- **Potomac Pedalers Touring Club**, 202-363-8687, www.bikepptc.org, leads local and getaway tours, including overnight trips; also, dozens of touring cue sheets are available on the club's web site.

- **Washington Area Bicyclist Association**, 202-628-2500 or www.waba.org, leads trips and offers commuter advice, education, and advocacy—sort of the AAA for cyclists.

See **Transportation** for more information about local bike amenities, including the rules for carrying your bike on the Metro. For a calendar of races and cross-country tours, see the Weekend section of the *Post* or *Spokes* magazine, available free at bike shops.

BOATING

If you look out the window as you cross the Potomac during morning rush hour, you'll see local crew teams practicing in their shells. At Washington Harbour in Georgetown, motor yachts put in for dockside partying on summer evenings. And south of Hains Point, at the mouth of the Anacostia, the Potomac is a wide estuary where sizeable sailboats can catch the wind. Several marinas rent wet and dry slips, and Potomac River boathouses rent canoes, kayaks, and rowboats; the paddleboats on the Tidal Basin, in the shadow of the Jefferson Memorial, are a favorite with kids.

Within a two-hour drive from the Beltway, you can raft, canoe, or kayak some of the finest whitewater on the East Coast, or go tubing on the calmer stretches. The upper Potomac, the New River, the Youghiogheny (pronounced "yuckaHAYnee"), Antietam Creek, the Shenandoah, and the Savage make a paddlers' mecca of Western Maryland and the Harper's Ferry area of West Virginia. Closer to home, the lower 22 miles of the C&O Canal, between Georgetown and Swain's Lock, are ideal for flat-water canoeing.

The Washington Boat Show is held every February at the Washington Convention Center. To shop for canoes and other human-powered river craft, see the Sports section classifieds in the *Washington Post* or the sporting goods stores listed in **Shopping for the Home**; most large retailers also offer rentals.

BOATHOUSES

- **Fletcher's Boat House**, 4940 Canal Road NW, 202-244-0461
- **Jack's Boats**, 3500 K Street NW, 202-337-9642
- **Lake Needwood Boathouse**, off Needwood Road near Muncaster Mill Road, Rockville, MD, 301-762-9500, www.mc-mncppc.org; 301-948-5053 (recording)
- **Swain's Lock**, Swain's Lock Road off River Road, Potomac, MD, 301-299-9006

- **Thompson Boat Center**, Rock Creek Parkway & Virginia Avenue NW, 202-333-9543, www.guestservices.com/tbc
- **Tidal Basin Boat House**, 1501 Maine Avenue SW, 202-484-0206

MARINAS & YACHT CLUBS

- **Alexandria City Marina**, Alexandria, VA, 703-868-4265
- **Belle Haven Marina/Mariner Sailing School**, Alexandria, VA, 703-768-0018, http://saildc.com
- **Buzzard Point Marina**, Anacostia River, 202-488-8400
- **Capital Yacht Club**, Washington Channel, 202-488-8110, www.capitalyachtclub.net
- **Columbia Island Marina**, Arlington, 202-347-0173, www.guestservices.com/cim
- **Gangplank Marina**, Washington Channel, 202-554-5000, www.gangplank.com
- **James Creek Marina**, Anacostia River, 202-544-8844
- **Washington Marina**, Washington Channel, 202-554-0222
- **Washington Sailing Marina**, Alexandria, VA, 703-548-9027, www.guestservices.com/cim
- **Washington Yacht Club**, Anacostia River, 202-543-2027

RIVER OUTFITTERS

These adventure travel centers offer guided trips, drop-off/pickup trips, and rentals:
- **River Riders**, 800-326-7238, www.riverriders.com
- **River & Trail Outfitters**, 301-695-5177, www.rivertrail.com
- **USA Raft**, 800-USA-RAFT, www.usaraft.com
- **Precision Rafting**, www.precisionrafting.com, 800-477-3723

The **Anacostia Watershed Society**, 301-699-6204, www.anacostia-aws.org, offers guided tours of the upper Anacostia River by canoe or pontoon boat.

BOWLING

Okay, Washington is different from the rest of the country: there are no public bowling alleys in the District of Columbia. None. **Bowl America** has seven locations in the suburbs:
- **Alexandria**, VA, 6450 Edsall Road, 703-354-3300; South Pickett and Duke streets, 703-751-1900

- **Fairfax**, VA, 9699 Lee Highway, 703-273-7700
- **Falls Church**, VA, 140 South Maple Street, 703-534-1370
- **Gaithersburg**, MD, 1101 Clopper Road, 301-330-5200
- **Silver Spring**, MD, Georgia Avenue and Cameron Street, 301-585-6990
- **Westwood**, VA, 5353 Westbard Avenue, 301-654-1320

  Rinaldi Lanes has two locations:
- **Arlington**, VA, 2945 Glebe Road, 703-684-5800
- **Riverdale**, MD, 6322 Kenilworth Avenue, 301-864-5940

EQUESTRIAN SPORTS

Northern Virginia is horse country, and most horse farms offer riding lessons. Visit www.virginiahorse.com/links for a list of farms and equestrian organizations. In Maryland, for training in equestrian events, visit the **Prince George's Equestrian Center,** 301-952-7900, in Upper Marlboro, where Pennsylvania Avenue meets US Route 301. Closer to home, there are several public riding stables:

- **Meadowbrook Stables**, East-West Highway & Meadowbrook Lane, Chevy Chase, MD, 301-589-9026
- **Rock Creek Park Horse Centre**, 5100 Glover Road NW, 202-362-0117
- **Wheaton Regional Park Stables**, 1101 Glenallen Avenue, Wheaton, MD, 301-622-3311

  The **Potomac Polo Club**, 301-972-7757, can refer you to opportunities to get involved with the "sport of kings," and there are occasional polo matches on the Mall near the Lincoln Memorial on Sundays during the summer.

FISHING

In season, the Weekend section of the *Washington Post* runs a weekly fishing report listing water levels, temperatures, and what's biting in area streams and impoundments. The Chesapeake Bay gave Maryland its state tourism slogan, "Maryland is for Crabs," and the blue crab makes its way well into the lower Potomac River. Check with local wildlife authorities for details about fishing licenses and limits on certain protected species—especially striped bass, also known as rockfish, the official state fish of Maryland. Also ask about environmental advisories—shellfish in certain areas have elevated levels of mercury, and the Chesapeake Bay fish population has been battling the *Pfiesteria* virus for several years.

- **Maryland Department of Natural Resources**, general information, 877-620-8367 or www.dnr.state.md.us; boating, hunting and fishing licenses, 410-879-4500; fish health hotline, 888-584-3110

- **Virginia Department of Conservation & Recreation**, 800-933-7275, www.dcr.state.va.us

GOLF

In addition to elite country clubs such as Congressional and Burning Tree, the Washington area has dozens of public golf courses, both commercial and community. Most area golf courses accept reservations online through www.teetimes.com.

DISTRICT OF COLUMBIA

- **East Potomac Park Golf Course & Driving Range**, 202-554-7660
- **Langston Golf Course & Driving Range**, 202-397-8638
- **Rock Creek Park Golf Course**, 202-882-7332

MARYLAND

- **Bowie Golf & Country Club**, Bowie, 301-262-8141
- **Enterprise Golf Course**, Mitchellville, 301-249-2040
- **Falls Road Golf Course**, Potomac, 301-299-5156
- **Glenn Dale Country Club**, Bowie, 301-262-1166
- **Henson Creek Golf Course**, Fort Washington, 301-567-4646 (no tee times; open weekdays 7 a.m., weekends from 6:30 a.m., until dark)
- **Lake Arbor Golf Course**, Bowie, 301-336-7771
- **Laytonsville Golf Course**, Laytonsville, 301-948-5288
- **Little Bennett Golf Course**, Clarksburg, 301-601-9209
- **Needwood Golf Course**, Rockville, 301-948-1075
- **Northwest Golf Course**, Wheaton, 301-598-6100
- **Paint Branch Golf Course**, College Park, 301-935-0330
- **Poolesville Golf Course**, 301-428-8143
- **Prince George's County Youth Golf Training Center**, Landover, 301-772-2527
- **Sligo Creek Golf Course**, Silver Spring, 301-585-6006
- **White Oak Golf Course**, Silver Spring, 301-593-6910

VIRGINIA

To reserve a tee time at one of these Fairfax County golf courses, call 877-776-3272 anytime, up to 48 hours in advance; teetimes.com users can make reservations up to two weeks in advance. For more information, visit www.co.fairfax.va.us/parks/golf.
- **Burke Lake Golf Course**, Fairfax Station, 703-323-1641

- **Greendale Golf Course**, Alexandria, 703-971-3788
- **Jefferson District Golf Course**, Falls Church, 703-573-0444
- **Oak Marr Golf Complex**, Oakton, 703-255-5390
- **Pinecrest Golf Course**, Alexandria, 703-941-1061
- **Pleasant Valley Golfers Club**, Chantilly, 703-631-7904
- **Twin Lakes Golf Course**, Clifton, 703-631-9372

HIKING

There are miles of hiking trails in Rock Creek Park, and in the section of the park north of Military Road you may forget you're in a city. The C&O Canal towpath offers easy walking all the way to the mountains of Western Maryland through the Potomac River valley, and both sides of the Potomac at Great Falls are meccas for weekend hikers. See the **Greenspace** chapter for more detail on these nearby parks. Within a two-hour drive from the Beltway, you can reach some of the most popular hiking and backpacking areas in the eastern United States.

Some especially good hiking areas near Washington follow; for trail atlases and hiking guides to these and other regional parks, visit the books department at REI or Hudson Trail Outfitters (see **Sporting Goods** in **Shopping for the Home**), or Patagonia at 1048 Wisconsin Avenue NW, 202-333-1776. Two little books published by the Appalachian Trail Conference will keep you busy with dozens of day hikes of 15 miles or less: *Circuit Hikes in Shenandoah National Park* and *Circuit Hikes In Virginia, West Virginia, Maryland, and Pennsylvania.*

- **Shenandoah National Park**: this 107-mile-long ridge 80 miles west of Washington is a favorite weekend getaway and, in the fall, parts of the park are actually overcrowded. Old Rag Mountain draws rock scramblers to its low timberline and massive cliffs, and the parking area at the trailhead is usually full on weekends in the summer. If you avoid the most crowded areas and times, you can immerse yourself in the woods of two dozen mountainsides, teeming with wildlife, waterfalls, and vistas. Call 540-999-3500 or visit www.nps.gov/shen.
- **The Appalachian Trail**: the "A.T." passes through Maryland about 60 miles north of Washington, crossing the Potomac near Harper's Ferry, where Maryland, Virginia, and West Virginia meet at the mouth of the Shenandoah River. Turn right and walk to Mt. Katahdin in Maine, 1,200 miles north; turn left and walk to Springer Mountain in Georgia, 900 miles south. Guidebooks are available at most bookstores and outfitters; for more information, contact the **Appalachian Trail Conference** at 304-535-6331 or www.atconf.org.
- **Prince William Forest Park**: less than 20 miles south of the Beltway, just off Interstate 95, this woodland park in the headwaters of Quantico

Creek is one of the area's best-kept secrets. You can spend hours on the park's 35 miles of trail and see plenty of deer, and few, if any, people. Call 703-221-7181 or visit www.nps.gov/prwi.

- **Cunningham Falls State Park/Catoctin State Park**: these two Maryland state parks, about two hours' drive north of Washington, offer easy day hikes and attract a lot of families. In Catoctin State Park, you might glimpse a high chain link fence deep in the woods—it marks the perimeter of Camp David, the secluded weekend retreat of every president since Eisenhower. Call 301-271-7574 or visit www.dnr.state.md.us/publiclands.
- **Manassas National Battlefield Park**: you can retrace the steps of Stonewall Jackson and Robert E. Lee through the swamps, meadows and woods of Bull Run, on scrupulously preserved hallowed ground barely 15 miles west of the Beltway. Call 703-361-1339 or visit www.nps.gov/mana.

These groups organize **hiking and backpacking trips**:
- **Appalachian Mountain Club**, 202-298-1488
- **Capital Hiking Club**, 703-578-1942
- **Northern Virginia Hiking Club**, 703-440-1805
- **Potomac Appalachian Trail Club**, 703-242-0965, www.patc.net
- **Sierra Club**, 202-547-2326
- **Washington Women Outdoors**, 301-864-3070

ICE SKATING

The Washington equivalent of going skating at Rockefeller Center is the fountain in the sculpture garden of the National Gallery of Art at 7th Street and Constitution Avenue NW. The rink is operated for the National Park Service by Guest Services, 202-289-3361, www.guestservices.com/skating.

The Gardens Ice House in Laurel, 301-953-0100, is a year-round skating facility with one ice rink in the summer and three in the winter. During the summer, two rinks are used for in-line and roller skating.

Most ice rinks are open from October through March and have certain hours set aside for hockey or figure skating; all provide skate rentals and lockers.
- **Cabin John Ice Rink**, 10610 Westlake Drive, Rockville, MD, 301-365-0585
- **Fairfax Ice Arena**, 3779 Pickett Road, Fairfax, VA, 703-323-1131
- **Fort Dupont Ice Rink**, 3779 Ely Place SE, 202-584-5007
- **Herbert Wells Ice Rink**, 5211 Paint Branch Parkway, College Park, MD, 301-277-3719 or 301-277-0654 (recorded information)
- **Mt. Vernon RECenter**, 2017 Belle View Boulevard, Alexandria, VA, 703-768-3224
- **Pershing Park** (outdoors), 14th Street and Pennsylvania Avenue NW, 202-737-6938

- **Tucker Road Ice Rink**, 1770 Tucker Road, Fort Washington, MD, 301-248-2508
- **Wheaton Ice Arena**, Arcola and Orebaugh avenues, Wheaton, MD, 301-649-2250

IN-LINE & ROLLER SKATING

Park rangers vigorously defend the grounds of national monuments from in-line skaters, but there are many other places to go, including the paved bike trails along the Potomac River and Rock Creek. Since the mid-1990s when the US Secret Service, citing security concerns, blocked motor vehicle traffic on Pennsylvania Avenue NW in front of the White House, the block has been taken over by in-line skaters and street hockey players. **Washington Area Rollerskaters**, 202-466-5005 or www.skatedc.org, can provide information about events and lessons. Their site includes links to thousands of local and general resources for in-line and roller skaters and street hockey enthusiasts. City Bikes, REI, and the Ski Center rent in-line skates—see **Sporting Goods** in the **Shopping for the Home** chapter.

ROCK CLIMBING

There are 50-foot cliffs just five miles outside the Beltway, looming over the Mather Gorge below Great Falls of the Potomac. Great Falls National Park on the Virginia side and C&O Canal National Historical Park on the Maryland side are meccas for technical climbing and rock scrambling. See the **Greenspace** chapter for more information.

For serious climbers, the ideal weekend getaway is the Spruce Knob-Seneca Rocks National Recreation Area in West Virginia, about 200 miles away; the area is renowned for the grandest rock arches and pillars east of Utah. Call the visitors' center at 304-567-2827 or the ranger station at 304-257-4488, or visit http://wvweb.com/www/nra.

For indoor climbing or lessons, go to **Sportrock Climbing Center**: 1408 Southlawn Lane, Rockville, MD, 301-ROCK-111; 5308 Eisenhower Avenue, Alexandria, VA, 703-212-ROCK. **Wakefield Park RECenter** (see **Health Clubs** below) also has an indoor climbing wall.

RUNNING

For training or casual jogging, the Mall, the Towpath, the banks of the Potomac, and the shaded, rolling hills of Rock Creek are as good as it gets; for more competitive running, the *Washington Post's* Weekend section lists 10-Ks, 5-milers, and "fun runs." See the chapter, **A Washington Year**, for information about the Marine Corps Marathon and the Army 10-Miler. For more ideas, or to join a group, contact:

- **American Running & Fitness Association**, 301-913-9517
- **Capitol Hill Runners**, 301-283-0821
- **D.C. Road Runners**, 703-241-0395
- **Reston Runners**, 703-437-3668
- **Washington Running Club**, 703-536-7764

SOCCER

Especially popular among children and teens, soccer is gaining a share of grownups' recreation time too. Contact one of the regional soccer associations for information about clubs and leagues:

- **Metro D.C./Virginia Soccer Association**, www.mdcvsa.org
- **Virginia Youth Soccer Association**, 703-494-0030, www.vysa.org
- **Maryland State Youth Soccer Association**, 410-987-7898, msysa@aol.com

SWIMMING

Every summer, when temperatures pass 100° and the humidity is described by professional meteorologists as "oppressive," we see TV and newspaper images of people taking a desperate dip in the fountains of Dupont Circle or Freedom Plaza, or in the slimy and shallow Reflecting Pool on the Mall. Fortunately, there are plenty of public swimming pools and private swim clubs in the area, including heated indoor pools for winter training.

There are a few **public beaches** on the Chesapeake Bay (Sandy Point and Calvert Cliffs, 877-620-8367), and US Route 50 is one long traffic jam every weekend from Memorial Day to Labor Day as Washingtonians flock to Ocean City, MD and Rehoboth Beach, DE. For a rustic seashore alternative to the resort scene, visit Assateague Island National Seashore located just south of Ocean City. See **Quick Getaways** for more information.

Generally, outdoor pools are open from Memorial Day to Labor Day, or from the last day of school in June to the first weekday of September. Most public pools charge a nominal fee to residents and a slightly higher fee, typically around $5, to guests; ask about family discounts, season passes, and discounts for youth and seniors.

PUBLIC SWIMMING POOLS

- **D.C. Department of Parks & Recreation** operates 34 outdoor pools and six indoor pools. Call the Aquatics Division at 202-576-6436 or visit http://dpr.dc.gov.
- **Montgomery County Department of Recreation** operates six outdoor pools and four indoor pools. Call the Aquatic Programs office at 240-777-6860 or visit www.co.mo.md.us.
- **Prince George's County Department of Parks & Recreation** operates 10 outdoor lap pools; the indoor **Bickford Natatorium** at Prince George's Community College; the indoor **Theresa Banks Complex** in Glenarden, with a lap pool and wave pool; and four "splash parks" with waterslides, fountains, and other fun pool features. Call 301-699-2400 or visit www.pgparks.com.
- The **Arlington County Department of Parks, Recreation & Community Resources** operates indoor pools at Wakefield, Washington and Lee, and Yorktown high schools. Call 703-228-3338 or visit www.co.arlington.va.us/prcr.
- **Fairfax County pools** are located at county RECenters—see **Health Clubs** below.
- The **Alexandria Department of Recreation, Parks & Cultural Activities** operates two full-sized pools for residents of all ages and four "neighborhood pools" for children 13 and under. Call 703-838-4843 or visit www.ci.alexandria.va.us/rpca.

COMMUNITY & PRIVATE SWIM CLUBS

Most large apartment buildings and even some office buildings have pools for tenants, condo association members, and their guests. In addition, some municipalities have community pools with inexpensive membership fees for residents, and a few private swim clubs such as Kenmont and Burke are known for fiercely competitive swim teams. The Curl Burke Swim Club has produced a few Olympic athletes, including local hero Tom Dolan.
- **Burke Swim & Racquet Club**, 6001 Burke Commons Lane, 703-250-1299, www.cubu.org/burke
- **Cheverly Swim & Racquet Club**, 5600 Euclid Street, 301-773-4814, www.cheverlypool.com
- **Garrett Park Pool Association**, Cambria & Keswick avenues, 301-946-0175, www.garrettpark.org
- **Greenbelt Aquatic & Fitness Center**, 101 Center Way Road, 301-397-2204

- **Hillandale Swim & Tennis Association**, 10116 Green Forest Drive, Silver Spring, www.playhsta.com
- **Kenmont Swim & Tennis Club**, 2900 Faulkner Place, Kensington, 301-933-0047, www.kenmontpool.homestead.com
- **Rockville Municipal Swim Center**, 355 Martins Lane, 301-309-3040

See also **Health Clubs** below, as most gyms and YMCAs have indoor pools. Many colleges and high schools with swimming pools make their facilities available to the community during the summer and on weekends. Contact the college and university athletic offices listed under **Collegiate Sports** above or visit the **Potomac Valley Swimmers** web site listing all regulation pools, public and private, in the Washington area: www.pvswim.org.

SCUBA & SKIN DIVING

You won't get much field practice around town, but if you're planning a trip to Florida or Hawaii, you can get scuba and snorkeling lessons at these diving shops:

- **American Sport Divers**, 12100 Nebel Street, Rockville, MD, 301-881-4208
- **Divemasters Scuba Center**, 109 East Diamond Avenue, Gaithersburg, MD, 301-670-0535
- **Dive Shop**, 3013 Nutley Street, Fairfax, VA, 703-698-7220
- **National Diving Center**, 4932 Wisconsin Avenue NW, 202-636-6123

TENNIS

Public tennis courts abound in Rock Creek Park, along the Anacostia and Northwest Branch, and in countless neighborhood parks; in agreeable weather, all you need to do is grab a court and play. In the winter, you'll need reservations to play at an indoor tennis facility—there are only two inside the Beltway (East Potomac Park and Rock Creek Park) and a handful in the suburbs:

- **Cabin John Regional Park**, 7801 Democracy Boulevard, Bethesda, MD, 301-469-7300
- **Cosca Regional Park**, 11000 Thrift Road, Clinton, MD, 301-868-6462
- **East Potomac Park Tennis Center**, 1090 Ohio Drive SW, 202-554-5962
- **Fairland Sports & Aquatics Complex**, 13950 Old Gunpowder Road, Laurel, MD, 301-953-0030

- **Rock Creek Park Tennis Center**, 16th & Kennedy streets NW, 202-722-5949
- **Watkins Regional Park**, 301 Watkins Park Drive, Upper Marlboro, MD, 301-218-6870
- **Wheaton Regional Park**, 11715 Orebaugh Avenue, Wheaton, MD, 301-649-4049

The **Southeast Tennis & Learning Center** in Congress Heights is now open; student and youth programs have priority use of its indoor and outdoor courts; accessible by the general public in the evenings. 202-645-6242

For information about tennis lessons, clinics, and tournaments, contact the **Washington Tennis Association**, 202-722-0067 or www.tennisnetwork. com/USTA-DC. For youth programs call the **Washington Tennis & Education Foundation**, 202-291-9888 or www.wtef.org.

ULTIMATE & DISC GOLF

You can usually find a pickup game of Ultimate on the Mall, the Ellipse, or any college campus. For information about leagues and tournaments, contact the **Ultimate Players Association** at 800-872-4384 or www.upa.org.

There is a public disc golf course on Paint Branch Parkway in College Park, near the Metro station and College Park Airport. For information, call 301-445-4500 or visit www.pgparks.com/places and select "specialized sports facilities."

VOLLEYBALL

During the summer, there's always a pickup game somewhere on the Mall or in East Potomac Park. For a list of area leagues and tournaments, contact **USA Volleyball**, Chesapeake Region, 301-270-0710.

HEALTH CLUBS AND RECENTERS

If you live in an apartment complex or work in a large office building you might have access to a fitness center or weight room at little or no cost. If not, or if you prefer a health club with a wider range of amenities and services, you're never far from a full range of gyms and fitness centers. Most feature weight machines, stationary bikes, racquetball, swimming, aerobics, kickboxing, yoga, and all the latest trendy workouts; many clubs also offer personal trainers and "boot camp" regimens.

Generally, in the suburbs, you'll find "the Y" and the big three chains: Bally, Sport & Health, and Washington Sports Clubs. Downtown, you'll find more independent clubs, many of which double as social centers for urban singles.

- **Bally Total Fitness**, 12 locations, 800-695-8111, www.ballyfitness.com
- **The Center Club**, 4300 King Street, Alexandria, VA, 703-820-8900
- **City Fitness**, 3525 Connecticut Avenue NW, 202-537-0539
- **Club Fitness at Washington Center**, 1001 G Street NW, 202-637-4747
- **D.C. Jewish Community Center**, 1529 16th Street NW, 202-518-9400, www.dcjcc.org
- **Franklin Plaza Health Club**, 1200 K Street NW, 202-408-5645
- **Gold's Gym & Aerobics Center**, eight locations, 202-554-4653 or 202-364-4653, www.goldsgym.com
- **Muscle Beach D.C.**, 202-328-5201, www.musclebeachdc.com
- **One to One Fitness Center**, 1722 I Street NW, 202-452-1861; 555 13th Street NW, 202-383-8765; 7929 Westpark Drive, Tysons Corner, VA, 703-848-0881
- **Results-The Gym**, 1612 U Street NW, 202-518-0001, www.resultsthegym.com
- **Sport & Health Clubs**, 23 locations, 800-882-5827, www.sportandhealth.com
- **Washington Sports Clubs**, 12 locations, 888-343-4WSC or 202-547-2255, www.washingtonsports.com
- **YMCA of Metropolitan Washington**, 17 locations, 800-473-YMCA or 202-232-6700, www.ymcawashdc.org

Fairfax County **RECenters** are comprehensive recreation and fitness centers featuring swimming pools, fitness rooms, spas, and racquetball courts. Other amenities, from volleyball courts to darkrooms and pottery studios, vary from one location to another. For county residents, admission is $5.50/day, with discounts for youth and seniors; without proof of residence, admission is $7.50/day. For more information, visit www.co.fairfax.va.us/parks/recenters.

- **Alexandria**: George Washington RECenter, 8426 Old Mt. Vernon Road, 703-780-8894; Mt. Vernon RECenter, 2017 Belle View Boulevard, 703-768-3224
- **Annandale**: Wakefield RECenter, 8100 Braddock Road, 703-321-7081
- **Falls Church**: Providence RECenter, 7525 Marc Drive, 703-698-1351
- **Franconia**: Lee District RECenter, 6601 Telegraph Road, 703-922-9841
- **McLean**: Spring Hill RECenter, 1239 Spring Hill Road, 703-827-0989
- **Oakton**: Oak Marr RECenter, Jermantown Road near Route 123, 703-281-6501
- **Springfield**: South Run RECenter, 7550 Reservation Drive, 703-866-0566

WASHINGTON D.C., WITH ITS HALF A MILLION PEOPLE, IS ALSO home to several wild bald eagles, and hundreds of deer. The city's web of broad, tree-lined avenues and grand plazas, laid out by architect Pierre L'Enfant in 1790, supplies vast green spaces and supports a surprising array of wildlife. You'll find parks and open spaces, large and small, famous and obscure, dotting the landscape—parks with hiking and biking trails, parks with statues and benches, parks with playgrounds and ball fields, even parks for dogs. D.C. citizens and lawmakers are so proud of their green havens and sweeping boulevards they have kept L'Enfant's plan largely intact for more than two centuries.

And D.C. is not alone in preserving green space. State and local governments in Maryland and Virginia protect tens of thousands of acres of woodland, riverside, marsh, and meadow for public enjoyment. Some private estates dating from colonial days invite visitors to formal gardens or secluded nature preserves. From Rock Creek Park, the 5,000-acre crown jewel of the region's natural areas, to the dozens of tiny wedge-shaped traffic medians crowned by statues honoring little-remembered frontiersmen, the region's parks are generally well-maintained, safe, and inviting.

Unless otherwise noted, the parks listed here are open daily from dawn to dusk and are free, although there may be fees for some events and attractions within. For those visiting national parks, a national parks pass is available from the National Parks Foundation at 888-GO-PARKS or www.nationalparks.org; the $50 pass gives you, your immediate family, and your vehicle and passengers one year of free entry to any national park sites charging admission. For an additional $15, the pass can be upgraded to cover other Department of Interior sites such as national wildlife refuges; also, special lifetime passes are available for seniors and persons with disabilities.

GENERAL INFORMATION

- **D.C. Department of Parks & Recreation** (playgrounds, ball fields and recreation centers), 202-673-7660, http://dpr.dc.gov
- **Maryland Department of Natural Resources** (state parks and forests), 877-620-8367, www.dnr.state.md.us
- **Maryland-National Capital Park & Planning Commission** (local parks in the Maryland suburbs), 301-495-4600, www.mncppc.org
- **National Park Service**, National Capital Area, 202-690-5185, www.nps.gov
- **Northern Virginia Regional Park Authority** (local parks in the Virginia suburbs), 703-352-5900, www.nvrpa.org
- **Virginia Department of Conservation & Recreation** (state parks and forests), 800-933-7275, www.dcr.state.va.us

County and city park and recreation departments are listed under **Participant Sports** in the **Sports and Recreation** chapter.

MAJOR REGIONAL PARKS

These are huge green spaces that span more than one jurisdiction.

ROCK CREEK PARK

Flowing almost 30 miles from Laytonsville, MD to Georgetown, Rock Creek is filled with wooded parkland, sheltered trails, picnic groves, athletic fields, and several pockets of deep woods where you can quickly forget your proximity to the Beltway and the halls of government. A paved bike path follows the creek for much of its length, and on Sundays, Beach Drive—the park's main thoroughfare, and nowhere near a beach—is closed to motor vehicles and set aside for human-powered wheels.

Some of the park's major attractions warrant their own listings elsewhere in this book: Carter Barron Amphitheater, in **Cultural Life**; tennis and golf amenities, in **Sports and Recreation**; and the National Zoo, in this chapter. Near Gaithersburg, the creek is impounded to form Lake Needwood and Lake Frank, suburban family meccas for fishing and boating. And in D.C., you can tour Pierce Mill, 202-426-6908, a gristmill whose waterwheel turned grindstones from the 1820s well into the 1990s.

Deer sometimes wander out of the park along Military Road NW in the District and throughout central Montgomery County; closer to the stream itself, the native trout have all but vanished, but frogs, snakes, salamanders, and turtles abound, and the woods are home to songbirds, owls, woodpeckers, raccoons, muskrats, and an occasional fox. A tributary stream in

Cleveland Park is one of the few known habitats of the tiny Hays Spring amphipod—not exactly cute and furry, but the flea-like mud dweller is a uniquely Washingtonian creature.

Rock Creek Park is maintained by the National Park Service in D.C. and by the Maryland-National Capital Park & Planning Commission in Maryland.

C&O CANAL NATIONAL HISTORICAL PARK

If you were among the first to explore the internet, you may recall that the frontier of cyberspace in 1990 was navigated by "ftp" and "gopher" technology, and the World Wide Web was an eccentric fad. In the early 19th century, innovators like Jefferson and John Quincy Adams were boosters of the barge canal, and little did they know that commercial railroads would connect the capital to the Ohio River before the Chesapeake & Ohio Canal could even be completed.

The artificial waterway along the eastern banks of the rocky Potomac did carry mule-drawn barges between Georgetown and the coal town of Cumberland, MD until the early 20th century. In the 1970s, Supreme Court Justice William O. Douglas led the fight to preserve the ruins of the canal and restore the mules' towpath for hiking, biking, and jogging. Justice Douglas led hikes along the full length of the 185-mile towpath, a feat you can replicate today.

The southern 22 miles of the canal are fully restored; you can rent canoes at Swain's Lock in Potomac or Fletcher's in Georgetown (see **Boating** in **Sports and Recreation**) or ride a sightseeing barge from the visitors' centers in Georgetown, 202-653-5190, or Great Falls, 301-413-0720. To the north, two major feats of early American engineering are preserved along the canal: the seven-arch stone aqueduct carrying the canal across the Monocacy River near Dickerson, and the 3/4-mile Paw Paw Tunnel through a mountain west of Hancock.

ANACOSTIA RIVER

Washington's "other" river is lined with federal and local parkland that links with Sligo Creek Park and Northeast Branch Park to preserve nearly uninterrupted ribbons of greenspace from Hains Point all the way to Wheaton and Beltsville. At least one mating pair of bald eagles lives here, and an eaglet was born in D.C. in 2000. The Anacostia's headwaters include Greenbelt Park, 301-344-3944, one of the largest stands of forest in any Beltway county, and two of the region's outdoor crown jewels: the National Arboretum and Kenilworth Aquatic Gardens, both listed elsewhere in this chapter. Sligo Creek Park features a paved bike path connecting Northwest Branch Park in Hyattsville to Wheaton Regional Park (see **Wheaton** in the **Neighborhood Profiles**); on Sundays, Sligo Creek Parkway is closed to motor vehicles, providing a less crowded alternative to Rock Creek Park.

DISTRICT OF COLUMBIA

- **The Mall and surrounding area**: America's front yard, the Mall stretches from the Ulysses S. Grant Memorial Pool, just west of the Capitol, to the Potomac River by the Lincoln Memorial. East of the Washington Monument, the Mall is crowded with people sunbathing or playing Frisbee or football—except when it's crowded instead with protesters, or with hordes of people celebrating the Fourth of July, Earth Day, or an inauguration. The Monument grounds are unofficially reserved for kite flying, and on any windy weekend, you can gawk at elaborate Chinese dragons and giant box kites, many purchased at the National Air & Space Museum nearby. To the west, on either side of the Reflecting Pool, the Mall encompasses the Vietnam Veterans Memorial, the Korean War Memorial, the War Memorial Bandstand honoring veterans of World War I, and the Bicentennial Pond and Memorial, dedicated to the signers of the Declaration of Independence. These national shrines, like the Lincoln Memorial, need no introduction—they're always open and there's never a line or a fee. The only exception is the Washington Monument: to visit the observation deck, you need a free ticket assigning you an entry time. Tickets are available at the kiosk on the 15th Street side of the Monument grounds, or, for a small fee, you can order them in advance from Ticketmaster, 202-432-SEAT. For more information, call 202-426-6840 or visit www.nps.gov/wamo. Between the monument grounds and the White House is the Ellipse, a vast lawn that is home to the National Christmas Tree and the annual Pageant of Peace (see **A Washington Year**). Stroll around this area with your *ADC Street Atlas*, and you'll find small, obscure monuments to, among others, the Boy Scouts, Albert Einstein, and Archie Butt, a White House aide who sacrificed his life for others aboard the Titanic.
- **East & West Potomac Park**: baseball diamonds, a golf course, bike paths, and plenty of fishing spots line the Potomac waterfront between the Lincoln Memorial and Hains Point, where the shallow Potomac swallows the Anacostia and becomes a broad, deep tidewater river. The east and west segments of the waterfront are divided by the inlet of the Tidal Basin. At the southern tip of East Potomac Park, Hains Point affords unique views of the Washington skyline and the river, and there's always a steady breeze. One of the most interesting pieces of statuary in this city of statues is here: Seward Johnson's sculpture "Awakening,"

where a buried giant yawns and stretches just before rising from the ground. Call 202-554-7660 for information about the golf course and other amenities.

- **Woodland Parks**: from the air, D.C. looks as if a green octopus had picked the city up and squeezed. Throughout the city, especially near Rock Creek and the Anacostia River, long strips of woodland line tiny streams and valleys. Few residents live more than a 15-minute walk from some kind of nature preserve. Major parks between the Potomac and Rock Creek include **Battery Kemble** in Foxhall; **Glover Archbold** and **Whitehaven** west of Wisconsin Avenue NW; and **Soapstone Valley**, **Melvin C. Hazen**, and **Klingle Valley** along Connecticut Avenue NW. Major parks east of the Anacostia River include **Oxon Run** off Wheeler Road SE, **Fort Stanton** off W Street SE, **Stanton** along Pennsylvania and Alabama avenues SE, and the 400-acre **Fort Dupont** off Minnesota Avenue NE. Throughout the city, your *ADC Street Atlas* will show dozens of smaller neighborhood parks—some no more than a city block. Many are the sites of old Civil War forts. A special gem is Theodore Roosevelt Island, 88 acres of woods and marsh in the middle of the Potomac, between the Kennedy Center and Rosslyn. If you can ignore the planes landing at Reagan National Airport nearby, and the Teddy Roosevelt Bridge carrying I-66 across the south end of the island, this is a fun little patch of wilderness. It's accessible only by a footbridge from the Virginia side, with its own parking area off the George Washington Parkway. The only man-made feature on the island—besides hiking trails—is a monument honoring the island's namesake.
- **Formal Gardens**: one of the most spectacular and least visited spots in Washington is **Dumbarton Oaks**, the estate that hosted the founding summit of the UN. The Georgetown mansion is now a museum of Byzantine art, and the grounds encompass 16 acres of lovely old gardens. The estate is owned by Harvard University and is open to the public at no charge, 2 to 5 p.m. daily except holidays. The entrance is at 32nd and R streets NW. For more information, call 202-339-6401 or see www.doaks.org. The 57-acre grounds of the **National Cathedral** (see **Places of Worship**), including the Bishop's Garden, are open daily. Near the cathedral's sundial, look for the Glastonbury Tree—according to legend, it blooms only at Christmas and when royalty visits. With an appointment, you can visit the gardens and orchid greenhouse of the **Hillwood Mansion** in Van Ness, 202-686-5807, and the traditional gardens of the **Japanese Embassy** on Embassy Row, 202-238-6700. The **Franciscan Monastery** in Brookland welcomes visitors to its gardens and catacombs at 1400 Quincy Street NE. The grounds of the **Capitol**, and the park connecting the Capitol to Union Station, are a living museum of native and exotic trees, with many trees bearing plaques

marking them as biological specimens planted by the architect of the Capitol or as memorials to great lawmakers. The Cherokee nation planted a sequoia here in 1970 to honor the bicentennial of Chief Sequoia.

- **Dog Parks**: several neighborhood parks have gained a reputation as unofficial dog-walking parks—and, by some accounts, meeting spots for dog-loving singles. See the **Pets** section in **Getting Settled** for more details.
- **National Zoological Park**: administratively part of the Smithsonian Institution and physically part of Rock Creek Park, the National Zoo was built in 1890 to house a herd of bison given to the Smithsonian. Today, the 175-acre zoo is a world leader in conservation biology as well as a tourist destination for three million people a year. This is not an old-fashioned zoo where animals are robbed of their dignity in austere cages; the Smithsonian has created artificial habitats that mimic the animals' native ecosystems. Visitors flock to see rare white Bengal tigers, komodo dragons, playful sea lions and polar bears, prairie dogs, and orangutans who commute from their home to their school by swinging from cables high above the human crowds. Two new giant pandas, Tian Tian and Mei Xiang, arrived in 2000 to follow in the pawsteps of the zoo's most beloved residents in the 20th century, the pair of pandas given to President Nixon by Chairman Mao. Entrances are at 3001 Connecticut Avenue NW, on Harvard Street NW, and on Beach Drive in Rock Creek Park. There are free shuttle vans from the Woodley Park-Zoo/Adams Morgan Metro station on the Red Line. For more information, call 202-673-4800 or visit http://si.edu/natzoo.
- **Malcolm X Park**: still known by older residents as Meridian Hill Park, Malcolm X Park separates Adams Morgan from Columbia Heights, and uptown from downtown. High macadam walls, with recessed fountains and stairwells, enclose this oasis of gardens, fountains, and soccer fields. A statue of Joan of Arc gazes southward to a panoramic view of Washington—an insider's choice vantage for the Fourth of July fireworks. (Other evenings, the park is renowned as the gay red-light district; officially it is closed after dark.) In the 1980s, the park was effectively off limits to all but drug dealers and users; a group now called Washington Parks & People resolved to make the park a community gathering place again, and it is. During the summer, neighborhood bands play by the lower fountain and local painters peddle their works. Overlooking the northeast corner of the park, an old embassy building now houses the Josephine Butler Parks Center, where some two dozen community nonprofits share offices and meeting space. The old embassy ballrooms are a favorite venue for local fundraising dances and political receptions. Josephine Butler is remembered by longtime Washingtonians for her tireless efforts to improve D.C. communities,

whether cleaning up neighborhood parks such as this one, promoting the performing arts, or working to make the residential parts of D.C. the 51st state. Washington Parks & People runs the center in her memory and continues to augment National Park Service stewardship of the park. For more information, call 202-387-9128.

- **National Arboretum & Kenilworth Aquatic Gardens**: straddling the Anacostia River south of New York Avenue NE, the National Arboretum and Kenilworth Aquatic Gardens are cherished by local naturalists and neglected by almost everyone else. The Arboretum is the USDA's tree preserve, a research facility in the form of a 450-acre park. On foot or bicycle, you can explore hundreds of species of labeled trees and shrubs, some nearly extinct in the wild; of the National Bonsai Collection housed in a pavilion here, naturalists Bill and Phyllis Thomas tell tourists that "this collection alone is worth a trip to Washington." Classes, workshops, and guided tours are available with reservations; call 202-399-5400 or visit www.ars-grin.gov/ars/Beltsville/na. Entrance is on New York Avenue NE near Bladensburg Road. Kenilworth Aquatic Gardens, across the river, is a wetlands park where private 19th-century gardens of water lilies have been allowed to spread naturally; the National Park Service has added cuttings from rare lotus plants and river grasses from all over the world. One Amazon lily here produces leaves six feet in diameter; another is a descendant of a millennium-old Chinese lotus. The entrance for walking visitors is on Douglas Street NW off Kenilworth Avenue, just inside the District; but purists insist that the best way to see the gardens is to paddle your kayak or canoe in from the Anacostia. For more information, call 202-426-6905 or visit www.nps.gov/nace/keaq. On weekends and federal holidays, the Arboretum is served by Metrobus route X6 from Union Station.

THE SUBURBS

In the counties neighboring D.C. there are more than 1,200 distinct parks, and even a brief overview would require a whole book; several such books are cited in the **Washington Reading List**. Here are some of the most interesting parks located within a few miles of the Beltway:

- **Glen Echo Park**: easily mistaken for a storybook village, Glen Echo Park is a campus of pavilions and odd little buildings that once housed amusement park rides and attractions; a working antique carousel is the only overt relic of those days. Now the grounds, run by the National Park Service, are used mainly for craft studios, dance classes, children's theater, and art festivals. Discovery Creek Children's Museum, a nature center and wildlife clinic, is located here, 202-364-3111 or www.discoverycreek.org; so is the historic home of American Red Cross founder

Clara Barton. Entrance is on MacArthur Boulevard at Goldsboro Road west of Bethesda. For more information, call 301-492-6245 or see www.nps.gov/glec.

- **Great Falls**: cultural anthropologist Jack Weatherford studied Congress as a tribe, and wrote in *Tribes on the Hill* that Washington has been a significant crossroads of activity since prehistoric times, and that it is no accident that the nation's capital is situated just below the geological "fall line" where a major river leaps off the Piedmont onto the coastal plain. Twenty thousand years ago, tribes of mastodon hunters settled here because the swamps between the Potomac and Anacostia were an intersection of the beasts' north-south and east-west migratory routes. The Potomac, roaring over 80-foot boulders into the Mather Gorge, is an arresting sight. Every year, a few people underestimate the river's might, ignore the posted warnings, venture too far onto the wet rocks near the falls, and vanish under the rapids. Expert kayakers can shoot the rapids in the gorge below the falls; above the falls stick to the designated overlooks. The Virginia side is Great Falls National Park, off Old Dominion Drive and Georgetown Pike; call 703-285-2965 or visit www.nps.gov/grfa. Admission is $4 per vehicle or $2 per person. Opens at 10 a.m. daily; closes at 4 p.m. in the winter, in the summer at 5 p.m. weekdays, and 6 p.m. weekends. The Maryland side is part of C&O Canal National Historical Park, listed above.
- **Seneca Creek State Park**: a forested link from Gaithersburg to the Potomac, Seneca Creek State Park protects some 4,500 acres along 12 miles of creek. In addition to the usual deer, foxes, raccoons, and other adaptive species, the more elusive bobcat and wild turkey have been seen here. You might also spot 300-year-old cypress trees, a seismic fault line, and evidence of the Native Americans who lived here 12,000 years ago. For more information, call 301-924-2127.
- **Patuxent River Parks**: several detached sections of parkland line the Patuxent River, at the eastern boundaries of Montgomery and Prince George's counties. The tranquil river is ideal for canoeing and fishing. Some notable sections of the park include the **Triadelphia Reservoir**, north of Brighton Dam Road off New Hampshire Avenue in Brookeville; the **T. Howard Duckett Reservoir** off US Route 29; **Patuxent Wildlife Research Center**, off the Baltimore-Washington Parkway just beyond Beltsville; **Merkle Wildlife Management Area** in Croom; and **Jug Bay Wetlands Sanctuary** near Upper Marlboro. In Montgomery County, call 301-489-4646 for information about fishing and boating on the reservoirs, or call the Washington Suburban Sanitary Commission at 301-699-4000. In Prince George's County, call 301-627-7074. Reservations are required for visits to certain ecologically sensitive areas.

- **Dyke Marsh**: south of Alexandria, Dyke Marsh is a 385-acre specimen of the pristine banks of the Potomac. Reached from the Belle Haven Marina access road from the George Washington Parkway, this wetlands preserve offers some of the best bird watching on the Potomac. For more information, call the superintendent of the George Washington Parkway at 703-289-2500, www.nps.gov/gwmp.
- **Mason Neck**: Telegraph Road south of Alexandria leads to some places not suited to casual exploration—Fort Belvoir Proving Ground, Davison US Army Airfield, and the old D.C. prison at Lorton. Just south of these gray spaces, though, are some well-preserved greenspaces along the Potomac and the north shore of the Occoquan River: **Pohick Bay Regional Park**, taking its name from the Algonquin word for wetlands; **Mason Neck State Park**; and **Mason Neck National Wildlife Refuge**, 703-690-1297. These contiguous areas feature thriving marshes and hemlock forest, and nesting bald eagles as well as migratory birds. Located along Gunston Road off US Route 1.
- **Dranesville & Potomac Overlook Parks**: for the best views of the Potomac between Great Falls and Mt. Vernon, go for a walk in **Dranesville District Park**, 703-941-5008, in Fairfax County, off Georgetown Pike just outside the Beltway, or **Potomac Overlook Regional Park**, 703-278-8880, in Arlington County, on Marcey Road off Military Road. Dranesville is secluded and largely undeveloped; Potomac Overlook features a nature center and archaeological sites exploring a Native American settlement.
- **National Colonial Farm**: this working demonstration farm is a model of environmentally advanced agriculture inspired by an era when all farming was organic. Crop varieties and edible wild plants harvested in colonial days are grown and studied here, as is the American chestnut tree—once the mighty Eastern counterpart to the California redwood, the chestnut was rendered nearly extinct by a blight in the mid-20th century. The chestnut grove here is part of an effort to cultivate a resistant variety. The farm site offers workshops and children's activities, and is open to visitors on weekends all year. The park is open daily, dawn to dusk. Located off Bryan Point Road in Accokeek, and accessible by ferry from Mt. Vernon across the Potomac. For information, call the Accokeek Foundation, 301-283-2113, or visit www.accokeek.org.
- **Gravelly Point**: one of the most surprising natural areas in Washington is the parkland surrounding a lagoon between the Pentagon and National Airport. On the inland side of the lagoon, **Roaches Run Waterfowl Sanctuary** attracts migrating geese, ducks, herons, and egrets, despite the railroad tracks and I-395 just yards away. At the inlet of the lagoon, locals know the Gravelly Point

picnic area as an offbeat place to bring a date—the great views of the Washington skyline are interrupted every few minutes as you get buzzed by jets landing on Reagan National Airport's main runway, just across the narrow inlet. For more information, call the superintendent of the George Washington Parkway at 703-557-8991.

HAZARDS

There are only two inherently dangerous (wild) animals in the Washington area: the poisonous copperhead snake and the deer tick. There are several other creatures that can ruin a camping trip, though, and which warrant some precautions:

- **Copperheads** live in woods and meadows, and are not often seen; as the name suggests, their skin conceals them among russet leaves. If you do spot one, you can recognize it (if you want to get this close) by the diamond-shaped head and small pits below the eyes. Like all North American snakes, copperheads are shy and generally bite only if provoked.

- **Deer ticks** transmit Lyme disease, an aggressive form of arthritis that can become debilitating and even attack internal organs. After any outing, especially in wooded areas, check yourself and your children and pets for ticks—the deer tick is about half the size of the more common, and less dangerous, dog tick. After a few days, deer tick bites begin to swell and usually take on a distinctive red "bulls eye" appearance; get immediate medical attention, especially for small children. Precaution: wear insect repellent and keep your head and ankles covered.

- **Mosquitoes** have been known to spread disease occasionally, though the familiar itchy welts are their usual calling cards. In the summer of 2000, the West Nile virus, carried by birds and then spread by mosquito bites, first appeared in the mid-Atlantic region. In response, some communities sprayed pesticides to control mosquitoes. Rest assured, while deadly for a very few, the West Nile virus in humans is usually no worse than the flu, and many object to the powerful insect sprays used to control mosquitoes. Even without exotic virus scares, Washington is built on swamp land, and ravenous mosquitoes abound in the summer. Precaution: get used to mosquito bites. Insect repellent helps, but we're outnumbered!

- **Gypsy Moths**; these tree-eating pests were introduced to North America by accident in the late 19th century and have been damaging forests ever since. The young caterpillars feed on leaves—almost any kind of leaves, but especially oak and other hardwoods—in the spring and early summer. If you have a yard with trees in it, you can protect them with inexpensive (or even homemade) caterpillar traps. Visit one of the home and garden stores listed in **Shopping for the Home**, or see www.gypsy-moth.com.

- **Bears** thrive in areas just 100 miles from the White House, especially in Shenandoah National Park and in the mountains of Western Maryland. Generally they want your food, not you, and they can and do pull car doors open to get it. The American black bear seldom attacks people—just don't step between a mother and her cub. Precaution: if you're camping overnight—even in a cabin—keep your food in a drawstring bag hung from a tree.

- **Rabies carriers** include raccoons as well as mice and rats—which do not distinguish between "good" and "bad" neighborhoods. Some bats carry rabies, but the brown bats fluttering above D.C. at sunset eat insects and do not attack people. The city's ubiquitous gray squirrels (and the occasional black squirrel) do not carry rabies. Precaution: don't try to approach or feed raccoons.

- *Giardia* are microbes inhabiting most streams and spring water in the mountains near Washington; when ingested, the bug can cause months of nausea, diarrhea, and stomach pain. Precaution: no matter how pristine the water looks, run it through a filter rated for giardia. The microbe lives in a hard capsule and, unlike most bacteria, can survive boiling.

- **Poison ivy** flourishes near running water, and its oils can cause a tenacious rash and blistering. Remember what young scouts say about wild plants with three leaves per stem: "Leaves of three, let it be." Precaution: wear high-top shoes and tall socks; if you are exposed to poison ivy, avoid spreading the oil to other parts of your body.

OTHER FLORA AND FAUNA

Inside the Beltway, you can see squirrels and pigeons every day, and robins and other migratory birds in the spring and summer. Occasionally, you might see a garter snake, rabbit, hawk, eagle, or owl; and on summer evenings from twilight to midnight, you can see the yellow flickers of the firefly beetle or "lightning bug." Around streams and ponds, look for frogs, turtles, and beavers; on larger ponds and rivers, especially along the Anacostia, you can see herons and cranes fishing in the shallows, along with plenty of ducks and geese.

You might be surprised to see seagulls circling above suburban parking lots—large paved spaces sometimes create air currents that remind the birds of the Chesapeake Bay, and they feed on litter. An occasional fox, opossum, or bobcat might show up in the outer suburbs or larger woodland parks, but mostly these creatures are elusive. You will see skunks sometimes and smell them fairly often, and in deep woods, you might glimpse a wild turkey.

The arrival of spring is marked by yellow forsythia and white dogwood blossoms, with oak and gingko trees dropping their distinctive seeds later in the summer. Tulip poplar, white pine, Virginia pine, magnolia, white birch, and dozens more broadleaf and evergreen trees thrive in Washington's temperate climate, and cultivated plants like azalea proliferate in many front yards. No patch of grass is immune to dandelions in the spring, and no cove of the Potomac south of Hains Point is immune to jellyfish in August; it's up to you whether those are nuisances or natural features of the place where you now live.

Visit www.audubonnaturalist.org for more information about non-human residents of the Washington area.

THERE ARE THREE SAFE GENERALIZATIONS THAT CAN BE MADE ABOUT Washington's weather: the summers are horrendously humid, the winters are slushy and icy, and the exceptions outnumber the rules. In March, temperatures can go from a freezing 30° to 80°, and back, within a few days. In truth, you can expect a week or two of 3-digit temperatures in late July or early August, and a week or two in January when you may need to take precautions against frozen pipes. Thunderstorms in February aren't unheard-of, nor light snow in April. Despite these rather dramatic exceptions, Washington has four predictable seasons—including a colorful, breezy fall and a delightful spring of dogwood and cherry blossoms.

August, on the other hand, is simply hell. It's hard to convey how humid it gets here—it's described as "oppressive" by weather forecasters, and you never quite get used to it. One longtime resident who grew up in Michigan says this is the only place where you need to take a shower after you get out of the shower. Lucky Washingtonians leave town every August, and central air conditioning is a big selling point in real estate listings. There is some cooling relief in the summer evenings, when you can almost set your watch by the 5 o'clock thunderstorms that ripple through. These are created when the warm western air bounces over the Blue Ridge Mountains and lands on top of Washington. Several times a year these storms intensify and remind us that nature bats last: the news photo of a car crushed under a fallen tree limb, the banner across the bottom of the TV screen listing counties under a tornado watch, and the widespread power failures are all summertime rituals. A few small tornadoes are spotted each year within 100 miles of Washington, and one actually hit suburban College Park in 2001.

The other weather-related ritual comes each winter with the local edition of the evening news, which include reports from grocery stores where people wait in hour-long lines to stock up on milk and toilet paper because a snowstorm is coming, quickly followed by reports from Reagan National

Airport, where flights have been cancelled, and where someone from Buffalo or Minneapolis is explaining that Washingtonians are all a bunch of wimps. Whatever—it's true, the Washington area does not cope well with snow. Schools close at the drop of a flake, and it only takes 12 inches to close all but the most essential elements of the federal government. But winter is only occasionally paralyzing—devotees of sledding and snowball fights will be satisfied only once or twice in a typical year. Most often the D.C. area experiences precipitation in the form of falling slush, called a "wintry mix" by local meteorologists. With temperatures often hovering just around freezing, winter storms drop ever-changing combinations of rain, snow, and sleet. When freezing rain leaves a sheet of ice on the city, watch out—the trees are beautiful, but the streets and ice-encrusted power lines can be deadly.

FLOODING

Once every five years or so, a hurricane makes its way up the Atlantic coast and grazes the Washington area. Even the mightiest Class V hurricane, by the time it reaches this far inland, has blown out most of its destructive wind—by the time it reaches the Chesapeake Bay, it's mostly heavy rain. Flooding here is more often caused when a winter storm dumps a foot of snow on the Potomac watershed and it all melts within a week or two.

In Old Town Alexandria, authorities and neighbors scramble to protect the low-lying streets with sandbags. Most other homes and businesses along the Potomac are secure, except in the unusual 100-year floods, such as those after Hurricane Agnes visited in 1972. Hurricanes Gloria and Hugo, more recently, tore away chunks of the retaining wall of the C&O Canal, putting much of the beloved towpath out of commission while the National Park Service groped for funding to restore it. This type of flooding happens roughly once a decade.

Flash flooding, which occurs after ordinary heavy thunderstorms, can push little suburban streams over their banks and into people's basements; and the occasional clogged storm drain can trap rainwater on city streets and paralyze traffic. If you live in a basement apartment or near a stream, you might want flood insurance.

LOCAL VARIATION

The counties bordering the District extend almost 40 miles from the White House. The northern part of Montgomery County, the western reaches of Fairfax, and southern Prince George's County have different climates, affected by their proximity to the mountains or the Chesapeake Bay, and by their distance from the "heat island" created by a major city.

If you live in southern Montgomery County, you might wonder why county schools are closed when there are barely three inches of snow on the ground; well, it's because northern Montgomery County got eight inches of snow. There's a perennial debate about splitting counties into different snow emergency zones, but school districts remain committed to a uniform school calendar throughout each county—and each county includes a certain number of snow days, usually five, in its calendar; once they're used up, the school year must be extended in June. (In the District, schools close when there's even a good *chance* of snow, because the city is notoriously inept at snow removal. A major snowstorm can make or break the political future of a mayor, so there are constant efforts to improve the snow emergency plan.)

Washington is right in the middle of the zone where winter precipitation changes from snow to rain; a common forecast is for "snow in the northern and western suburbs, rain to the south and east." That line coincides roughly with I-95, and in the summer, thunderstorms can wreak havoc west of I-95 and go unnoticed to the east.

The heat island effect means that temperatures are always a few degrees higher inside the Beltway than in the outer suburbs. Depending on where you lived before coming here, there might be a few other terms that are new to you: wind chill, an estimate of how much colder it feels on account of the wind; heat index, an estimate of how much hotter it feels on account of the humidity; and heating degree days, a measure of the severity of the winter—and the cost in heating fuel. (Heating degree days measure the difference between the average temperature and 65° F. For example, to calculate the number of heating degree days in a given month, a meteorologist will add 5 for each day on which the average temperature was 60° F, 10 for each day on which the average temperature was 55° F, and so on. January here averages around 945 heating degree days; April averages 270. Utility companies use this information to estimate fuel costs.)

SNOW EMERGENCIES

Major thoroughfares in the District and suburbs are marked with signs that say "SNOW EMERGENCY ROUTE." When snow causes hazardous road conditions, local authorities may declare a "snow emergency," making it illegal to drive on Snow Emergency Routes without snow tires or chains. If your vehicle gets stuck in the snow and you are not properly equipped, you may get a ticket. A snow emergency also allows taxi drivers to add a surcharge.

In icy conditions that don't quite force schools to close, local school districts will declare a late opening—schools will open one or two hours late in order to avoid mixing school buses with rush-hour traffic. Schools and some federal offices may close early if a snowstorm hits during the day.

Along with school closings, you will hear announcements on the radio saying the federal government has announced "liberal leave," which means government employees may take personal leave time without having scheduled it in advance. And many private employers follow the lead of the government—closing when the government closes, allowing employees to use discretionary leave when the government does.

The District and most neighboring jurisdictions have laws that require you to remove snow from the sidewalk in front of your house, and clear a path to your mailbox or front door, within 24 hours after the snow stops falling.

Finally, if you've moved here from a warm climate, learn how to prevent water pipes from breaking in cold weather. Few homes have insulated plumbing; if yours doesn't, whenever the temperature is expected to be in the 20s (Fahrenheit) for 24 hours or more, leave a little trickle of water dripping from the tap farthest from the point where the water pipe enters your house. Yes, it is wasteful—but much less wasteful than an avoidable broken pipe. (You can catch the water in a bucket and use it later.)

AIR POLLUTION

The Washington area has never been in compliance with the federal Clean Air Act, which limits the number of days per year a jurisdiction may exceed certain pollution levels. Here, the culprit is ozone—unlike the high-altitude ozone that protects us from the Sun's ultraviolet radiation, ground-level ozone is an unwelcome byproduct of auto exhaust and industrial emissions. Ozone is a key ingredient in urban smog, and is a respiratory irritant that can cause problems for people with asthma, seniors, and people doing strenuous exercise outdoors.

Air quality is monitored by the Metropolitan Washington Council of Governments (COG), a partnership of counties, municipalities, and state and federal agencies addressing regional issues such as transportation and suburban sprawl. The COG air quality index is included in most weather reports, along with pollen advisories for those with allergies, and ozone alerts are issued during the summer "ozone season," May-August. Under federal guidelines, COG declares "Code Yellow" days warning those who are susceptible to ozone-related problems to avoid any heavy exertion outdoors. "Code Orange" days warn susceptible persons to stay inside as much as possible; and everyone should avoid spending more than eight hours outside. On a "Code Red" day everyone is advised to stay inside. The region typically experiences three to five Code Red days per year.

For more information about regional air quality, visit www.mwcog.org/dep/air or call COG's Air Quality Hotline at 202-962-3299.

STATISTICS

Just for the record, here are the official average temperatures and precipitation totals for each month, compiled by the National Weather Service from every year on record at Reagan National Airport. The temperatures are rounded to the nearest degree, and the precipitation totals are rounded to the nearest inch. Remember, though, that these are averages; the "average" temperature in February may be in the high thirties, but there are plenty of evenings when temperatures in the low twenties make it a serious effort to wait for a bus. On a humid afternoon in July when it's 98° out, you don't care that the statistical average temperature is a mild 80°. And remember that three inches of precipitation in January is not the same as three inches in June—the same amount of water that falls as an inch of rain can fall as 5 to 15 inches of snow.

	Temperature (F)	Precipitation
January	33° to 36°	2" to 3"
February	36° to 39°	2" to 3"
March	46° to 48°	2.5" to 3.5"
April	55° to 57°	2" to 3"
May	65° to 67°	3" to 4"
June	74° to 76°	2" to 4"
July	79° to 80°	2.5" to 4"
August	77° to 81°	2.5" to 4.5"
September	70° to 72°	1.5" to 4"
October	58° to 61°	2" to 3.5"
November	48° to 51°	2" to 3.5"
December	38° to 41°	2" to 3.5"

WEATHER REPORTS & FORECASTS

Washingtonian's favorite TV weather forecaster is Channel 4's Bob Ryan, whose team collects highly localized data from weather stations set up in elementary schools around the region. During a major snowstorm, or the occasional hurricane, Ryan and his colleagues just might be the most influential people in the nation's capital.

In addition to local broadcast news and The Weather Channel, you can call 936-1212 (no area code needed) to get an hourly weather report sponsored by Verizon. For travel forecasts, marine advisories, sunrise/sunset, tides, and other details, see the weather page in the Metro section of the *Washington Post* or visit the weather page at www.nbc4.com. If you use e-mail, a wireless phone, a pager, or a PDA, you can subscribe to services that send you customized weather alerts. A free service available from www.weather.com sends you a message announcing any weather advisories or warnings affecting your immediate area. You can also get detailed weather information, including a huge library of current satellite images, from the National Weather Service at www.nws.noaa.gov.

THE NIGHT SKY

If you move here from a rural area or small town, you may complain that you can't see the stars; if you move here from New York City, you will be dazzled—especially on a clear winter night or after a heavy storm has rinsed the smog out of the air. In the inner suburbs and the outermost parts of the District, on residential side streets away from the orange glare of sodium-vapor streetlights, you can pick out constellations like Orion and the Big Dipper; in the outer suburbs, you can see much more—even meteor showers and passing satellites. Venus and Jupiter are easily mistaken for airplanes until you see that they're not moving. You'll have to take a road trip to see the glowing band of the Milky Way, but from most of the Washington area, you can see enough bright stars to get your bearings.

Aspiring astronomers can call 202-357-2000 for the Air & Space Museum's weekly recorded message explaining where and when to spot planets and first-magnitude stars; also, the museum's Albert Einstein Planetarium offers virtual tours of the night sky. For upcoming satellite passes visible from your exact location, visit www.heavens-above.com.

I F YOU CAME FROM A SMALL TOWN, YOU MAY HAVE GONE TO *the* Methodist church, *the* Catholic church, or *the* synagogue. No problem. But in Washington, you will find dozens of each, plus Buddhist viharas, Muslim mosques, Ethiopian Orthodox churches, Korean Baptist churches, and a whole suburban town built by the Seventh-Day Adventist Church. Moravians, Mennonites, Swedenborgians, Antiochans, Armenian Apostolics, Byzantine Catholics, and Huguenots each have congregations here. The golden spires of the Washington Mormon Temple rise like Oz from the trees of Rock Creek Park. The Gothic towers and gargoyles of the Washington National Cathedral look like they belong in 16th-century Europe, as does the brightly painted dome of the Basilica of the National Shrine of the Immaculate Conception. And amid the constant buzz of downtown traffic, around the corner from a Staples office supply store, you can attend services at the New York Avenue Presbyterian Church, just as Abraham Lincoln did when he lived in Washington.

CHOOSING A PLACE OF WORSHIP

If you belong to a congregation in your old hometown, your religious leader might be able to refer you to a kindred congregation in Washington. On Saturdays, the Religion section in the *Washington Post* includes a page of classified ads which lists places of worship and their weekly and daily services; also, the Yellow Pages has extensive listings under "Churches" and "Synagogues." The phone book listings are arranged by denomination and include sections for nondenominational, interdenominational, and independent churches, as well as metaphysical and spiritual science centers.

These interfaith agencies, representing congregations working together to address hunger, homelessness, and other urban problems, might be able to refer you to a congregation that fulfills your spiritual needs:

- **Council of Churches of Greater Washington**, 202-722-9240
- **InterFaith Conference of Metropolitan Washington**, 202-234-6300
- **Washington Interfaith Network**, 202-518-0815

The **National Council of Churches**, 212-870-2227, www.ncccusa.org, publishes the *Yearbook of American & Canadian Churches*, a directory listing of thousands of Christian churches. Order one for $35 at 888-870-3325 or browse the directory links at www.electronicchurch.org.

Other online directories of churches—generally limited to Christian denominations—include http://dcregistry.com/churches, http://netministries.org, http://churches.net, and www.forministry.com. Synagogues serving all branches of Judaism are listed at www.jewish.com.

Of course, in all but the largest churches—those that draw congregations from miles around—the character of the neighborhood will give you a good idea of the character of services. Catholic services at Blessed Sacrament in Chevy Chase are very different from Catholic services at St. Augustine in Shaw; and a Baptist church in the outer suburbs might have a busy youth ministry and family counseling center, while a sister church in the inner city might devote its social ministries to a soup kitchen or homeless shelter. If you're attracted to a place of worship far from your home, remember to check weekend bus and Metro schedules, or allow time for heavy traffic near larger churches.

HISTORIC CHURCHES

These are grand places of worship that draw many visitors of all faiths—for worship, concerts, tours emphasizing art and architecture, special bookstores and gift shops, or just for curiosity.

- **Washington National Cathedral**, Wisconsin & Massachusetts avenues NW, 202-966-2171 (general information) or 202-537-6200 (services); www.cathedral.org/cathedral, is a functioning Episcopal church—home of the Episcopal Diocese of Washington—and, at the same time, a universal house of worship honoring faith traditions from all over the world. If you look around carefully, or ask a tour guide, you will find embedded stones from the Appian Way, Jerusalem, and the Moon; and, yes, one of the thousands of different gargoyles and grotesques is carved in the image of Darth Vader. The Bishop's Garden and the "close," or grounds, of the cathedral are inviting in their own right, and on a nice day, you will probably see lots of people with easels and charcoal or paint, trying to capture the grandeur of the Gothic buttresses and the boxwood hedges.

- **Basilica of the National Shrine of the Immaculate Conception**, 4th Street & Michigan Avenue NE, 202-526-8300, www.nationalshrine.com; the flagship Roman Catholic church in the US, the National Shrine is one of the ten largest churches in the world, with dozens of chapels under its distinctive multicolored dome. The Pope confers the designation of "basilica" on churches of special historic or cultural significance, and rare peregrine falcons have designated this basilica a nesting place.
- **Washington Islamic Center**, 2551 Massachusetts Avenue NW, 202-332-8343; with Arabic minarets towering above the trees along Embassy Row and onion-shaped archways trimmed in turquoise and gold, "The Mosque" can make you do a double-take and believe, for a moment, you're in Riyadh or Istanbul. This is the oldest genuine mosque, built facing Mecca, in the United States. In 2001, after the terrorist attacks that destroyed the World Trade Center and damaged the Pentagon, President George W. Bush paid a historic visit here to promise the Muslim community that the nation's war against terrorism would not be a war against Islam.
- **Washington Mormon Temple**, Stoneybrook Drive & Beach Drive, Kensington, 301-587-0144; the towering, castle-like temple of the Church of Jesus Christ of Latter-Day Saints is a major landmark along the Beltway, inspiring a graffiti artist to caption the looming edifice by painting, on an overpass across the highway, "Surrender Dorothy." Only baptized Mormons are allowed inside the temple itself, but a visitor center on the grounds hosts concerts and lectures. In December, the wooded grounds are lit by thousands of tiny white Christmas lights in the trees, casting a halo on cloudy skies; choirs and a live nativity draw crowds to the visitor center.
- **National Presbyterian Church**, 4101 Nebraska Avenue NW, 202-537-0800, www.natpresch.org; the flagship Presbyterian church in the US, the National Presbyterian Church and National Presbyterian Center occupy a sleek modern sanctuary just off Embassy Row.
- **St. Matthew's Cathedral**, 1725 Rhode Island Avenue NW, 202-347-3215, www.stmatthewscathedral.org; the Cathedral of St. Matthew the Apostle is the mother church of the Catholic Archdiocese of Washington, and under the distinctive green dome, Pope John Paul II celebrated mass here in 1979. The annual Red Mass in the fall seeks divine guidance for the legal profession, and is attended by members of the Supreme Court, the Cabinet, and Congress.
- **St. John's Episcopal Church**, 16th & H streets NW, 202-347-8766; standing just across Lafayette Square from the White House, St. John's is known as the "Church of the Presidents"—for more than a century, every President has attended services here.

CHURCHES IN THE COMMUNITY

Most congregations have volunteer programs and community outreach services, but here are just a few of the larger churches whose charitable ministries play a big role in D.C. civic life:

- **All Souls Unitarian Church**, 16th & Harvard streets NW, 202-332-5266
- **First Congregational Church**, 945 G Street NW, 202-628-4317
- **Friends Meeting of Washington**, 2111 Florida Avenue NW, 202-483-3310
- **Scripture Cathedral**, 8th & O streets NW, 202-483-9400
- **Shiloh Baptist Church**, 1500 9th Street NW, 202-232-4000
- **St**. **Aloysius Parish**, 19 I Street NW, 202-336-7200
- **St**. **Augustine Catholic Church**, 15th & V streets NW, 202-265-1470
- **Union Temple Baptist Church**, 12th & W streets SE, 202-678-8822
- **United House of Prayer for All People**, 601 M Street NW, 202-289-1916

RESOURCES

These faith-based agencies are a good place to start as you look for your place of worship. There are thousands of possibilities here—large and small, grand and simple, conservative and liberal, famous and obscure—from major Baptist and Unitarian Universalist churches with a thousand members and roots dating to the Underground Railroad to little Pentecostal storefronts and service-oriented urban ministries, to far eastern meditation centers. This is by no means a complete list, and no substitute for the listings in the newspaper and phone book, but these religious denominations have regional or national directories online or major information centers in Washington:

- **African Methodist Episcopal**: www.amecnet.org or Second Episcopal District, www.amec2nd.org, 202-842-3788
- **Baptist**: American Baptist Churches Mission Center, www.abc-usa.org, 800-ABC-3USA
- **Baha'i**: D.C. Baha'i Center, 800-22-UNITE or 202-291-5532, www.dcbahai.org
- **Brethren**: Southeast Christian Fellowship, 202-581-3387
- **Buddhist, Theravadan**: Buddhist Vihara Society, 202-723-0773, www.vihara.org
- **Buddhist, Zen**: Zen Buddhist Society of Washington, 202-829-1966
- **Christian Methodist Episcopal**: Seventh Episcopal District, www.cmesonline.org, 202-829-8070
- **Christian Science**: 202-783-4325 (recorded information)
- **Episcopal/Anglican**: www.us.net/edow, 800-642-4427 or 202-537-6555

- **Friends (Quakers)**: Baltimore Yearly Meeting, 800-962-4766 or 301-774-7663, www.bym-rsf.org; regional offices for DC, MD, VA and Southern PA
- **Hare Krishna**: Food for Life, 301-983-6826, www.ffl.org
- **Hindu**: Gandhi Memorial Center & Golden Lotus Temple, 202-229-3871
- **Islamic (Muslim)**: Idara Dawat-O-Irshad, 703-256-8622, www.irshad.org
- **Jewish, Conservative**: United Synagogue of Conservative Judaism, 301-230-0801, http://uscj.org
- **Jewish, Orthodox**: Orthodox Union, 212-807-7888, www.ou.org
- **Jewish, Reconstructionist**: Jewish Reconstructionist Federation, 301-206-2332, www.jrf.org
- **Jewish, Reform**: Union of American Hebrew Congregations, http://uahc.org/conglist, 888-842-8242 or 202-232-4242
- **Jehovah's Witnesses**: Washington, D.C. Central Unit, 202-832-9177
- **Latter-Day Saints (Mormons)**: www.mormon.com; Washington Mormon Temple, 301-587-0144
- **Lutheran, Evangelical**: Evangelical Lutheran Church in America, 800-638-3522, www.elca.org
- **Lutheran, Missouri Synod**: 888-843-5267, www.lcms.org
- **Mennonite**: Washington Community Fellowship, 202-543-1926
- **Methodist, United**: Washington Episcopal Area, 202-546-3110
- **Moravian**: Moravian Church in America, 800-732-0591, www.moravian.org
- **Orthodox**: Orthodox Church in America, www.oca.org; Orthodox Christian Foundation, www.ocf.org
- **Nazarene**: National Church of the Nazarene, 202-723-3252
- **Pentecostal, Assemblies of God**: General Council of the Assemblies of God, www.agfinder.org, 417-862-2781
- **Pentecostal, Church of God in Christ**: www.cogic.org
- **Pentecostal, International**: 405-787-7110, www.iphc.org
- **Presbyterian**: National Presbyterian Center, 202-537-0800, www.natpresch.org
- **Roman Catholic**: Catholic Information Center, 202-783-2062, www.catholic.net
- **Scientology**: Founding Church of Scientology, 202-667-6245, http://foundingchurch.scientology.org
- **Seventh-Day Adventist**: Columbia Union Conference, 301-596-0800, www.columbiaunion.org
- **Unitarian Universalist**: Unitarian Universalist Association of Congregations, 617-742-2100, www.uua.org
- **United Church of Christ**: Office of General Ministries, 216-736-2100, www.ucc.org
- **Wesleyan**: Chesapeake Wesleyan District, 410-571-9235

GAY & LESBIAN SPIRITUAL GROUPS

The *Washington Blade* (see **Newspapers and Magazines** in **Getting Settled**) runs a calendar of religious services and congregations that welcome the gay and lesbian community, and there are plenty. Some additional resources for gay and lesbian people of faith are:

- **Bet Mishpachah Gay & Lesbian Synagogue**, 202-833-1638
- **Dignity—Gay & Lesbian Catholics, Families, and Friends**, 703-912-1662
- **Gay & Lesbian Unitarians**, 301-776-6891
- **Metropolitan Community Church**, 202-638-7373, www.mccdc.com

NEW AGE & SPIRITUALITY

For a comprehensive guide to New Age spiritual centers, ayurveda, meditation, mysticism, Pagan, shamanist, yoga, and Wiccan spiritual resources, pick up a copy of *Pathways* magazine at any health food store or bookstore. A free quarterly, each new issue of *Pathways* disappears quickly; you might want to subscribe for $10. Also available online at www.pathwaysmag.com or call 301-656-3127.

WASHINGTONIANS PERFORM ROUGHLY HALF A MILLION HOURS of volunteer service every year—tutoring, coaching youth sports, cleaning up neighborhood streams and parks, selling tickets to the local symphony, giving museum tours, staffing libraries and rescue squads, supporting political campaigns, serving food to the needy, repairing inner-city homes and schools, painting over graffiti, and the list goes on. At some of the most prominent soup kitchens and shelters, those who want to volunteer on Thanksgiving or Christmas actually need to make reservations in advance. The other 363 days of the year, there's no shortage of places that will welcome your contributions of physical labor, professional skills, or the time and the dedication to stuff envelopes and make phone calls.

Volunteering is a great way to meet people in your new community. Any national organization you've supported in the past undoubtedly has a chapter in Washington, and for any cause that captures your interest, there's probably a community organization here too. If you attended a big university or prominent small college, there's probably an alumni officer here—a volunteer opportunity in its own right as well as a source of ideas. If you join a religious congregation, ask about community service programs. If you don't know where to begin, check out *Finding Fun & Friends in Washington: An Uncommon Guide to Common Interests* by Roberta Gettesman. These resources can also help you find ways to volunteer:

- **Greater D.C. Cares** works with dozens of community organizations to arrange monthly or occasional volunteer opportunities for groups or families. Individual members may team up to participate in group projects, and many employers organize workplace volunteer projects through the service: 202-289-7378, www.dc-cares.org.

- *Washingtonian* **Online** lists volunteer opportunities at www.washingtonian.com/schools.

- **The *Washington Post*** on Thursdays, in the D.C. Extra and suburban Extra sections, lists volunteer opportunities and donations needed at a variety of local charities.
- **DoingSomething** organizes groups to be matched with local charities for a variety of service projects: 202-393-5051, www.doingsomething.org.
- **Just Cauz** is an informal network of young professionals organizing charity happy hours and volunteer opportunities that support D.C. community services. Visit www.justcauz.org.
- **Washington Needs You** is an online directory of volunteer opportunities and a catalog of gifts sold to benefit local charities: www.needsyou.org.

VOLUNTEER BUREAUS

Volunteer bureaus are city or county agencies that keep track of current and permanent volunteer opportunities at area nursing homes, soup kitchens, libraries, animal shelters, museums and more:

- **Montgomery County Volunteer & Community Service Center**, 240-777-2600, www.montgomeryvolunteer.org
- **Prince George's Voluntary Action Center**, 301-699-2800
- **Arlington County Volunteer Office,** 703-228-5811, www.co.arlington.va.us/volunteer
- **Volunteer Center of Fairfax County**, 703-246-3460, www.volunteerfairfax.org
- **Alexandria Volunteer Bureau**, 703-836-2176, www.alexandriavolunteers.org

For information on volunteer agencies in outlying areas, agencies specializing in senior and retired volunteers, or links to state and national service programs, contact the **Governor's Office on Service & Volunteerism** (Maryland) at 410-767-4803 or www.gosv.state.md.us, or the **Virginia Office of Volunteerism** at 800-777-8293 or www.dss.state.va.us/community/volunteer.

AREA CAUSES

Here is just a sample of the kinds of organizations in constant need of volunteer help. Some have structured volunteer programs with training sessions and schedules; others are grateful when you walk in off the street and help sort donated books or clothing for an hour. In addition to the organizations listed in this chapter, keep in mind that many of the community institutions listed elsewhere in this book rely on volunteers:

- Political organizations—see **Getting Settled**

- Food co-ops and farmers' markets—see **Shopping for the Home**
- Parks and trails—see **Greenspace**
- Children's programs—see **Child Care & Education**
- Animal shelters—see **Getting Settled**
- Thrift stores—see **Shopping for the Home**
- Services for people with disabilities—see **Helpful Services**
- Neighborhood festivals and special events—see **Neighborhood Profiles** and **A Washington Year**
- Practically every institution listed in **Cultural Life** and **Sports and Recreation**

Note that you may be greeted with caution when you offer your services to an agency that deals directly with children. Don't take it personally; since you care enough about children to volunteer in an after-school program or summer camp, you understand the agency's duty to check your references and perhaps run a criminal background check.

If you have special skills—legal or medical training, web design, desktop publishing, writing and editing, or accounting, or if you have a license to drive large trucks and buses, experience facilitating meetings, or a background in catering and you know how to prepare meals for 400 people—be sure to mention them. Don't be shy. Any non-profit organization will be happy to hear from you.

AIDS & HIV

- **ACT UP/DC**, 202-547-9404, www.actupdc.org
- **D.C. AIDS Information Hotline**, 202-332-2437, www.wwc.org
- **D.C. AIDS Ride**, 800-825-1000, www.aidsride.org
- **Food & Friends**, 202-488-8278, www.foodandfriends.org
- **Prevention Works!** 202-939-7820, e-mail: prevworks@mindspring.com

ALCOHOL ABUSE

- **Alcoholics Anonymous**, 202-966-9115, www.aa-dc.org
- **Alcolicos Anonimos de Habla Hispana**, 202-797-9738
- **Mothers Against Drunk Driving**, Greater Washington, 202-374-2487, www.madd.org

CHILDREN/YOUTH SERVICES

- **Boys & Girls Clubs of Greater Washington**, 301-562-2001, www.bgcgw.org
- **Children's Defense Fund**, 202-628-8787, www.childrensdefense.org

- **Court Appointed Special Advocate Program**, 202-328-2191, http://casa.volunteermatch.org
- **D.C. SCORES**, 202-234-4103, www.americascores.org/dc
- **For Love of Children**, 202-462-8686, www.flocdc.org
- **Higher Achievement Program**, 202-842-5116, www.higherachieve-ment.org
- **KaBoom!**, 202-659-0215, ext. 225, www.kaboom.org
- **Sasha Bruce Youthwork**, 202-675-9340, www.needsyou.org

CRIME PREVENTION

- **Metropolitan Police Department Auxiliary**, 202-727-4314
- Contact your local police station listed in the **Neighborhood Profiles** for information about neighborhood-based Citizens On Patrol or "Orange Hats" programs.

SENIOR CARE & SERVICES

- **Geriatric Day Care Center**, Downtown Cluster of Congregations, 202-347-7527
- **IONA Senior Services**, 202-966-1055, www.iona.org
- **Meals On Wheels**, 202-966-8111 or call 800-677-1116 to find the nearest local program

ENVIRONMENTAL PROTECTION

- **Anacostia Watershed Society**, 301-699-6204, www.anacostiaws.org
- **Arlingtonians for a Clean Environment**, 703-228-6427, www.capac-cess.org
- **Audubon Naturalist Society**, 301-652-9188, www.audubonnatural-ist.org
- **Clean Water Action**, 202-895-0420, www.cleanwateraction.org
- **Coalition for Smarter Growth**, 202-588-5570, www.smartergrowth.net
- **Community Alliance for Youth Action** (CAYA), 202-986-0206, www.empoweryouth.org
- **Earth Conservation Corps**, 202-554-1960, www.earthconcorps.org
- **Earthjustice Legal Defense Fund**, 202-667-4500, www.earthjustice.org
- **Friends of the Earth**, 202-783-7400, www.foe.org
- **Greenpeace**, 202-462-1177, www.greenpeaceusa.org
- **National Park Service**, National Capital Region, 202-619-7077, www.nps.gov/ncro

- **Sierra Club**, New Columbia Chapter, 202-488-0505, www.sierra-club.org
- **Washington Parks & People**, 202-462-7275, www.dcregistry.com/users/washingtonparks
- **Washington Regional Network for Livable Communities**, 202-667-5445, www.washingtonregion.net

GAY, LESBIAN, BISEXUAL & TRANSGENDER SERVICES

- **BiNetwork D.C.**, 202-828-3080, www.ogburn.net/bndc
- **Gay & Lesbian Activists Alliance**, 202-667-5139, www.glaa.org
- **Gay & Lesbian Alliance Against Defamation**, 202-986-1360, www.glaad.org
- **Parents and Friends of Lesbians & Gays (P-FLAG)**, 202-638-3852, www.pflagdc.org
- **Pride at Work**, Baltimore-Washington, 202-434-1150 ext. 6, www.igc.org/prideatwork
- **Sexual Minorities Youth Assistance League**, 202-546-5940, www.smyal.org

HEALTH & HOSPITALS

Researchers at NIH and other institutions are always recruiting volunteers for clinical trials. If you meet the physical requirements for a particular study, you can make a contribution to medical science and often receive a stipend and free physical checkups during the study. Check the *Washington City Paper* classifieds.

- **American Cancer Society**, 202-483-2600, www.cancer.org
- **American Heart Association**, National Capital Area Council, 202-686-6888, www.americanheart.org/dc
- **American Lung Association of D.C.**, 202-682-5864, www.aladc.org
- **Center for Science in the Public Interest**, 202-332-9110, www.cspinet.org
- **Children's National Medical Center**, 202-884-2063, www.cnmc.org
- **Hospice of Washington**, 202-966-3720, www.washingtonhome.org
- **Hospital for Sick Children**, 202-832-4400 or 800-226-4444, www.hfscsite.org
- **National Rehabilitation Hospital**, 202-877-1000, www.nrhrehab.org
- **Whitman-Walker Clinic**, 202-797-3500, www.wwc.org

HUNGER & HOMELESSNESS

- **Bread for the City**, 202-265-2400, www.breadforthecity.org
- **Capital Area Food Bank**, 202-526-5344
- **Coalition for the Homeless**, 202-347-8870, www.dccfh.org
- **Community for Creative Nonviolence (CCNV)**, 202-393-1909, http://users.erols.com/ccnv
- **D.C. Central Kitchen**, 202-234-0707, www.dccentralkitchen.org
- **D.C. Habitat for Humanity**, 202-610-2355, www.dchabitat.org
- **Homes Not Jails**, 202-297-4430, www.homesnotjails.org/dc
- **Martha's Table**, 202-328-6008, www.marthastable.org
- **So Others Might Eat**, 202-797-8806, www.some.org

INTERNATIONAL

- **Amnesty International**, Mid-Atlantic Region, 202-544-0200, http://amnestyusa.org
- **Ayuda Inc.**, 202-387-0324
- **Calvary Bilingual Multicultural Education Center**, 202-332-4200, www.cbmlc.org
- **Casa del Pueblo**, 202-332-3422, www.faithumcmd.org
- **Central American Refugee Center**, 202-328-9799
- **Hostelling International**, 202-737-2333, www.hiwashingtondc.org
- **Latin American Youth Center**, 202-319-2225, www.layc-dc.org
- **Meridian International Center**, 202-667-6800, www.meridian.org
- **Spanish Education Development Center**, 202-462-8848
- **Washington Inner-City Self Help (WISH)**, 202-332-8800
- **Youth for Understanding Host Families**, 800-872-0200, www.youthforunderstanding.org

LEGAL AID

- **Bread for the City Legal Clinic**, 202-265-2400
- **D.C. Public Defender Service**, 202-628-1200, www.lawbbs.net/gideon
- **Legal Aid Society of D.C.**, 202-628-1161, www.legalaiddc.org
- **Legal Counsel for the Elderly**, 202-434-2170; www.aarp.org/foundation
- **National Lawyers Guild**, 202-296-5600 or 212-627-2656, www.nlg.org
- **Neighborhood Legal Services Program**, 202-682-2720, www.nls.org
- **Washington Legal Clinic for the Homeless**, 202-872-1494, www.legalclinic.org

LITERACY

- **D.C. Reading Is Fundamental**, 202-638-6053 (Northwest office), 202-561-0800 (Southeast office), www.rif.org
- **Everybody Wins!**, 202-624-3957, www.everybodywinsdc.org
- **Junior League of Washington**, 202-337-2001, www.jlw.org
- **Literacy Volunteers of America**, 202-387-1772, www.songline.com/lva
- **Washington Literacy Council**, 202-387-9029, http://users. erols.com/washlc

MEN'S SERVICES

- **Men Can Stop Rape**, 202-265-6530, www.mencanstoprape.org
- **MenCenter**, 202-393-3300, http://pages.zdnet.com/mencenter
- **Washington, D.C. Men's Council**, 703-536-7681, www.angelfire. com/biz/dcmen

MENTORING & CAREER DEVELOPMENT

- **Byte Back**, 202-529-3395, www.byteback.org
- **City Vision**, 202-272-2448, http://nbm.org
- **Environmentors Project**, 202-347-5300, www.environmentors.org
- **Service Corps of Retired Executives (SCORE)**, 202-205-6762, www.score.org
- **Suited for Change**, 202-293-0351, www.suitedforchange.org

PEACE & SOCIAL JUSTICE

- **Children's Creative Response to Conflict,** 301-270-1005, www.crcca.org
- **D.C. Peace & Economic Justice Program**, American Friends Service Committee, 202-265-7997, www.afsc.org
- **Gray Panthers of Metropolitan Washington**, 202-347-9541, www.angelfire.com/pe/DCGrayPanthers
- **Peace Action**, 202-862-9740, www.peace-action.org
- **Physicians for Social Responsibility**, 202-898-0150, www.psr.org
- **20/20 Vision**, 202-833-2020, www.2020vision.org
- **Washington Peace Center**, 202-234-2000, www.washingtonpeacecenter.org

POLITICS & CITIZENSHIP

Contact your local board of elections, listed in **Getting Settled**, for information about serving as a precinct worker, election judge, or voter registrar.
- **Alliance for Democracy**, 888-466-8233, www.thealliancefordemocracy.org
- **American Civil Liberties Union**, National Capital Area, 202-457-0800, www.aclu-nca.org
- **Common Cause**, 202-833-1200, www.commoncause.org
- **League of Women Voters**, 202-429-1965, www.lwv.org
- **Stand Up for Democracy**, 202-232-2500, www.standupfordemocracy.org
- **US Public Interest Research Group**, 202-546-9707, www.uspirg.org

TRANSPORTATION

During big snowstorms, area hospitals need people who own vehicles with 4-wheel drive and all-weather tires to be on call to transport doctors and ambulatory patients. Local news broadcasts announce the appropriate hotlines during snow emergencies.
- **Metropolitan Washington Council of Governments Carpool Line**, 800-745-7433
- **Travelers Aid**, 202-546-1127, www.travelersaid.org
- **Washington Area Bicyclist Association**, 202-628-2500, www.waba.org

VETERANS

- **American Legion**, 202-861-2700, www.legion.org
- **Disabled American Veterans**, 202-554-3501, www.dav.org
- **National Gulf War Resource Center**, 301-585-4000, www.ngwrc.org
- **Veterans of Foreign Wars**, Washington Office, 202-543-2239, www.vfw.org

WOMEN'S SERVICES

- **Calvary Women's Services**, 202-783-6651, www.calvaryservices.org
- **D.C. Rape Crisis Center**, 202-232-0789, www.dcrcc.org
- **House of Ruth**, 202-667-7001, www.houseofruth.org
- **My Sister's Place**, 202-529-5261, www.mysistersplace.com
- **Planned Parenthood of Metropolitan Washington**, 202-347-8500, www.ppmw.org

- **Washington Area Clinic Defense Task Force**, 202-797-6577, www.wacdtf.org
- **The Women's Center**, 703-281-2657, www.thewomenscenter.org

VOLUNTEER WORK DAYS

JANUARY

- **Martin Luther King Day of Service** is a nationwide volunteer program observing the Martin Luther King Jr. holiday as "a day on, not a day off." Contact the Corporation for National Service at 202-606-5000 or www.mlkday.org.

APRIL

- **Earth Day** activities in hundreds of communities are listed at www.earthday.net.
- **Christmas in April/Sukkot in April** is a workday to repair the homes of senior citizens and low-income families: 202-362-1611, www.christmasinaprildc.org.
- **Hands On D.C.** is an annual workathon in which thousands of people help renovate inner-city schools and collect pledges from sponsors to endow scholarship funds in those schools: 202-667-5808, www.hands-ondc.org.

MAY

- **Greater D.C. Cares Day** (formerly the Servathon): 202-289-7378, www.dc-cares.org

OCTOBER

- **Make a Difference Day** is a nationwide volunteer mobilization sponsored by *USA Weekend* magazine and the Points of Light Foundation: 800-416-3824, http://usaweekend.com/diffday

DECEMBER

- The **D.C. Jewish Community Center** organizes volunteers every December to "temp" on Christmas Day for receptionists, concierges, and other service workers who would otherwise have to work: 202-518-9400, www.dcjcc.org

CHARITABLE GIVING

Residents of the District, Maryland, and Virginia gave $6.35 billion to charity in 1998, according to IRS statistics. Those figures include the gifts of major philanthropists, but many small donations add up; thousands of Washingtonians give to charity through the United Way (or, for federal workers, the Combined Federal Campaign). One easy way to give is to choose a credit card or long distance phone service that gives a percentage of its receipts to charity—many large charities have their own affinity cards issued in partnership with financial institutions, and Working Assets provides credit cards, long distance service, and investment services that pay annual dividends to nonprofits selected each year by account holders. For details, contact Working Assets at 800-537-3777 (for credit cards) or 800-788-0898 (for long distance), or visit www.workingforchange.com.

During the annual United Way/Combined Federal Campaign in the fall, you'll see posters at Metro stations and bus stops advertising the work of local charities and their CFC number, requesting that you set up a voluntary weekly payroll deduction, in any amount you specify.

Charitable Choices, www.charitablechoices.org, publishes an annual booklet profiling CFC charities meeting certain standards of fiscal responsibility and low ratio of overhead to program spending—but note: among the charities meeting those standards, only those paying a fee are listed in the guide. Other sources of information about specific charities include:

- **Council of Better Business Bureaus Philanthropic Advisory Service**, 703-276-0100, www.bbb.org
- **The Foundation Center**, 202-331-1400, www.foundationcenter.org
- **National Center for Charitable Statistics**, 202-261-5801, http://nccs.urban.org
- **National Committee for Responsive Philanthropy**, 202-387-9177, www.ncrp.org

Here are some charities and federated funds that address a variety of social needs:

- **Catholic Charities**, 703-549-1390, www.catholiccharitiesusa.org
- **Combined Federal Campaign of the National Capital Area**, 202-628-2263, www.cfcnca.org
- **Greater Washington Urban League**, 202-265-8200, www.gwul.org
- **Jewish Federation of Greater Washington**, 301-230-7200, www.jewishfedwash.org
- **Salvation Army**, 202-783-9085, www.salvationarmyusa.org
- **United Black Fund**, 202-783-9300, www.ubfinc.org

I N SOME PARTS OF THE WASHINGTON AREA, YOU CAN'T DO anything without a car; in other neighborhoods, a car would be more of a hassle than benefit. Generally, within the District a car is a lifestyle choice, not a necessity. In the inner suburbs, a car is decidedly useful—especially for a household with kids—but dedicated singles or couples can manage without one. Outside the Beltway, most communities are designed on a scale negotiable only by cars—don't expect to be within walking distance of a grocery store or other basics.

It's easy to travel between D.C. and the suburbs, or within D.C., by public transportation, but the real challenge for a growing number of commuters is the issue of travel between suburbs. Most new jobs in the region are concentrated in Northern Virginia: Tysons Corner, McLean, Dulles, and the Interstate 270 corridor in Maryland, making commuting between Maryland and Virginia an arduous grind no matter how you do it.

Washington's roads are more congested than any other in the nation except in Los Angeles, in terms of average commute times calculated by the Census Bureau. For roughly a quarter-million residents of the Washington area, the daily commute takes an hour or more in each direction; for more than a million residents, the commute is longer than half an hour.

How do you keep your commute from becoming a daily dose of stress? First, if you move here with a job lined up, keep the commute in mind as you look for a place to live. In heavy traffic, even a 15-minute commute can be frustrating. Likewise, if you find a home here and you're looking for a job, think twice about a long commute—if you feel stressed by the time you get to work, you'll not likely keep that job for long. Try to avoid driving to work alone; if public transportation doesn't work for you, consider carpooling. Or, if the route is safe and short enough, try riding a bike or walking to work.

Finally, you may be able to cut back on daily commuting. Ask your employer about telecommuting—working at home—at least one or two days a week. Many employers, especially federal agencies, are discovering that workers who don't have to commute every day are happier and more productive, wherever they do their jobs.

GETTING AROUND

BY METRORAIL

True to its reputation, Metrorail rapid transit—"the Metro"—is clean, safe and reliable. It's crowded at rush hour and after a game or concert at the MCI Center, and fares can add up quickly, but taking the Metro downtown from the suburbs is almost always cheaper and easier than finding and paying for parking.

On the 25th anniversary of Metrorail service, in March 2001, the *Washington Post* commented, "The Metro system has become—among many other things—a gathering place, a unifier, a matchmaker, a land developer, an economic power and a community planner." The *Post* reported that Metro trains carry 600,000 passengers a day and keep 270,000 cars off the area's congested roads, saving 12 million gallons of gasoline each year. In fact, the Metro is almost too popular; transit officials are worried that, by 2020, the system will be paralyzed by overcrowding.

Visitors often say the Metro system isn't user-friendly, but if you just read the instructions and maps, you'll quickly get tired of hearing such complaints. All the information you need is located just inside the entrance to any station: a big, easy-to-read map of the system; a detailed street map of the neighborhood surrounding the station; schedules for bus routes serving the station; a chart showing travel times and fares to every other station; and, most important if you're going out at night, a sign showing the departure times of the last train leaving the station in each direction. (Metrorail closes around 12:30 a.m. except on Friday and Saturday nights, when it closes around 2 a.m.)

The farecard vending machines need not be intimidating either. These magnetic cards can be encoded with any amount of money from $1.10 to $39.95. Look at the destination chart on the station manager's kiosk to see how much money you'll need to put on your card, or just put at least $20 on it and receive a 10% bonus. Your farecard will let you through the station gates and will deduct the proper fare when you exit. If, at your destination, you discover that there's not enough value on the card to pay for your trip, you can add money at the "Exitfare" machine.

Fares range from $1.10 to $3.25 depending on the length of your trip and time of day—they're lower during off-peak times (rush hour is 5:30 to 9:30 a.m. and 3 to 7 p.m.). An all-day Metrorail pass is available for $5 on weekends and after 9:30 a.m. on weekdays.

If you will be transferring from the Metro to a bus, get a bus transfer from the dispenser at the station where you board the Metro—the transfer shows the time and the station, and is proof to the bus driver that you paid a Metro fare. This will give you an 85-cent discount on the bus. There is no discount for transferring from the bus to the Metro.

Most suburban stations have parking lots, but many fill up early on weekdays. Every station has feeder bus routes and a "Kiss & Ride" loop for passengers getting dropped off or picked up.

For more information, call the **Washington Metropolitan Area Transit Authority (Metro)** at 202-637-7000 and plan to spend a few minutes on hold, or visit www.wmata.com.

BY BUS

The **Metrobus** system is the main feeder bus line serving all Metrorail stations throughout D.C. and the Maryland and Virginia suburbs. These regional buses also connect to local bus systems in suburban counties.

In 1999, Metrobus fares were simplified and, in many cases, reduced. With only two exceptions the Metrobus fare is $1.10 on all routes at all times. "Express" routes making long trips into the outer suburbs are $2, and routes connecting to the Anacostia Metro station are 60 cents. Gone, too, is the complicated old system of bus-to-bus transfers. Now you are offered a free "transfer" (time-stamped transfer pass) when you board any public bus in the area, and it's good for unlimited trips of equal or lesser value on any local bus system in the area for the next two hours. A regional all-day bus pass is $2.50.

- **Ride On** buses serve Montgomery County and connect to the Metro Red Line. Fares are 90 cents during off-peak times and $1.10 during rush hour. 240-777-7433, www.rideonbus.com
- **The BUS** routes serve Prince George's County. 301-883-5683
- **Fairfax Connector** buses connect the west end of the Metro Orange Line to Tysons Corner, Reston and Herndon. Most fares are 50 cents. 703-339-7200, www.fairfaxconnector.com
- **DASH** buses serve Alexandria, including the Pentagon, from the south ends of the Metro Blue and Yellow lines. Most fares are $1. 703-370-DASH
- **ART** (Arlington Transit) buses serve Crystal City Metro station on weekdays, and cost 50 cents during rush hour. At off-peak times or with a Metrorail transfer, it's free. 703-228-RIDE, www.commuterpage.com

- **OmniRide** buses serve the outer Virginia suburbs in Prince William County, south of the Franconia-Springfield Metro station, on weekdays. Most fares are $1.75—these are long trips. 703-730-OMNI, www.omniride.com

Information about many smaller bus and commuter van lines serving the outer suburbs is available at www.commuterpage.com.

PASSES & DISCOUNTS

Weekly and monthly bus passes allow unlimited travel on Metrorail or Metrobus, and some are good on both bus and rail. Pick up a brochure at any station listing the various combination bus/rail passes and figure out your particular transit needs; generally, the passes save you money if you commute five days a week and make a few trips in addition to your daily commute. For many frequent riders, though, the main benefit is convenience.

- **SmarTrip** cards are permanent plastic farecards that can be encoded with up to $180 (plus the 10% bonus). You can "register" your SmarTrip card and, in the event that it is lost or stolen, it will be replaced with a new card encoded with the value of your card at the time you reported it missing. If your card's remaining value is less than the fare for your trip, you can go into "overdraft" and leave the station, add money later, and the balance will be deducted from your next trip. You can also transfer the value of a regular farecard, up to $7, to your SmarTrip card; and, for those who enjoy unnecessary technological bells and whistles, the SmarTrip card lets you touch a scanner on the station gate instead of running your card through the old-fashioned card-reading slot.

- **Metrochek** is a fare voucher issued through employers as a fringe benefit. Many employers offer free parking as an employee benefit; if you commute by bus or Metro, ask your employer about Metrochek. If your employer doesn't participate in the Metrochek program, consider asking for the cash equivalent of a parking space. If you need proof of commuting expenses in order to be reimbursed by an employer or client, you can buy passes at the Metro Sales Office or the Commuter Store and get a receipt; also, some farecard vending machines accept credit cards and dispense receipts.

- Metrobus **tokens** are available in packs of 10 or 20 and are handy if you aren't in the habit of making sure you have exact change. They're sold in clear plastic bags, so you can inspect them before buying to make sure none of them is a Salvadoran 5-centavo coin, which is exactly the same size and color.

  Metro passes, maps, and schedules are available at:

- **Metro Sales Office**, inside the Metro Center station on the Red, Blue and Orange Lines
- **WMATA (Metro) Headquarters**, 600 5th Street NW, 202-637-7000, www.wmata.com
- **Commuter Express** retail store, 8401 Colesville Road, Suite 150, 301-770-7665
- **The Commuter Store**, Ballston Common Mall, 703-528-3541; Crystal City Underground Shops, 703-413-4287; Rosslyn Metro Center, 703-525-1995
- **Online** at www.commuterpage.com (information) and www.commuterdirect.com (purchases)

In addition, many supermarkets sell bus and Metrorail passes at the customer service counter.

RIDER ETIQUETTE

It's illegal to eat or drink on the Metro, on buses, or in stations, and the law is enforced. (Tourists may get off with a warning, but your local ID will tell the authorities you should know better.) Seats facing sideways must be offered to elderly or disabled passengers.

On station escalators, though it's officially discouraged, people who want to walk do so on the left side, and those who want to ride stand to the right. Posted and recorded announcements about escalator safety may seem like schoolmarmish fussing (watch out for loose clothing, untied shoelaces, etc.), but in fact people have been seriously injured on Metro station escalators, all in easily preventable accidents.

If there are no seats available on a crowded train, stand as far from the doors as you can so you don't block people getting on and off. If you're near a door and people are pushing to get off the train, you can help a lot by stepping off the train and getting back on after the rush. You won't miss the train. On the other hand, there's always someone who sprints to get a foot or a briefcase in the door just after the loud, obnoxious electronic chimes make it very clear that the doors are closing and it's time to step back and wait for the next train—which, during rush hour, is usually just a minute or two behind.

You will spot the seasoned commuters the first time you ride a Metro train on a weekday: they've mastered the art of tuning out background noise so they can read the latest John Grisham novel, and they're wearing business suits and tennis shoes—at the office, they will change into office shoes. You might also notice them walking the length of the platform while waiting for the train—you know you're getting assimilated when you know just where to board the train in order to be near the escalator at your destination.

BY COMMUTER TRAIN

Maryland Rail Commute (MARC) and Virginia Rail Express (VRE) commuter trains from Union Station, just off Capitol Hill, serve Baltimore and its far suburbs, Brunswick, MD, and Manassas and Fredericksburg, VA. Buses connect Frederick, MD to the Brunswick line. Suburban sprawl is not quite so advanced that those places qualify as part of the Washington area, but these trains may be a good option for commuting from the outer suburbs, like Gaithersburg or Bowie. And a weekday MARC fare to Baltimore is less than $11 round trip, compared to $36 for an Amtrak ticket. MARC trains also serve Baltimore/Washington International Airport, so ground transportation to BWI—at least on weekdays—is much cheaper than to busier Dulles Airport. Special MARC trains run at night when the Baltimore Orioles play home games at Camden Yards.

Single-trip tickets and monthly passes are sold at Union Station and during rush hour at other stations; for a few dollars extra, you can pay the fare aboard the train.

- **MARC**, 800-325-RAIL; www.mtamaryland.com
- **VRE**, 703-684-1001; www.vre.org

BY CAR

On major thoroughfares, rush hour can last from 6 to 9:30 a.m. and 4 to 7 p.m. Most local radio stations carry traffic reports every 10 to 15 minutes during rush hour. Chronic traffic jams occur at several points on the Capital Beltway, including both Potomac River crossings, and along Interstates 95 and 270. The dreaded "mixing bowl"—the junction of I-95, I-395, and the Beltway in Springfield, VA—is cited by AAA as one of the ten most congested interchanges in the country; with construction in progress to ease the pressure, it will get worse for several years before it gets better.

Heavy traffic isn't limited to highways. Most major streets carry more traffic at peak times than urban planners ever imagined, but at least it's moving traffic—unless there's an accident. Always have an alternative route in mind and pay attention to traffic reports.

The Capital Beltway is not as confusing as it may seem. Yes, part of it is marked I-95 and all of it is marked I-495, but most signs on approaching highways just say "Beltway." Traffic reporters and a few signs refer to the Inner Loop and the Outer Loop, which are simply the clockwise (inner) and counterclockwise (outer) sides of the divided highway.

There are only two toll highways in the Washington area, both connecting the Virginia suburbs with outlying Dulles International Airport: the Dulles Toll Road and the privately operated Dulles Greenway. Potomac and

Anacostia River bridges in the area are toll-free. There is one toll crossing: White's Ferry, a quaint old working auto ferry on the Potomac River between Leesburg, VA and Poolesville, MD—but it's more of a scenic attraction than a commuter thoroughfare.

If you're driving in the city, especially near Embassy Row north of Dupont Circle, keep in mind: foreign diplomats have immunity from prosecution, and are not bound by local laws requiring drivers to carry liability insurance. For cars with diplomatic license plates, traffic laws and parking restrictions are pretty much optional.

Newcomers from snowy climates are often quick to point out that Washingtonians don't know how to drive in snow, or how to remove it. Even though the whole city practically shuts down with a few inches of snow, accidents are common. If you get stuck on roads marked "Snow Emergency Route" during a declared snow emergency (read: when it's snowing) and your vehicle isn't fitted with snow tires or chains, you may get a ticket.

On Thursdays, check out "Dr. Gridlock," a traffic advice column in the *Washington Post*, also available online at www.washingtonpost.com. For information about vehicle registrations, residential parking permits, insurance, and driver's licenses, see **Getting Settled**.

CARPOOLS AND SLUG LINES

Carpooling saves you money and eases congestion on area roads, which in turn saves you time. It also allows you to take advantage of reserved "high-occupancy vehicle" (HOV) lanes, for cars with three or more occupants. If your workplace or a nearby coffee shop has a bulletin board, you might find a carpool partner posted. Otherwise, try calling the **Ride Finders Network**, 800-745-RIDE, or the **Metropolitan Washington Council of Governments Carpool Line**, 800-745-7433. In Northern Virginia, call **Fairfax County RideSources**, 703-324-1111.

The "**slug line**" is a local tradition, an unofficial ride-sharing program that might be described as ritualized hitchhiking (but it's much safer). Since 1969, with the first designation of HOV lanes on highways from Northern Virginia to D.C., commuters seeking a ride downtown have been gathering in certain parking lots in Virginia to form impromptu carpools, and gathering at certain pickup points in downtown D.C. for evening carpools back across the river. Visit www.slug-line.com for the current list of pickup locations and a guide to slug line etiquette.

The **Guaranteed Ride Home** program is a project of Commuter Connections. Register with Commuter Connections at www.commuter-connections.org or call 800-745-RIDE. If you take a carpool or mass transit to work and an emergency or unscheduled overtime prevents you from getting home the same way, you'll be given a ride home or be reimbursed for taxi fare.

CAR SHARING

If you need a car occasionally but not often enough to own one, consider joining a car-sharing network: **Flexcar**, 202-296-1359, www.flexcar.com or **Zipcar**, 866-494-7227, www.zipcar.com. Members share a fleet of cars kept at designated Metro stations; whenever you need a car, for an hour or a week, just make reservations by phone and you'll be billed for the time and mileage. The fees include gas, insurance, and the cost of maintenance. New to Washington, the car-sharing system has been successful in Portland, Oregon and Seattle as well as in Europe.

TAXIS

In D.C., taxis don't have meters. Instead, the city is divided into zones and sub-zones, and the fare is based on the number of zones between pickup and drop-off. The zone system was intended to standardize fares and prevent drivers from taking advantage of out-of-town passengers; instead, despite the zone maps prominently displayed in every D.C. taxi, passengers complain that the system is confusing. Indeed, the maps don't show any landmarks—just the streets that mark zone boundaries—so you need to be familiar with the city's major roads in order to find your current location on the zone map.

There is perennial talk of returning to a meter system, but drivers object to the cost of new equipment; plus, the zone system works to the advantage of passengers riding through heavy traffic, when meters would charge for idle time as well as distance. There are flat surcharges for rush hour, for extra passengers, and during declared snow emergencies.

Cab drivers are required to display their license at all times, and to use air conditioning at the passenger's request from May 15 to October 15 and heat from October 16 to May 14. Smoking is prohibited. Drivers may stop and pick up additional passengers while you're in the vehicle.

Every cab displays the passenger's bill of rights, which affirms that any paying customer has a right to be taken to any location within the District. Still, many taxi drivers refuse to drive to addresses in rough neighborhoods, and some refuse to pick up passengers whom they deem suspicious; though illegal, such practices are fairly common.

Unless you look "suspicious," you should have no problem hailing a cab on a major thoroughfare in the District. Except at Metro stations, you shouldn't count on hailing a cab in the suburbs. Call:

- **Arlington Yellow Cab**, 703-522-2222
- **Barwood**, 301-984-1900
- **Capitol Cab**, 202-546-2400
- **Dial Taxicab Radio Services**, 202-829-4222
- **Diamond Cab**, 202-387-6200
- **Fairfax Yellow Cab**, 703-534-1111

- **Red Top Cab of Arlington**, 202-328-3333
- **Yellow Cab of D.C.**, 202-544-1212

In the suburbs, taxis use meters that charge for distance, idle time, and extra passengers. If you take a Maryland or Virginia cab into the District, you'll pay the metered rates within the District; if you take a District cab into the suburbs, your fare will be based on mileage—and most drivers will quote a fare at the beginning of the trip.

Allow at least half an hour if you're calling a cab at rush hour or in bad weather. Most cab companies will accept credit cards, if you give your number to the dispatcher when you call, and all will provide receipts on request.

CAR RENTALS

These national chains rent cars, minivans, and pickup trucks on a daily or weekly basis, and most have pickup and drop-off points throughout the Washington area—though selection is better at airports and Union Station. Of these, only Alamo and National will rent cars to drivers under 25 years old. If you don't have a major credit card, forget it.

- **Alamo**, 800-327-9633, www.alamo.com
- **Avis**, 800-831-2847, www.avis.com
- **Budget**, 800-527-0700, www.budgetdc.com
- **Dollar**, 800-800-4000, www.dollar.com
- **Enterprise**, 800-736-8222, www.enterprise.com
- **Hertz**, 800-654-3131, www.hertz.com
- **National**, 800-227-7368, www.nationalcar.com
- **Thrifty**, 800-847-4389, www.thrifty.com

BY BIKE

Many Washingtonians commute by bike, sometimes in a business suit and bike helmet. Bicycles are vehicles, according to law—unless there's a sign expressly prohibiting bikes, cyclists are entitled to use the road and are required to obey the same traffic signs, signals, and rules as motor vehicles. In most jurisdictions, minors are required to wear helmets, and in downtown traffic, everyone should.

Except during rush hour, you may bring a bicycle on the Metrorail. Bikes are allowed only on the last car of each train and only at the ends of the car, with only one bike at each end (i.e., no more than two bikes on the train at any time). You must hold onto your bike (no kickstands). If the train is evacuated due to an emergency, you must place your bike on a seat, out of the way, and leave it behind. Cyclists under 16 must be accompanied by an adult. Most stations have bike racks outside, and some have bike lockers, which can be leased for $70/year or $45/six months, plus a $10 key deposit. For locker rentals, call 202-962-1116 or visit www.wmata.com. There's a waiting list at most stations.

With the exception of some Ride On buses in Montgomery County, you can't take your bike on the bus.

Bicycle shops are listed under Bicycling in **Sports and Recreation**, and sporting goods stores are listed in **Shopping for the Home**.

ON FOOT

If you live in a downtown neighborhood like Dupont Circle or Adams Morgan, many errands might take longer by car than on foot, once you take traffic and parking into account. You'll see city dwellers with their own folding carts for grocery shopping, and lawyers dragging thick files on a luggage cart. In the downtown business district, you even see buttoned-down executives on folding scooters borrowed from their kids.

On many street corners in D.C., and on busy streets in the suburbs, you have to press a button to activate the pedestrian crossing signal. Look for a little gray or yellow box with a button in the middle, on a pole about waist high.

Walk D.C. is a clearinghouse promoting pedestrian safety and amenities in the Washington area. For more information call 202-744-0595 or visit www.walkdc.org.

TELECOMMUTING

Telecommuting, or telework, is gaining currency as an alternative to commuting. Some employers allow, even encourage, employees to work at home one or two days a week if their jobs make it feasible. A large company or government agency with some employees telecommuting each day can ultimately save money on expensive office space as well as parking or transit benefits. In the outlying suburbs, there are a few "telework centers" where you can rent office space by the day or the hour, so you can use a computer with a fast internet connection, a fax machine, copier, mailroom and office supplies without trekking inside the Beltway to do it. Ask whether your employer has a telework policy, or contact the Metropolitan Washington Council of Governments at 202-962-3200 or www.mwcog.org for information about setting up a telework arrangement. The web site also lists telework centers.

ON THE DRAWING BOARD

As this book goes to press, new Metrorail stations are planned along Central Avenue in Prince George's County and on New York Avenue NE north of Union Station. A private company, Potomac RiverJet, is planning to launch a fleet of **commuter boats** eventually linking Georgetown, Alexandria, the Washington Navy Yard, and points south as far as Woodbridge, VA. And, in a city that was served by streetcars for more than 100 years, the District government is studying proposals to bring back the **electric trolley**. Light rail lines are being considered along three routes: one looping from Georgetown to Capitol Hill via the Kennedy Center, one from R.F.K. Stadium to Woodley Park via Florida Avenue, and one from Silver Spring to the Southwest waterfront via Georgia Avenue NW. For updates on these new amenities, talk to a real estate agent or visit one of the commuter stores or web sites listed under **Passes and Discounts** above.

REGIONAL/NATIONAL TRANSPORT

AMTRAK

Amtrak passenger trains stop at Union Station and BWI Airport, and some also stop in New Carrollton, MD or Silver Spring. Union Station is a major stop on the rail line from Atlanta to Boston, and long-haul trains stop here to switch from a diesel locomotive for points south to an electric locomotive for the Northeast.

The express Metroliner to New York is frequent and expensive (usually around $120 each way), and the high-speed Acela to Boston reaches speeds of 150 m.p.h. where track conditions permit.

Go to www.amtrak.com or call 800-872-7245 for more information. Online, check their rail sale section for regional specials.

BUSES

Greyhound and Peter Pan Trailways buses serve the Greyhound bus terminal at 1st and L streets NE, a few blocks from Union Station (but an unsavory walk at night). This is the cheapest way to get to other East Coast cities without driving—New York is $39 one way, Atlanta $57, and Boston $63. Some Greyhound routes also stop in Silver Spring, Arlington, or Springfield.

- **Greyhound**, 800-231-2222; www.greyhound.com
- **Peter Pan Trailways**, 800-343-9999; www.peterpanbus.com

AIRPORTS & AIRLINES

It may never again be possible to use one of the Washington area's three major airports without remembering September 11 and the plane that struck the Pentagon, just a few hundred yards from Reagan National Airport. New security measures make air travel to and from Washington safer and less convenient; so far, few passengers have complained.

Call your airline to find out how much carry-on baggage you may bring—for many domestic flights it's just one bag—and for the latest policies on curbside check-in. Anything sharp (even nail clippers, nail files, and tweezers) must be packed in checked luggage or it will be confiscated. Random searches and interviews may remain common practice for years to come, so arrive well before your flight; many travel experts say to allow at least two hours. If you're being dropped off or picked up, the farewells or reunions will have to take place in the main lobby of the terminal—only ticketed passengers are allowed past the security checkpoints.

Because of its proximity to the White House, one special restriction applies to flights to and from National: all passengers must remain seated for the first 30 minutes of any outbound flight and the last 30 minutes of any inbound flight. There are no exceptions, so plan restroom breaks accordingly, especially if you're traveling with kids.

Reagan National Airport, is still called "National Airport" by everyone except weather announcers and travel industry professionals. (When Congress renamed the airport in 1998, liberals and conservatives alike pointed out that it was already named after a former president, President Washington.) Its short runway limits the size of aircraft it can handle, but a new terminal and tower handle the crowds—the busy airport, just a few minutes from downtown by cab or Metro, has shuttles every half hour to New York and Boston. For more information, call 703-417-8000 or go to www.metwashairports.com.

Domestic airlines serving Reagan National include:

- **America West**, 800-235-9292, www.americawest.com
- **American**, 800-433-7300, www.aa.com
- **Continental**, 800-523-3273, www.continental.com
- **Delta**, 800-221-1212, www.delta.com
- **Delta Express**, 800-325-5205, www.flydlx.com
- **Midwest Express**, 800-452-2022, www.midwestexpress.com
- **Northwest**, 800-225-2525, www.nwa.com
- **TWA**, 800-892-2746, www.twa.com
- **United**, 800-241-6522, www.united.com
- **US Airways/US Airways Express**, 800-428-4322, www.usairways.com

Dulles International Airport, is dominated by the renowned and beautiful glass-sided terminal designed by I.M. Pei. The National Air & Space Museum is building an annex here, scheduled to open in 2003, to house artifacts too big for the downtown museum, including the space shuttle *Enterprise* and the bomber *Enola Gay*. Long runways make Dulles the heavy-duty international airport in the region, with regular flights to Tokyo, and Concorde service to Britain and France. For most domestic flights, you'll board a unique "mobile lounge"—a giant bus whose height adjusts to connect to aircraft gates—to ride across the tarmac to a midfield terminal. Outlying Dulles is an expensive cab ride west of the city, but Metrobus route 5A serves the airport from L'Enfant Plaza and Rosslyn Metro stations. There are also many vans and shuttle services from downtown. For more information, call 703-661-2700 or go to www.metwashairports.com. For ground transportation, call Washington Flyer at 703-661-8230 (taxi) or 703-685-1400 (bus).

Domestic airlines serving Dulles include:

- **AirTran Airways**, 800-247-8726, www.airtran.com
- **America West**, 800-235-9292, www.americawest.com
- **American**, 800-433-7300, www.aa.com
- **Atlantic Coast**, 703-707-8550, www.atlanticcoast.com
- **Continental**, 800-523-3273, www.continental.com
- **Delta**, 800-221-1212, www.delta.com
- **Delta Express**, 800-325-5205, www.flydlx.com
- **MetroJet**, 888-368-7653, www.usairways.com/metrojet
- **Northwest**, 800-225-2525, www.nwa.com
- **TWA**, 800-892-2746, www.twa.com
- **United**, 800-241-6522, www.united.com
- **US Airways/US Airways Express**, 800-428-4322, www.usairways.com
- **Virgin Atlantic**, 800-862-8621, www.virgin-atlantic.com

Baltimore/Washington International Airport, is closer to Baltimore than to Washington and, unlike Dulles, is just beginning to grow its own business district. Its remote location generally means cheaper flights, though, especially on the no-frills Southwest Airlines. Metrobus route B30 makes $2 express trips from the Greenbelt Metro station. The airport is also accessible by rail: MARC and Amtrak trains stop nearby, and frequent shuttle buses run between the airport and the BWI Rail Station. On weekdays, the airport is just $5 away from Union Station by MARC. For more information, call 301-261-1000 or go to www.bwiairport.com. For information about ground transportation, call 800-258-3826 (SuperShuttle).

Domestic airlines serving BWI include:

- **America West**, 800-235-9292, www.americawest.com
- **American**, 800-433-7300, www.aa.com
- **Continental**, 800-523-3273, www.continental.com
- **Delta**, 800-221-1212, www.delta.com
- **MetroJet**, 888-368-7653, www.usairways.com/metrojet
- **Northwest**, 800-225-2525, www.nwa.com
- **Southwest**, 800-435-9792, www.iflyswa.com
- **TWA**, 800-892-2746, www.twa.com
- **United**, 800-241-6522, www.united.com
- **US Airways/US Airways Express**, 800-428-4322, www.usairways.com

I N A CITY WHOSE BIGGEST PRIVATE INDUSTRY IS TOURISM, HOTEL space is diverse and plentiful, from no-frills motels along I-95 to historic grand hotels like the Willard and the Hay-Adams. The most exclusive crash pad in the nation is Blair House at 16th and Pennsylvania, across the street from the White House. To stay there, you must be an official guest of the President—a visiting king or prime minister, for example, or a President-elect preparing to move in.

For the rest of us, there are options at every level of price, luxury, convenience, and service. When tourists and conventions crowd the downtown hotels, consider staying at a bed & breakfast, a hostel, or a hotel in the suburbs—most hotels offer shuttle service to the nearest Metro station.

Room rates here are among the highest in the nation, but the seasonal fluctuations are the same as elsewhere: lowest in the winter, and when you book a room well in advance. Always ask about discount offers—many aren't advertised and may change from day to day—and discounts for seniors, veterans, military personnel, and AAA members are common. However, no combination of discounts or good timing will be likely to get you into a big hotel in the District for less than $100 a night; a room in a first-class hotel can easily command $350 or more. Prices aren't quite as high in the suburbs, or in quirky little downtown hotels such as the Tabard Inn or the Brickskeller. Also, in the suburbs, you escape the 14.5% hotel room tax assessed by the District, which pays for the new convention center.

Just for kicks, note: the historic Jenny Lind Suite in the corner dome of the Willard Inter-Continental, with a round window framing the view of the Washington Monument, goes for a little over $3,000 a night. For most of the 19th century, this hotel did the job of Blair House today—it was the accommodation for heads of state and the incoming President-elect. In the days before civil service, when the President personally appointed every federal clerk and bureaucrat, job-seekers would loiter in the Willard's lobby hoping to bend the new President's ear for a moment. Yes, this is where lobbying was invented.

Top-of-the-line hotels will pamper you, anticipating your every need—for a price, of course. Big convention hotels, either downtown or in the Crystal City section of Arlington, offer the most amenities—including restaurants and shops, health clubs, short-term newspaper subscriptions, and a "business center" with internet stations, fax machines, and copiers.

Cheaper than luxury hotels and nicer than convention hotels, bed & breakfast guesthouses aren't just for country getaways. Many historic mansions downtown, especially between Georgetown and Logan Circle, have been turned into B&Bs where $70 to $100 will buy better accommodations and hospitality than at many hotels.

If you need temporary lodgings for more than a few weeks, an extended-stay hotel or even a sublet might suit you better. Few hotel rooms have kitchens, and few hotels have self-service laundry rooms, which are offered at an extended-stay facility. If your timing is good, you might be able to rent a condo or house for a few months—or even line up a house-sitting deal, taking care of pets and plants and doing housekeeping chores in exchange for free housing. Look in the *Washington City Paper* or **Finding a Place to Live** for leads on rentals and housesitting.

The listings in this chapter are just a sample of the types of accommodations available in a city where 25,000 hotel rooms collectively see more than 20 million visitors each year. For more complete listings, check the Yellow Pages or the District's tourism web site, www.washington.org, where you can search by price range and location. If you're a member of AAA, don't forget you can get a AAA travel guide—with updated hotel and motel listings—for free.

DISCOUNT RESERVATIONS

If you do end up in a traditional hotel, there are several ways to save money. Ask a travel agent about promotions—most Washington residents have never heard of "Winterfest," a tourist-oriented series of shopping and entertainment packages between Thanksgiving and Valentine's Day, as it's marketed only outside the Washington area and on www.washington.org. Also try these national reservation services, which offer their own discounts:

- **Capitol Reservations**, call 800-VISIT-DC or go to www.washington.org and select "Book a Hotel."
- **Central Reservation Service**, 800-555-7555, www.centralhotelreservations.com
- **Hotel Discounts/Hotel Reservations Network**, call 800-823-9652 or go to www.washington.org and select "Book a Hotel."

- **Quikbook**, 800-789-9887, www.quikbook.com
- **Washington D.C. Accommodations**, 800-554-2220 or 202-289-2220

Note that some reservation services charge cancellation fees or require advance payment, and their discounts usually cannot be combined with promotions offered by hotels, credit card affinities, or other organizations.

LODGINGS

At any hotel, room rates vary based on the time of year, which are highest between Memorial Day and Labor Day, lowest from January (in inauguration years, February) through mid-March. Rates can be higher on weekends than on weekdays, and some hotels offer lower rates for longer stays. Of course, the rate per person is higher in single-occupancy rooms than in doubles or triples, and the savings on rooms booked several months in advance can be significant.

The letter "U" after a listing denotes union hotels whose workers are represented by Hotel & Restaurant Employees Local 25, AFL-CIO.

LUXURY HOTELS

Expect to pay at least $250 per night at these landmark hotels—and more, sometimes hundreds more, for a view or a suite. But also expect impeccable service, elegant surroundings, and, with some, a sense of history.

- **Four Seasons**, 2800 Pennsylvania Avenue NW, 800-332-3442 or 202-342-0444; in a city where elegance is often synonymous with historic vintage, this modern Georgetown hotel is as elegant as postwar properties get. Consistently among the top-ranked hotels in the nation for service, luxury, and dining.
- **Hay-Adams**, 16th & H streets NW, 800-424-5054 or 202-638-6600; these exclusive rooms—individually decorated with antiques, silk, and molded plaster, and some offering views of the White House—have attracted visiting luminaries since Amelia Earhart, Charles Lindbergh, and Ethel Barrymore stayed here in the 1920s. Among locals, the Hay-Adams is known for afternoon tea and as a studied specimen of architecture in the Italian Renaissance style. (U)
- **Henley Park Hotel**, 926 Massachusetts Avenue NW, 202-638-5200; a beautiful little hotel in an elegant historic building near the new convention center offers a pleasant alternative to standard convention hotels.
- **Hotel Washington**, 15th Street & Pennsylvania Avenue NW, 202-638-5900, www.hotelwashington.com; the stately hotel a block from the White House promises "a front row seat for the parade of history," and often delivers. (U)

- **Jefferson Hotel**, 1200 16th Street NW, 202-347-2200; this historic and pricey hotel features antique furniture, canopy beds, fireplaces, and a discreet register of famous guests who need to be close to the White House. (U)
- **Loews L'Enfant Plaza Hotel**, 480 L'Enfant Plaza SW, 800-235-6397 or 202-484-1000; this modern high-rise offers spacious suites, first-class service, and a location on the working side of the federal district—near the headquarters of three cabinet departments, plus NASA, the GSA, and the FAA. (U)
- **Renaissance Mayflower**, 1127 Connecticut Avenue NW, 800-228-7697 or 202-347-3000, www.renaissancehotels.com; two weeks after this beaux-arts hotel opened, President Coolidge held his inaugural ball here; later, FDR wrote his "nothing to fear but fear itself" speech here. Other names that have appeared on the guest register include Churchill, Truman, and Eisenhower. (U)
- **Ritz-Carlton**, 1150 22nd Street NW, 202-835-0500, www.ritz-carlton.com; renovated for the 21st century, this four-star hotel still has featherbeds in every room, but also high-speed internet lines.
- **Swissotel Washington, TheWatergate**, 2650 Virginia Avenue NW, 202-965-2300, www.swissotel.com; it's not just the scene of Washington's most famous crime—the Watergate is a complex of luxury apartments, shops, a four-star French restaurant, and this four-star hotel to match. (U)
- **Willard Inter-Continental**, 14th Street and Pennsylvania Avenue NW, 800-442-7375 or 202-628-9100; even in Washington, it's hard to pack more history—or more elegance—into one commercial building.
- **Washington Monarch Hotel**, 2401 M Street NW, 877-222-2266 or 202-429-2400, www.washingtonmonarch.com; from the classic luxurious surroundings, you wouldn't necessarily expect high-speed internet connections in every room, but you get them. Some suites, with names like the Lafayette or the Shenandoah, have bigger living and dining rooms than you'll find in some apartments.

LARGE HOTELS

Most of these are chain hotels and will be familiar, but a few stand out: the Marriott Wardman Park, still known to locals as "the Sheraton," is the city's largest hotel, a vast uptown citadel with 1,345 rooms; nearby, overlooking Rock Creek Park, the elegant Omni Shoreham is a favorite venue for high school proms; the J.W. Marriott, a block from the White House and across the street from the Treasury Department, offers luxury, prestige, and a coveted view of parades and fireworks; and the Hilton Washington's sleek 1960s contours are instantly recognizable to those who remember the evening news footage of President Reagan and three aides surviving John Hinckley's ambush there in 1981.

As a Washington resident, you're likely to visit the Hilton, the Wardman Park, the Shoreham, and a few Hyatts and Doubletrees sooner or later for conferences, luncheons, dances, and meetings. Even with competition from a convention center and the spacious, if aging, D.C. Armory, these hotels are always hosting some national conference or trade show.

Expect to pay $100 to $250 a night.

- **Best Western**, 800-528-1234, www.bestwestern.com; three locations in D.C., 10 in the suburbs
- **Crowne Plaza**, 14th and K streets NW, 202-682-0111
- **Doubletree Hotels & Guest Suites**, 800-222-8733, www.double-treehotels.com; three locations in D.C., two in the suburbs
- **Embassy Suites**, 800-362-2779, www.embassy-suites.com; two locations in D.C., three in the suburbs
- **Hilton Hotels**, 800-445-8667, www.hilton.com; four locations in D.C., five in the suburbs; some (U)
- **Holiday Inn**, 800-465-4329, www.holiday-inn.com; five locations in D.C., nine in the suburbs; some (U)
- **Hyatt Hotels & Resorts**, 800-233-1234, www.hyatt.com; three locations in D.C., six in the suburbs; Hyatt Regency (U)
- **Marriott Hotels**, 800-228-9290, www.marriott.com; eight locations in D.C., 11 in the suburbs, including Courtyard by Marriott suites and Residence Inn extended-stay hotels; Marriott Wardman Park (U)
- **Omni Shoreham**, 2500 Calvert Street NW, 800-843-6664 or 202-234-0700, www.omnihotels.com; (U)
- **Quality Inn & Suites**, 800-228-5151, www.qualityinn.com; 1315 16th Street NW, 202-232-8000; 1501 Arlington Boulevard, Arlington, 703-524-5000
- **Radisson**, 800-333-3333 or www.radisson.com: Radisson Barcelo, 2121 P Street NW, 202-293-3100; Radisson Plaza at Mark Center, 5000 Seminary Road, Alexandria, 703-845-1010
- **Washington Plaza Hotel**, 10 Thomas Circle NW, 202-842-1300
- **Wyndham Hotels**, 800-WYNDHAM or www.wyndham.com: Wyndham Bristol, 2430 Pennsylvania Avenue NW, 202-955-6400; Wyndham City Center, 1143 New Hampshire Avenue NW, 202-772-0800; Wyndham Vista, 1400 M Street NW, 202-457-0604

SMALL HOTELS

These are smaller hotels that attract tourists and couples rather than the business travelers who stay in the big chain hotels. If you book ahead and ask about promotions, you might get into one of these establishments for as little as $70 a night, and even the premium rooms are less expensive than those at luxury hotels—though the service and atmosphere can be just as charming.

- **Brickskeller Inn**, 1523 22nd Street NW, 202-293-1885; a bargain if you don't mind sharing a bathroom with a neighboring room, this Continental-style guesthouse is also home of The Brickskeller saloon, serving more than 700 kinds of beer from around the world—some imported exclusively to "The Brick."
- **Topaz Hotel**, 1733 N Street NW, 202-393-3000; upscale suites at bargain rates on a nice residential street near Dupont Circle.
- **Capital Hotels** offer the style and amenities of a luxury hotel at (slightly) lower rates: St. Gregory, 2033 M Street NW, 800-829-5034 or 202-223-0580, www.stgegoryhotelwdc.com; St. James Suites, 950 24th Street NW, 800-852-8512 or 202-659-4492, www.stjamesuitewdc.com; The Governor's House Hotel, 1615 Rhode Island Avenue NW, 800-821-4367 or 202-333-0227, www.governorshousewdc.com. (U)
- **Capitol Hill Suites**, 200 C Street SE, 202-543-6000; modern suites with kitchenettes for the price of single rooms in the business district.
- **Carlyle Suites**, 1771 New Hampshire Avenue NW, 800-964-5377 or 202-234-3200; named the city's "Official Art Deco Hotel" by the Art Deco Society of America; spacious suites at rates competitive with double rooms.
- **Center City Travelodge**, 1201 13th Street NW, 202-682-5300, www.travelodge.com; modern hotel with good rates, free breakfast, and convenient downtown location.
- **Channel Inn**, 650 Water Street SW, 202-554-2400, www.channelinn.com; "Washington's Only Waterfront Hotel" overlooks Washington Channel and Hains Point.
- **The Churchill**, 1914 Connecticut Avenue NW, 202-797-2000, www.meristar.com; this elegant high-rise features big rooms and an attractive location between Dupont Circle and Embassy Row.
- **Clarion Hampshire**, 1310 New Hampshire Avenue NW, 202-296-7600, www.clarionhampshiredc.com; bargain rates, convenient to Georgetown and Dupont Circle, and guests have privileges at neighborhood health clubs.
- **Georgetown Inn**, 1310 Wisconsin Avenue NW, 202-333-8900: www.georgetowninn.com; upscale rooms and suites in the heart of Georgetown.
- **Hotel Harrington**, 12th & E streets NW, 202-628-8140, www.hotel-harrington.com (U); popular tourist hotel downtown with student discounts; with low rates and established reputation, it fills up quickly in the summer.
- **Hotel Lombardy**, 2019 I Street NW, 202-828-2600, www.hotellombardy.com; suites with kitchens at rates comparable to plain rooms in larger hotels.

- **Morrison-Clark Inn**, 1015 L Street NW, 202-898-1200; the city's only inn listed on the National Register of Historic Places, this elegant hotel, with antique furnishings and a highly-rated restaurant, is one of the most luxurious hotels in its price range.
- **The Normandy Inn**, 2118 Wyoming Avenue NW, 202-483-1350; elegant Kalorama location convenient to Dupont Circle and Adams Morgan.
- **Phoenix Park Hotel**, 520 North Capitol Street NW, 202-638-6900, www.pparkhotel.com; decorated in the style of an Irish manor, this Capitol Hill hotel has *two* popular Irish pubs in its storefront. (U)
- **The River Inn**, 924 25th Street NW, 202-337-7600, www.theriverinn.com; convenient to George Washington University and the State Department.
- **Savoy Suites**, 2505 Wisconsin Avenue NW, 800-944-5377 or 202-337-9700; Georgetown cousin of Dupont Circle's Carlyle Suites.
- **Tabard Inn**, 1739 N Street NW, 202-785-1277; country-style inn whose courtyard restaurant is always crowded for its famous Sunday brunch. Some rooms have shared baths, but may be the best bargains in downtown D.C.
- **Washington Court Hotel**, 525 New Jersey Avenue NW, 800-321-3010 or 202-628-2100; steps from Union Station, many rooms here offer views of the Capitol five blocks away.

BUDGET HOTELS & MOTELS

At these no-frills establishments, you can almost always get a room for less than $100, and sometimes as little as $30 or $40. Naturally, the locations aren't the most convenient, but the savings will cover a lot more than your bus fare.
- **Adams Inn**, 1744 Lanier Place NW, 202-745-3600, www.adamsinn.com
- **The Braxton Hotel**, 1440 Rhode Island Avenue NW, 800-350-5759, 202-232-7800, www.braxtonhotel.com
- **Days Inn**, 800-329-7466, www.daysinn.com; four locations in the suburbs
- **Econo Lodge**, 6800 Lee Highway, Arlington, 703-538-5300, www.econolodge.com
- **Howard Johnson Hotels & Lodges**, 800-446-4656, www.hojo.com; two locations in D.C., one in the suburbs
- **Ramada**, 9113 Baltimore Avenue, College Park, 800-228-2828 or 301-345-4900, www.ramada.com
- **Red Roof Inns**, 800-THE-ROOF, www.redroof.com; one location in D.C., seven in the suburbs
- **Super 8**, 501 New York Avenue NE, 800-800-8000 or 202-543-7400, www.super8.com

EXTENDED-STAY HOTELS

It could take a few months to find the perfect home. Perhaps the most conve-nient arrangement while you're searching is an extended-stay hotel. These facilities, also called corporate apartments, offer furnished suites by the day, week, or month. **Smith Corporate Living**, 888-234-STAY, and **Bridge Street Accommodations**, 800-776-5057 or www.bridgestreet.com, have dozens of locations in the area. Other extended-stay hotels, and apartment buildings that rent furnished units on a short-term basis include:

- **Alexandria Suites Hotel**, 420 North Van Dorn Street, Alexandria, 202-333-6564, www.alexandriasuites.com
- **The Barton House**, 2525 North 10th Street, Arlington, 703-525-2600
- **Bragg Towers**, 99 South Bragg Street, Alexandria, 703-354-6300
- **The Chastleton**, 1701 16th Street NW, 202-387-8101, www.apart-ments.com/chastleton
- **The Remington**, 661 24th Street NW, 202-223-4512, www.reming-ton-dc.com
- **Residence Inn by Marriott**, 2120 P Street NW, 202-466-6800; 1199 Vermont Avenue NW, 202-898-1100, www.residenceinn.com
- **The Virginian**, 1500 Arlington Boulevard, Arlington, 703-522-9600
- **The Woodner**, 3636 16th Street NW, 202-328-2800

HOTELS AND THE AMERICANS WITH DISABILITIES ACT

According to Wheels Up! Wheelchair Travel Specialists, www.wheelsup.com, "Disabled access to our capital city rates high marks in just about every respect. Hotels (though pricey) offer many ADA standard accommoda-tions—including a few with roll-in showers instead of the more-common bathtub with handrails. And budget-minded visitors can find accessible rooms not far outside the District (Arlington, Alexandria, the Maryland sub-urbs) at much more reasonable prices."

All large hotels, and most smaller hotels downtown, meet or exceed Americans with Disabilities Act standards for wheelchair access, Braille sig-nage, audible elevator signals, audiovisual fire alarms, and trained support staff. Top-tier luxury hotels emphasize personal service and will expertly accommodate any guest's needs; smaller hotels—especially in historic buildings—may or may not be fully equipped for special needs. Ask when you make reservations—almost all hotels in the Washington area have at least a few wheelchair-friendly rooms, and most rooms in the Hilton, Hyatt, and Marriott chains are fully accessible.

The "Know Before You Go" page at **www.halftheplanet.com** includes a small, but detailed, list of accessible hotels and restaurants. A longer list with less detail is available from the **Endependence Center of**

Northern Virginia at www.ecnv.org/touristfaq. **Travelocity**, www.travelocity.com, and **Travelweb**, www.travelweb.com, let you search for wheelchair-accessible hotels.

B&BS

Bed & breakfast guesthouses, or "B&Bs," can be great bargains on luxurious accommodations and great service—or they can be disappointing rip-offs. Most B&Bs are "quaint" or "eccentric," but there's good quaint and bad quaint. The 21 properties affiliated with **Bed & Breakfast Accommodations** are a good bet, and they're almost all well-appointed quarters in postcard-ready mansions. Call 202-328-3510 or visit www.bnbaccom.com. The **Bed & Breakfast League**, 202-363-7767, also handles bookings for guest rooms in affiliated historic homes. Other reputable B&Bs include:

- **The Dupont at The Circle**, 1604 19th Street NW, 888-412-0100 or 202-332-5251, www.dupontatthecircle.com
- **Embassy Inn**, 1627 16th Street NW, 202-234-7800
- **Hereford House**, 604 South Carolina Avenue SE, 202-543-0102
- **Kalorama Guest House at Kalorama Park**, 1854 Mintwood Place NW, 202-667-6369
- **Kalorama Guest House at Woodley Park**, 2700 Cathedral Avenue NW, 202-328-0860
- **Windsor Inn**, 1842 16th Street NW, 800-423-9111 or 202-667-0300

HOSTELS & DORMITORIES

There's only one official **youth hostel** in D.C. displaying the Hostelling International/American Youth Hostels medallion, at 1009 11th Street NW, 202-737-2333 or www.hiwashingtondc.org. You can stay there for $25 a night—or less, in the off season—if you have a current membership card ($25/year). In peak season, however, official youth hostels reserve the right to bump domestic travelers in favor of international guests.

If you belong to a church or faith-based organization, check to see if there are any affiliated guesthouses in Washington—most welcome respectful visitors of all faiths, but do not advertise except in denominational magazines or newsletters. Quiet, inexpensive semi-private lodgings are available in two Quaker guesthouses: the **William Penn House** on Capitol Hill, 202-543-5560, www.quaker.org/penn-house, and **Davis House** off Dupont Circle, 202-232-3196. Dorm rooms are sometimes available at **Wesley Theological Seminary** at American University, 202-885-8600, and women between the ages of 18-34 can rent rooms at the **Young Women's Christian Home** on Capitol Hill, 202-546-3255. The following are additional options:

COMMERCIAL HOSTELS

Like non-profit youth hostels, these places offer communal or semi-private lodgings at the lowest prices available. Some have curfews or other limitations; on the other hand, some provide breakfast.

- **Allen Lee Hotel,** 2224 F Street NW, 202-331-1224, www.allenleehotel.com; inexpensive lodgings near George Washington University; some rooms with shared bath; 2-week minimum
- **Columbia Guest House**, 2005 Columbia Road NW, 202-265-4006; probably the cheapest rooms within a few blocks of Adams Morgan and Dupont Circle
- **International Guest House**, 1441 Kennedy Street NW, 202-726-5808, www.bedandbreakfast.com; European-style hostel with dorms, curfews, communal bathrooms, and a 20-minute bus ride from downtown, but for $25/night or $160/week you get breakfast and afternoon tea. One-week limit for US citizens, two weeks for international guests.

COLLEGE DORMS

During the summer, if space is available, most area colleges and universities rent rooms in student housing. Dorm rooms for paying tenants are no different from those for students: you share a bathroom with the rest of the hall, you get a small room with basic furnishings, and you might not be allowed to have alcoholic beverages on the premises. Rates are slightly higher than at hostels and lower than anywhere else. Of course, priority goes to enrolled students and participants in summer programs or conferences on campus, but some space is generally available between late May and mid-August. Contact:

- **American University Residential Life & Housing Services** (4-week minimum), 202-885-3370, www.american.edu/other.depts/reslife
- **Catholic University of America Summer Housing & Conferences**, 202-319-5277, http://summer.cua.edu
- **Gallaudet University Visitors Center**, 202-651-5000 (voice & TTY), www.gallaudet.edu
- **George Washington University Community Living & Learning Center**, Summer Housing Services, 202-994-9193, http://gwired.gwu.edu/cllc
- **Georgetown University Conference & Guest Services**, 202-687-4560, www.georgetown.edu/housing/summer
- **Howard University Office of Residence Life**, 202-806-6131, www.howard.edu/residence
- **University of Maryland–College Park Conference & Visitor Services**, 301-314-7884, www.inform.umd.edu/CampusInfo/Departments/guest

TEMPORARY OFFICE SPACE

"Office clubs" or "executive suites," listed in the Yellow Pages under "Office & Desk Space Rental," provide offices, cubicles, or meeting rooms by the hour, day, or month; rental usually includes access to internet and fax lines, phones and receptionists, copiers, a mailroom, and even on-site professional services such as accounting and desktop publishing. These facilities might be the perfect base camp if you have come to Washington with plans to set up a new business or to make an important presentation to prospective clients here.

Of course, the cheapest office space (aside from your own home) is usually a sublet from another business or organization. Walk or drive around a neighborhood you're interested in and look for signs.

NOW THAT YOU LIVE IN ONE OF THE WORLD'S MOST POPULAR tourist destinations, where will you go on vacation? In the winter or when you have out-of-town guests, you can visit the Smithsonian museums, the monuments, and the touristy side of Washington, but when the summer hordes of tourists clog the Smithsonian Metro station, you might want to head for the mountains or the beach.

Classified ads in *Washingtonian* magazine and the *Washington City Paper* list beach houses and mountain cabins for rent, and *Washingtonian* and the *Washington Post* Sunday magazine run seasonal issues focusing on weekend getaways, which carry extra advertising from bed-and-breakfast lodgings, resorts, and destination towns.

For travelers on a budget, the bulletin boards or student newspaper classifieds at area colleges and universities are replete with people seeking rideshares to New York, Richmond, and other day-trip destinations. The advertiser might be offering gas money to share a ride or offering a ride to share expenses.

BLUE RIDGE MOUNTAINS

Just 80 miles west of the Lincoln Memorial, a much larger stone figure looms 4,000 feet above the Shenandoah Valley: Stony Man Mountain, one of the high points (in more than one sense) of Shenandoah National Park. It resembles the face of a sleeping giant when viewed from scenic Skyline Drive along the park's 107-mile ridge. An easy nature trail leads to the cliffs, with great views across the Shenandoah Valley to the west and, on a clear day, the next few ridges of the Appalachians.

Bookstores and hiking outfitters in the Washington area offer a selection of hiking guides to Shenandoah's waterfalls and granite peaks. In the fall, you might find the parking lot at the head of a popular trail overcrowded with D.C. license plates as city dwellers clamor for a dose of autumn leaves. Look especially for *Circuit Hikes in Shenandoah National*

Park, published by the Potomac Appalachian Trail Club, and *The New Appalachian Trail* by Edward B. Garvey.

South of the park, the Blue Ridge Parkway makes a 469-mile scenic link between Shenandoah and Great Smoky Mountains National Park on the Tennessee/North Carolina border. Looking west from Shenandoah, you can see Massanutten Mountain, the near edge of the vast George Washington National Forest; the south end of the long, narrow mountain features the closest ski slopes to Washington. To the north, where the Blue Ridge meets the Allegheny range, Western Maryland offers some of the finest whitewater paddling in the mid-Atlantic—the Youghioheny River, Antietam Creek, and the lower Shenandoah (which flows south to north).

Throughout the Blue Ridge Mountains, the valleys and foothills are teeming with quaint little towns famous for antique shopping. New Market and Sperryville, along US Route 211 in Virginia, are the most fertile antiquing grounds. The Shenandoah Valley is also renowned for its caverns, vast limestone chambers in the porous rock of the ancient riverbed. Of the cave systems open to tourists, Luray Caverns are the most famous, perhaps because of the unique Stalacpipe Organ, where natural rock formations are played like the tines of a music box.

For more information on these and other attractions, contact:

- **Shenandoah National Park**, 540-999-3500, www.nps.gov/shen; National Park Service camping reservations, 800-365-2267 or http://reservations.nps.gov
- **George Washington National Forest**, 540-740-8310 or www.southernregion.fs.fed.us/gwj; National Forest Service camping reservations, 877-444-6777, www.reserveusa.com
- **Shenandoah Valley Travel Association**, 877-VISIT-SV, www.svta.org
- **Blue Ridge Parkway**, 828-298-0398, www.nps.gov/blri

See the **Greenspace** and **Sports & Recreation** chapters for more information about parks, camping, hiking, and paddling.

BEACHES

From Memorial Day to Labor Day, US Route 50 east of Washington becomes one long traffic jam as Washingtonians flock to the shore—mostly to the boardwalk resorts of Ocean City, MD and Rehoboth Beach, DE. Generally speaking, Ocean City attracts a college crowd and Rehoboth is popular with gay men. Both offer boardwalk culture exactly as you would expect: saltwater taffy, skee-ball arcades, fries and funnel cakes, R-rated t-shirts, and plenty of volleyball.

Those who prefer a rustic beach should head south from Ocean City to Assateague Island, a protected National Seashore and home to the famous wild horses who have flourished here since a long-forgotten wreck of a Spanish galleon. The island is also home to the endangered piping plover and other rare shorebirds. North of Rehoboth Beach, Cape Henlopen, DE and Cape May, NJ, connected by ferries across the mouth of the Delaware Bay, also offer shorebirds a carefully preserved dune habitat.

About four hours northeast of the Beltway is Atlantic City, NJ, the Las Vegas of the East, where there is also a traditional boardwalk, but that's not why people go. It's all about slot machines, blackjack, roulette, keno, and other opportunities to donate some of your money to Donald Trump; and, in the evening, you can catch the same acts you associate with Vegas— Don Rickles, Tom Jones, and others trying to fill the Sinatra gap. You already know all the street names here, by the way—this is where Monopoly was invented, and the only square on the Monopoly board you won't find in real-life Atlantic City is "Go."

- **Ocean City Visitor Office**, 800-GO-OCEAN, www.ocean-city.com
- **Rehoboth Beach**, 800-441-1329, www.rehoboth.com
- **Assateague Island National Seashore**, 410-641-1441, www.nps.gov/asis
- **Cape May**, 609-884-5508, www.covesoft.com/capemay
- **Cape Henlopen State Park**, 301-645-8983, www.destateparks.com
- **Atlantic City**, 888-AC-VISIT, www.atlantic-city-online.com

AMUSEMENT PARKS

You don't have to drive far to ride classic roller coasters and splash in a giant wave pool. There are world-class thrill rides and amusements right in the suburbs, at Six Flags America in Largo, MD, on Central Avenue east of Route 193. Locals might still refer to the place by one of its former names, "Wild World" or "Adventure World," as it has had a few facelifts. Roller-coaster enthusiasts may want to take a few longer trips, though, after checking out the ride reviews at www.ultimaterollercoaster.com. Nearby parks include:

- **Busch Gardens—The Old Country & Water Country USA**, Williamsburg, VA, 757-253-3350, www.buschgardens.com
- **DelGrosso's Amusement Park**, near Pittsburgh, PA, 866-684-3538, www.delgrossos.com
- **Hersheypark**, Hershey, PA, 800-HERSHEY, www.hersheypa.com
- **Paramount Kings Dominion**, near Richmond, VA, 804-876-5561, www.kingsdominion.com
- **Six Flags America**, Largo, 301-249-1500, www.sixflags.com/america
- **Six Flags Great Adventure & Hurricane Harbor**, Jackson, NJ, 732-928-1821, www.sixflags.com/greatadventure

A day at an amusement park can be a very expensive proposition for a family, but there's never any reason to pay full price to go to Six Flags

America or Kings Dominion. There's always a grocery store or drugstore giving out coupons, or get some friends together for a group rate.

Children who aren't quite old enough to appreciate visceral thrill rides might enjoy the tamer attractions at **Sesame Place**, near Philadelphia, 215-752-7070, www.sesameplace.com—a Sesame Street theme park—or **Dutch Wonderland** in Lancaster, PA, 717-291-1888, www.dutchwonderland.com.

Preservationists are working to restore **The Enchanted Forest**, a defunct theme park in Ellicott City, MD that once delighted younger kids with boat rides, giant slides and playhouses inspired by nursery rhymes and fairytales.

SOUTHEASTERN PENNSYLVANIA

Drive an hour north of Baltimore and you'll need to keep an eye out for horse-drawn buggies. These days, the low-tech Amish sects grudgingly stick reflective orange triangles on their black carriages, but they adhere to a religious order that forbids them from having telephones in their homes, putting rubber tires on their tractors, or fighting. They did introduce pretzels to this side of the Atlantic, and name-brand snack foods such as Snyder and Utz hail from Amish country and bear Amish family names.

Lancaster County is the heart of "Pennsylvania Dutch" country (a name based on a mistake in translation—the Amish are of German descent, or Deutsche), and there is an influence of Amish culture in York, Reading, and Hanover. Moravians and Quakers, both descendants of the same pacifist Anabaptist movement as the Amish, also settled here; in addition to Amish shoofly pie and snickerdoodles, you'll find spiky Moravian stars adorning front porches, and Moravian sugar cakes at old-fashioned general stores. Historic markers identify many farms and old buildings as sites on the Underground Railroad, the 19th-century network of "safe houses" where Quaker abolitionists helped slaves run to freedom.

This is also outlet shopping country, where day trippers from Baltimore and Philadelphia scour outlet malls in search of designer dresses and coats at a fraction of the retail price.

- **Lancaster County**, 800-PA-DUTCH, www.padutchcountry.com
- **York**, PA, 888-858-YORK, www.yorkpa.org
- **Reading/Berks County**, 800-443-6610, www.readingberkspa.com

COLONIAL SITES

D.C. residents are fond of pointing out that the District is legally a colony today, but "colonial heritage" generally doesn't refer to the four cornerstones of the District. Within three hours' drive, you can visit:

- **Williamsburg**, VA, 800-HISTORY, www.history.org; this restored 17th century settlement is a living museum, where music students from

William & Mary don colonial dress to play the same hornpipes and reels that entertained the Redcoats back in the day. Here, on May 15, 1776, the colonial Virginia assembly met and decided to send a resolution to the Continental Congress proposing that the 13 colonies declare their independence from England. They took down the British flag and replaced it with the flag of the Grand Union—which today flies over Williamsburg every year from May 15 to July 4.

- **St. Mary's City, MD**, 800-762-1634, www.stmaryscity.org; older than Williamsburg and less touristy, this partially restored settlement is where the colony of Maryland was founded in 1634. An ancestor of the First Amendment was born here—the first religious tolerance law made by Europeans in North America. Ongoing archaeological work here makes headlines every few years, and in the early 1990s a metal coffin from colonial times was found to contain scientific pay-dirt: pristine samples of the 17th century atmosphere, never touched by car exhaust or factory smoke. The bluffs above the St. Mary's River, and the rocky beaches of nearby Point Lookout State Park, offer some of the most spectacular sunsets within a day's drive of Washington.

- **Jamestown, VA**, 888-593-4682, www.historyisfun.org; the first recorded European settlement in North America. Almost 200 years later, in nearby Yorktown, Gen. Cornwallis surrendered King George's colonies to Gen. Washington.

- **Monticello, VA**, 804-984-9822, www.monticello.org; the mansion on the back of the nickel, designed by and for architect Thomas Jefferson in his spare time.

CIVIL WAR SITES

A diner north of Frederick, MD is known as Barbara Fritchie's, and patrons are reminded that she was the Maryland woman who defied Jackson's Confederate troops on the march, as recalled by poet John Greenleaf Whittier. "Shoot, if you must, this old gray head, but spare your country's flag," she said. Moved by her gallantry, General Stonewall Jackson turned to his rebels, stating "Who touches a hair of yon gray head dies like a dog; march on." Whether that story is embellished or not, the Civil War raged through Northern Virginia, Western Maryland, and well into Pennsylvania for four years before the destruction of supply lines from Atlanta led to General Lee's surrender at Appomattox. The flash point that started it all is just a 90-minute drive or a short train ride north of the Beltway. Where the Shenandoah meets the Potomac, and Maryland, Virginia, and West Virginia come together is Harper's Ferry, site of John Brown's raid in preparation for, Brown believed, an epic conflagration.

- **Antietam, MD**, 301-432-5124, www.nps.gov/anti; this tranquil riverside field, looking much as it did in 1862, was the scene of a pivotal battle that slowed Gen. Lee's army, deterred the British from recognizing the Confederate nation, and opened the door for the Emancipation Proclamation.

- **Fredericksburg, VA**, 800-678-4748, www.fredericksburgva.com; this is where Clara Barton and Walt Whitman tended casualties of the Spotsylvania and Chancellorsville battles; the city itself preserves a walkable old town section near the Rappahannock River.
- **Gettysburg, PA**, 717-334-6274, www.gettysburg.com; Gettysburg National Military Park, 717-334-1124, www.nps.gov/gett; the bloodiest battle ever fought on American soil drew President Lincoln here to dedicate the cemetery with the words now chiseled in stone at the Lincoln Memorial. The battlefield itself is well-preserved, and the town offers many interpretive attractions—including a wax museum, a 360-degree panoramic painting, an observation tower, and a narration of the battle over a giant map illuminating troop movements.
- **Harper's Ferry, WV**, 304-535-6298, www.nps.gov/hafe; the town, nestled between two rivers, was declared by maverick abolitionist John Brown to be the provisional capital of the United States after he seized the federal armory there to equip his posse of freed slaves for the battle he envisioned. Before touring the well-preserved historic town, stop on the Maryland side of the Potomac at the Maryland Heights trailhead on Route 340 and take a leisurely walk up the hill; the postcards in town are no substitute for seeing that view for yourself.
- **Manassas National Battlefield Park**, 703-361-1339, www.nps.gov/mana; Bull Run is a quiet little creek with a cute little stone bridge that was twice the object of bloodshed. It was during the first battle here that Gen. Thomas Jackson stonewalled the Union troops and earned his nickname. Except for the highway across it, the battlefield hasn't changed much—in the mid-1990s, preservationists forced the Walt Disney Co. to cancel plans for an American history theme park here. This is a day trip, not a weekend getaway—indeed, the city of Manassas is practically a suburb of Washington.

NEW YORK

With a Greyhound bus almost every hour, several airlines offering hourly shuttles during the day, and new high-speed train service via Amtrak, you can easily go see a Broadway show in the evening and still go to work in Washington the next morning—or, check out www.nycvisit.com for a guide to accommodations in the Big Apple. It's a nice place to visit, but it's not the nation's capital. In New York, you actually have to *pay* to get into the museums!

BEACH & MOUNTAIN HOUSES

Check the classified ads in *Washingtonian* magazine, the *City Paper*, and the *Post* Sunday magazine for opportunities to rent, sublet, share, or even buy a vacation home. A cabin in the mountains can be quite inexpensive, if you plan to use it enough to get your money's worth; buying a beachfront house or condo may pay for itself through rentals.

In beach communities, you should have no trouble finding a rental agent or broker to help you lease or buy property. If you're looking outside the major beach resorts listed in this chapter, search http://officialcitysites.org for the appropriate community web site—if you're buying a place of your own or buying into a timeshare arrangement, you'll want to look at web sites created by and for residents, not visitors.

TRAVEL BARGAINS

With the emergence of online ticket agents such as www.expedia.com and www.lowestfare.com, it's easy to shop around for the lowest scheduled fares; but if you're headed to a common destination, start with the *City Paper* classifieds—there's always someone selling unwanted airline tickets to Chicago or Atlanta, train tickets to New York, or bus tickets to Atlantic City. Airfares are lower from BWI than from Dulles and National airports, and lower to busy destinations than to smaller cities.

Most colleges and universities have at least an unofficial "ride board," where travelers in need of a ride, or vice versa, can post their needs and browse for potential matches. Ride-sharing ads appear in the *City Paper* too.

For a list of small, independent accommodations, pick up a directory of bed-and-breakfast inns at any major bookstore or visit www.travelassist.com/reg. Rates are often much lower than at hotels and motels, and you get much nicer rooms and hospitality than the same money would buy at a hotel.

Council Travel, 800-2-COUNCIL or www.counciltravel.com, is a full-service travel agency specializing in budget travel for students as well as young-at-heart travelers who are more interested in adventure than tightly scripted tour packages. Locations are, naturally, on or near university campuses: 3301 M Street NW, 202-337-6464; 4400 Massachusetts Avenue NW, 202-244-7330; and 7401 Baltimore Avenue, College Park, 301-779-1172.

Finally, please be assured that you're never too old for a **youth hostel**. The 4,500 friendly, inexpensive, no-frills lodgings around the world that display the Hostelling International symbol are open to anyone with a friendly attitude and a current membership card, available for $25/year. Visit the American Youth Hostels retail store and travel agency at 1108 K Street NW, 202-783-4943, or go to www.hiayh.org.

A DD UP THE EVENTS HOSTED BY THE MUSEUMS, LIBRARIES, theaters, parks and monuments, neighborhood associations, congregations, charities and civic groups, not to mention athletic venues, multiply them by the cities and counties that make up the D.C. area, and you'll understand why residents here complain that there's not enough time.

Check the newspapers for features and listings of upcoming events. The *Washington City Paper* and the "Weekend" section of the *Washington Post* (Fridays) are the best places to look for upcoming concerts, gallery and museum openings, plays, readings, lectures, tours, craft fairs, and other special events; for book signings and discussions, check the "Book World" section of the *Post* on Sundays. On the first Sunday of the month, the "Style" section of the *Post* lists charity galas. The *Common Denominator* is good for civic events in the District. The *Washington Business Journal* covers conventions and trade shows. (Speaking of conventions and trade shows, note that the Washington Convention Center listed below is the "old" convention center, on New York Avenue NW, between 9th and 11th streets; the new convention center at Mt. Vernon Square is expected to open sometime in 2003.) Also check the **Neighborhood Profiles** for additional listings of community festivals—street fairs, town birthdays, and other folksy events that are popular with local residents and make for fun, inexpensive outings. The neighborhood events listed here are those that draw big crowds.

If a location is not listed below, it's because the location changes from year to year. For more information about these festivities, check the *Post* or the *City Paper* a week or two before the event.

JANUARY

- **Martin Luther King Jr. Day** observance, Lincoln Memorial, 202-619-7222; the annual ceremony culminates with a broadcast of Dr. King's "I Have a Dream" speech.

- **Sugarloaf Crafts Festival**, Capital Expo Center, Chantilly, 301-990-1400, www.sugarloafcrafts.com; more than 300 artisans gather from all over the US and Canada for this huge fair.
- **Wammie Awards**, www.wamadc.com, 703-237-9500; nominees and past honorees perform at the Washington Area Music Association's annual awards gala.

FEBRUARY

- **Chinese New Year** celebration, Chinatown, 202-638-1041; D.C.'s Chinatown becomes a week-long ethnic festival culminating in a parade under the Friendship Arch at 7th & H streets NW. *Metro: Gallery Place-Chinatown*
- **Frederick Douglass' birthday observance**, Frederick Douglass House, 202-426-5961; Black History Month is commemorated with a tribute to the abolitionist leader at his historic home in Anacostia. *Metro: Bus W6/W8 from Anacostia*
- **Lincoln's Birthday observance**, Lincoln Memorial, 202-619-7222; with fanfare from military bands, the President lays a wreath at the memorial and a prominent speaker delivers the Gettysburg Address.
- **Washington Boat Show**, Washington Convention Center, 703-823-7960; if you're looking for a new yacht, this is the place. *Metro: Gallery Place-Chinatown*
- **Washington's Birthday observance**, Mt. Vernon, 703-780-2000; Old Town Alexandria, 703-838-4200; Washington Monument grounds, 202-619-7222; festivities include a parade and ceremony at George Washington's estate, with a performance by the US Army Fife & Drum Corps; a parade in Alexandria in the shadow of the Masonic memorial to Washington (*Metro: King Street*); and a musical tribute at the Sylvan Theatre at the Washington Monument. *Metro: Smithsonian*

MARCH

- **Environmental Film Festival**, various locations, 202-342-2564; museums, government agencies, and nature centers host two weeks of documentary and dramatic films about environmental issues and endangered places.
- **Helen Hayes Awards**, 202-337-4572, www.helenhayes.org; Washington's theater community—called the nation's second-largest by *Variety* magazine—honors its best performances at this Washington Theatre Awards Society gala named after the venerated District native.

- **Smithsonian Kite Festival**, Washington Monument grounds, 202-357-2700 (sometimes in early April); kite enthusiasts show off their most elaborate kites and stunt skills. *Metro: Smithsonian*
- **St. Patrick's Day Parade**, along Constitution Avenue NW; all the pubs are overcrowded on March 17, but there's plenty of room to celebrate along the parade route. *Metro: Archives-Navy Memorial or Federal Triangle*

APRIL

- **African-American Family Celebration**, National Zoo, 202-673-4717; the Easter Monday festival at the Zoo features music, dance, and interactive activities for all ages. *Metro: Woodley Park-Zoo/Adams Morgan*
- **Cherry Blossom Festival**, Tidal Basin, 202-547-1500, www.gwjapan.com/cherry; crowning a week of entertainment, games, and a 10-K under the blooming cherry trees, the city's largest annual parade marches down Constitution Avenue. *Metro: Federal Triangle*
- **Christmas in April/Sukkot in April**, various locations, 202-362-1611, www.christmasinaprildc.org; volunteers make repairs to the homes of senior citizens and low-income families, and in community centers, shelters, and inner-city schools.
- **Earth Day** celebration, The Mall and various locations, 206-876-2000, www.earthday.net (global directory of Earth Day events). The big-tent environmental exposition, with its big-name entertainment, is held every five years, but many communities hold smaller Earth Day fairs where you can find out more about local environmental groups and how to lend a hand.
- **Hands On D.C.**, various locations, 202-667-5808, www.handsondc.org; teams of volunteers give a day's work to neighborhood schools—and raise money for scholarships from sponsors supporting their efforts.
- **Smithsonian Craft Show**, 202-357-2700; artisans from all over the country compete to be selected for this exhibition and sale.
- **Take Back the Night** march and rally, Dupont Circle, 202-232-0789; this annual protest against domestic violence is the signature event of Sexual Assault Awareness Month. *Metro: Dupont Circle*
- **WAMA Crosstown Jam**, various locations, 202-338-1134, www.wamadc.com; a weekend of concerts by hundreds of local musicians at dozens of clubs and coffeehouses around town raises money for the Washington Area Music Association.
- **Washington International Film Festival**, various locations, 202-724-5613; area theaters, museums, and libraries host special screenings of national and international films.
- **White House Easter Egg Roll**, 202-456-2200, www.nps.gov/whho; this Easter Monday tradition happens on the South Lawn of the White

House. Open to children ages three to six, accompanied by an adult. Free, but tickets are required—visit the information kiosk on the Ellipse south of the White House. *Metro: McPherson Square*

MAY

- **Andrews Air Force Base Air Show**, Beltway & Suitland Road, 301-981-1110; this flying parade includes the Thunderbirds fighter aerobatics team, the B-2 stealth bomber, and vintage and modern military aircraft.
- **Cathedral Flower Mart**, Washington National Cathedral, 202-537-6200, www.cathedral.org/cathedral; this flower show and sale features cuttings from the Bishop's Garden. *Metro: 30 series bus from Tenleytown or N series from Dupont Circle*
- **Chesapeake Bay Bridge Walk**, 877-229-7726; just for kicks, once a year, pedestrians are allowed on the high suspension bridge across a 4.3-mile-wide neck of the Bay. For a small fee, a shuttle bus will bring you back across.
- **Greater D.C. Cares Day**, various locations, 202-289-7378, www.dc-cares.org; thousands of volunteers spend the day helping to improve neighborhood schools, parks, and low-income housing. To support the ongoing work of Greater D.C. Cares, each participant collects pledges from sponsors, as in a walkathon.
- **Memorial Day** observances, Arlington National Cemetery, 703-607-8052; Vietnam Veterans Memorial, 202-393-0090; The Mall, 202-619-7222; the President lays a wreath at the Tomb of the Unknowns (Metro: Arlington Cemetery). Similar ceremonies are held at the Vietnam Veterans Memorial. The National Symphony Orchestra plays a free concert at the Capitol end of The Mall, and the Rolling Thunder motorcycle parade along Constitution Avenue honors POW and MIA soldiers.
- **Takoma Park Jazz Festival**, 301-589-4433, http://cityoftakoma-park.org/organizations; dozens of local jazz artists fill six stages all day, and it's free. *Metro: shuttle bus from Takoma*
- **Unifest**, Martin Luther King Jr. Avenue SE, 202-678-8822; a two-day street festival celebrates Anacostia. *Metro: Anacostia*
- **WHFStival**, PSINet Stadium in Baltimore, 202-234-SEAT, www.whfs.com; WHFS-FM hosts an all-day lineup of alternative rock bands—sort of a one-day Lollapalooza.

JUNE

- **Alexandria Red Cross Waterfront Festival**, 703-549-8300; in the nation's largest outdoor event to benefit the American Red Cross, Alexandria's nautical heritage is celebrated with a weekend of arts and entertainment to welcome vintage tall ships. *Metro: bus 28A/28B from King Street*

- **Capital Jazz Fest**, various locations, 301-218-0404; big-name jazz artists gather at venues in and around Washington for three days of celebration.
- **Capital Pride**, Freedom Plaza, 13th Street & Pennsylvania Avenue NW, www.capitalpride.org; a parade honoring the gay, lesbian, bisexual, and transgender community—and friends—culminates at a street festival with big-name entertainment. *Metro: Federal Triangle*
- **Dupont-Kalorama Museum Walk**, various locations between Dupont Circle and Calvert Street NW, 202-667-0441, www.dkmuseums.com; a weekend of free admission and special activities at a dozen private museums.
- **Juneteenth**, various locations; a traditional celebration of the Emancipation, Juneteenth is observed on June 19 with vigils, parades, and festivals at Freedom Plaza, the Capitol, and the Frederick Douglass House. An emerging new holiday—specific events and sponsors vary each year.
- **Kemper Open**, Avenel, Bethesda, MD, 202-432-7328, www.pgatour.com (sometimes in late May); world-class golfers compete in this PGA Tour event.
- **Louisiana Swamp Romp**, Wolf Trap, 703-218-6500; hoo-wee, the Washington area has its own annual festival of zydeco music and dance.
- **Mt**. **Pleasant Day**, along Mt. Pleasant Street NW; one of the city's biggest and oldest annual street fairs celebrates this Latino neighborhood. *Metro: bus 42 from Dupont Circle*
- **National Capital Barbecue Battle**, Pennsylvania Avenue NW, 301-860-0630; sample the entries by restaurants and amateurs in the regional barbecue contest. *Metro: Federal Triangle*
- **Potomac Celtic Festival**, Morven Park, Leesburg, VA, 800-752-6118; traditional and modern music, dance and crafts celebrate the Celtic cultures of Ireland, Scotland, Cape Breton, and even Celtic France and Spain.
- **Shakespeare Free-for-All**, Carter Barron Amphitheater, 202-547-3230; the Shakespeare Theater Company gives free performances of a different Shakespeare play each year. Harry Hamlin, Kelly McGillis, and Franchelle Stewart Dorn are among recent stars of the festival. Advance tickets are required and go quickly, four to a customer. *Metro: bus S2/S4 from Silver Spring*
- **Smithsonian Festival of American Folklife**, The Mall, 202-357-2700 (continues through the Fourth of July); interactive exhibits, craft demonstrations, music, and storytelling in a tent city celebrate the history and cultural diversity of the US. *Metro: Smithsonian*
- **Wolf Trap Jazz & Blues Festival**, Wolf Trap, 703-218-6500; famous and up-and-coming artists fill several stages for four days of concerts.

JULY

- **A Capital Fourth**, The Mall; the fireworks at the Washington Monument are accompanied by a free National Symphony Orchestra concert on the west lawn of the Capitol, ending a full day of pop, jazz, country, and patriotic concerts on the Mall. *Metro: Smithsonian*
- **Bastille Day** celebration, along Pennsylvania Avenue NW, 202-296-7200; waiters and waitresses with full trays race from Les Halles restaurant at 12th and Pennsylvania to the Capitol and back *Metro: Archives-Navy Memorial*
- **D.C. AIDS Ride**, 800-825-1000, www.aidsride.org; this four-day, 330-mile bike ride from Raleigh, NC draws thousands to cheer at the finish line. Participants raise money for local charities serving people with HIV/AIDS.
- **Screen on the Green**, Monday evenings on the Washington Monument grounds, www.screenonthegreen.com; weather permitting (don't count on it, during thunderstorm season), see classic American films on a giant outdoor screen. *Metro: Smithsonian*
- **Latino Festival**, along Pennsylvania Avenue NW, 202-835-1555; a parade and a weekend of festivities showcase the large and diverse Latino community in Washington. *Metro: Archives-Navy Memorial or Federal Triangle*
- **Legg Mason Tennis Classic**, William H.G. Fitzgerald Tennis Stadium, Rock Creek Park, www.leggmasontennisclassic.com; world-class tennis pros come to Washington. *Metro: bus S2/S4 from Silver Spring*
- **Minnesota Avenue Day**, Minnesota Avenue and Benning Road NE, 202-397-7300; this summertime street festival is second only to Unifest as the largest neighborhood celebration "east of the river." *Metro: Minnesota Avenue*
- **Virginia Scottish Games**, Alexandria, 703-912-1943; a festival of Scottish heritage featuring traditional music, dancing, and food—including real haggis.
- **Washington Theater Festival**, Source Theatre and other locations, http://users.starpower.net/sourcetheatre, 202-462-1073 (continues in August); rising stars in the local theater community present dozens of new plays and staged readings at the Source and other participating theaters. The series culminates in the 10-Minute Play Competition, with a different set of short plays every night for a week.

AUGUST

- **Governor's Cup**, from Annapolis to St. Mary's City, MD, 301-862-0380; the most prestigious yacht race on the Chesapeake is also one of the biggest overnight regattas on the East Coast.

- **Maryland Renaissance Festival**, Crownsville, MD, 410-266-7304 (through October); one of the nation's largest Renaissance fairs, "RenFest" celebrates the Tudor era with games, pageantry, food, mead and jousting—the official state sport of Maryland.
- **Montgomery County Agricultural Fair**, Gaithersburg Fairgrounds, 301-926-3100; a classic county fair, right out of *Charlotte's Web*, with animal and harvest shows, carnival games, rides, cotton candy, and funnel cakes. *Ride-On bus: 55/59 from Rockville*
- **Stone Soul Picnic**, RFK Stadium, 202-547-9077; the all-day free festival is the biggest annual soul concert in the mid-Atlantic region.

SEPTEMBER

- **Adams Morgan Day**, 202-332-3292; only Mt. Pleasant Day rivals the size of this annual street festival, organized by neighborhood businesses. Watch the *InTowner* or the *City Paper* for details. *Metro: Bus 42 from Dupont Circle*
- **Arts On Foot**, locations throughout Penn Quarter, www.artsonfoot.org; in the downtown gallery district dozens of public and private galleries and studios hold open houses. Also look for street performances, a "Cooking as Art" demonstration, the Shakespeare Theater's annual sale of used props, and sidewalk sales by local artists. *Metro: Gallery Place-Chinatown or Metro Center*
- **Black Family Reunion**, The Mall, 202-737-0120; this huge two-day festival celebrates African-American culture with entertainment, food, games, and exhibits. *Metro: Smithsonian*
- **Capital Soulfest**, www.soulfest.com; older and younger generations of big-name soul and R&B artists perform at an all-day concert and party.
- **D.C. Blues Festival**, Carter Barron Amphitheater, 202-828-3028; D.C. Blues Society artists offer a day and evening of free concerts. *Metro: bus S2/S4 from Silver Spring*
- **Elderfest**, Freedom Plaza, 13th Street and Pennsylvania Avenue NW, 202-289-1510; this celebration and expo for the senior community features entertainment, exhibits, and free health screenings. *Metro: Federal Triangle*
- **International Children's Festival,** Wolf Trap, 703-642-0862; young performing artists from the Washington area and around the world present a weekend of family entertainment.
- **Kennedy Center Open House**, 202-467-4600, www.kennedy-center.com; the nation's living museum of the arts and memorial to President Kennedy offers a full day of free performances on its seven stages. *Metro: Foggy Bottom-GWU*

- **Prince George's County Fair**, Prince George's Equestrian Center, 301-579-2598; half an hour's drive from the Capitol, Pennsylvania Avenue becomes a country road through rolling fields and horse farms. This land is among the first places where Native Americans cultivated tobacco. A traditional agricultural fair honors the agrarian history of Prince George's County.
- **Takoma Park Folk Festival**, www.tpff.org; local folk musicians and dancers representing traditions from all over the world gather for a day of free performances on six stages. *Metro: shuttle bus from Takoma*
- **Washington Irish Festival**, Gaithersburg Fairgrounds, 301-565-0654; this festival, organized by the National Council for Traditional Arts, is deemed "among the best anywhere in the world" by *Irish Echo* magazine. *Ride-On bus: 55/59 from Rockville*

OCTOBER

- **Army Ten Miler**, 202-685-3361; *Runner's World* magazine calls it one of the top 100 races in the nation: a flat course through the monumental city, which attracts some 16,000 runners each year. Register early.
- **Art-o-Matic**, www.artomatic.org, 202-661-7589; hundreds of local visual and performing artists and filmmakers show and sell their work in this all-volunteer, month-long, grassroots exhibition.
- **Halloween Drag Races**, 17th and Q streets NW; Washington's gay community and friends celebrate Halloween off Dupont Circle with contests for drag queens in high heels. *Metro: Dupont Circle*
- **Marine Corps Marathon**, www.marinemarathon.com; you don't have to be a Marine, but you do have to register early and be able to run a 26.2 mile loop, from the Marine Corps Memorial (the "Iwo Jima Memorial") in Rosslyn to Capitol Hill and back.
- **Herndon Folk Festival**, Town Green, Herndon, VA, 703-435-6868; local folk musicians, dancers, and craftspeople fill three stages for a day of free performances.
- **Reel Affirmations**, various locations, www.reelaffirmations.org; dozens of venues show films of gay and lesbian interest in this week-long film festival.
- **Takoma Park Street Fair,** along Carroll Avenue, Takoma Park, MD; Old Town merchants, artisans, community organizations, and musicians celebrate the community. *Metro: Takoma*
- **Taste of D.C.**, along Pennsylvania Avenue NW, 202-724-5430; a three-day street festival where dozens of D.C. restaurants offer samples of their fare. *Metro: Federal Triangle*

- **Washington International Horse Show**, MCI Center, 7th & F streets NW, 301-840-0281; a week of indoor equestrian competition brings competitors from all over the world into downtown Washington. *Metro: Gallery Place-Chinatown*

NOVEMBER

- **Goodwill Industries Book Sale**, Washington Convention Center, 202-636-4225; a convention hall is filled with over 200,000 inexpensive books, CDs, and videotapes; on the last day, you pay a flat price for each shopping bag you fill. *Metro: Gallery Place-Chinatown*
- **Veterans Day**; memorial events throughout D.C.

DECEMBER

- *A Christmas Carol* **at Ford's Theater**, 202-347-4833, www.fordstheatre.org; the classic tale is staged every year at the historic venue. *Metro: Metro Center*
- **The Christmas Revels**, Warner Theatre, 202-432-SEAT; Old World carols, dances, and mummers' plays are performed by a lively chorus in period garb. *Metro: Metro Center*
- **First Night Alexandria**, 703-836-1526; **First Night Montgomery**, Silver Spring, 240-777-6821; these family-oriented public New Year's Eve celebrations include music, games, dances, and no alcohol.
- **Kennedy Center Holiday Festival**, 202-467-4600; the Kennedy Center itself is wrapped in a giant red ribbon, and the gift inside is a month of free holiday performances, including a Christmas Eve "Messiah" sing-along. *Metro: Foggy Bottom-GWU*
- **Pageant of Peace**, The Ellipse, 202-208-1631, www.nps.gov/whho/pageant; music and family activities celebrate the lighting of the National Christmas Tree and the smaller trees representing each state and territory.
- **Wildlife Arts Festival**, Woodend, Chevy Chase, MD, 301-652-9188; the Audubon Naturalist Society kicks off the holiday season with a sale of works by local artists to benefit regional conservation efforts.

WASHINGTON AREA GUIDES

- **Arcadia** publishes a series of guidebooks for neighborhood walking tours, written by local historians and providing detailed and informative notes.

- *D.C. for Free* by Brian Butler, Mustang Publishers, 1997; the cost of living may be high, but the cost of playing isn't. This book will keep you busy for years exploring museums, parks, and offbeat attractions that cost no more than bus fare.

- *The Everything Guide to Washington, D.C.* by Lori Perkins, Adams Media Corp., 2000; you'll want a tourist guide for detailed information about the museums and monuments that can fill as many weekends as you can spare, and to help you host visiting friends and family; there are dozens of guidebooks, and this is one of the most knowledgeable.

- *Finding Fun & Friends in Washington: An Uncommon Guide to Common Interests* by Roberta Gettesman, Piccolo Press, 1996; if you're into tai chi, Civil War reenactments, volunteering for the orchestra box office, gourmet vegetarian cooking, sailing, or just about any other hobby, this encyclopedia of Washington social opportunities will help you get "in the loop."

- *Going Places With Children in Washington, D.C.*, Green Acres School, 1998; this comprehensive family-oriented guide to the city includes touristy and offbeat activities.

- *Greater Washington Area Bicycle Atlas*, Jim McCarthy & Sharon Gang, Washington Area Bicyclist Association & Hostelling International 1998; WABA knows bike routes, and these ride notes are expertly tested in detail.

- *Natural Washington* by Richard L. Berman & Deborah McBride, EPM Publications; parks and natural areas from Manassas to the Bay are profiled in detail in this knowledgeable pocket guide.

- ***The New Washington One-Day Trip Book*** by Jane Ockershausen, EPM Publications, 1992; even Washington workaholics get to sneak away once in a while, and this book suggests dozens of quick road trips, arranged by season.
- ***The Pub, Club & Grub Guide to Washington, D.C.*** by Zena Polin & Steve Gatward, Patmos Press, 2000; over 220 bars and nightclubs are profiled in this detailed directory.
- ***StationMasters***, Bowring Cartographic, 1996; this little booklet contains maps of the immediate areas surrounding each Metro station, identifying key buildings and points of interest.

D.C. HISTORY

- ***Above Washington*** by Robert W. Cameron, Cameron & Co., 1981; there are lots of coffee-table picture books of Washington, but this one stands out. Though it's a bit dated, it emphasizes aerial photos of living neighborhoods as well as national landmarks, and includes a section of "then and now" photos of historic neighborhoods.
- ***A Cartoon History of the District of Columbia*** by Patrick M. Reynolds, Red Rose Studio, 1995; the histories of D.C. neighborhoods, and the lives of the people whose names they bear, are recounted in this anthology of "Flashbacks" cartoons that appear in the Sunday comics in the *Washington Post*. A second collection *D.C. Neighborhoods*, was published in 2000.
- ***Captive Capital: Colonial Life in Modern Washington*** by Sam Smith, Indiana University Press, 1974; one of the founders of the D.C. Statehood Party looks at the civil rights movement from the perspective of half a million Americans still lacking the right to govern their own local affairs.
- ***Civil War to Civil Rights; Washington D. C.'s Downtown Heritage Trail*** by Richard T. Busch and Kathryn Schneider Smith, Howell Press, 2001; these self-guided walking tours visit famous and off-beat sites in downtown D.C. that have played important roles in the history of the city and the nation.
- ***A Literary Map of Metropolitan Washington, D.C.*** by Martha Hopkins and Sheila Harrington, Women's National Book Association, 2001; a folding map created in partnership with the Library of Congress shows important sites in the city's literary history, including the homes and graves of famous authors who lived here.
- ***The Names of Washington, D.C.*** by Dex Nilsson, Twinbrook Communications, 1998; Dupont, Logan, Thomas, and Scott aren't just traffic circles, and Col. Brooks and Col. Shaw have neighborhoods named after them for a reason. This history book recounts these too-often-neglected stories.

- **On This Spot** by Douglas Evelyn & Paul Dickson, National Geographic Society, 1999; every neighborhood, if not every block, in D.C. has a story, but not every historic place has a marker or a brochure to explain its significance. This book fills you in on a lot of arcane history.
- **Washington Album: A Pictorial History of the Nation's Capital** by Bob Levey and Jane Freundel Levey, Washington Post Books, 2000; like Bob Levey's daily column in the *Post*, this book reflects a city of real people and real neighborhoods, not just monuments and tourist attractions.

BIOGRAPHIES & MEMOIRS

Some of these people grew up in Washington and made their mark on the world; others came here and made their mark on the city. But they all walked the streets of your new hometown.

- **Red Auerbach**: *Seeing Red* by Dan Shaughnessy and Larry Bird, Crown Publishers, 1994; the legendary Boston Celtics coach grew up in Washington, attended George Washington University, and coached high school basketball here until his first pro coaching job—with the old Washington Capitols NBA franchise.
- **Clara Barton**: *Professional Angel* by Elizabeth Brown Pryor, University of Pennsylvania Press, 1998; *Woman of Valor* by Stephen B. Oates, Free Press, 1995
- **Sammy Baugh**: *Sammy Baugh, Best There Ever Was* by Whitt Canning, Masters Press, 1998; the Washington Redskins' first quarterback held the job longer than anyone else has, and they didn't wear face masks in those days.
- **Mary McLeod Bethune**: *Building a Better World* (collected writings edited by Audrey Thomas McCluskey), Indiana University Press, 2000; often described as one of the most influential African-American women in history, the Shaw resident founded the National Council of Negro Women and some of the earliest schools for African-American girls.
- **Alexander Graham Bell**: *The Life and Times of the Man Who Invented the Telephone,* by Edwin S. Grosvenor and Morgan Wesson, Harry N. Abrams, 1997
- **Ben Bradlee**: *A Good Life* (autobiography), Simon & Schuster, 1995; the Watergate-era *Washington Post* editor has been one of the most prominent figures in social and political Washington since he was JFK's friend and neighbor in Georgetown in the 1950s.
- **William O. Douglas**: *My Wilderness: East to Katahdin* (memoir), Doubleday, 1961; in this collection of essays, the Supreme Court Justice and accomplished hiker recounts, among other adventures, his travels along the C&O Canal—one of the most eloquent narratives ever written about natural areas in greater Washington.

- **Frederick Douglass**: *Narrative of the Life, My Bondage and My Freedom* (autobiography), 1845
- **Daniel Drayton**: *Personal Memoir*, Negro University Press, 1969; in 1848, this local merchant—along with Paul Jennings, a former slave employed by Sen. Daniel Webster—led a sensational attempt to smuggle 77 slaves to freedom. Originally published in 1855 under the title *Personal Memoir of Daniel Dreyton...*
- **Duke Ellington**: *Music Is My Mistress* (autobiography), Da Capo Press, 1976; *Beyond Category: The Life and Genius of Duke Ellington* by John Edward Hasse, Da Capo Press, 1995
- **Katharine Graham**: *Personal History* (autobiography), Vintage Books, 1998; *Power, Privilege, and the Post: The Katharine Graham Story* by Carol Felsenthal, Seven Stories Press, 1999; *Katharine the Great: Katharine Graham and Her Washington Post Empire* by Deborah Davis, Institute for Media Analysis, June 1991
- **Helen Hayes**: *My Life in Three Acts* (autobiography with Katherine Hatch), Harcourt, 1990; the "first lady" of Washington theater is the namesake of the most prestigious theater awards off Broadway.
- **Walter Johnson**: *Walter Johnson: Baseball's Big Train* by Henry W. Thomas, Farragut Publishing, 1995; an Amazon.com review says it all— "How good a pitcher was Washington Senator ace Walter Johnson? Babe Ruth, Ty Cobb, and Joe Jackson considered him the best ever ... no one's ever come close to his mark of 110 shutouts."
- **Al Jolson**: *Al Jolson* by James Fisher, Greenwood Publishing Group, 1994; the Washington-born entertainer is often criticized by modern audiences for appearing in black face makeup as a 19th-century minstrel, but in fact he singlehandedly put an end to that medium and used his stardom to introduce many other innovations in stage performance—long before he starred in the first "talking" movie, *The Jazz Singer*, loosely based on his own career.
- **Pierre L'Enfant**: *The Life of Pierre Charles L'Enfant* by Hans Paul Caemmerer, Da Capo Press, 1970
- **Vince Lombardi**: *When Pride Still Mattered* by David Maraniss, Simon & Schuster, 1999; best known as the coach of the Green Bay Packers, Lombardi ended his coaching days here with the Redskins in the early 1970s.
- **Frederick Law Olmsted**: *A Clearing in the Distance* by Witold Rybezynski, Scribner, 1999
- **Robert Gould Shaw**: *Blue-Eyed Child of Fortune* (letters collected by Russell Duncan), University of Georgia Press, 1999; a friend of Lincoln's son, Col. Shaw commanded the first African-American regiment in the US Army, and the heart of D.C. now bears his name.
- **John Philip Sousa**: *Marching Along, Recollections of Men, Women and Music* (memoir) 1928; reissued by Integrity Press, 1994; the

Washingtonian composer is one of the few individuals in history who is widely credited with introducing an entire genre of music—the march written for brass band.

- **Mike Tidwell**: *In the Shadow of the White House* (memoir), Prima Communications, 1992; a local drug-abuse counselor, now a travel writer for the *Washington Post*, recounts the 1980s crack epidemic.
- **Doug Williams**: *Quarterblack: Shattering the NFL Myth* (memoir with Bruce Hunter), Bonus Books, 1990; the Washington Redskins quarterback was the first African-American to lead a team to victory in the Super Bowl.

Of course, political biographies and memoirs also offer unique perspectives on the city and its culture. Perhaps the most fascinating—and certainly the most revealing—glimpses of "inside the Beltway" society are those in the memoirs of Watergate figures such as H.R. Haldeman, John Dean, Jeb Magruder, and the *Washington Post* duo of Bob Woodward and local native Carl Bernstein.

Finally, there's one person who had a profound impact on Washington without ever even visiting the city: **James Smithson**, the British chemist who left his money to the United States to endow a facility in Washington: for the increase and diffusion of knowledge." Since 1846, the Smithsonian Institution has grown into one of the most revered scholarly organizations in the world, and it includes several of the world's most popular museums. The Smithsonian released an official biography, *James Smithson and His Bequest*, in 1879; a more contemporary portrait is offered in *James Smithson and the Smithsonian Story* by Leonard J. Carmichael and J.C. Long, Putnam, 1965.

CHILDREN

- *Independent School Guide for Washington, D.C. and Surrounding Area*, published by Independent School Guides, is the most comprehensive directory of private and parochial schools.
- *Raising Your Child in Washington*, Washington Parent/Piccolo Press, 1995; from schools and childcare to summer camps and soccer leagues, this book anticipates your questions, because it's edited by people who have been there.
- *Underground Train* by Mary Quattlebaum, illustrated by Cat Bowman Smith, Yearling Books, 1997; this delightful children's book teaches toddlers what to expect from their first ride on the Metro.
- *Dreamland: A Lullaby* and *Halley Came to Jackson* (both HarperCollins) are children's books by Mary-Chapin Carpenter, the native Washingtonian country music star, who still lives in Georgetown.

FICTION

Washington shows up in many classic and contemporary novels—especially in works by Tom Clancy, Gore Vidal, and Allen Drury. In the 1959 Pulitzer Prize novel *Advise and Consent,* Drury wrote of Washington:

> It is a city of temporaries, a city of just-arriveds and only-visitings, built on the shifting sands of politics, filled with people passing through. They may stay fifty years, they may love, marry, settle down, build homes, raise families, and die beside the Potomac, but they usually feel, and frequently they will tell you, that they are just here for a little while. Someday soon they will be going home. They do go home, but it is only for visits, or for a brief span of staying-away; and once the visits or the brief spans are over ('It's so nice to get away from Washington, it's so inbred; so nice to get out in the country and find out what people are really thinking') they hurry back to their lodestone and their star, their self-hypnotized, self-mesmerized, self-enamored, self-propelling, wonderful city they cannot live away from or, once it has claimed them, live without.

Drury also knew his way around the streets of D.C., and the halls of power. But not all novels set in Washington revolve around politics. Check out these thrillers:

- ***Dark*** by Kenji Jasper, Broadway Books, 2001; the first novel by a 25-year-old District native is a coming-of-age story set in Shaw, with a young protagonist trying to escape the violent street life for which he seems destined.
- ***Dupont Circle*** by Paul Kafka-Gibbons, Houghton Mifflin, 2001; of the novel and the neighborhood, Kafka-Gibbons writes: "In Dupont Circle poor meets rich, old meets young, gay meets straight, native meets new arrival, and the peoples, styles, and languages all squish together to form America."
- ***The Exorcist*** by William Peter Blatty, 1971; the classic horror novel, reissued by HarperCollins in 1993, is loosely based on actual events that took place in the quiet Maryland suburbs along the upper Anacostia River.
- ***Who's Afraid of Virginia Ham?*** by Phyllis Richman, HarperCollins, 2001; the third whodunit by the longtime *Washington Post* food critic is a sequel to *Murder on the Gravy Train* (2000) and *The Butter Did It* (1998).

DIRECTORIES & REFERENCE BOOKS

- **ADC** publishes a series of excellent detailed street atlases of the District and neighboring counties, showing zip codes, Metro lines, post offices, and other useful details. The index includes special sections for parks, schools, police and fire stations, and other points of interest. The regional atlas covering the entire area discussed in this book is a substantial investment, but worth it.

- **Opportunities in Public Affairs** from Brubach Publishing is a must if you're looking for work on the Hill, on K Street (lobbying), or in the non-profit sector; for more specialized listings, subscribe to *Environmental Career Opportunities, International Career Opportunities,* or *Opportunities in Arts & Media.* These are not classified ads—many of the listings are based on insider knowledge not published anywhere else. The subscription rates may seem pricey, but this is the next best thing to having a personal "mole" in hundreds of agencies and companies. (Don't buy these papers at newsstands—subscribers will have a week's head start on you. Call 301-571-0102 or visit www.brubach.com.)

- **Washington 2002** (or the current year) is the definitive annual directory of key players—people and institutions—in government, business, and non-profits. It's an expensive tome, and you probably don't need to own a copy unless you're a journalist or politico, but it's good to be familiar with your public library's copy. Same goes for the *Media Yellow Book,* the *Congressional Yellow Book,* and other volumes in the Leadership Directories series.

- **Washington Business Journal Book of Lists** is an annual compilation of the Top 25 lists that appear in the *Washington Business Journal* every week—collectively, a "who's who" of the Washington area's leading companies in every field from aerospace to interior design.

- **Zagat Survey Washington D.C. & Baltimore Restaurants** is an annual summary of reader evaluations of hundreds of area restaurants. Thorough cross-indexing—not just by cuisine, neighborhood, and price range, but also outdoor seating, fireplaces, late hours, and dress codes—make up for the lack of detail.

- Finally, don't forget the **Yellow Pages** and the **White Pages**—both have front sections full of useful consumer information about local services; recorded information by phone about everything from auto repairs to heart surgery to news headlines to soap opera updates; stadium and theater seating charts; and everything you need to know about your local phone service, including troubleshooting and do-it-yourself repairs.

AGING

- **D.C. Office on Aging**, 202-724-5625; http://dcoa.dc.gov
- **Maryland Department of Aging**, 800-243-3425 or 410-767-1100, www.mdoa.state.md.us
- **Virginia Department of Aging**, 800-552-3402, www.aging.state. va.us
- **American Association of Retired Persons**, (**AARP**) 202-434-2277, www.aarp.org
- **Elder Care Locator**, US Administration on Aging, 800-677-1116
- **Legal Counsel for the Elderly**, 202-434-2170, www.aarp.org/foundation
- **National Council on Aging**, 202-479-1200, www.ncoa.org
- **Social Security**, 800-772-1213, www.ssa.gov
- **Medicare Hotline**, 800-MEDICARE

ANIMALS

LICENSING AND ANIMAL CONTROL

Where there is no separate number listed for dog licenses, contact the animal control agency:
- **D.C. Animal Control Shelter**, 202-576-6664
- **Montgomery County Police**, Division of Animal Control and Humane Treatment, 301-279-1249, www.co.mo.md.us/services/police/animal
- **Prince George's County Animal Control Commission**, 301-883-6009
- **Arlington County Dog Licenses**, 703-228-3255, www.co.arlington.va.us/treas

383

- **Fairfax County Animal Control**, 703-830-3310, www.co.fairfax.va.us/ps/ac
- **Fairfax County Dog Licenses**, 703-222-8234, www.co.fairfax.va.us/dta
- **Alexandria Police - Animal Control/Protection Service**, 703-838-4774

SHELTERS

- **Washington Humane Society**, 202-723-5730, www.washhumane.org
- **Washington Animal Rescue League**, 202-726-2556, www.warl.org
- **Montgomery County Humane Society**, 240-773-5054, www.mchumane.org
- **Animal Welfare League of Arlington**, 703-931-9241, www.awla.org
- **Fairfax County Animal Shelter**, 703-830-1100, www.co.fairfax.va.us/ps/ac
- **Alexandria Animal Shelter**, 703-838-4775, www.adoptapet.com/adoptapet

AUTOMOBILES

STATE LICENSING & REGISTRATION

- **D.C. Department of Motor Vehicles**, 202-727-5000, http://dmv.washingtondc.gov
- **Maryland Motor Vehicle Administration**, 800-950-1682, www.mva.state.md.us
- **Virginia Department of Motor Vehicles**, 866-DMV-LINE, www.dmv.state.va.us

LOCAL REGISTRATION & PARKING PERMITS

- **Arlington County**, 703-228-3135, www.co.arlington.va.us
- **Fairfax County**, 703-222-8234, www.co.fairfax.va.us
- **Alexandria**, 703-838-4560; ci.alexandria.va.us

TOWED AUTOMOBILES

- **D.C. Impound Lot**, 202-727-5000
- **Montgomery County Police**, 301-840-2454 or 301-279-8000
- **Prince George's County Police**, 301-772-4740
- **Arlington County Police**, 703-228-4040

- **Fairfax County Police Traffic Division**, 703-280-0587
- **Alexandria Code Enforcement Bureau**, 703-838-4360

BIRTH & DEATH CERTIFICATES

- **District of Columbia**, 202-442-9009
- **Maryland**, 410-764-3069; Montgomery County office, 240-777-9460; Prince George's County office, 301-952-4576
- **Virginia**, 804-662-6200; Fairfax County office, 703-246-712

CONSUMER PROTECTION

- **D.C. Office of the Corporation Counsel**, 202-442-9828
- **Maryland Office of the Attorney General**, Consumer Protection Division, 410-528-8662 (complaint hotline), 410-576-6550 (consumer information)
- **Virginia Department of Agriculture and Consumer Services**, Office of Consumer Affairs, 804-786-2042 or 800-552-9963
- **Better Business Bureau of Metro Washington D.C.**, 202-393-8000, www.dc.bbb.org
- **Consumer Product Safety Commission**, 800-638-2772, www.cpsc.gov
- **Federal Communications Commission**, 888-225-5322, www.fcc.gov
- **Federal Consumer Information Center**, 800-688-9889, www.pueblo.gsa.gov
- **Federal Trade Commission**, 202-382-4357, www.ftc.gov
- **Scambusters**, www.scambusters.org

See **Getting Settled** for regulatory agencies that oversee cable TV companies.

CRISIS HOTLINES

ALCOHOL & DRUG ABUSE

- **Alcoholics Anonymous**, 202-966-9115, www.aa-dc.org
- **Alcolicos Anonimos de Habla Hispana**, 202-797-9738, www.aa-dc.org
- **D.C. Alcohol Prevention & Recovery Administration**, 202-673-6618
- **D.C. Central Intake Division**, 202-727-5163
- **D.C. Office of Tobacco Control**, 202-442-5433
- **Second Genesis**, 202-234-6800
- **Montgomery County Department of Health & Human Services**, 301-762-5613

- **Prince George's County Department of Health**, 301-883-7853 (addictions)
- **Arlington County Alcohol and Drug Treatment Programs**, 703-228-4900
- **Fairfax County Alcohol & Drug Services**, 703-359-7040 (general information); 703-222-4145 (intake)
- **Alexandria Health Department**, 703-329-2000

BATTERED WOMEN SHELTERS & HOTLINES

- **My Sister's Place**, 202-529-5991, www.mysistersplace.org
- **House of Ruth**, 202-347-2777, www.houseofruth.org

CHILD ABUSE HOTLINES

- **District of Columbia**, 202-671-7233
- **Montgomery County**, 301-315-4000
- **Prince George's County**, 301-699-8605
- **Arlington County**, 703-228-1500
- **Fairfax County**, 703-324-7400
- **Alexandria**, 703-838-0800
- **Childhelp USA**, 800-422-4453
- **National Center for Missing & Exploited Children**, 800-843-5678

HUMAN SERVICES

- **D.C. Child & Family Services Agency**, 202-698-6220
- **D.C. CFSA Foster Parent & Adoption Recruitment**, 202-671-5683
- **Focus Adolescent Services** (referrals), 877-362-8727, www.focusas.com

RAPE CRISIS

- **D.C. Rape Crisis Center**, 202-333-7273, www.dcrcc.org
- **Sexual Assault Follow-up Program**, D.C. Department of Health, 202-727-4906
- **Montgomery County Sexual Assault Crisis Line**, 301-315-4357
- **Arlington Violence Intervention Program**, 703-228-4848
- **Fairfax County Rape Crisis Hotline**, 703-360-7273
- **Alexandria Sexual Assault Response & Awareness**, 703-683-7273

SUICIDE PREVENTION

- **D.C. Hotline**, 202-223-2255

YOUTH CRISIS & RUNAWAYS

- **Child Quest International Hotline**, 800-248-8020
- **Covenant House Nineline**, 800-999-9999, www.covenanthouse.org
- **Girls & Boys Town Hotline**, 800-448-3000, www.boystown.org
- **Sasha Bruce Youthwork Crisis Hotline**, 202-547-7777, www.needsyou.org
- **Street Survival Project**, 800-942-8382

HUMAN RIGHTS

- **D.C. Commission on Human Rights**, 202-727-0656
- **Maryland Commission on Human Relations**, 800-637-6247 or 410-767-8600, www.mchr.state.md.us
- **Virginia Council on Human Rights**, 804-225-2292, www.chr.state.va.us
- **Montgomery County Human Relations Commission**, 202-777-8450
- **Prince George's County Human Relations Commission**, 301-883-6170
- **Arlington County Human Rights Commission**, 703-358-3929
- **Fairfax County Human Rights Commission**, 703-324-2953
- **Alexandria Office of Human Rights**, 703-838-6390
- **US Department of Justice**, Civil Rights Division, 202-514-2000; 800-514-0301 (disability matters); 800-896-7743 (housing)

ELECTED OFFICIALS & MUNICIPALITIES

ELECTED OFFICIALS

- **Mayor of the District of Columbia**, 202-727-2980, http://dc.gov/mayor
- **D.C. Council**, 202-724-8000, www.dccouncil.washington.dc.us
- **D.C. Advisory Neighborhood Commissions**, 202-727-2525, http://anc.washingtondc.gov
- **Governor of Maryland**, 410-974-3901 or 800-811-8336, www.gov.state.md.us

- **Governor of Virginia**, 804-786-2211, www.thedigitaldominion.com
- **Maryland General Assembly**, 301-970-5400 or 800-492-7122, http://mlis.state.md.us
- **Virginia General Assembly**, 804-698-7410 (Senate), 804-698-1500 (House), 800-889-0229 (comment line)
- **Montgomery County Executive**, 240-777-2500, www.co.mo.md.us/executive
- **Montgomery County Council**, 240-777-7900, www.co.mo.md.us/council
- **Prince George's County Executive**, 301-952-4131, www.goprince-georgescounty.com
- **Prince George's County Council**, 301-952-3600, www.goprincege-orgescounty.com/council
- **Arlington County Board**, 703-228-3130, www.co.arlington.va.us
- **Fairfax County Board of Supervisors**, 703-324-2000, www.co.fair-fax.va.us
- **Alexandria City Council**, 703-838-4500, www.ci.alexandria.va.us
- **US House of Representatives**, 202-224-3121, www.house.gov
- **US Senate**, 202-224-3121, www.senate.gov
- **White House**, 202-456-1111 (comment line); 202-456-1414 (general information), www.whitehouse.gov

AREA MUNICIPALITIES

- **Alexandria**, 703-838-4500, www.ci.alexandria.va.us
- **Bethesda**, www.bethesda.org
- **Berwyn Heights**, 301-474-5000, http://berwyn-heights.com
- **Bladensburg**, 301-927-7048, www.bladensburg.com
- **Bowie**, 301-262-6200, www.cityofbowie.org
- **Brentwood**, 301-927-7395
- **Cheverly**, 301-773-8360, www.cheverly.com
- **Chevy Chase**, 301-654-7144, www.townofchevychase.org
- **Chevy Chase Village**, 301-654-7300, www.ccvillage.org
- **College Park**, 301-864-8666, www.inform.umd.edu/collegepark
- **Colmar Manor**, 301-277-4920
- **Cottage City**, 301-779-2161
- **District of Columbia**, 202-727-1000, www.washingtondc.gov
- **Edmondston**, 301-699-8806
- **Fairfax**, 703-385-7855, www.ci.fairfax.va.us
- **Falls Church**, 703-248-5014, www.ci.falls-church.va.us
- **Gaithersburg**, 301-258-6300, www.ci.gaithersburg.md.us
- **Garrett Park**, 301-933-7488, www.garrettpark.org
- **Greenbelt**, 301-474-8000, www.ci.greenbelt.md.us

- **Herndon**, 703-435-6800, www.town.herndon.va.us
- **Hyattsville**, 301-985-5000, www.hyattsville.org
- **Laurel**, 301-725-5300, www.laurel.md.us
- **Mt. Rainier**, 301-985-6585, http://users.erols.com/mrainier
- **North Brentwood**, 301-699-9699
- **Reston**, http://reston.org, www.restonweb.com
- **Riverdale Park**, 301-927-6381, www.ci.riverdale-park.md.us
- **Rockville**, 301-309-3000, www.ci.rockville.md.us
- **Somerset**, www.townofsomerset.com
- **Silver Spring**, www.silverspringcenter.com
- **Takoma Park**, 301-270-1700, www.cityoftakomapark.org
- **University Park**, 301-927-2997, www.upmd.org
- **Vienna**, 703-255-6300, www.ci.vienna.va.us
- **Washington Grove**, 301-926-2256, www.washgrov.sailorsite.net
- **Wheaton**, www.wheatonnet.com

Check the **Further Afield** section following the **Neighborhood Profiles** for additional city and county web sites. For cities and towns not profiled in this book, visit: http://officialcitysites.org.

AREA COUNTIES

- **Montgomery County**, www.co.mo.md.us
- **Prince George's County**, www.goprincegeorgescounty.com
- **Arlington County**, www.co.arlington.va.us
- **Fairfax County**, www.co.fairfax.va.us

STATE/DISTRICT GUIDES

- **District of Columbia**, www.dclibrary.org/community
- **Maryland**, www.sailor.lib.md.us
- **Virginia**, www.vipnet.org

EMERGENCY

- **Fire, Police, Medical**, 911
- **National Capital Poison Control Center**, 202-625-3333 or 800-492-2414
- **Federal Emergency Management Agency**, Disaster Assistance Information, 800-525-0321, www.fema.gov

See listings below for **Police** and **Utility Emergencies**.

ENTERTAINMENT

- **All Sports & Concerts**, 301-595-4009 or 800-786-8425, www.ascticket.com
- **Encore Tickets**, 301-718-2525, www.encoretix.com
- **Ticketmaster**, 202-432-SEAT or 800-551-SEAT, www.ticketmaster.com
- **Tickets.com**, www.tickets.com
- ***Washington City Paper***, www.washingtoncitypaper.com
- ***Washington Post Weekend***, http://eg.washingtonpost.com

GARBAGE & RECYCLING

- **D.C. Department of Public Works**, 202-727-1000, http://dpw.dc.gov
- **Montgomery County Solid Waste Services Division**, 240-777-6410, www.dpwt.com
- **Prince George's County Department of Environmental Resources**, 301-952-7630 (garbage), 301-883-5045 (recycling); www.goprincegeorgescounty.com/services
- **Arlington County Department of Environmental Services**, 703-228-6570, www.co.arlington.va.us/des
- **Fairfax County Department of Public Works & Environmental Services**, 703-550-3481, www.co.fairfax.va.us/dpwes
- **Alexandria Division of Solid Waste**, 703-751-5130, www.ci.alexandria.va.us/solidwaste

HEALTH & MEDICAL CARE

CHILDHOOD LEAD POISONING PREVENTION

- **D.C. Lead Poisoning Prevention Program**, 202-535-2690
- **Maryland Lead Program**, 800-776-2706
- **Lead-Safe Virginia**, 877-668-7987 or 804-225-4463

DEPARTMENTS OF HEALTH, HOTLINES

- **D.C. AIDS Information Hotline**, 202-332-2437, www.wwc.org
- **D.C. Department of Health**, 202-442-5999, www.dchealth.com
- **Bureau of Cancer Control**, 202-442-5905
- **Bureau of Diabetes Control**, 202-442-9157
- **Immunization Information**, 202-576-7130
- **Sexually Transmitted Diseases Clinic**, 202-698-4050
- **Medicaid/D.C. Department of Human Services**, 202-463-6211

- **Maryland Department of Health & Mental Hygiene**, 877-463-3464 or 410-767-6860; www.dhmh.state.md.us
- **Virginia Department of Health**, Arlington District Office, 703-228-4992; Fairfax District Office, 703-246-2479, www.vdh.state.va.us
- **US Department of Health and Human Services**, 800-336-4797, www.hhs.gov
- **Montgomery County Department of Health & Human Services**, 240-777-1245, www.co.mo.md.us/services/hhs
- **Prince George's County Department of Health**, 301-883-7834
- **Arlington County Department of Human Services**, 703-228-1300, www.co.arlington.va.us/dhs
- **Fairfax County Department of Health**, 703-246-2411, www.co.fairfax.va.us
- **Alexandria Health Department**, 703-838-4400, www.ci.alexandria.va.us/city/health

MEDICAL/DENTAL REFERRALS

- **General Practitioners**, 800-DOCTORS or 202-DOCTORS
- **Specialists**, 800-776-2378; http://www.abms.org
- **Alternative Practitioners**, www.pathwaysmag.com
- **Dentists**, 202-547-7613

MENTAL HEALTH

- **D.C. Commission of Mental Health Services**, Central Intake Division, 202-673-9040
- **Maryland Mental Health System**, 800-888-1965
- **Virginia Office of Mental Health**, Northern Virginia Mental Health Institute, 703-207-7103, www.nvmhi.state.va.us

WORKERS' COMPENSATION COMMISSION

- **Maryland**, 410-767-0900
- **Virginia**, 804-367-8600

HOUSING

- **D.C. Building & Land Regulation Administration**, 202-442-4460, www.dcra.gov/main
- **Rental Housing Commission**, 202-442-8949
- **Housing Regulation & Enforcement Division**, 202-442-4620
- **Historic Preservation Review Board**, 202-442-4570

- **D.C. Tenants Advocacy Coalition** (TENAC), 202-628-3688
- **Montgomery County Department of Housing & Community Affairs**, 240-777-3600 (general information); 240-777-3636 (consumer affairs), www.co.mo.md.us/services/hca
- **Prince George's County Department of Housing**, 301-883-5500
- **Arlington County Housing Information Center**, 703-228-3765, www.co.arlington.va.us/cphd
- **Fairfax County Tenant-Landlord Commission**, 703-222-8435, www.co.fairfax.va.us
- **Alexandria Office of Housing**, 703-838-4545, www.ci.alexandria.va.us/city/housing
- **Fair Housing Information Clearinghouse**, 800-343-3442
- **Fair Housing Council of Greater Washington**, 202-289-5360 or 800-603-3247, www.fairhousing.org
- **US Department of Fair Housing and Discrimination**, 800-477-5977, www.fairhousing.com
- **Fire Prevention Division**, D.C. Fire & EMS Department, 202-727-1614

INTERNET SERVICE PROVIDERS

- **America Online**, 800-827-6364, www.aol.com
- **AT&T WorldNet**, 800-967-5363, www.att.net
- **Earthlink**, 800-EARTHLINK, www.earthlink.net
- **Erol's**, 888-GO-EROLS, www.erols.com
- **Juno Online Services**, 800-879-5866, www.juno.com
- **Microsoft Network**, 800-426-9400, www.msn.com
- **SmartNet Internet Services**, 301-470-3400, www.smart.net
- **Starpower Communications**, 888-782-7313, www.starpower.net
- **Verizon Internet**, 800-NET-2026, www.bellatlantic.net

LABOR

- **US Department of Labor**, Fair Labor Standards Enforcement, 202-219-7043
- **Equal Employment Opportunities Commission**, 202-663-4900, www.eeoc.gov
- **Occupational Safety & Health Administration**, 202-219-8148, www.osha.gov

LEGAL REFERRAL

- **D.C. Bar Legal Service Sourcebook**, 202-737-4700, www.dcbar.org

- **Maryland State Bar**, www.msba.org/public; Lawyer Referral Service, Montgomery County Bar Association, 301-279-9100; Prince George's County Bar Association, 301-952-1440
- **Virginia State Bar Lawyers Referral**, 800 552-7977 or 804-775-0808, www.vsb.org
- **D.C. Public Defender Service**, 202-628-1200, www.lawbbs.net/gideon
- **Legal Aid Society of D.C.**, 202-628-1161, www.legalaiddc.org
- **Neighborhood Legal Services Program**, 202-682-2720, www.nls.org

LIBRARIES

- **District of Columbia**, 202-727-0321, http://dclibrary.org
- **Montgomery County**, 240-777-0002, www.montgomerylibrary.org
- **Prince George's County**, 301-699-3500, www.prge.lib.md.us
- **Arlington County**, 703-823-5295, www.co.arlington.va.us
- **Fairfax County**, 703-324-3100, www.co.fairfax.va.us/library
- **Alexandria**, 703-519-5900, www.alexandria.lib.va.us

LOTTERY

- **D.C. Lottery**, 202-645-8000, www.dclottery.com
- **Maryland Lottery**, 888-333-5923, www.msla.sailorsite.net
- **Virginia Lottery**, 703-494-1501, www.valottery.com

MARRIAGE LICENSES

- **District of Columbia**, 202-879-4840
- **Montgomery County**, 240-777-9460
- **Prince George's County**, 301-952-3288
- **Northern Virginia**, 703-691-7320

NEWSPAPER SUBSCRIPTIONS

- *The Washington Post*, 202-334-6100, www.washingtonpost.com
- *The Washington Times*, 202-636-3333, www.washtimes.com
- *The Common Denominator*, 202-635-6397, www.thecommonde-nominator.com
- **Journal Newspapers**, 703-846-8500, www.jrnl.com
- **Gazette Newspapers**, 301-607-1015, www.gazette.net
- **Times Community Newspapers**, 703-437-5400, www.timescom-munity.com

- *Montgomery Sentinel*, 301-838-0788, www.thesentinel.com
- *Prince George's Sentinel*, 301-306-9500, www.thesentinel.com

See **Getting Settled** for special-interest and free community newspapers.

PARKS & RECREATION

- **National Park Service**, National Capital Area, 202-690-5185, www.nps.gov
- **Maryland Department of Natural Resources**, 877-620-8367, www.dnr.state.md.us
- **Virginia Department of Conservation & Recreation**, 800-933-7275, www.dcr.state.va.us
- **Maryland-National Capital Park & Planning Commission**, 301-495-4600, www.mncppc.org
- **Northern Virginia Regional Park Authority**, 703-352-5900, www.nvrpa.org
- **D.C. Department of Parks & Recreation**, 202-673-7660, http://dpr.dc.gov
- **Montgomery County Department of Recreation**, 301-217-6790, www.mc-mncppc.org
- **Prince George's County Department of Parks & Recreation**, 301-699-2400, www.pgparks.com
- **Arlington County Department of Parks, Recreation & Community Resources**, 703-228-3338, www.co.arlington.va.us/prcr
- **Fairfax County Park Authority**, 703-324-8702, www.co.fairfax.va.us/parks
- **Alexandria Department of Recreation, Parks & Cultural Activities**, 703-638-4345, www.ci.alexandria.va.us/rpca

POLICE

- **Emergency**, 911
- **Crime Solvers** (anonymous), 202-393-2222
- **D.C. Metropolitan Police Department**, 202-727-1010, http://mpdc.dc.gov
- **Montgomery County Police Department**, 301-279-8000, www.co.mo.md.us/services/police
- **Prince George's County Police Department**, 301-772-4740, www.goprincegeorgescounty.com/safety/police
- **Arlington County Police Department**, 703-228-4252, www.co.arlington.va.us/police

- **Fairfax County Police Department**, 703-691-2131, www.co.fairfax.va.us/ps/police
- **Alexandria Police Department**, 703-838-4444, http://ci.alexandria.va.us/police
- **Maryland State Police**, Central Region, 410-799-0458; College Park, 301-345-3101; Rockville, 301-279-2388
- **Virginia State Police**, 804-674-2000; Division 7 (Northern Virginia), 703-323-4500, www.vsp.state.va.us
- **Bureau of Alcohol, Tobacco & Firearms**, 202-927-7777 or 800-283-4867
- **Federal Bureau of Investigation**, 202-324-3000, www.fbi.gov
- **US Capitol Police**, 202-228-2800
- **US Coast Guard Search & Rescue**, 800-418-7314
- **US Marshals Service**, 202-353-0600, D.C. evictions, 202-616-8633
- **US Park Police**, 202-619-7310
- **US Secret Service Uniformed Division**, 202-395-2020

POST OFFICE

- **US Postal Service General Information**, 800-275-8777, www.usps.com
- **Consumer Affairs & Complaints**, 202-636-1400
- **Post Office Box Information**, 202-636-1532
- **Zip Code & Postage Information**, 202-635-5300

ROAD CONDITIONS/TRAFFIC INFORMATION

- **SmarTraveler**, 202-863-1313; www.smartraveler.com
- **Virginia Department of Transportation Hotline**, 800-367-7623
- **Maryland Beach Traffic**, 800-541-9595
- **MapQuest** online traffic reports, www.mapquest.com

SCHOOL DISTRICTS

- **D.C. Public Schools**, 202-724-4222; www.k12.dc.us
- **D.C. Public Charter Schools**, 202-328-2660; www.dcpubliccharter.com
- **Montgomery County**, 301-279-3000; www.mcps.k12.md.us
- **Prince George's County**, 301-952-6300, www.pgcps.pg.k12.md.us
- **Arlington County**, 703-228-6008; www.arlington.k12.va.us
- **Fairfax County**, 703-246-2502; www.fcps.k12.va.us
- **Alexandria**, 703-824-6600, www.acps.k12.va.us
- **Falls Church Public Schools**, 803 West Broad Street, Falls Church; 703-248-5600; www.fccps.k12.va.us

SHIPPING SERVICES

- **Airborne Express**, 800-247-2676, www.airborne.com
- **DHL Worldwide Express**, 800-225-5345, www.dhl-usa.com
- **FedEx**, 800-238-5355, www.fedex.com/us
- **FedEx Ground** (formerly RPS), 800-238-5355, www.fedex.com/us
- **United Parcel Service**, 800-742-5877, www.ups.com
- **US Postal Service Express Mail**, 800-222-1811, www.usps.com

SOCIAL SECURITY ADMINISTRATION

- Toll free: 800-772-1213, TTY, 800-325-0778 (both 7 a.m. to 7 p.m., Monday-Friday)
- Web site: **www.ssa.gov**; click "contact us" to locate the nearest office.

SPORTS

PROFESSIONAL

- **Baltimore Orioles** (AL), 202-296-2473, www.theorioles.com
- **Bowie Baysox** (minor league baseball), 301-805-6000, www.baysox.com
- **D.C. Divas** (NWFL), 703-541-2247; www.dcdivas.com
- **D.C. United** (MLS), 703-478-6600, www.dcunited.com
- **Frederick Keys** (minor league baseball), 301-662-0088, www.frederickkeys.com
- **Potomac Cannons** (minor league baseball), 703-590-2311, www.potomaccannons.com
- **Washington Capitals** (NHL), 202-661-5050, www.washingtoncaps.com
- **Washington Freedom** (WUSA), 202-432-SEAT, www.washingtonfreedom.com
- **Washington Mystics** (WNBA), 202-661-5050, www.wnba.com/mystics
- **Washington Redskins** (NFL), 202-546-2222, www.redskins.com
- **Washington Wizards** (NBA), 202-661-5050, www.nba.com/wizards

COLLEGIATE

- **Catholic University Cardinals**, 202-319-5286, http://athletics.cua.edu
- **George Mason Patriots**, 202-432-SEAT, www.gmusports.com
- **George Washington Colonials**, 202-994-6650, www.gwsports.com
- **Georgetown Hoyas**, 202-687-7159, www.guhoyas.com
- **Howard Bison**, 202-806-7198, www.bisonmania.com

- **Marymount Saints**, 703-284-1619, www.marymount.edu/ssa/athletic
- **Maryland Terrapins**, 301-314-8587, umterps.fansonly.com
- **Navy Midshipmen**, 800-US-4-NAVY, www.usna.edu/athletics

TAXES

- **Internal Revenue Service**, 800-829-1040 (help) or 800-829-4477 (recorded information), www.irs.gov
- **D.C. Chief Financial Officer**, 202-727-2476, www.cfo.washingtondc.gov
- **Maryland Comptroller of the Treasury**, 800-MD-TAXES, http://individuals.marylandtaxes.com
- **Virginia Department of Taxation**, 804-367-8031 (information), 888-268-2829 (forms), www.tax.state.va.us
- **D.C. Board of Real Property Assessments & Appeals**, 202-727-6860
- **Maryland Department of Assessments & Taxation**, Montgomery County office, 301-279-1431; Prince George's County office, 301-952-2500, www.dat.state.md.us
- **Arlington County Department of Real Estate Assessments**, 703-228-3920; www.co.arlington.va.us/dmf
- **Fairfax County Tax Information**, 703-222-8234; www.co.fairfax.va.us/dta
- **Alexandria Department of Real Estate Assessments**, 703-838-4646, www.ci.alexandria.va.us/city/realestate

TELEPHONE SERVICE

LOCAL

- **Verizon**, 202-346-1000 (D.C.), 301-954-6260 (Maryland), 703-876-7000 (Virginia), www.verizon.com
- **Capital Telecom**, 800-673-2400, www.captel.com
- **Close Call America**, 800-845-2215, www.closecallamerica.com
- **Qwest**, 800-860-2255, www.qwest.net
- **RCN**, 888-782-7313, www.rcn.com
- **Verizon Avenue**, 866-892-8368, www.onepointcom.com

LONG DISTANCE

- **AT&T**, 800-222-0300, www.att.com
- **MCI WorldCom**, 800-950-5555, www.mci.com

- **Cable & Wireless**, 888-454-4264, www.cw.com
- **Sprint**, 800-877-7746, www.sprint.com
- **Verizon**, 800-343-2092, www.verizon.net
- **Winstar**, 888-WINSTAR, www.winstar.com
- **Working Assets Long Distance**, 800-788-0898, www.workingforchange.com

WIRELESS

- **AT&T Wireless**, 800-IMAGINE, www.attws.com
- **Cingular**, 866-CINGULAR, www.cingular.com
- **Metrocall**, 703-660-6677, www.metrocall.com
- **Nextel**, 800-NEXTEL9, www.nextel.com
- **Verizon Wireless**, 202-624-0072 or 202-296-4400, www.verizonwireless.com
- **VMC Communications**, 301-261-2165 or 703-532-9100, www.freecell-phone.com
- **VoiceStream**, 800-937-8997, www.voicestream.com
- **Sprint PCS**, 202-496-9400, www.sprintpcs.com

DIRECTORY ASSISTANCE

- **Local and long-distance numbers**, 411
- **Toll-free numbers**, 800-555-1212
- **www.555-1212.com**
- **www.altavista.com**
- **www.anywho.com**
- **www.bigbook.com**
- **www.people.yahoo.com**
- **www.switchboard.com**
- **www.whowhere.lycos.com**
- **www.worldpages.com**
- **www.zip2.com**

TELEVISION—CABLE/DISH

- **District Cablevision**, 202-635-5100
- **Comcast Cable, Montgomery**, 301-424-4400
- **Comcast Cable, Arlington**, 703-841-7700
- **Cox Communications, Fairfax**, 703-378-8400
- **Comcast Cable, Alexandria**, 703-823-3000
- **DirecTV**, 800-237-5988
- **Dish Network**, 800-333-DISH

- **Jones Communications, Alexandria**, 703-823-3000
- **Starpower Communications**, 703-321-8000

TIME

- **Time of Day**, 844-2525 (any local area code)
- **US Naval Observatory Atomic Clock**, 202-762-1401

TOURISM & TRAVEL

- **International Association for Medical Assistance to Travelers**, 716-754-4883
- **Travelers Aid**, 202-546-1127; www.travelersaid.org
- **Washington, D.C. Convention & Visitors Association**, 202-789-7000, www.washington.org
- **Washington D.C. Visitor Information Center**, 202-328-4748, www.dcvisit.com
- **Maryland Office of Tourism Development**, 800-634-7386, www.mdisfun.org
- **US Customs Service**, 202-354-1000, www.customs.gov
- **Virginia Tourism Corporation**, 800-321-3244, www.virginia.org

TRANSPORTATION

AIRPORTS

- **Reagan National Airport** general information, 703-417-8000, www.metwashairports.com
- **Dulles International Airport** general information, 703-661-2700, www.metwashairports.com; ground transportation, 703-661-8230 (taxi) or 703-685-1400 (bus)
- **Baltimore/Washington International Airport** general information, 301-261-1000; ground transportation, 800-435-9284, www.bwiairport.com

CARPOOLING

- **Ride Finders Network**, 800-745-RIDE
- **Metropolitan Washington Council of Governments**, Carpool Line, 800-745-7433
- **Fairfax County RideSources**, 703-324-1111
- **Slug Line information**, www.slug-line.com

COMMUTER RESOURCES

- **Guaranteed Ride Home**, 800-745-RIDE, www.commuterconnections.org
- **Telecommuting Information**, Metropolitan Washington Council of Governments, 202-962-3200, www.mwcog.org
- **Washington Area Bicyclist Association**, 202-628-2500, www.waba.org

For more commuter resources, visit www.commuterpage.com.

COMMUTER TRAINS

- **MARC**, 800-325-RAIL, www.mtamaryland.com
- **Virginia Railway Express**, 703-684-1001, www.vre.org

COUNTY BUSES

- **Ride On** (Montgomery County), 240-777-7433, www.rideonbus.com
- **The BUS** (Prince George's County), 301-883-5683
- **Fairfax Connector**, 703-339-7200, www.fairfaxconnector.com
- **DASH** (Alexandria), 703-370-DASH
- **ART** (Arlington), 703-228-RIDE, www.commuterpage.com

METRORAIL/METROBUS

- **General Information**, 202-637-7000, www.wmata.com
- **Weekly & Monthly Passes**, www.commuterdirect.com
- **Student Fares** (D.C. Public Schools), 202-671-0537
- **Senior & Disabled Fares**, 202-962-1245

NATIONAL TRAIN & BUS SERVICE

- **Greyhound**, 800-231-2222, www.greyhound.com
- **Peter Pan-Trailways**, 800-343-9999, www.peterpanbus.com
- **Amtrak**, 800-USA-RAIL, www.amtrak.com

TAXIS

- **Capitol**, 202-546-2400
- **Dial**, 202-829-4222
- **Diamond**, 202-387-6200

- **Red Top**, 202-328-3333
- **Yellow Cab**, 202-544-1212

Suburban taxicab companies are listed in the **Transportation** chapter.

UTILITIES

EMERGENCIES

- **Gas Leaks**, 703-750-1000
- **Downed Power Lines**, 202-872-2000
- **Power Failures**, 877-737-2662; life-threatening emergency, 202-872-3432
- **Water & Sewer Leaks**, D.C., 202-612-3400
- **Toxic Spills**, 800-424-8802
- **Locate Buried Gas Lines**, Miss Utility Hotline, 800-257-7777, www.missutility.net

ENERGY

- **Potomac Electric Power Company (Pepco)**, 202-833-7500, www.pepco.com
- **Dominion Virginia Power**, 703-934-9660, www.dom.com
- **Washington Gas Energy Services**, 888-236-9437 or www.wges.com.
- **PowerChoice/Pepco Energy Services**, 800-ENERGY-9, www.powerchoice.com/residential

WATER

- **D.C. Water & Sewer Authority**, 202-354-3600, www.dcwasa.com
- **Washington Suburban Sanitary Commission**, 301-206-4001 or 800-634-8400, www.wssc.dst.md.us.
- **Arlington County Department of Public Works**, 703-228-3636, www.co.arlington.va.us/dpw
- **Fairfax County Water Authority**, 703-698-5800, www.fcwa.org
- **Virginia-American Water Co., Alexandria**, 703-549-7080, www.vawc.com/alex
- **Falls Church Public Utilities Division**, 703-248-5071, www.ci.falls-church.va.us

PUBLIC SERVICE COMMISSION

- **District of Columbia**, 202-626-5100, www.dcpsc.org
- **Maryland**, 410-767-8028 or 800-492-0474, www.pcs.state.md.uc
- **Virginia**, 804-371-9141 or 800-552-7945, www.state.va.us/scc

VOTER REGISTRATION

- **D.C. Board of Elections & Ethics**, 202-727-2525, www.dcboee.org
- **Maryland State Board of Elections**, 800-222-8683, www.elections.state.md.us
- **Virginia State Board of Elections**, 800-552-9745, www.sbe.state.va.us
- **Montgomery County Board of Elections**, 240-777-VOTE, www.co.mo.md.us/services/elections
- **Prince George's County Board of Elections**, 301-627-2814, www.goprincegeorgescounty.com
- **Arlington County Registrar of Voters**, 703-228-3456, www.co.arlington.va.us/voters
- **Fairfax County Electoral Board & General Registrar**, 703-324-4700, www.co.fairfax.va.us/eb
- **Alexandria Office of Voter Registration**, 703-838-4050, www.alexandriavoter.org

WEATHER

- **Verizon Weather Recording**, 936-1212 (any local area code)
- **Air Quality Hotline**, 202-962-3299
- **National Weather Service** online, www.nws.noaa.gov

WOMEN

- **Maryland Commission for Women**, 800-332-6347 or 410-260-6047, www.dhr.state.md.us/mcw
- **Montgomery County Commission for Women** - Counseling & Career Center, 301-279-1800, www.co.mo.md.us/services/cfw
- **Arlington County Commission on the Status of Women**, 703-228-5995, www.co.arlington.va.us/cbo/women
- **Fairfax County Office for Women**, 703-324-5730
- **Alexandria Commission for Women**, 703-838-5030

ABOUT THE AUTHOR

MIKE LIVINGSTON was born in D.C. and has spent most of his life within a mile of the Beltway. He is a freelance editor and writer whose clients include the Citizen Policies Institute, Conservation International, *Legal Times*, Nonprofit Watch, the Points of Light Foundation, and the *Washington Business Journal*. He helped establish Sarah House, a non-profit organization serving children in public housing and homeless shelters. In 1998, he was the Green Party candidate for D.C.'s "shadow" congressional seat. Mike lives in Brightwood and does not own a car. He extends special thanks to Susan Doran, Lorin Kleinman, and Greg Smith for their support during the revision of this book—it is because of such people that Washington is an exciting place to live, work, and play.

READER RESPONSE FORM

We would appreciate your comments regarding this third edition of the *Newcomer's Handbook®* *for Moving to Washington D.C.* If you've found any mistakes or omissions or if you would just like to express your opinion about the guide, please let us know. We will consider any suggestions for possible inclusion in our next edition, and if we use your comments, we'll send you a *free* copy of our next edition. Please send this response form to:

Reader Response Department
First Books
6750 SW Franklin, Suite A
Portland, OR 97223 USA

Comments:

_____

_____

_____

_____

_____

_____

_____

_____

Name: _____

Address _____

_____

_____

Telephone (_____) _____

6750 SW Franklin, Suite A
Portland, OR 97223
503-968-6777
www.firstbooks.com

FIRST BOOKS

NEWCOMER'S HANDBOOK

ORDER FORM ®

THE ORIGINAL, ALWAYS UPDATED, ABSOLUTELY INVALUABLE GUIDES FOR PEOPLE MOVING TO A CITY!

Find out about neigborhoods, apartment and house hunting, money matters, deposits/leases, getting settled, helpful services, shopping for the home, places of worship, cultural life, sports/recreation, volunteering, green space, schools and education, transportation, temporary lodgings and useful telephone numbers!

	# COPIES	TOTAL
Newcomer's Handbook® for Atlanta	_____ x $17.95	$_____
Newcomer's Handbook® for Boston	_____ x $18.95	$_____
Newcomer's Handbook® for Chicago	_____ x $18.95	$_____
Newcomer's Handbook® for London	_____ x $20.95	$_____
Newcomer's Handbook® for Los Angeles	_____ x $17.95	$_____
Newcomer's Handbook® for Minneapolis-St. Paul	_____ x $20.95	$_____
Newcomer's Handbook® for New York City	_____ x $19.95	$_____
Newcomer's Handbook® for San Francisco	_____ x $20.95	$_____
Newcomer's Handbook® for Seattle	_____ x $18.95	$_____
Newcomer's Handbook® for Washington D.C.	_____ x $21.95	$_____
	SUBTOTAL	$_____
POSTAGE & HANDLING (*$7.00 first book, $1.00 each add'l.*)		$_____
	TOTAL	$_____

SHIP TO:

Name _____

Title _____

Company _____

Address _____

City _____ State _____ Zip _____

Phone Number (_____) _____

FIRST BOOKS

Send this order form and a check or money order payable to:
First Books

First Books, Mail Order Department
6750 SW Franklin, Suite A, Portland, OR 97223
Allow 1-2 weeks for delivery

METRORAIL MAP